DISTORTING THE LAW

THE CHICAGO SERIES IN LAW AND SOCIETY

Edited by William M. O'Barr and John M. Conley

DISTORTING THE LAW

Politics, Media, and the Litigation Crisis

WILLIAM HALTOM AND MICHAEL MCCANN

THE UNIVERSITY OF CHICAGO PRESS

Chicago and London

WILLIAM HALTOM is a professor in the Department of Politics and Government at the University of Puget Sound. He is the author of *Reporting on the Courts: How Mass Media Report Judicial Actions* (1998).

MICHAEL MCCANN is the Gordon Hirabayashi Professor for the Advancement of Citizenship and director of the Comparative and Society Studies Center at the University of Washington, Seattle. He is the author of *Taking Reform Seriously: Perspectives on Public Interest Liberalism* (1986) and *Rights at Work: Pay Equity Reform and the Politics of Legal Mobilization* (1994), the latter published by the University of Chicago Press; he is also a coeditor of *Judging the Constitution: Critical Essays on Judicial Lawmaking,* with Gerald L. Houseman (1989).

The University of Chicago Press, Chicago 60637
The University of Chicago Press, Ltd., London
© 2004 by The University of Chicago
All rights reserved. Published 2004
Printed in the United States of America

13 12 11 10 09 08 07 06 05 04   1 2 3 4

ISBN: 0-226-31463-4 (cloth)
ISBN: 0-226-31464-2 (paper)

Library of Congress Cataloging-in-Publication Data
Haltom, William.
   Distorting the law : politics, media, and the litigation crisis / William Haltom
and Michael McCann.
      p. cm.—(The Chicago series in law and society)
   Includes bibliographical references and index.
   ISBN 0-226-31463-4 (cloth : alk. paper)—ISBN 0-226-31464-2 (pbk. : alk. paper)
   1. Actions and defenses—Press coverage—United States. 2. Torts—Press
Coverage—United States. 3. Law in mass media—United States. 4. Law and
politics. 5. Sociological jurisprudence. I. McCann, Michael J. II. Title. III. Series.
KF380.H35 2004
346.7303—dc22

                                                            2004001268

♾ The paper used in this publication meets the minimum requirements of the
American National Standard for Information Sciences—Permanence of Paper for
Printed Library Materials, ANSI Z39.48-1992.

From Michael,
to Donna, with love and devotion always

From Bill,
to three women who agreeably but insistently speak their minds:
Patricia Anderson, Carolyn Haltom, and Karen Porter

Contents

Preface

This book began with a casual conversation about the much-publicized McDonald's coffee case. Our common interest in the curious case no doubt reflected in part our mutual ties to the University of Washington, where one of us (Haltom) finished up a Ph.D. and the other (McCann) started out as an assistant professor at about the same time. Both of us participated in a vibrant intellectual community of scholars at UW interested in law and society, mass media, and political culture. We were each especially interested in how legal knowledge, and hence law itself, is constructed and produced in modern mass-mediated culture. At the same time, our quite different types of previous research provided us varying angles on the subject. One of us, Haltom, had undertaken extensive study concerning newspaper coverage of judicial action; he was skilled at compiling and parsing statistical data sets, and given to fretting over how to make his methodological cuts into empirical reality as sharp as possible. The other, McCann, specialized in theory-driven, qualitative, interpretive studies of legal mobilization and disputing by social movements and individuals; he reveled in exploring the elusive topic of legal consciousness. While we each straddled the fence dividing rival approaches to social constructionist analysis, Haltom leaned a bit more toward the realist, positivist side while McCann tilted more consistently to the post-structuralist and post-positivist side. Both of us were inclined to be detail-oriented, but we assessed and obsessed about details very differently. Our discussions progressively clarified these differences as well as the commonalities of intellectual style and understanding that fused into our common project.

Eventually a general question emerged: How did it come about that prominent elites—politicians, media pundits, news reporters, celebrities, comedians, cartoonists, film makers, novelists, and other producers of mass culture—routinely blame a myriad of social ills on an epidemic of litigiousness among American citizens and their lawyers? Our thinking about this question was influenced by a substantial body of social science literature strongly suggesting that this conventional wisdom about a litigation crisis greatly simplifies and distorts our understanding of legal practice. But our specific concerns developed along subtly different lines. Why did the common sense about the lawsuit crisis emerge and become so prominent when it did? What social forces drive this mass-produced cultural logic? Why is it that this new common sense seems to resonate so powerfully in our culture, especially at this historical moment? What do these practices of blaming lawyers and litigants mean for social life, politics, and law itself? What are the implications of these practices for those concerned about struggles for justice and democracy? Those are the types of issues that most concerned us as we designed our study.

Our plans for developing these questions into a larger project on media coverage of litigation crystallized into an ambitious, multidimensional research proposal submitted to the National Science Foundation. We were eventually awarded generous funding (award SES-9818581), for which we are very grateful. Recognizing that we then were committed to constructing a book, moreover, we doubled our ambitions to include related analysis of the political debate over tort reform (chapters 2–4) that engaged so many of our colleagues in sociolegal study. From this synthesis developed our attention to the instrumental, institutional, and ideological factors shaping the mass production of legal knowledge. The legacy of collaboration that produced this book over six or more years has been a strange and wonderful adventure.

Additional funding for the expanded project was provided from several sources. Bill thanks the University of Puget Sound both for the John Lantz Senior Sabbatical Fellowship and for the sabbatical enhancements that enabled him to travel, research, and interview. Michael thanks the Royalty Research Fund and Gordon Hirabayashi Professorship for the Advancement of Citizenship at the University of Washington for various forms of financial support.

We have been blessed with considerable assistance from many people in the long process of research and writing. Above all, we owe a very great deal to a corps of extraordinary graduate students at the University of Washington. Judy Aks worked with us in formulating the original research design, and then supervised for two years the systematic content analysis of media articles. Anne Bloom was enormously helpful in mapping tort reform debates and tort reform players; she aided us in contacting key individuals for interviews as well as in understanding their perspectives at many points. Jeffrey Dudas worked on the media content analysis from early on and was responsible for most of the study of the tobacco litigation coverage. All three students contributed ideas, interpretations, and interest along the way. Lisa Horan, Peter Hovde, Iza Hussin, Vincent Jungkunz, Scott Lemieux, and Claire Rasmussen each contributed as well in various regards during the project.

An even larger group of undergraduates provided invaluable assistance in coding newspaper reports. They endured dull training sessions and the tedium of reading endless news articles to produce much of the data at the heart of our analysis. This group included Serena Dolly, Lise Dorfsman, Tara Elfering, Matt Judge, Terra Nevitt, Todd Reichert, Kate Reynolds, Brian Schiewe, Andrea Visveshwarn, Danielle Walker, and Michelle Wolfe.

Many people—tort reform advocates, consumer advocates, trial lawyers, social scientists, journalists—gave us their time and thoughts despite very busy schedules. Some are named in the following pages, while others preferred anonymity; many just go unnamed. We are thankful to all of them.

Many professional colleagues provided input at various points, first on our many conference presentations and then on manuscript chapters. Several individuals deserve special mention. Thomas Burke provided early copies of his book manuscript on related issues, access to several invaluable interviews that we quote extensively, incisive insights about our project, and some last-minute corrections of the book manuscript. By contrast, Stuart Scheingold provided little direct input to this study, but his scholarship over several decades greatly influenced our thinking in infinite indirect ways. David Engel and Charles Epp proved to be extraordinarily careful, thoughtful, and gracious reviewers whose comments were extremely useful in the late phases of revising the manuscript.

We also benefited from commentary by many others scholars, including: Lance Bennett, John Brigham, Lief Carter, Ann Crigler, Stephen Daniels, Lauren Edelman, Howard Erlanger, Patricia Ewick, Malcolm Feeley, Marc Galanter, John Gilliom, Howard Gillman, Jon Goldberg-Hiller, Christine Harrington, Roger Hartley, Bryan Jones, Robert Kagan, Bert Kritzer, Richard Lempert, Robert MacCoun, Joanne Martin, Neal Milner, A. Susan Owen, Douglas Reed, Austin Sarat, Susan Silbey, Helena Silverstein, Jonathan Simon, Elliot Slotnick, Mark Smith, Theodore Taranovski, and John Wilkerson. The intellectual community in the Comparative Law and Society Studies Center at the University of Washington—Katherine Beckett, Angelina Godoy, Steven Herbert, George Lovell, Jamie Mayerfeld, Joel Migdal, Arzoo Osanloo, Patrick Rivers, Andrea Simpson, Susan Whiting, and others—provided a terrific source of commentary and stimulation, for which McCann in particular is grateful.

David Bemelmans did a splendid job as copy editor in slimming down and touching up our prose. The staff at the University of Chicago Press was great in every way. In particular, John Tryneski once again demonstrated why he is among the best editors in the university press publishing business. He showed interest early on in our ideas and much patience over two years while we continued to delay submissions of any text for reading. He then secured reviews, provided a contract, and initiated production with great dispatch. All the time he was intellectually engaged and personally delightful.

Finally, we publicly thank one another. We suspect that collaboration between the two of us produced a manuscript that took twice as long to develop and is nearly twice the number of pages than would have been the case had either of us alone undertaken the project. But we enjoyed it twice as much as our previous books written alone and we learned a great deal about ourselves in the process. We are amused, and a bit amazed, by the fact that we are better friends now than when we started. Because we reject mass culture's simplistic moral stories about excessive blaming and claiming, however, we feel free to assign the book's faults to each other, and to bring legal action if necessary to establish or to deny relative responsibility for errors.

CHAPTER ONE

The Social Production of Legal Knowledge

Judith Haimes, a self-proclaimed psychic, was awarded close to $1 million by a Philadelphia jury on [sic] March 1986 after she said that a C.A.T. scan at Temple University Hospital made her lose her psychic abilities.

The above item appeared under the heading "Strange Lawsuits" on a popular Web site titled "Jokes, Jokes, Jokes from Everywhere . . ." in May 2001.[1] This single-sentence account is one version of a widely circulated narrative concerning events that had taken place several years earlier. Judith Richardson Haimes had indeed filed a medical malpractice claim after suffering a severe allergic reaction to an injection of dye prior to a CAT scan at Temple University Hospital in 1976.[2] As the jury heard it in the 1986 civil trial, the thirty-three-year-old Ms. Haimes warned the radiologist that she had previously experienced strong allergic reactions and had been admonished to avoid iodine-based dyes. The plaintiff testified that the radiologist, Dr. Judith Hart, dismissed the warning as "ridiculous." After the doctor persisted and proposed to experiment with a small dose of the dye, Haimes finally relented. Almost immediately, the patient went into anaphylactic shock and experienced severe pain, later testifying that she felt "as if my head was going to explode" *(Haimes v. Temple University Hospital and Hart)*. Another doctor quickly intervened, although the effects of this remedial action were later disputed. Haimes suffered from extreme nausea and vomiting along with the intense headaches for several days; welts and hives that initially appeared on her body lingered for sev-

---

1. www.abp1.com/2humor/jokes/page1.html. See also Hobbie 1992.

2. Ms. Haimes was undergoing tests to discover the nature and cause of tumors on her ear.

eral weeks. She testified that acute headaches continued thereafter whenever she attempted deep mental concentration.

Judith Haimes sought legal relief from the doctor and hospital for the
immediate pain and other consequences of the dye injection as well as for
the protracted, debilitating headaches that ended her practice as a professional psychic. National and local law enforcement officials affirmed that
the plaintiff in the past had aided them in solving crimes through use of
her unusual gifts, a legacy well documented for some time by Philadelphia
media. At the conclusion of the four-day trial, however, Pennsylvania state
court judge Leon Katz instructed the jury to ignore the latter component
of her claim because Haimes failed to produce any expert testimony linking the injection of dye to her continuing headaches and alleged loss of income. Only her claim for immediate pain and suffering from the allergic
reaction was to be considered. The jury returned within three quarters
of an hour and awarded Haines what would have become $986,000—that
is, $600,000 damages plus accrued interest. The defendant immediately
moved to set aside the judgment. Four and a half months later, Judge Katz
agreed, denying the award as "grossly excessive" and ordering a new trial.
A second trial in 1989 was dismissed when the new judge ruled that the
plaintiff's medical expert lacked qualifications. That ruling was affirmed in
1991 by a divided Pennsylvania Superior Court. In the end, Judith Haimes
never received a cent for her civil claim of injury, much less adequate medical care for her malady.[3]

Although interest in the lawsuit receded quietly, the original story
developed a robust life of its own in American mass culture and politics.
Initial coverage of the case in major national newspapers, wire services,
and professional journals was brief but highlighted the enormous sum of
money that the jury had awarded, ostensibly for the bizarre claim of the
plaintiff.[4] The *Los Angeles Times* (1986a) headline was typical: "Says Her
Powers Vanished, 'Psychic' Awarded $988,000 in Hospital CAT-Scan Law-
suit." The *New York Times* (1986) was pithier: "Woman Wins $1 Million in
Psychic Power Suit." Local newspapers freely traded pretenses of objectivity for derisive humor about the case. Headlines such as "Jury Sees $1M for
Psychic," "But Didn't She Know before She Got There?" and "Psychic 'Sees'
Victory, but Loses Her Powers" were featured prominently in dailies.[5]

3. Our account of events surrounding the lawsuit is based on academic and journalistic
sources, interviews with the plaintiff, Haimes's personal records, and her husband's book
about the event (Haimes 1990). For more details, consult the Web site (www.lawslore.info)
that accompanies this volume.
4. See, for example, *Los Angeles Times* 1986a; DiGirolamo 1986a, 1986b; Tulsky 1986.
5. *Philadelphia Daily News,* March 28, 1986, pp. 1, 3; *St. Petersburg Evening Independent,*
March 28, 1986, p. 1; *Clearwater Sun,* March 29, 1986, p. 1A.

News reports announcing the dismissal of the award were soon overtaken by published accounts that selectively translated the event into an entertaining morality tale about excessive litigiousness. One such account in *Playboy*, titled "Psychic Whiplash," began:

"In those days, we didn't have insurance," said Mel Brooks in character as the 2000-Year-Old Man. He was explaining what people did 20 centuries ago when they were run down by a lion. "You just lay there till you got better." In these greedy times, it seems, all you have to do is lie there until a personal-injury lawyer spots you, get the name of the lion's insurance company and litigate for the kind of money that has to be moved around on hand trucks.[6]

The fable quickly became a symbol for the thriving national tort reform movement. In a speech that was widely distributed and published in *Vital Speeches of the Day*, Robert Malott, a corporate CEO and chair of the Business Roundtable, cited the anecdote about the psychic along with other incidents as examples of jury awards that "strain credulity" (Malott 1986). A *Washington Post* editorial entitled "Liability Reform Is Coming" contended in the same vein that "jury awards such as the one for the Philadelphia psychic that shock the public . . . aid the cause of the reformers."[7] The story provided the lead example for articles at home and abroad about President Reagan's commitment to "rein in galloping damages" awards in tort cases (see *London Times*, April 3, 1986, p. 9A). In 1987, a year after the verdict, Reagan invoked the story at a luncheon of physicians and surgeons to assail a legal system gone awry at the expense of deserving citizens, including new mothers and their children.

Last year a jury awarded one woman a million dollars in damages. She claimed that a CAT scan had destroyed her psychic powers. (Laughter.) Well, recently a new trial was ordered in that case, but the excesses of the courts have taken their toll. As a result, in some parts of the country, women haven't been able to find doctors to deliver their babies, and other medical services have become scarce and expensive. (Galanter 1998b, 727)

The tale continued to circulate during subsequent years in publications aimed at professional business managers and policy elites. Pundit Peter

---

6. Vetter 1986. To be fair, this story assaults insurance companies and lawyers with equal disdain.

7. *Washington Post*, April 1, 1986, p. A18.

Huber repeated the anecdote in his widely recognized book *Galileo's Revenge* (1991a, 4) and companion *Forbes* article (1991b) as a classic case of "junk science" that routinely permeates our courts. Somehow Huber transformed an unorthodox malpractice claim that was thrown out of court for lack of expert evidence into an example of routine failure by the civil courts and subversion of the law by fraudulent science. President Bush's Council on Competitiveness (1991) soon thereafter drew on Huber's transformed tale, this time trimming recognition that the case had been dismissed while emphasizing that the award represented "commonplace" abuses of the civil legal system. Indeed, one business executive in a Washington, D.C. public relations and lobbying firm advised that an effective challenge to trial lawyers was to "make Judith Haimes into as notorious a public figure as Willie Horton was in the 1988 presidential campaign" (Galanter 1998b, 729; see also Nye 1992). The story was later recounted prominently in tort reform advocate Walter Olson's high-profile volume *The Litigation Explosion: What Happened When America Unleashed the Lawsuit* (1991) and, based on Olson's account, Charles J. Sykes's *A Nation of Victims: The Decay of American Character* (1992). In both instances the Haimes case again was invoked as a "typical" example of the two closely related epidemics in American culture clearly signaled by each book's respective title. Harvard Law professor W. Kip Viscusi similarly opened a 1991 book—*Reforming Products Liability*—with an account of the "outrageous" episode that was intended to support his argument for systematic tort reform.

Once widely legitimated by prominent public intellectuals, the Haimes story was freely recycled in the mass media by journalists and reform advocates alike to illustrate commonsense charges about an inefficient, irrational, morally inverted legal system. For example, a *Time* magazine cover story entitled "Busybodies and Crybabies: What's Happening to the American Character" focused on the moralistic message preached in the speeches and books mentioned above, and especially in Sykes's subtitle. "Hypersensitivity and special pleading are making a travesty of the virtues that used to be known as individual responsibility and common sense," read the byline of the story that made Walter Olson's account of Haimes's ordeal the leading example of "the new area of litigious behavior that has blossomed and might be labeled emotional tort law" (Birnbaum 1991).[8]

---

8. This focus on individual moral character is usually suspect for actual plaintiffs in legal horror stories. Judith Haimes, for example, only decided to file a claim after her son was killed in a car accident, an event that she believed with great remorse she might have foreseen and prevented had she not been disabled. Moreover, Haimes and her husband, Allen, are

Alternative accounts stressing how the actual facts should have rendered the Haimes case a non-event were generated as well, to be sure. Members of the plaintiffs' bar issued rebuttals in professional journals and official Web pages that attempted to demystify the tall tale by telling "the way it really was," emphasizing that the initial jury award and eventually the case itself were dismissed (Hengstler 1986; Strasser 1987; see ATLA Web page). Ralph Nader and Wesley Smith cited the story in their 1996 muckraking book on corporate lawyers as but one of many "tort deform anecdotes" that are promulgated to mislead the public about the civil legal system. "Corporate propagandists simply refuse to let the actual facts get in the way," the authors protested (1996, 275). Social scientists and other scholars in the nation's law schools likewise challenged the story (Saks 1992). Law professor Marc Galanter in particular made the attention given to the Haimes story the lead case study in one of his many law review articles aiming to unmask tort reform rhetoric during the 1990s. He, like other social scientists, emphasized not only that the facts of the popular account were wrong or misleading, but also that the initial jury award was highly atypical of jury actions generally (1998b; Daniels and Martin 1995).

However, legal professionals and social scientists tended to publish their challenges to the tort reform movement in law reviews, professional journals, and other esoteric scholarly venues that few citizens or policymakers read. By contrast, populist tort reformers, although often writing for targeted audiences, managed to find much more popular outlets for their narratives. The derisive accounts of the Haimes case, for example, were widely cited in articles, editorials, letters, and book reviews published in the general print media as well as in popular books, as cited above (see also Perkins 1992; Dirck 1993; Griffin 1996). The fact that a popular president and a later president's special advisory council publicly repeated the story amplified the anecdote further, infusing it with sufficient cultural vitality to thrive into the new millennium.

Common Sense about Law in the United States

The "strange lawsuit" portrayed above indeed has become a well-known "joke," as our opening reference suggested. Yet we hope to demonstrate in this book that anecdotal narratives like this one, which we label "tort

---

well-known community activists in a variety of philanthropic causes, especially related to support for popular music as well as to public education about the Holocaust through work with survivors. That the Haimes's community involvement included work with the Democratic Party may have figured into their stigmatization, however.

tales,"[9] convey serious meaning and exercise pervasive interpretive power in modern American society. Years of retelling have made the CAT scan episode a favored narrative among the widely circulating horror stories about frivolous lawsuits, greedy lawyers, shameless plaintiffs, and duped jurors. These narratives, we argue, are one important component in a powerful tradition of legal lore permeating contemporary mass culture. Tort tales in the news complement and feed on the relentless litany of lawyer jokes (Galanter 1998a), humorous caricatures of litigious attorneys that populate movie and television screens (Bergman and Asimow 1996; Denvir 1996; Jarvis and Joseph 1998), bombastic moralizing by prominent public intellectuals about excessive "rights talk" (Boot 1998; Glendon 1991; Olson 1991), and ritualized daily discourse among citizens bemoaning lawyers, litigation, and legalization (Greenhouse, Yngvesson, and Engel 1994; Miller and Sarat 1980–81). Indeed, assumptions about an "epidemic" of civil litigation, a surfeit of rights claiming, and a legal system run amok became conventional wisdom in late-twentieth-century America. The underlying logic was succinctly expressed in the title of Philip K. Howard's widely publicized 1994 book *The Death of Common Sense: How Law Is Suffocating America.* And these pervasive allegations about civil law are but one dimension of a larger assault on rights entitlements, legal challenges to hierarchy, and democratic appeals to courts that have fueled the culture wars in American society over the past several decades.[10] The aforementioned comparison of Judith Haimes to Willie Horton well represents the linkage among familiar stories regarding law's routine subversion by uncivil action.[11] Such connections provide just one example of how mass media seize on dramatic anomalies as a way of normalizing the atypical so that it becomes, over time, a matter of "common sense."

These negative narratives and notions about civil law, and tort law in particular, have permeated our official political discourse. President Rea-

9. "Tort tale" is not recent coinage. It dates at least back to a debunking of a fundraising letter sent out by the American Tort Reform Association (Strasser 1987).

10. The term "culture wars" refers to a prominent mode of political contestation in contemporary society, characterized two important defining features: (1) competing visions concerning the proper relationship between individual responsibility and the collective "moral community," and (2) the focus on mass cultural forms of knowledge production (education, television, movies, newspapers, advertising, etc.) as the primary sites of this contest for influence. See generally Hunter 1991. On links of recent moral battles to long-standing American traditions, see Morone 2003. For an interesting analysis of divisions at the heart of contemporary "moral politics," see Lakoff 2002.

11. Willie Horton is an African American male who, after he kidnapped a couple and raped the female while on furlough following a murder conviction, became an enduring symbol for liberals' "softness" on the crime issue during the 1988 presidential election. See Beckett 1997.

gan's propensity to recount tort tales and lament an excess of lawyers was echoed by Vice President Dan Quayle (1994). The same general themes have been reiterated in various tones by prominent jurists and a host of national and state politicians. Indeed, highly visible campaigns for tort law reform swept the country following the mid-1980s, bringing about changes at the state level through legislation, initiatives, and referenda. The alleged conventional wisdom informing these crusades was clearly articulated in the mid-1990s when the Republican-led "Contract with America" promised tort reform and led to the federal Common Sense Legal Reforms Act of 1995 (H.R. 10) and Common Sense Product Liability Legal Reform Act (H.R. 956 1996).[12] President George W. Bush proudly made the assault on trial lawyers and reform of tort law a prominent part of his legacy as Texas governor in the latter part of this time period. In fact, Bush, his Democratic rival, and both parties' vice-presidential candidates all unabashedly embraced the cause of national tort reform in the 2000 presidential election. The only figure in the electoral contest to challenge this conventional wisdom was Ralph Nader, who garnered about 3 percent of the national vote.

LAW, KNOWLEDGE, POWER: A PROFILE OF OUR PROJECT

A Social Constructionist Account

One reading of the legacy described above—what might be called the "realist account"—emphasizes the considerable gap between the facts of actual events, such as Judith Haimes's legal encounters, and the inaccurately embellished legends about those experiences that circulate in the mass media and political culture. Relying heavily on statistical studies of legal disputing, many realist sociolegal scholars have demonstrated how the tort reform campaign has been built on "baseless fictions" and unrepresentative stories. For example, scholarly experts have documented that plaintiffs rarely win large judgments against corporations for defective products (Koenig and Rustad 1993), that the volume of products liability and medical malpractice cases has not increased greatly in recent decades, and that the actions of legal agents—litigants, lawyers, juries, judges—gener-

---

12. We use the term "common sense" throughout our analysis for three interrelated reasons: (1) it is the label that pop reformers repeatedly claim for their position as part of their effort to normalize or legitimate their selective constructions; (2) reformers and bystanders routinely invoke or appropriate long-familiar cultural discourses and values for their purposes; and (3) in more critical analytical terms, this "common sense" tends to support various hierarchical relations and agendas, even while it *can* be constructed to resist or contest dominant relations as well (see McCann 1994, chap. 8).

ally produce reasonable outcomes (Daniels and Martin 1995). Consequently, realists tend to criticize tort reforms as misguided and even harmful. This perspective captures two meanings of our book title. Whereas business-supported reformers routinely *dis* torts[13] in contemporary society, realist scholars labor to demonstrate how those claims radically *distort* empirical truth about legal practice. Such twisted and unfounded ideas persist, realist academics contend, largely because well-funded business advocates have successfully infiltrated the media, mobilized support of policy elites, and beguiled the mass public with their message. By exposing the fantastic fictions of popular culture with facts garnered from social science research, realist scholars thus have aimed to provide an "antidote" to misleading legal anecdotes.[14]

We find much of value in the realist account. Indeed, our analysis summarizes these scholarly studies, adds new evidence mostly supporting their position, tacitly endorses many of their conclusions, and thus indirectly fortifies much but not all of the realist's case against tort reform rhetoric. As our opening example of the dye-injected psychic illustrates, there is a lot of bunk out there and we are happy to join the chorus of debunkers. In many regards, our study thus builds on and complements the projects of other sociolegal scholars.

But we also find the typical realist argument inadequate for addressing a variety of important empirical and interpretive questions. For example, have tort reformers actually succeeded in saturating the press with their tales of unleashed legality? How often and why do the media report and circulate misleading stories about tort law? Are aberrant tort tales, such as the highly misleading Haimes fable, the primary or most important source of media contributions to the conventional wisdom? How and how much do the mass media report ordinary instances of civil litigation? Why might elites and the general public accept or embrace tort tales if they are so atypical and inaccurate? Why have social scientists, plaintiffs' lawyers, and other opponents been unsuccessful in challenging faulty fables and suspect sense about law? To what extent have realist scholars themselves been participants in tort reform politics? Finally, what are the primary implications of the new common sense, and how do such narratives about the lawsuit crisis matter? These are the core questions that most concern us in this study and justify our particular social constructionist approach to exploring them.

---

13. We invoke the *New Oxford American Dictionary*'s definition of "dis": (v) to act or speak in a disrespectful way toward.

14. Galanter 1996b. See chapter 3 for a full review.

In more affirmative terms, our study advances three general lines of argument that together produce a more complex political account:

- *Critical scholarly challenges that focus on inaccurate, evasive, and unrepresentative characterizations of tort law in the prevailing litigation-crisis narratives miss, and often obscure, the narratives' compelling ideological grounding.* We argue that the reigning common sense, which tort reformers cultivate and exploit, expresses normative appeals to deeply rooted values and moralistic homilies as well as empirical claims about legal practice. These appeals to enduring moral values, we contend, are one facet of a broader jeremiad bitterly contesting the rights-based politics that arose in the 1960s.[15]
- *We emphasize the relatively independent proclivities of mass media even more than the strategic political efforts of reform advocates as key factors in the complex process of knowledge production.* The institutionalized predilections driving entertainment-oriented mass media, including especially "real world" news reporting, shape the style and content of legal knowledge production. As such, routinely dramatized, personalized media representations parallel simplistic tort tales and reinforce the moralism of reform rhetoric, imbuing both with a casual familiarity that is difficult to challenge.
- *The prevailing common sense about the lawsuit crisis inhibits sophisticated democratic discourse regarding public policy as well as the prerogatives of unaccountable corporate power.* We address two particular dimensions of this undemocratic impact. First, our study highlights agenda-setting dynamics by which policy discourse and public opinion are diverted by default concerns about proliferating legalism from attention to actual changes in legal practice, important public problems, and plausible policy responses to such problems. Second, we suggest that the prevailing legal lore nurtures pervasive cultural pressures that encourage various types of legal action and, especially, inaction—by lawyers, judges, jurors, administrators, injured citizens, risk-calculating consumers, and the like—in response to everyday harms. Prevailing norms stigmatize certain types of action while privileging others, disciplining citizens into enacting the visions celebrated by romantic reformers.

15. Our analysis shares the view with rogue cultural analysts that social scientists pay far too little attention to the moralistic dimensions of American politics. See, for example, Lakoff 2002; Morone 2003.

Our critical project thus aims less to take sides in partisan debates about tort reform than to focus on how the core logics tapped by those debates matter for law, politics, and power more broadly in contemporary American society. We seek not to substitute a more rigorously derived empirical truth for mass-produced commonsense truth so much as to analyze critically the origins, character, and effects of the latter. Our analysis emphasizes in particular that familiar laments about excessive litigiousness are not an isolated trend, but rather are closely connected to the moralistic "culture wars" waged in the United States during the late twentieth and early twenty-first centuries. This connection helps to explain the mass appeal of narratives invoking the lawsuit crisis and their implications for supporting status-quo hierarchies in contemporary society. We further suggest that, if the pervasive legal hypochondria is to be treated, engagement with the substantive moral logic of tort tales through the forms and idioms that dominate mass political culture must be part of the treatment. At the least, such an engagement demands the cultivation of compelling counternarratives that creatively draw on alternative ideological traditions in our cultural repertoire (Ewick and Silbey 1995; Sarat 2000a; Sarat and Simon 2001). Our project here is not to develop at length such challenges or counternarratives but to anticipate some of the visions that have so far been stifled by legal lore.

Legality and Legal Culture

Interrogating the cultural politics of the lawsuit crisis is just one aim of our study, however. We also emphasize at the outset that this book's more general subject is law and legal culture. Indeed, to a large extent the lawsuit crisis provides but one provocative and consequential case study for investigating the dynamics of the creation of legal knowledge in mass society. Our approach again departs from the familiar realist tendency to distinguish between law and society as separate spheres (Sarat 2000a; Sarat and Simon 2001). As we see it, it is insufficient to recognize simply that "popular culture as reflected in the media, is not, and cannot be taken as, an accurate mirror of the actual state of living law" (Friedman 1989, 1588). Instead, our project builds on a rich tradition of study that envisions law itself as diverse forms of specialized knowledge that permeate and structure practices throughout contemporary society. Such forms of legal knowledge, it is commonly recognized, are inherently indeterminate, fluid, contingent, and contested. Legal norms and narratives are routinely reconstructed and mobilized by different actors in varying contexts. This understanding thus points to yet another meaning of our book title. In short, *law is inherently distorted—twisted, manipulated, reshaped—into multiple forms by ordinary practical activity.* The emphasis of this perspective is not on how empirical facts are violated so much as on how certain legal narratives develop, circulate, and come to be accepted as a truth of social life, while many other plausible legal constructions are discarded, displaced, or diminished.

Analysis regarding mass media constructions of law thus represents a logical extension of legal study that addresses commonplace knowledge about law in routine social interaction (Silbey and Sarat 1987). As Ewick and Silbey (1998) argue,

> The law seems to have a prominent cultural presence . . . , occupying a good part of our nation's popular media, providing grist for both news and entertainment. . . . Thus law is experienced as both strange and familiar; an episodic event and a constant feature of our lives; deadly serious and a source of humor and entertainment; irrelevant to our daily lives and centrally implicated in the way those lives are organized and lived. (17)

So prominent is this relationship that political scientist Douglas Reed (1999) has given the provocative label of "juridico-entertainment complex" to the sum of mass media representations—from news reporting to "real" documentaries to fictional dramas and comedies—regarding police, lawyers, judges, legal disputing, courtroom trials, and the like that saturate and inform contemporary mass culture (see also Chase 1986b; Macauley 1989).

Such narratives of legal practice not only take on a life of their own in mass culture, we suggest. In addition, alluring stories that circulate in the media *about* law often pervade and profoundly reshape—or, again, *distort*—legal policymaking and ordinary legal practice itself. Accounts of disputing practices or courtroom dramas thus may vary in important ways among practicing attorneys, sitting judges, plaintiffs and defendants, scholars, news journalists, screenwriters, novelists, and even comedians or cartoonists, but they all contribute to a complexly constructed "reality" of cultural understandings that we identify with law or legality.[16] As such, knowledge of and about law is routinely produced, reproduced, and reconstructed through the complex circuitry of mass-mediated culture.

At the same time, we frankly acknowledge the limitations of our study.

---

16. Edelman, Abraham, and Erlanger (1992, 47) make a similar point. While acknowledging that the mass character of the construction of legal knowledge has changed over time, our approach rejects the proposition (see Sherwin 2000) that law and popular culture ever were separate and that the line today is "vanishing."

It is important to emphasize that our direct focus in this book is the mass production of legal knowledge rather than the variable ways in which that knowledge becomes meaningful in the legal consciousness of variously situated citizens.[17] We fully recognize that news narratives, tort tales, and manufactured versions of common sense can be constructed (*distorted*, again, one might say) to mean different things by different people in different situations. To gauge the range and distribution of these variable, context-specific understandings would require a very different type of study from that we undertake here. Moreover, it is undeniable that a wide variety of legal knowledges and narratives circulates in modern society. In fact, we identify some of the accounts about law that challenge, complicate, deepen, or undermine the significance of the specific critical narratives about the litigation explosion and excessive rights claiming at the core of this study.

Nevertheless, our project complements in important ways studies that focus attention on the legal consciousness of citizens (Ewick and Silbey 1998; McCann and March 1995; Merry 1990; Nielsen 2004). Our study addresses complex ways in which legal lore develops and circulates among policymakers, lobbyists, the intelligentsia, journalists, and other elites. Moreover, we analyze at length a set of familiar narratives, scripts, and logics that mediate between official law and everyday legality, "writing" conventional legal referents into the lives of citizens (see Mezey 2001). To the extent that these widely circulated story lines figure prominently in the cognitive archives from which media-attentive citizens actively construct

17. Two specific choices of terminology are worth noting here. First, we use the term "mass" rather than "popular" culture to emphasize the corporate logics of mass media at work in cultural production processes (see Kammen 1999; Daniels and Martin 2000). Legal knowledge is constructed at all levels of social life, but our primary focus is limited to the important processes of systemically manufactured knowledge about civil legal practice. Likewise, we use the term "lore" to connote a particular form of legal understanding for related reasons. That term usually refers to bodies of knowledge about a topic that are shared among specific populations. The word is commonly used in the compound form of "folklore." In many ways, folklore, and "folk knowledge," connote the types of familiar, didactic, and often humorously stigmatizing narrative logics that we investigate. See, for example, Bird 1976; Brunvand 1968; Burns 1969; Cohen 1987; Dundes 1990; Fine 1992; McLuhan 1951; and, among sociolegal scholars, Steiner, Bowers, and Sarat 1999. However, the addition of the prefix "folk" implies origins and primary transmission of that knowledge through informal oral traditions by ordinary people. While the power of narratives in ordinary discourse is part of our larger story, our empirical focus again is more on the institutionalized production and transmission of knowledge in our complex, technocratically administered, profit-driven corporate society. Our use of the term "circuitry" to refer to the transmission of this mass knowledge throughout social life owes much to Foucault, although we again underline the corporate aspects of knowledge production and the hierarchies served by these processes.

legal meaning, the narratives we identify can be expected to matter a great deal. Finally, we develop and illustrate with evidence several ways of thinking about the impact of mass-produced legal knowledge. All in all, we suggest, the *common plays of law* generated through the circuitry of media culture surely infuse and inform the *common place of law* in everyday experience (Ewick and Silbey 1998). Mass-manufactured legal knowledge constitutes and reconstitutes law itself. As such, we cautiously ascribe to these stories of proliferating litigation *hegemonic* status, in that they seem to be pervasive, they tend to be taken for granted as truth by many citizens, they define the terms of contesting truth for others, and they thus for the most part work to uphold status-quo relations in society (see Hayden 1991).[18]

KNOWLEDGE PRODUCTION AS A PROCESS

Social constructionist analysis typically interrogates knowledge and meaning within varying cultural contexts. Such analysis often proceeds by critical interpretation of selected social texts. This book critically examines a wide variety of texts, including especially newspaper articles but also speeches, pamphlets, Web site material, articles, books, and other propaganda by political activists; scholarly articles and books; television and radio news reports; paid advertisements; movies and television entertainment shows; and interviews with political activists, lawyers, news reporters, and scholars. In this interpretive venture, we attempt to find common patterns in the narrative form and knowledge content that are produced and disseminated about civil legal practice in the contemporary United States.

Our interest transcends simply investigating discrete texts in this way, however. Rather, we are primarily interested in examining the multiple, interrelated paths through which such knowledge is created, disseminated, and entrenched in cultural practice. *Our particular approach thus emphasizes that the social construction of legal knowledge is a complex, dynamic, multidimensional process.* We posit three general dimensions—the instrumental, the institutional, and the ideological—of social practice that are important for analyzing these intricate cultural processes of narrative production.[19] While analytically discrete, these dimensions refer not to

18. One of us has defined hegemony as "the aggregate of socio-cultural-political forces that generate consent and induce acquiescence to power" (McCann 1994, 304). See Lears 1985; Ewick and Silbey 1998.

19. Our emphasis on "production" of knowledge implies a continuous process of construction, reconstruction, and dissemination in various public forums.

separate practices but rather to concurrent, interrelated aspects of ongoing social activity that constitute the dynamic process. This is to say that, in our scheme, we do not understand social actions as simply instrumental *or* institutional *or* ideological. Instead, we understand virtually all practices by means of a triangulation among the instrumental *and* the institutional *and* the ideological. By attending to these interrelated dimensions of power in social practices iterated over time, we hope to grasp the complex character of legal knowledge production processes through the circuitry of modern mass culture.[20]

Instrumental Designs: Political Contests and Forms of Knowledge

Our focus on the *instrumental* aspects of social practice shares much in common with realist frameworks and essentially takes individual actors or groups of actors as the units of analysis. We use the term "instrumental" in conventional ways to refer to the development and enactment of calculated designs by such social actors to achieve various self-identified social goals. Attention to the instrumental dimension of action thus emphasizes in particular the tactical or strategic aspects of social practice and especially those that are manifest in political contests among differently situated groups of actors. One especially significant aspect of most instrumental contests is the effort of some parties to control, or to influence, what others do or do not know and count or discount as relevant knowledge (Schattschneider 1960; Baumgartner and Jones 1993).

We note at the outset a dilemma intrinsic to the study of instrumental action. In short, attention to the strategic dimensions of action raises questions about whether such actors are sincere and honest in their aims or whether their words and actions intend to hide other less lofty motivations, like profit or partisan advantage. Our position is that most strategic action entails elements of both sincerity and manipulativeness in varying combinations that are difficult to untangle. We are prepared to accept that most actors believe, often profoundly, in the values and ideas that they advocate. Because they care so deeply, however, they also are willing to manipulate those values and ideas to convince others, even if this involves duplicitous acts of commission such as exaggeration or falsification and omission in communication. In other words, not only are sincerity and deception often interrelated, but constructions of interests and ideology

---

20. "The dimensions of power . . . must be seen as interrelated in the totality of their impact . . . such that each dimension serves to re-enforce the strength of the other" (Gaventa 1980, 20–21).

tend to be mutually constitutive in practice. For the most part, we take seriously the words of activists by probing the deeper logics that they express, linking them to actors' social positions and actions, and speculating about the interests that those logics render sensible and serve. At various points, we underline the palpable duplicity of some speech acts while still calling attention to the power of ideas at stake for actors and their audiences.

Our study addresses specifically the instrumental designs of those primary actors aiming to convince the mass public that our civil tort law system is or is not badly in need of fundamental reform. In the first part (chapters 2–4), we focus on three groups of instrumental actors who were introduced in the opening pages as dominating the contest over tort reform, and who generally have influenced the way we imagine the workings of our contemporary civil legal system. Our analysis of each group emphasizes not only the policy logic but the specific forms of evidentiary knowledge marshaled to advance that position and the venues in which that knowledge is communicated. In particular, we emphasize the different characteristics of anecdotal, case study, and statistical evidence regarding legal practice.

The first group of instrumental actors in our account is referred to generally as "populist tort reformers."[21] This label refers to a disparate cadre of corporate-sponsored policy elites, intellectuals, public relations specialists, lobbyists, media personalities, and their elected allies who have led the charge to identify and correct glaring inadequacies in our civil legal system. As noted above, their instrumental campaigns have relied heavily on disseminating simplistic anecdotes along with moralistic rhetoric to alarm the mass public about a litigation explosion by greedy, rights-obsessed plaintiffs and lawyers extorting innocent business corporations and undermining communal norms of civility. We, as do other sociolegal scholars, presume that the primary motivation of such reformers is the insulation of corporations from liability for harm and the commitment to secure, if not enlarged, profits. We also argue, however, that the movement is led by highly skilled advocates who deeply believe in the moral logics supporting the legal reforms that they champion. Indeed, such moralistic commitments link pop tort reformers to the broader agendas of neoliberal

---

21. We use the term "populist," or "pop," to distinguish media-oriented moralists from the diverse array of sophisticated policy advocates for specific tort reforms. It is tempting to label pop reformers as "conservatives." While most reformers are business supported, policy advocates range across the partisan spectrum and some do not fit the moralistic profiles we identify as pop or romantic advocates.

and New Right culture warriors.[22] Hence, we call attention to the complex, variable ways that material and moral motivations of political actors often merge.

The other two instrumental campaigns have emerged largely in response to the tort reform movement. One tactical crusade has been waged by personal injury lawyers, or the "plaintiffs' bar"—that group of attorneys and their allies who regularly represent plaintiffs in personal injury litigation and have expended considerable resources fighting against tort reform in legislatures and courts across the nation over recent decades. Two important points about this campaign are especially relevant to our analysis. The first is that plaintiffs' lawyers have invested heavily in a "stealth" strategy of insider political influence and largely opted out of the contest for influencing public discourse and opinion. We explore a number of reasons for this strategic response, not least of which include lawyers' resignation about the power of the conventional wisdom and their own divisions among themselves. Moreover, the limited public response of lawyers has been posed primarily in terms of challenging the "real" factual basis of legal horror stories. Sometimes these responses are complex and detailed case studies, but more often they echo the thin anecdotal renderings and partial, inflammatory, or dismissive tone of reformers and moralistic counterparts in the media.[23]

Finally, we also are interested in the role of realist sociolegal scholars in disputing tort reformers' claims. In one sense, it is misleading to label these scholars' challenges as "instrumental," in that they undeniably are committed to norms of intellectual rigor and professional academic respectability. Yet such scholars typically display relatively greater confidence and even disdain in their retorts than do the personal injury lawyers who are under assault. One reason for this is that most scholars can cite copious social scientific data demonstrating that tort reformers' allegations about a litigation explosion, wildly irresponsible juries, and the like are highly misleading about actual patterns of legal practice. As such, the scholars can have it both ways: they can be impartial social scientists com-

22. We use the term "neoliberal" to identify advocates of pro-business, market-oriented, antiregulatory values and visions of socioeconomic organization and public policy. New Right (or neoconservative) advocates, by contrast, focus on conservative social values; they vigorously oppose "liberal collectivism" and a cultural worldview that is said to diminish "religiosity, morality, individual responsibility, and family authority" (McGirr 2001, 10). The two visions share a common commitment to the ethos of individual discipline and self-governance—core values that permeate the current discourse about the lawsuit crisis.

23. For an informed Associated Press study dramatizing the salience of instrumental interest-group activity and campaign spending around issues of tort liability and the lawsuit crisis in Congress, see Salant 2003.

mitted to rigorous empirical research methodologies *and* partisan advocates confidently trumpeting the implications of findings that those methods produce. However, we also suggest that the professional commitments of scholars to specialized forms of statistical knowledge presented in largely esoteric law reviews and academic journals render their instrumental impact in public life as relatively modest (see Rhode 1999, 140). In other words, their very claim to authority as professional experts has limited the scholars' public visibility, accessibility, and influence in the battle to shape cultural knowledge of law.

Our discussion of these various groups together highlights the contested character of legal narratives and knowledge as well as the relationship of that specific contest to the larger culture wars in early-twenty-first America. Attention to these instrumental actors also clarifies one major theme of our explanation regarding why some accounts or logics win out over others in the mass media and throughout popular culture. When one group, like pop tort reformers, focuses on shaping the public agenda around core moral concerns, while primary opponents focus their energies in more esoteric pursuits, we should not be surprised when the former group has substantially greater success. Finally, these studies also suggest that some forms of knowledge are more likely to prevail than others in contemporary mass-media culture.

Institutional Practices: News Reporting Conventions

Political actors seeking to expand their influence in public life routinely conduct their activities within institutional venues. In contemporary American politics, most political advocacy groups undertake multidimensional strategies that direct energies into multiple institutional settings. Each institutional setting, moreover, is governed by rules, norms, conventions, and relational structures that encourage, invite, and reward various modes of interaction, while discouraging, disadvantaging, stifling, or excluding others. As Schattschneider put it, each venue expresses its own *mobilization of bias* "in favor of the exploitation of certain types of conflict and the suppression of others. . . . Some issues are organized into politics while others are organized out" (1960, 71; see also Bachrach and Baratz 1970). As such, instrumental efforts to wield influence in turn tend to be highly influenced and shaped by the constellation of conventions, relations, and practices in each specific institutional setting.

We explore a variety of institutional venues in which battles over tort reform have been waged over recent decades in the United States. However, we commit the second part of this book primarily to the study of one institutional venue of great power in modern society: the mass media.

While we cast our analytical net widely at times, we focus most directly and extensively on practices of news reporting, especially but not exclusively in the print media. We focus on the print media for three reasons. First, the print media shape the agenda for other news media and for mass culture generally. As Downie and Kaiser (2002) summarize:

> In America's towns and cities, the local newspaper sets the news agenda. A few major newspapers do the same for the national news media. . . . Television news depends on newspapers, as its practitioners freely attest. Radio news is often lifted right out of the newspapers. Government officials and politicians understand the primacy of newspapers and regularly go to newspaper reporters first with important or complicated information. The news organizations maintained by newspapers are what make America's . . . press meaningful. (64)[24]

Second, it has been argued that, while citizens tend to view television news as part of the entertainment medium in which it is embedded, newspaper accounts are viewed as far more serious and reliable, more true and objective (Salomon 1979, 1984; Neuman, Just, and Crigler 1992). In this sense, constructions of legal reality by the print media may be most consequential in that they provide the foundational knowledge that makes other constructions more "real." Finally, newspapers also are, fortunately, electronically accessible, rendering them available for the type of systematic analysis that we have undertaken. It is important to highlight that our unit of analysis is not personal predilections of individual journalists so much as the standardized conventions that govern the systematic production of familiar narrative logics, selected story lines, and solicited commentary in the news that journalists report. This focus does not deny that reporters and editors exercise considerable discretion and even bring their own instrumental designs and ideas to their work. However, institutional analysis assumes that such discretion is significantly delimited and shaped by the shared contexts and learned routines of everyday work activity in an orderly, profit-driven corporate environment and moralistic culture.[25]

24. See also Cook 1998, 79; Epstein 1973, 140–3.

25. Martha Feldman has suggested the concept of "order without design" to make sense of modern news reporting. See Bennett 1996, 12–13, 33. Our argument here is not that news reporters are determined by routines, nor is it that their personal motives—job security, promotion, raises, respect, and so forth—play no role. Rather, we suggest that institutionalized news reporting practices dramatically channel those personal interests and designs into particular directions in their work activity.

Our study follows the lead of many media scholars in contending that such news gathering and reporting practices best account for the systematic slants of the news. On the one hand, analysts explain, reporters work for corporate organizations that need to sell advertising, thus putting a premium on news that is accessible, intriguing, even entertaining. Journalists can distinguish themselves and advance their careers by variously combining different mixes of these virtues in their reporting, but most journalists learn to be sensitive to both general professional norms and the need to enhance their organization's capacity to provide what they think readers want to read, see, or hear.[26] On the other hand, reporters must regularly operate under constraints of severely limited time, money, and access to information. News reporting is a high-pressure, short-deadline job that privileges reliance on work routines, conventions, and formulas to simplify the choices that must be made and to standardize the operating procedures of information gathering and presentation. As Thomas Patterson (1993) and other scholars have shown, American journalists in particular follow very similar processes in deciding what events to report, how to report them, and which authorities to consult in the process.

The specific institutional pressures placed on journalists by professional norms, organizational demands, and news sources have been documented at length elsewhere (Bennett 2001; Patterson 1993; Tuchman 1978). Most important for our inquiry, instead, are the established formulas, scripts, and logics themselves that shape routine selection of events and modes of presenting those events as news in the present age of *infotainment*. We follow in particular the argument of Lance Bennett (2001) that journalistic reliance on standardized norms privileges news narratives that dramatize, personalize, fragment, and normalize the presentation of events and relationships, thus reconstructing complex social relations and policy issues in simplistic, systematically skewed ways. Legal scholar Deborah Rhode (1999, 139) argues that this is especially important with regard to portrayals of legal matters, emphasizing that the "way that journalists frame their coverage helps reshape the legal world that they claim only to represent."

The second part of this book (chapters 5–7) presents copious evidence demonstrating how news accounts of civil litigation fit the features described by Bennett while ignoring critical information regarding the fac-

---

26. Communications scholar Doug Underwood has written that "[t]oday's market-savvy newspapers are planned and packaged to 'give readers what they want'; newspaper content is geared to the results of readership surveys, and newsroom organization has been reshaped by newspaper managers whose commitment to the marketing ethic is hardly distinguishable from their version of what journalism is" (1993, xii).

tual and normative complexity of events. This systematic selectivity is apparent with regard both to *which* events are reported as news and to *how* they are included in news accounts. We shall see that the practices of news reporting shape the instrumental efforts of policy activists to reach the public through news media as well as represent a quasi-autonomous force in knowledge production that variously expresses, parallels, mutes, and contradicts the messages of various players in the tort reform policy contest for public influence. As noted already, however, the general conclusion that emerges from our study is that the simplistic, fragmentary *form* and dramatized, personalized, decontextualized *content* of most news reporting about civil litigation parallels to a remarkable degree the simplistic, anecdotal moral accounts and titillating tales routinely circulated by tort reformers. Documenting this homology between the tort reform message and ordinary media constructions of legal practice, along with the undeniable instrumental impact of reformers on media reporting, is at the heart of our argument about the production of the reigning legal lore.

We also examine the interrelationship between newsgathering practices and the institutionalized constraints of the legal process itself. For one thing, the sheer length, complexity, and uncertainty of legal proceedings deter most journalists from coverage of routine civil trials. As a result, critical processes of fact presentation, evidentiary interpretation, and principled legal argument typically escape news coverage of civil disputes. Reporting focuses instead on claims and counterclaims of parties preceding trials and following judgments or settlements, thus reinforcing perceptions about the adversarial, interest-oriented character of contests and the arbitrary character—the alleged "litigation lottery"—of outcomes. Even more important, the common practices of judicially enforceable confidentiality agreements and protective orders binding parties to negotiated settlements significantly restrict information about corporate negligence, calculations, deceptions, and practices that harm the citizenry. Silenced plaintiffs and their attorneys who know the most thus are denied from sharing their knowledge with reporters and the public. In this way, institutionalized news conventions and legal processes together shape and limit what the public knows about legal practice. As such, our study underlines the arguments of other scholars that the news media and law are interrelated, often mutually supportive institutional forms "representing order" and maintaining social control in mass society (Ericson et al. 1991).

When recognition of these factors is joined to additional data showing that reform-minded "authorities" are well represented in both spot news and feature stories, it is not difficult to understand how piecemeal, pejorative images and understandings of our legal system have developed considerable interpretive power in the juridico-entertainment complex informing mass society (Reed 1999). This understanding points to a final meaning of our book title. "Distorting the law" refers to the familiar amplification of simple, fuzzy, but often titillating narratives about the litigation explosion that is so common in contemporary mass-mediated culture, which in turn muffles alternative signals and reshapes the very forms of practical legal activity and meaning construction throughout society. While granting passing attention to some of the much-analyzed fictional portrayals of law in these media, we focus on news production precisely because its narrative representations tend to be accepted as those most "real" and legitimate by readers. This especially seems true with regard to the familiar moral lessons drawn by citizens from news reporting (Neuman, Just, and Crigler 1992). As such, news reporting provides a foundation of legal knowledge on which additional images and information from entertainment media and savvy reform propaganda build the edifice of manufactured lore about the litigation crisis.

Ideological Factors: The Pull of the Individualist Ethic

We also consider, finally, the role of *ideology* as a force at work concurrently in both instrumental calculation and institutional practices. By the term "ideology," we suggest neither the familiar behavioral equivalent of individual "attitudes" nor the structuralist conception of seamless, closed, static, coherent sets of abstract ideas that "determine" thinking and action. Rather, we envision ideology as definable but indeterminate cultural logics from which humans actively construct meaning and make sense of things. We emphasize that ideology tends to be generated dynamically through practical interaction; it involves ongoing processes of cultural practice "by which meaning is produced, challenged, reproduced, transformed" (Ewick and Silbey 1998, 225). In this sense, ideology refers to intersubjective conventions that constitute social life less by dictating or impeding thought than by inviting, encouraging, privileging, and facilitating certain types of interpretive constructions over others. Ideology matters because every way of seeing, understanding, and doing is a way of *not* seeing, *not* understanding, and *not* doing.

Moreover, ideology always embodies "a particular arrangement of power and affects life chances in a manner different from that of some other ideology or arrangement of power" (Ewick and Silbey 1998, 226). We are particularly interested in how certain inherited ideological configurations have been mobilized to sustain prevailing arrangements and dominant power hierarchies in America. At the same time, ideological configurations not only are indeterminate but often are replete with internal tensions, contradictions, and possibilities that enable considerable "play" in construction. Different parties often wage contests for influence across similar ideological terrain, constructing common themes into divergent, even clashing visions. Our study of the construction of legal lore thus both maps how various ideological themes have (and have not) been variously constructed to characterize tort law "reality" and analyzes why some of these constructions have emerged as more compelling than others. Because inherited ideological conventions figure variously into citizen formulations of interest as well as organizational practices, we interweave attention to ideology with discussions of instrumental and institutional dimensions throughout the study rather than isolate analysis in separate chapters.

Specifically, we are interested in how powerful, if indeterminate, norms of "individual responsibility" and populist antipathy toward formal state intervention in socioeconomic life figure into the dominant stories and arguments regarding tort law practice. We refer especially to the specific "ethic of individualism" that "emphasizes self-reliance, toughness, and autonomy—qualities that are posed as being central to progress and 'getting along' in a market economy" (Greenhouse, Yngvesson, and Engel 1994, 173). Somewhat paradoxically, such ideas about individual responsibility have been invoked both to stigmatize certain types of legally authorized rights claims by citizens and to affirm inherently romantic, even nostalgic images of shared *moral community* in contemporary America. Norms celebrating personal responsibility both provide a common value bonding citizens together in shared life *and* sustain a disciplinary ethos encouraging individuals to regulate themselves so as to minimize the need for state legal regulation. Communal order thus depends in both senses on morally self-governing, self-reliant individuals (Rose 1999).[27] As we shall see, this connection is often made through literal and metaphorical reference to organic *bodies*—to the importance of personal responsibility for the safety of one's material body and public conduct that is critical to the well-being of the collective body politic.

The invocation of this individualistic ideological construction is critical to understanding the moral power of the reigning common sense about tort law. We show in coming pages how both popular news accounts and prominent pundits together have reinforced inherited inclinations to blame social problems on pathologies of individual irresponsibility, negli-

---

27. The tendency to define social issues in terms of individual moral character or capacities, often linked to the celebration of a "moral community" comprised by responsible agents, is at the substantive core of our characterization of pop reformers as "moralists." In this view, excessive legalism and rights claiming signify moral failure or weakness in aggregates of individual agents.

gence, and greed among plaintiffs or their attorneys obsessed with rights claiming, rather than on incidents of corporate irresponsibility or the deficiencies of our public regulatory and insurance systems.[28] As such, familiar legal constructions of social relations in terms of individual choices and private contracts by citizen subjects are repeatedly reconstructed and reinforced by the cultural stories that we Americans tell ourselves *about* law, law's promises, and law's failures. At the same time, alternative conceptions of responsibility privileging citizen rights and entitlements sometimes enter into popular accounts, thus providing contrary meanings that implicitly or explicitly cut against the grain of pro-business reformers' critiques. In short, the ideologies of individualism and anti-statism play out quite complexly in both overt political clashes over tort reform and routine public constructions of legal events in our culture.

This specific analysis of individualistic and anti-statist ideologies is linked to broadly ranging discourses of governance about the changing "politics of risk" in advanced liberal capitalist societies. As contemporary scholars have argued, neoliberal regimes have experienced important strategic shifts in cultural discourses and technologies regarding personal security (Rose 1999; Baker and Simon 2002). Specifically, the logic of social insurance schemes and collective regulatory intervention that developed throughout much of the twentieth century, and which together informed many changes in tort law since the 1960s, no longer is viewed positively in terms of

> a socializing and responsibilizing principle of solidarity: not only does it not provide adequate security; not only does it represent a drain on individual incomes and on national finances; it also stifles responsibility, inhibits risk taking, and induces dependency. . . . Hence all individuals, not just the well off, would benefit if they took *upon themselves* the responsibility for their own security and that of their families. (Rose 1999, 159)

The discursive elements of individualist ideology may be quite traditional in American society, but their recent constructions within our contemporary social life and cultural politics signal new developments that merit attention in the following pages. Specifically, we note the linkage of these specific renderings of individualistic, anti-statist moral principles by romantic tort reformers to parallel assaults on welfare entitlement, affirma-

---

28. Scholars have similarly demonstrated how individualistic accounts trump "structural" analysis in public discourse about street crime (Scheingold 1984, 1991; Beckett 1997) and welfare policy (Gilens 1999).

tive action, anti-discrimination claims by gays and lesbians, fairness in the criminal justice system, and other basic rights at the heart of recent culture wars in the United States. This again underlines the connection of the lawsuit crisis to the neoconservative forces driving the culture wars over the last half century: claimants of consumer rights to redress for injury are stigmatized as "undeserving" in much the same was as are the welfare poor, the unemployed, the homeless, juvenile delinquents, "bad" girls, subversives, street criminals, and other "deviants" in American society. Equally destructive, in this moral vision, are the lawyers who encourage rights-claiming by such undeserving types. Moreover, while tales of the lawsuit crisis *dis* tort claimants as lacking moral discipline in facially impersonal, abstract terms, we suggest that the assault has implications for class, race, and gender hierarchies similar to more direct attacks on specific groups. Finally, narratives about the lawsuit crisis participate in the culture wars by focusing on mass media as both the end and means of producing legal knowledge and moral disciplinary power.

The Complexities of Cultural Knowledge Production

Our analysis regarding the general processes that produce common legal knowledge and its deployment in reinterpreting the lawsuit crisis incorporates all three of these analytical dimensions—the instrumental, the institutional, and the ideological. The general argument of this book, in short, is that the simplistic narratives disseminated by policy-driven tort reformers have at once reinforced and been reinforced by everyday news reporting along with enduring ideological commitments endorsing individual responsibility and disparaging legalistic state paternalism. Legal knowledge thus has resulted only in small part from the reformers' instrumental efforts to saturate the news with their message. After all, as illustrated by our opening account of the case involving Judith Haimes, the overwhelming bulk of tort reformers' "evidence," including their much touted tort tales, originates in print or electronic news. We thus emphasize how the institutionally driven production of infotainment—in most cases uninformed by trial records, by key evidence legally shielded from public disclosure, or by scholarship documenting larger patterns of practice—circulates both trivial stories and serious news that highlight seemingly arbitrary high-stakes civil litigation against corporate producers and professionals.

At the same time, news reporters have afforded business-friendly reformers easy institutional access for continually recycling old stories through op-ed articles and adding critical spin to breaking news, further reinforcing for readers and reporters alike the pervasive subtexts regarding a dramatic litigation explosion that permeates popular culture. Meanwhile, instrumental efforts of lawyers and academic experts to challenge the narrative have been compelling and well funded in many regards, but they have tended to be waged in forms and forums that enjoy only limited exposure in mass culture. The result is that ordinary news institutions, popular entertainment conventions, and pro-business advocates have worked in both parallel and convergent, independent and interactive, ways to sustain ideologically loaded cultural narratives portraying the irrational tort litigation lottery complex. This process over time has been cumulative and interactive but uneven and shifting, as multiple narratives and counternarratives of imagined events circulate throughout mass culture, fundamentally reconstructing legal knowledge and practice. We thus illustrate, for example, how political debates concerning high profile tobacco litigation in the 1990s directly follow cultural constructions of legal disputing during the previous decades. All in all, our goal is not just to reinterpret the evolution of the lawsuit crisis, but to render this complex process of interrelated instrumental, institutional, and ideological factors shaping knowledge production in the juridico-entertainment establishment more comprehensible and, frankly, more unsettling than have previous scholarly accounts.

MOBILIZING EVIDENCE: A PLURALISTIC APPROACH

Our ambitious project builds on a variety of different, often competing scholarly traditions of sociolegal analysis. This curious mix not only synthesizes realist and social constructivist interpretations, but it employs traditional methods of data collection in the service of a process-based, post-positivist epistemological orientation to knowledge production outlined above. This unusual integration of eclectic approaches to the subject deserves some brief attention at the outset.

The empirical evidence we offer generally reflects the quite varied modes of mass communication about law. For example, our effort to trace tort reform advocacy involves analyzing a disparate array of communicative media, including: newspaper and radio commentary; official pamphlets; Web site text; speeches and position statements; intellectual books; professional journal articles; and the like. Given the diversity of such media, we have chosen relatively unsystematic, perhaps even impressionistic, qualitative techniques for identifying substantive themes and evidentiary logics in movement advocacy. Our coverage of scholarly studies regarding tort litigation practices as well as advocacy by personal injury lawyers likewise reflects the different evidentiary logics employed by these actors, ranging from extensive statistical studies to simple anecdotes.

In the second part of the book, by contrast, we engage in quite systematic studies of media reporting, including quantitative results of content analysis regarding: a large data set of patterns in print news reports regarding tort, and especially products liability, litigation over a nineteen-year period; detailed newsworth practices and ideological themes at work in multiple-media coverage of the McDonald's coffee case; and changing policy themes in print news coverage about tobacco litigation. Even in these sections, however, our specific coding techniques vary significantly to make sense of different data sources, narrative logics, and analytical questions. Moreover, less formal qualitative content analyses of specific news accounts, editorials, and feature stories from each of these data sets are included as well. Our final chapter compounds this diversity by presenting a wide array of both qualitative and quantitative data sources as well as diverse conceptual perspectives to demonstrate how prevailing legal narratives matter for social life.

Chapter 5 provides details regarding our systematic content analysis of news articles. In addition, we refer readers to our Web site that makes available our data for general examination and offers much additional commentary about what those data do and do not reveal here.[29] The Web site also provides commentary regarding a host of related issues and electronic links to many Web sites relevant to the subject of this book.

Finally, a brief word about interviews is in order. We conducted nearly fifty interviews over four years, roughly half with journalists and half with political advocates in the tort reform debates. Our primary goals in these interviews were to gain insights and information for our study rather than to engage interviewees as subjects of direct study. As such, the interviews were not conducted systematically, in uniform fashion. Most interviews were taped and transcribed, however, and we chose to use in the following text a very few quotes from interviewees—most anonymously—to illustrate or support specific interpretive points.

We firmly believe that this effort to present multiple types of data within an integrated conceptual scheme holds considerable merit. We follow the basic principle of *triangulation* in the mobilization of evidence as well as in conceptual analysis. If one assumes that all existing modes of knowledge are intrinsically selective, partial, and problematic, then a sensible response by social scientists is to rely on multiple types of data that are attuned to the diverse social phenomena under consideration, that offset the limitations of each mode separately, and that together provide a more complex view of the elusive phenomena at stake. We further believe that such a complex analysis is especially appropriate for our particular ex-

29. www.lawslore.info.

ercise in social constructionism, which explicitly engages, afer all, in critically interpreting multiple layers of interpretations by diverse others. When struggling to probe the imprecise, indeterminate processes of human communication, humility about the challenges and limits of our capacity to balance analytical rigor, coherence, and reliability seems warranted. The cost of such an approach, of course, is often manifest in severe limitations on the parsimony, elegance, and verifiability of the resulting study. We do apologize in advance to readers for the considerable amount of data and complexity that are included here. But we have no compunction about presenting a picture that is dense, detailed, and drenched in paradox, contradiction, and irony.

THE ORGANIZATION OF THE BOOK

We have outlined in previous pages the key elements and dimensions of this books' conceptual framework. We review here briefly the organizational logic of our chapter development in an effort to render our complex argument more accessible.

The book is organized into two primary parts, each with three chapters; these two parts are sandwiched between this introduction and a concluding chapter. Part 1 focuses primarily, but not exclusively, on the instrumental dimensions of the political contest over tort reform. Separate chapters profile the primary advocates, organizational roots, political tactics, and communicative practices of the three primary groups that we identify: pro-business tort reformers (chapter 2), sociolegal scholars who are critical of pop tort reform (chapter 3), and the plaintiffs' bar that likewise opposes tort reform (chapter 4). Each chapter gives special attention to the form and content of policy positions that the respective groups tend to project, analyzing both the evidentiary basis of these arguments and the degree to which these claims do or do not articulate with dominant ideological currents in American society. One key point of these chapters is to show that tort reformers have focused their campaign on saturating the mass-mediated public space with their message, a commitment that has not been matched by their opponents. For each of the latter groups, both professional norms and legally mandated nondisclosure restrict the public responses to business interests. A second key point is to show that critics of tort reform have generally won the battle of empirical claims but failed to counter consistently the reformers' simple, ideologically powerful moral vision. The result has been something of a mismatch in the contest over message articulation within mass political culture (Eisenberg and Henderson 1992).

Part 2 shifts from a primary focus on instrumental politics to the institutional terrain of modern mass media in which this arguably skewed contest has been waged.[30] Our basic goal in the three chapters that constitute this part is to examine media coverage of tort litigation and the complex mix of interrelated factors that figures into this production of legal knowledge in the news and beyond. Chapter 5 focuses on a large data set dissecting national newspaper reporting over nearly twenty years to identify systematic patterns of newsworth selection in what readers do and do not learn about civil legal practice. This chapter underlines the striking homology between ordinary news stories about civil litigation and the morally titillating tort tales beloved by the media and regularly retold by reformers. Chapter 6 probes this logic further by an in-depth analysis of the most famous news story that became a tort tale, the saga of the seventy-nine-year-old woman who sued McDonald's for burns caused by hot coffee. This case study not only advances more detailed content analysis of newsworth selection practices in both spot news and editorials, but it permits extensive treatment of the individualistic ideology at work in such stories as well as traces the diffusion of the legend among a wide variety of popular electronic news and entertainment media. Our position in this chapter, as in the entire book, is not that the hot coffee case was rightly decided by the jury or the judge. Rather, our point is that coverage by newspapers and eventual recycling of the story through the juridico-entertainment complex confirmed dramatically the moralistic rants of tort reformers while precluding intelligent, informed deliberation about the reasonableness of the specific legal outcome, its relative (in)significance for understanding our civil justice system, and its potential utility for identifying the larger failures of the U.S. regulatory/welfare state.

Chapter 7 takes up the complicated, changing legacy of tobacco litigation as reported in the news. Tobacco litigation is especially interesting in that neither business-supported tort reformers nor their adversaries have made it a major part of the public tort reform debate, even though recent "mass tort" class actions represent a radically new, extremely expensive, highly problematic form of legal regulation that tobacco companies have spent fortunes to defeat. We generally find that news coverage during the 1990s was attuned to changing legal narratives highlighting corporate deception and public health costs in ways that trumped the traditional "individual responsibility" narrative. However, business-initiated spin and

30. The title of part 2, "Reporting Legal Realities," captures the many sides of our analysis. According to the New Oxford American Dictionary, to report is to: (1) give a written account; (2) cover an event as a journalist; (3) indicate that something has been stated, although one cannot confirm its accuracy; (4) make a formal complaint to an authority; and (5) in law, provide a formal account of a case heard in a court.

newsworth framing inclinations ensured that the latter individualistic frame persisted. This default moral ethos was revitalized by increasing critical attention to huge attorney fees following successful plaintiff litigation in the late 1990s, thus inhibiting the triumph of narratives celebrating the contributions of the civil tort process to advancing justice and social welfare. This observation helps to explain why public opinion expressing great distrust toward tobacco companies also has been quite mixed about the litigation campaign generating both private and public financial redress. We also suggest how the focusing of attention on themes of individual responsibility and greedy lawyers effectively deflected critical attention away from the palpable abdication of government, not to mention corporate, responsibility regarding tobacco health dangers in previous decades.

Finally, the concluding chapter 8 summarizes our analysis and develops directly our more speculative argument regarding how the prevailing constructions of civil litigation in mass media culture matter for contemporary social relations. As noted above, we address first how law's lore shapes the politics of agenda setting in national life. Mass media representations of civil litigation practice not only implicitly confirm simplistic claims by tort reformers, we aver, but prevailing reporting practices facilitate efforts to redefine or derail a multitude of policy debates by elevating the fear of excessive litigation and lawyers' greed. We do not deny that the existing civil justice system is flawed in some fundamental ways and that some reforms are warranted. We acknowledge that, by themselves, jury trials of individual and class-action legal claims seldom are the optimal forums for making public policy regarding the dangers of faulty automobiles, scalding coffee, or incompetent doctors, much less the mass harms of asbestos, tobacco, and guns. Nevertheless, our point is that prevailing news coverage, popular narratives, and policy debates provide a highly inadequate knowledge base for understanding, much less judging, tort law institutional arrangements and practices. At the same time, the reigning legal lore tends to discourage public attention regarding the larger failures of our supposedly more "democratic" political institutions in providing basic citizen welfare and security—those very ends that litigation has, for better or worse, been mobilized to address in the contemporary age of global corporate power.

Second, we offer evidence suggesting that news reporting, widely circulated tort tales, lawyer jokes, and other popular representations combine to impose a moralistic discipline discouraging ordinary citizens from legal rights claiming while alarming managerial elites about exaggerated liability for their actions. In this sense, we develop a parallel between what Greenhouse, Yngvesson, and Engel (1994) refer to as "narratives of avoidance" among citizens in selected suburban communities and broader trends throughout the nation. This disciplinary discourse of law avoidance is not merely regulatory and constraining in its effects. Rather, our attention to how narratives are produced is matched by appreciation for their productive, or generative, capacities.[31] Narratives identifying and stigmatizing excessive litigiousness encourage a variety of actions—stoic conflict avoidance, self-healing, personal insurance schemes, informal dispute resolution, and the like—that moralistic reformers celebrate. As we see it, challenges by scholars, trial lawyers, and others to the factual accuracy of these negative legal narratives often overlook, and leave unchallenged, their power as romantic prescriptions for a community of cooperative, responsible, and self-reliant individuals, prescriptions that resonate powerfully throughout American society. In our view, such narrative logics again have significant implications for insulating corporate producers and professionals from legal accountability while, again, deflecting attention from the undemocratic, unresponsive character of modern welfare state governance. Challenges to tort law in this sense overlap with and fortify general assaults on the practices of ordinary citizens in claiming rights to secure lives and just remedies for harm.

31. "What makes power hold good, what makes it accepted, is simply the fact that it doesn't weigh on us as a force that says no, but that it traverses and produces things, it induces pleasures, forms knowledge, produces discourses. It needs to be considered as a productive network which runs through the whole social body, much more than as a negative instance whose function it is to repress" (Foucault 1980, 119).

PART ONE

Contesting Legal Realities

CHAPTER TWO

Pop Torts: Tales of Legal Degeneration and Moral Regeneration

When his electric power mower gets clogged with wet grass, a man turns it over and, without turning it off, reaches into the blade area and begins removing the clotted grass. He loses several fingers, sues the manufacturer . . . and wins. . . . Today the object is to collect—from someone. . . . There is usually someone else around with a "deep pocket" to pay. This entitlement mentality has a terrible, corrosive effect on American society. . . . It's time to restore the principles of self-reliance and personal responsibility to our civil justice system, and there are some practical reforms that will do this.

NEWSPAPER ADVERTISEMENT FOR AETNA LIFE AND CASUALTY

American life is increasingly characterized by plaintive insistence, I am a victim. . . . *The mantra of victims is the same:* I am not responsible; it's not my fault. . . . *In the law, the proliferation of causes of action has created a society whose leitmotif is the cry "Don't Blame Me!" . . . A substantial reform of tort liability could begin to roll back the tide of briefs, injunctions, and writs that has flooded the culture of victimization. . . . It's time to drop the crutch.*

CHARLES J. SYKES, *A NATION OF VICTIMS*

Litigation and its threat have begun to metastasize to virtually every sector of the economy. . . . Some boast that America is the most advanced of all nations in developing rights of redress. But in fact we are among the most backward, because our legal system does not redress the ills it inflicts itself.

WALTER K. OLSON, *THE LITIGATION EXPLOSION*

[L]aw cannot save us from ourselves. . . . Let judgment and conviction be important again. . . . Relying on ourselves is not, after all, a new ideology. It's just common sense.

PHILIP K. HOWARD, *THE DEATH OF COMMON SENSE*

We begin our review of instrumental politics with the campaigns of those activists who have widely publicized narratives about the litigation explosion to advance the cause of tort reform. Intellectuals, policy elites, politicians, and interest group partisans have advocated reforms of civil justice for decades, but the publicizers and popularizers on whom this chapter focuses have extended such advocacy among broader audiences to secure greater visibility for selected visions and versions of legal change. While the evidence supporting the broad charges of "pop" tort reformers has been contested from the start, their core message has proved quite alluring in contemporary mass culture. In fact, we contend that the very qualities that have drawn the most criticism from intellectuals have made the reform rhetoric more widespread and more memorable, producing an advantage in debates, deliberations, and other discourse. Our survey begins by outlining the basic logic of tort law, the important changes wrought in tort law practice in post–World War II America, and the political response of established interests seeking to reverse those developments. The second section provides a brief taxonomy of the tort reform movement—its organizational structure, strategic activities, financial base, and leadership network. We then proceed to outline the core forms and substance of knowledge communicated by pop tort reformers. These have included dramatic statistical claims, catchy phrases, protracted sermons on core ethical themes, and, perhaps most important, arresting anecdotal representations of legal failure. Running through all these forms of knowledge is a preoccupation with the forfeiting of individual responsibility that the modern, liberalized tort regime has encouraged and the need for a return to "commonsense" values and disciplined behavior. Our account concludes with some speculations about why these moralistic appeals seem to have struck a responsive chord in American mass culture. We assess the apparent effectiveness of these instrumental appeals specifically in terms of their fit with both the institutional proclivities of mass media and prevailing ideological currents in American political culture, themes that will be developed later in the book.

TORT LAW, TORT REGIMES, AND TORT REFORM

Some Basics of Tort Law

A tort is a legally actionable wrong that is neither criminal nor contractual. One commits a tort when one causes injury to persons or property by defaulting on some responsibility or expectation sanctioned by legislation or adjudication. Tort disputes are civil matters—unlike criminal matters, in which governments undertake to prove beyond a reasonable doubt that accused persons have violated with illicit intent duly enacted and carefully articulated laws backed by fines or imprisonment. In civil matters, some party or parties, perhaps including governmental officials or entities, blame others for failing to behave as a reasonable and responsible citizen would have done. If the misbehavior is said to have violated voluntary, explicit agreements, a dispute may take shape under the principles of contract law to establish what the disputants originally had agreed. Tort claims may include intentional harms, but far more often they involve accidental, unintended, and even unexpected harms resulting from (often poorly performed but) otherwise legitimate activity, including routine automobile accidents; unsafe facilities or property that result in personal injury; production of goods such as vehicles, drugs, clothing, food and the like that harm consumers; harmful by-products from production of goods, such as toxic chemicals in groundwater; and careless or incompetent practices by doctors or other professionals that result in physical infirmity, disability, or death. Complex social relations often will arguably involve criminal and civil laws and norms as well as contractual, quasi-contractual, and non-contractual understandings, but tort reforms concentrate on legal liabilities that do not follow from contracts or crimes.

Usually, the tort-victim and tort-feasor resolve conflicts short of securing legal representation or filing suit, so informal reconciliation or termination of disputes over liability for harm is the rule and formal tort cases are exceptions. If a matter reaches or threatens to reach a court, the aggrieved becomes a plaintiff, the party blamed becomes a defendant, and plaintiff and defendant repair to some more or less formal venue for resolution of the matter guided by tort doctrines. Those doctrines, shaped by judges or legislators over decades or centuries, detail circumstances under which the injured party may be able to shift a loss to another party or parties (Schuck 1991, 17). Despite the complexities and indeterminacies of competing principles, observers may identify the habitual judgments of courts and legislatures. Those habitual rulings constitute the tort regime: the harms about which decisionmakers will probably do something, the losses that this jury or that judge may recompense, and the costs that may be shifted to those who might better bear them.

Tort regimes, in practice, thus generate calculations of probabilities based on notions that "are as loose-jointed, context-sensitive, and openly relativistic as any principles to be found in the law. They do not simply accommodate social change; they *invite* the law to adapt to it" (Schuck 1991, 18; italics in original). Criminal law and contract law must be fairly predictable lest they fail to serve their core functions, but applications of tort law tend to be less foreseeable. Doctrines of criminal law almost always correspond to widely recognized mores, and principles of contract law aim to allow parties to an agreement to make law for themselves within broad social and moral perimeters. Because tort law frequently deals with unintended, unexpected, perhaps even unforeseeable consequences of often technically complex activity, tort principles usually are far more general and thus less explicit than either criminal laws or contract principles. Moreover, tort doctrines usually conserve the negotiations, accommodations, and compromises by which courts or legislatures produced tort decisions, with the result that tort "law" is seen to be more protean than other kinds of law, contrary to expectations that law should be settled. Consequently, tort rules in a given regime are sometimes unpredictable, the categorizations of facts unreliable, and the policies up for grabs. For most of American history, the discretion inherent in tort law arguably has worked in favor of the largest, most development-oriented enterprises and well-organized corporate interests (Horowitz 1979). Newly legislated regulatory and compensatory schemes—such as systematic workers' disability compensation, health insurance, zoning regulation, and environmental protection—have developed in various periods precisely to replace inadequate, piecemeal, inconsistent tort mechanisms.

The Historical Context of Contemporary Tort Reform

Changes in tort law have not been steady over time; rather, they have been mostly episodic, often responding to changes in and contests over core social relations. One important, unique period of change was the post–World War II era, when courts generally began to reduce the hurdles facing civil litigants—broadening standing, trimming immunities, abandoning the privity requirement in tort disputes—and enlarged the range of potential awards (Galanter 2002). These legal innovations were soon followed by a variety of social reform movements that actively mobilized law to make government, corporations, and select groups of professionals (doctors, for example) more responsive to, and responsible for, serious material injuries to consumers, minorities, women, the poor, and the environment. During the 1960s, prominent spokespersons at once exalted the promises of law for increasing civil justice in corporate America and decried the many barriers that impeded law's promise, including not least those from the legal profession. Reform leaders such as Ralph Nader inspired the "public interest law" movement and "access to justice" movement aiming to increase the responsibilities of powerful organizations both within and through the law.

These liberal public-interest movements developed a multidimensional strategy with four interrelated components: passing new forms of civil rights and "social" regulatory statutes such as OSHA, NEPA, and other consumer and environmental acts; litigating against government to enforce regulatory action authorized by these laws; litigating directly via tort and civil rights claims to challenge and to regulate the harmful practices of large enterprises and professionals; and drawing mass media attention to expose the wrongs and harms of unaccountable power in contemporary society (McCann 1986). All these tactics aimed to increase the levels of anticipatory deterrence as well as compensatory "insurance" against the proliferating "risks" that rendered citizen-consumers vulnerable to harm in contemporary corporate society (Baker and Simon 2002; Rose 1999). These developments emerged, moreover, at the same moment in the late 1960s that the number of lawyers in our nation began to increase dramatically, far beyond the rate of population growth. All in all, this era of legally focused, security-oriented reform politics contributed to what often is called the increasing "judicialization" of politics and regulatory policy in the United States (McCann 1986).

Specific alterations in the regime of tort law during this era were, not surprisingly, widely perceived to disadvantage substantively and substantially those powerful established interests who were formerly advantaged, insulated, or uninvolved. Expansions of liability put entrepreneurs and enterprises on notice that some losses formerly borne by customers or society were now more likely to be assigned to those adjudged better able to anticipate or to afford them, which in turn materially altered costs, risks, and profits that economic decisionmakers might anticipate—or now be unable to anticipate. This provided cause for alarm among many corporate producers and select groups of professional service providers, most notably doctors. By the 1970s, tort awards were alleged to be ever more extravagant and arbitrary, which critics argued made corporate planning difficult, business profits and even assets less secure, and consumers as well as producers vulnerable.

The proliferation of activities subject to strict liability, for example, reduced potential plaintiffs' burden of proving fault on the part of providers of goods or services. Joint and several liability made deep-pocketed defendants available to defray losses that otherwise might have gone uncompensated.[1] However, this occurred at the expense of private producers and public agencies, who feared that they would pay lavishly for fault that

---

1. Joint and several liability refers to the "condition in which rights and liabilities are shared among a group of people collectively and also individually. Thus, if defendants in a negligence suit are 'joint and severally' liable, all may be sued together or any one may be for full satisfaction of the injured party" (Gifis 1995, 111).

was only minimally theirs and that they would not be able to recoup such payments from more blameworthy defendants for the same reasons that plaintiffs could not—the defendants most at fault often had the least assets. Among the most concerned enterprises with large revenues at stake were insurance companies that might have to make good an increasing number of dubious claims and suspect lawsuits.

Modern class-action lawsuits further transformed the nature, meaning, and capacity of tort adjudication.[2] Victims who once had no shot at compensation now had access to the litigation battlefield through mass forms of legal representation. "Cause lawyers" representing the disadvantaged and other "progressive" interest groups strategically remade tort doctrines in court cases to remedy large-scale wrongs even as unaffiliated litigators invented novel actions and remedies in specific cases to ameliorate particularized injuries. The potential for big awards in class-action cases as well as the rapid growth in punitive damage awards generally together boosted the material as well as moral incentives for attorneys on contingency fees to take cases for group interests previously underrepresented in the political and legal system.[3] This shift in legal liability for harm was often perceived as not only new, but as inherently unpredictable, capricious, and unwarranted. As Victor Schwartz, a leading lawyer and lobbyist for the tort reform movement told us, "the standards of punitive damages in most states are so vague that no one could really tell you what they are. . . . When you say you will be punished if you are reckless or wanton or malicious or intentional and these waves of words come to a jury, it really can come down to whether they like you or not."

Having seen progressives wrest judgments, doctrinal changes, and notorious awards through novel tactics and ever-expansive strategies, corporate defendants and those who feared they would soon be civil defendants redoubled their public defenses within and beyond courtrooms. The tort reform movement in the 1970s developed to challenge, roll back, and otherwise reconstruct this expanded liability regime of tort law.

---

2. A class action is a lawsuit brought by one person or group on behalf of many persons who have been, arguably, similarly injured. Class actions significantly enable nongovernmental legal advocates to overcome "free rider" problems in representing large, previously unorganized groups sharing a selective interest.

3. *Punitive damages* are commonly defined by contrast with *compensatory damages.* The latter are payments for actual damages suffered—medical bills, property repair, lost income or asset value, pain and suffering, and so forth. Punitive damages do not address losses of actual harm, but rather serve to punish the injuring party and to deter similar conduct generally in the future. Both types of remedies are distinguished from *injunctions,* which are orders for a party to act or refrain from acting in particular, injurious ways.

REFORMERS ON THE OFFENSIVE

Business-oriented reformers adopted a multidimensional strategy to advance their counterreform efforts. In keeping with the long-standing practices of business-friendly interests (Schattschneider 1960), tort reformers tended to use "insider politics" to readjust the tort regime and elements of tort law in legislatures, courts, and other councils of authority. They lobbied legislators, testified and otherwise provided information and ideas to investigators and formulators, published analyses and advocacy in elite journals, and argued vigorously but decorously before civic, business, academic, and especially governmental authorities for a return to commonsense standards of civil justice. Lobbying, testifying, and arguing articulated the negative consequences of the modern tort regime for national and local economies but accentuated the baneful effects of novel court decisions and settlements on national character as well. Although highly technical issues were necessarily raised, simple justice was as often invoked.

Over the last three decades, many reformers have complemented this insider politicking with additional efforts directed at what we call "pop tort reform." Pursuing strategies more common among business groups over the last decades of the twentieth century than before, pop tort reform "went public."[4] Pop reformers articulated their case ever more through mass media to condition public attitudes and to supply to the public information that would advance tort reforms. The use of "paid media" (advertisements that reformers pay newspapers or broadcasters to publish) and "free media" (publicity for which reformers do not pay media) has complemented the reformers' repertoire of influence.

This combination of tactics has greatly enhanced the capacity of pop tort reformers to shape knowledge about torts and the civil system. We distinguish analytically four aspects of this spreading of knowledge. First among essentials, *organization* protects mass-marketed reform from clashing messages, distracting disagreements about strategic themes, or other digressions. For messages to be mutually reinforcing and effective and energies to be complementary and targeted, organizations must draw on ample *financing,* and financial support itself must be obtained and man-

---

4. Political scientist Mark Smith notes a general strategic shift among business interests in the late twentieth century. "When it comes to *unifying* issues" like tort reform, he argues, "the most effective strategy for business involves shaping public mood" (2000, 194). Issues particular to specific business sectors, by contrast, are best advanced by different, often less publicly visible strategies.

aged in an organized and businesslike fashion. Beyond organizational and financial management, it follows, "outside" tort reformers must be able to rely on *leadership,* by which we mean personnel who exercise guidance of and control over the formulation and release of information. Organization, financing, and leadership are essential to the accomplishment of the pop tort reform mission, but *ideas* constitute that mission. Absent ideas that arrest attention, any knowledge imparted is more likely to sustain a trivia contest than a regime change. Although we next turn to consider organization, financing, and leadership separately, it was their strategic coordination in promulgating big, attractive ideas that enabled pop tort reformers to affect and to effect knowledge.

Organizing for Strategic Action

Because tort reform issued primarily from interests who perceived themselves to be damaged or endangered by changes in civil law, pop tort reform systematized efforts to reverse some legal developments and to ameliorate others through creation and dissemination of knowledge both comprehensible to ordinary citizens and consonant with reforms. To establish pop tort reform on a popularly accessible but intellectually imposing base, reformers drew on the prodigious outputs of the Manhattan Institute for Policy Research, a conservative think tank that has hosted such prominent intellectual trendsetters as George Gilder, Stephen and Abigail Thernstrom, and Charles Murray. The institute's monographs, articles in popular media, video recordings, and symposia have achieved great notice for pop tort reform ideas (Stefancic and Delgado 1996, 99). Just as important, however, may be the writings, writers, and ideas that the institute has funded, fostered, and furthered to augment the intellectual heft of the tort reform movement. We consider in turn the institute's contributions to popular and intellectual consideration of tort reform, remembering that successful movements find ways to make the popular and intellectual merge.

The central strategy of the institute's campaign has been to transform public opinion about the legal system. The think tank has explicitly committed itself to define the terms of discourse systematically as the primary means for "influencing the outcomes of the tort and civil justice debates" (Manhattan Institute internal memorandum, December 22, 1993). A 1986 Manhattan Institute memorandum, dated February 18, 1986 stated its understanding of how to shape debate:

- Journalists, like most other people, don't originate ideas so much as "absorb them, sometimes by direct contact with original thinkers but more often by exposure to their work."

- Liberal media bias is the product of systematic efforts by Left thinkers over several generations to influence reporters.
- "The printed word still plays a key role in informing national debate and reorienting popular thinking," thus requiring a continual flood of books, articles, and editorials by pro-business reformers to reshape the public agenda.
- "The competitive nature of journalism works to the favor of those with new ideas," thus providing opportunities for conservative thinkers with "well presented and properly marketed" ideas.
- "Communicating to a mass audience is a sophisticated business which is best left to the pros."
- "Throughout history, battles of ideas have usually been won by the offense," which privileges positive presentation of ideas that avoid or ignore rather than engage opponents.

Note that these six postulates appear to dichotomize between initiating activists and disseminating journalists. Practitioners actively impress their ideas on journalists. Journalists are presumed to absorb the influence of such ideas not quite passively but not very critically if and when ideas are presented and marketed deftly and professionally. Institute strategists reasoned that changes would result from the exertion of communicative force in one direction superior to force exerted in opposing directions. In this classic conception of instrumental group struggle, the press was presumed to absorb influence and pass messages along with great amplification and fidelity.

The Manhattan Institute also identified and supported public intellectuals to spread tort reform ideas. Most important, the think tank shaped debate by cultivating the "two gurus of the tort reform movement" (www .manhattan-institute.org, accessed August 7, 2002). They made Peter Huber their first "Civil Justice Fellow" and supported his writing of *Liability: The Legal Revolution and Its Consequences* and the follow-up *Galileo's Revenge: Junk Science in the Courtroom.* Through the institute's support and on the strength of his other literary and scholarly productions, Huber became the "academic superstar of the legal-reform movement," cited by Justice Sandra Day O'Connor (for whom he had clerked) and welcomed as frequent guest of the Senate Commerce Committee in the 1980s (Geyelin 1992). Although Huber's prominence followed from aggressive institute marketing of his books, copies of which were sent gratis to judges, law professors, and legislators (Geyelin 1992), one must not underestimate Huber's efforts to promote himself. Among Huber's greatest gifts was and is his ability to coin memorable phrases to convey otherwise difficult ideas. In *Galileo's Revenge,* for example, he launched the phrase "junk science"—

a term used to stigmatize manipulative use of dubious expert testimony regarding scientific research to advantage one's position in a trial—into the vernacular based on vignettes and debunking. Likewise, Huber's estimate of the annual cost to the economy of tort litigation—the "tort tax" discussed later in this chapter—caught Vice President Quayle's eye in *Forbes* magazine, in which Huber wrote a regular column. Huber has authored books with academic presses, but he made himself (with the help of the Manhattan Institute) a public intellectual by means of more popular media.

The institute has also touted Senior Fellow Walter K. Olson. *The Litigation Explosion: What Happened When America Unleashed the Lawsuit* is frequently mentioned by the institute to establish Mr. Olson's expertise. *The Rule of Lawyers: How the New Litigation Elite Threatens America's Rule of Law* furthered Olson's attack on lawyers and litigation. Like Huber, Olson has through his own exertions expanded the publicity accorded him by the institute. For example, he edits the Web site "overlawyered.com" to reach audiences through the Internet.

These two leading figures joined David Bernstein, Senior Fellow Michael Horowitz, and allied scholars like Jeffrey O'Connell (University of Virginia) and Lester Brickman (Cardozo School of Law) as the core leadership group of advocates. This corps has been active in a wide range of publicity and intellectual efforts, including publishing articles in law reviews and other academic journals as well as trade books; circulating working papers among policymakers; giving talks to influential organizations; and publishing articles and editorials throughout the specialized business and managerial press. Books well placed with commercial publishers secure visibility and credibility with relevant publics, and the institute works to secure favorable reviews and to distribute positive comments to potential book reviewers.

The Manhattan Institute also affords its staff opportunities to present their messages in controlled forums, away from the hurly-burly of academia or uncontrolled media. For example, on January 20, 1999, the institute hosted a luncheon conference entitled "Order in the Court: A Fresh Look at Litigation Reform in America" that featured Huber, Brickman, and Olson of the Manhattan staff but welcomed John Stossel of ABC News and former attorney general Richard Thornburgh. Collaboration with and organized presentations to sympathetic conferees improve the work of Manhattan personnel and provide attendees with the latest insights and reports. One analyst has claimed that the strength of the Manhattan Institute has been less in the generation of ideas and more in test-marketing ideas in the "Manhattan Forum" and provision to journalists of copy that touts tort reform (Chesebro 1993, 1710). Between 1986 and 1990, the institute sponsored twenty-three meetings on the reform of civil justice (Chesebro 1993, 1712 n. 336). "Civil Justice Memos" reach judges, law professors, politicos, and businesspeople. A senior fellow at the institute, Michael Horowitz, helped to design a "loser pays" proviso for a bill in the U.S. House of Representatives (Stefancic and Delgado 1996, 99). In sum, the Manhattan Institute and especially its Center for Legal Policy have suited ideas of pop tort reform to organization, financing, and personnel in a masterly manner.

If such efforts seem ordinary for a think tank, the "New Manhattan Project" shows the extraordinary savvy for marketing and publicity that guided the Manhattan Institute's efforts. The institute launched its "Project on Civil Justice Reform" in 1986 by inviting Richard Epstein (professor at the University of Chicago Law School) and Richard Willard (a leader of the Reagan administration's Tort Policy Working Group) to join Peter Huber (who had recently authored a law review article urging individuals to heed their own conduct more and worry about manufacturers' conduct less) to assess blame for the "liability crisis." According to Manhattan president William Hammett, the Institute then mailed a report of the proceedings to twenty-five thousand political, academic, media, and business leaders and hosted two follow-up workshops. The project's director Walter Olson wrote opinion pieces on the topic, at least one of which was mailed to more than a thousand CEOs (Chesebro 1993, 1705–8).

Instrumental and perhaps indispensable, the institute and its allied public intellectuals have organized a cerebral base for tort reforms, but they have relied on complementary forces to popularize the cause. The primary agent of systematization, creation, and dissemination of knowledge for pop reform[5] of civil justice has been the American Tort Reform Association (ATRA), which has coordinated more than three hundred corporate and trade groups and about forty state reform organizations. ATRA's conventional, "inside" politicking includes *lobbying* (e.g., assisting legislators with arguments, briefs, formulated legislation, credible witnesses, and speeches and speakers); *strategizing* (e.g., advising legislative and electoral leaders concerning tactics, phrasings, polls, and agenda items); *coordinating* (e.g., planning conferences, building coalitions, mobilizing corporate, trade, and interest groups); and *facilitating* (e.g., providing a clearinghouse

---

5. We insert here a caveat that ought to be unnecessary. We use "reform" *both* as the name that activists have given their own activities *and* as a reasonably neutral descriptor. We use "reform" in the sincere belief that most ideas adduced by tort reformers would change the form and functions of one or more tort regimes and tort law if not of the larger system of civil disputing. When we use "tort reform" we no more endorse reform in general or specific reforms than we assert the justice of results in what we call the "civil justice system" in conformity to usage.

for reform ideas and information for and among groups associated with tort reform or civil justice [Stefancic and Delgado 1996, 100–103]).

Crucial as such conventional politicking is, ATRA's most central role may be to formulate and reformulate "common sense" regarding torts in particular and civil justice in general. ATRA disseminates such common sense to peripheral allies and gathers common sense and instances of its violation from the hinterlands. ATRA formulates and communicates an evolving consensus regarding injustices and inefficiencies that the current tort regime promotes at great cost and peril to individual responsibility, economic efficiency, and reason. Its mastery of the arts of perception and persuasion has augmented ATRA's success at conventional politicking by publicizing and popularizing tort reform messages, but one underestimates ATRA if one overlooks the association's mediating between big ideas (such as those coming out of the Manhattan Institute and academia) and everyday impressions.

ATRA has subordinated idiosyncratic imperatives and private interests of its hundreds of constituents to define and to reinforce evolving "common sense" regarding torts. ATRA has supplied newsmakers and pundits with commonsense themes that propagate in free media information and interpretations that might seem less credible as part of paid media. What might be tarred as propaganda if found in an advertisement is more likely to be accepted as presumption in news reports or commentaries. In a weighty pamphlet rebutting the American Bar Association's attacks on pop tort reform *(Fact or Fiction? You Be the Judge)*, in regular news releases highlighting developments in tort reform, in its weekly fax alert *Legislative Watch,* in its quarterly newsletter *The Reformer,* in its semi-annual summary of legislative happenings *Tort Reform Record,* and in its annual legislative forecast, ATRA organizes efforts to shape opinion directly. Many of these attempts at public influence are reproduced at ATRA's Web site alongside compendia of "Litigation Horror Stories—Stories That Show a Legal System That's Out of Control," of "Loony Lawsuits," and other attention-grabbers. The association also distributes pamphlets and posters in public settings and has placed in-flight videos on airlines. These direct efforts coalesce around themes of pop tort reform, characterizing the civil justice system as out of control, unjust, and inefficient, while vilifying trial lawyers, fraudulent plaintiffs, and judges and jurors for undermining individual responsibility and moral character (Matthews 1995).

ATRA has supplemented its direct and obvious endeavors with those that are less direct and obvious via APCO, a subsidiary of Grey Global Group (Silverstein 1996). APCO has coordinated messages of localized groups and created appeals and advertisements while shielding its clients from exposure. The advertisements and appeals rely on research, polling, and focus groups to hone themes that the civil system is out of control, that ordinary people pay for the broken system, and that lawsuit abuse will only abate when ordinary people oppose it. For example, APCO created the "Jack and George" ad that featured former liberal presidential candidate George McGovern and former conservative presidential candidate Jack Kemp denouncing lawsuit abuse, and placed the ad on *The McLaughlin Group* and other opinion shows. APCO also originated "Heroes," an advertisement in which volunteer firefighters from Ohio opined that fear of liability suits might lead volunteers to hesitate, with disastrous consequences (Matthews 1995). APCO assisted lobbyists in targeting and timing these appeals to responsibility, morality, and reason.

Equally important to the tort reform enterprise are the many Citizens against Lawsuit Abuse (CALA) organizations that are locally based in a half dozen states around the nation. These nonprofit organizations portray themselves as populist uprisings of ordinary people who take the lead for tort reform legislation and education at the local level, often as part of larger coalitions. They are led by "citizen activists fed up with the high cost and injustice in our legal system," notes the ATRA Web site, confirming the close linkage and coordination with national tort reform entrepreneurs as well as local allies. Their mission statements vary little, and that of the California CALA is typical: "Our mission is to educate the public on the effects of lawsuit abuse in order to create a climate for reform of our civil justice system." Their specific goals are "to educate the public," "to stimulate debate," and "to serve as watchdog" over those who abuse the legal system. Like ATRA, CALA Web sites feature relevant news stories, position papers on "the facts," reform proposals, available speakers, links to related groups, and humorous examples of "bizarre" events in our failing legal system— "loony lawsuits," "wacky warning labels"—along with serious policy matters. CALAs have been instrumental advocates in some of the most creative and effective efforts to pass tort reform in the states through the legislative and even referenda process (see Burke 2002).

The network of tort reform and pop reform ideas, institutions, and initiatives extends beyond the Manhattan Institute, ATRA, APCO, and CALAs, but those organizations reveal the uncommon expertise necessary to organize, to publicize, and, indeed, to construct common sense.

Financing Reform Advocacy

The network of pop tort reform has, of course, depended greatly on the mobilization of money. Financial support must be secured from those who have resources, but those who have resources may not want their funding activities known for fear that they will face reprisals for their political actions. More to the point for pop reform, the private interests of financiers must not outshine the public interests tort reforms might serve. Fundraising has therefore commonly been handled delicately, lest the monetary medium become the media message.

Of course, some fundraising spin is politically axiomatic: modest contributions received from ordinary folk are emphasized, while larger amounts are not readily acknowledged. Far-flung associations of CALAs permit not merely helpful data but sustaining donations to flow from hinterlands to organizations. These moneys, when publicized, redound to the grassroots appeal of receiving organizations and underscore the importance of tort reforms to ordinary citizens. Bottom-up funds, of course, confer more credibility than solvency for major organizations, which depend as much or more on instrumental investments by affluent entities. For example, documents released as part of Big Tobacco's 1998 settlement showed that in 1995 half of ATRA's budget came from tobacco's coffers, much of the funds funneled through the Covington and Burling law firm (Deal and Doroshow 2000, 12–14). It was instrumentally counterproductive for such contributions to become known, and contributors often prefer anonymity. Tobacco money underwrote the APCO "Heroes" advertisement mentioned above on the condition that tobacco companies' role not be acknowledged.

ATRA and related tort reform advocacy groups and legal defense groups also have relied heavily on funding from wealthy individual patrons and foundations that traditionally have supported conservative, probusiness causes, including the John Olin Foundation, the Sarah Scaife Foundation, and the Starr Foundation. On top of the general funding of ATRA and allied national organizations and the targeted funding of CALAs and other local lobbyists, other crucial financing has been project-specific (Deal and Doroshow 2000, 24–26, 32–42). In 1995, for example, ATRA, the National Federation of Independent Businesses, Citizens for a Sound Economy, the American Council of Life Insurance, the U.S. Chamber of Commerce, and others sponsored advertisements for the Republicans' "Contract with America." Business and reform groups—including Aetna Life and Casualty, the Insurance Information Institute, and ATRA—sponsored a major advertising campaign in major national newspapers and radio during the 1980s. These ads typically featured bold headlines—"Sue City USA," "Sue-icidal Impulse," "Life without Risk," "Responsibility Repealed," "The Lawsuit Crisis Is Penalizing School Sports," "The Lawsuit Crisis Is Bad for Babies," "Justice for All?"—followed by stories illustrating the woes of a legal system gone awry (fig. 1). Some ads featured staged pictures (e.g., of empty swimming pools; of defunded sports teams or children's organizations; and of a bumper sticker reading "Go ahead. Hit me. I

Sue-icidal impulse

*6 in a Series on Civil Justice Reform

A woman attempts suicide by locking herself in the trunk of her car. Upon changing her mind and (luckily) being found, she sues the car maker.

When his electric power mower gets clogged with wet grass, a man turns it over and, without turning it off, reaches into the blade area and begins removing the clotted grass. He loses several fingers, sues the manufacturer...and wins.

A man stalls on an interstate highway. A woman stops to push him from the road, but she is rear-ended by a third and then a fourth car. She sues everybody. But only the original, stalled driver can pay. So the jury holds him liable. Judgment against him: $885,000.

Today, the object is to collect—from someone. If the unlawful are bankrupt, the unethical have disappeared, or the careless are dead, there is usually someone else around with a "deep pocket" to pay.

This entitlement mentality has a terrible, corrosive effect on American society. We teach our children to be responsible for their own actions. Then we turn around and show them a system which rewards irresponsibility. The system seems to be saying, "No matter what happens, somebody must pay—preferably somebody rich!"

It's time to restore the principles of self-reliance and personal responsibility to our civil justice system, and there are some practical reforms that will do this. A majority of Americans agree that we should restore fairness to our product liability laws so that manufacturers who comply with standards of good practice and warn of all known hazards aren't held liable for misuse or abuse of their products.

And nearly three-quarters of Americans believe we should limit liability to a defendant's own share of the damages suffered by an injured person. Clearly, it is time for change. I hope you will join me in working for meaningful reform of our civil justice system.

I welcome your thoughts and ideas on how we can work together to restore fairness and balance to this system. And I would be pleased to send you information on some of the efforts that already are under way.

> "The system seems to be saying, 'No matter what happens, somebody must pay—preferably somebody rich.'"

William O. Bailey
Vice Chairman
Aetna Life & Casualty
Hartford, CT 06156

Responsibility Repealed

*8 in a Series on Civil Justice Reform

In order for someone to haul you into court today, the product you make doesn't have to be defective or shoddily made. It just has to have some kind of inherent risk.

The classic example is the vaccine manufacturer who makes a product essential for millions, but harmful to a few. The constant threat of liability and the astronomical costs associated with litigation have stopped many manufacturers from producing life-saving vaccines.

And in today's legal environment, you can even be held retroactively liable for conduct that was considered careful, responsible and acceptable at the time it occurred.

Consider the Federal Superfund law. Should a company be liable for clean-up costs when it had followed accepted procedure at the time it disposed of waste? And should one company have to pick up the whole tab, even if it was only marginally responsible?

I've been dealing with the civil justice system for more than 30 years. In years past, I saw this system play a very valuable role in deterring careless and irresponsible behavior. The system once protected the careful and responsible from legal harassment, but not anymore. Our civil justice system has lost the ability to distinguish between the good guys and the bad guys.

We can have a liability system that recognizes responsible behavior. Let's restore the notion of fault to the system. Let's crack down on frivolous suits. And let's not impose liability and added costs on those who exercise due care in making a product.

The American people are ready for reforms like these and America is desperately in need of them. I hope you will join me in working for meaningful reform of our civil justice system.

I welcome your thoughts and ideas on how we can work together to restore balance to this system. And I would be pleased to send you information on efforts that already are under way.

> "Our civil justice system has lost the ability to distinguish between the good guys and the bad guys."

William O. Bailey
Vice Chairman
Aetna Life & Casualty
Hartford, CT 06156

need the money") followed by statements decrying lawsuit abuse and an address where pamphlets could be requested.

The direct expenditures by corporate allies to exert political influence generally are significant and deserve mention, even though those funds are not funneled directly through tort reform organizations and not all the funds are directed narrowly to the tort reform cause. For example, in the year 2000, the insurance industry spent $41 million in total electoral campaign contributions; the pharmaceuticals and health products industry spend $26 million, while tobacco contributed over $8 million.[6] Moreover, the tobacco industry spent a reported $58 million for lobbying government in 1998 alone, primarily to stop the McCain bill seeking a global settlement of tobacco litigation initiated by the states (see chapter 7). Seven and a half million dollars went to the leading Washington lobbying firm, Verner, Liipfert, Berhard, McPherson, and Hand (Derthick 2002, 137). An additional $40 million was also spent on radio and TV ads over several months to the defeat the bill (Kurtz 1998, A1). Lobbying expenditure by corporations involved in the tort reform campaign, much of it regarding issues directly related to tort reform, has been noteworthy as well. In 1999, the insurance industry spent $85.6 million for lobbying, while health care industry spend $197 million, which is more than twenty times the amount spent by trial lawyers.

Beyond direct efforts to influence public policy, we should also recognize the many indirect expenditures of huge amounts by big business to shape ideas relevant to the tort reform cause. For example, while big business was not happy about having to relinquish annually $10 billion or so in cigarette taxes to various levels of government, these revenues surely provided the tobacco industry a considerable amount of influence over political officials. We should also remember the stupendous sums of money spent on corporate advertising to sell products, images, and ideas to the American public. Perhaps most important again is the tobacco industry, which spent $2.5 billion in 1985 and nearly twice that ($4.6 billion) by 1991 to sell its noxious goods, company name, and "voluntaristic" values.

To a great extent, financing of pop tort reform organs and related causes reiterates the approach of opponents in the earlier progressive public-interest law movement, although the scale of mobilized resources by the former is immensely greater. "The most significant development since 1970 has been a new breed of public interest organizations fashioned closely after the older ones but, for the first time, founded, financed, and

6. Except where otherwise noted, all data on campaign contributions and lobbying expenditures in this paragraph come from the Center for Responsive Government Web site: www.opensecrets.org.asp.

presided over by the chief executives and counsel for such entities as Exxon, ARMCO, and General Motors, the chemical, mining, and construction industries, public and private utilities, national and international banks, the most powerful economic forces in America" (Houck 1984, 1420; see Smith 2000). Numerous analysts have pointed out how much the "Legal Right" learned from the "Legal Left" after the triumphs of the latter in the 1960s and 1970s. Prominent among the lessons were centralized collections and dispersals of funds to achieve effective targeting of money to where it would do the most good. Emulating pro-business public-interest organizations, pop tort reformers have spotlighted public interests in issues and ideas and downplayed any mercenary stakes that might elicit funds from affluent donors.

Leadership

Although the White House Council on Competitiveness in the 1980s naturally boosted the efforts of ATRA, APCO, CALAs, the Manhattan Institute, and others, perhaps its greatest contribution was sponsoring a highly visible leadership corps of the pop tort reform movement. The Competitiveness Council, which teemed with public officials, by design "went public," which in turn required spokespeople to reach the masses through advertising, electioneering, or other species of publicity. Vice President Dan Quayle and his council were very visible, thanks in part to proposals and slogans cribbed from businesspeople as well as public intellectuals (Queenan 1992). Other political leaders also helped expand knowledge of the tort reform movement, enhancing the outputs of organized and financially flush lobbies and groups. Solicitor General Kenneth Starr, federal judge and Clinton investigator as well as tobacco lawyer, supervised production of fifty recommendations for the overhaul of civil liability. The Starr Report recommended expansions of voluntary dispute resolution; reforms of pre-trial discovery, expert evidence, and punitive damages; and institution of "loser pays" and other remedies for frivolous litigating.

Still, intellectual, ideological, and moral contributions demanded additional political savvy if they were to become widely accepted knowledge. Covington and Burling, a Washington law firm, coordinated ATRA, the American International Group (AIG Insurance), Eli Lilly and Co., 3M Corporation, Morgan Stanley and Co., the National Coal Association, the National Federation of Independent Business, Philip Morris, RJR Nabisco, and the American Legislative Exchange Council into "Citizens for Civil Justice Reform" (CCJR) to back the Starr Report. CCJR and ATRA founder Martin Connor then did the advance work for Vice President Quayle, who promoted the Starr Report as a distinctive issue in the 1992 presidential campaign (Deal and Doroshow 2000, 9–10). These activities of the Competitiveness Council demonstrate how all-encompassing modern politicking can be when outside and inside, national and local, official and private efforts coalesce around systematized knowledge, unified themes, and an overarching ideological and moral vision—all matched to money and political know-how.

The Competitiveness Council imparted currency to various aspects of pop tort reform. However, scholarly and intellectual backing from the Manhattan Institute and allied scholars was similarly instrumental in garnering free media and popular notice. Some leaders have lent their credentials and expertise to tort reform and to pop reformers. One important figure is Victor Schwartz, a senior partner at the D.C. law firm Crowell and Moring. An opponent labeled Mr. Schwartz the "nation's most important tort-reform lobbyist" and an effective spokesperson for the association (Chesebro 1993, 1646). Schwartz wields particular authority because he has long involved himself in the contemporary tort regime and is co-author of the classic, often-updated law school casebook nicknamed "Schwartz on Torts." Beyond Schwartz, W. Kip Viscusi (the John F. Cogan Professor of Law at Harvard Law School) is probably the most prominent academic economist to undergird intellectual and pop tort reform. Economists surmised that proliferation of lawyers choked economies (Magee, Brock, and Young 1989). Samuel Jan Brakel and Stuart Taylor Jr. have authored law review or legal journalism articles to shore up tort ideas, issues, and initiatives. For knowledge of tort reform to spread, these intellectual leaders did not have to triumph singly or collectively in academic or intellectual media. Rather, their contribution was to show that pop tort reform was part of a set of ideas, interpretations, and issues taken seriously by imposing minds.

Political and intellectual mobilization of ideas and issues has enticed other writers and activists into the fray, and they in turn have spread pop tort ideas to less intellectual, less attentive publics. Titles alone tell the tale. Philip K. Howard directly dealt with civil law and tort issues in his highly acclaimed *The Death of Common Sense: How Law Is Suffocating America,* and again in *The Collapse of the Common Good: How America's Lawsuit Culture Undermines Our Freedom* (previously published as *The Lost Art of Drawing the Line: How Fairness Went Too Far*) early in the twenty-first century. Max Boot, writer of a column in the *Wall Street Journal,* penned a polemic against courts and judges in which he lampooned the civil justice system *(Out of Order: Arrogance, Corruption and Incompetence on the Bench).* In 1992 Charles J. Sykes offered *A Nation of Victims: The Decay of the American Character,* pertaining but not limited to civil plaintiffs who pronounce themselves victimized for fun and profit. Patrick Garry *(A Na-*

tion of Adversaries: How the Litigation Explosion Is Reshaping America) published in 1997 a book friendly to tort reform and brimming with anecdotes and arguments.

Legislating to Advance and Preserve Reform

While a massive effort to construct public knowledge and to shape public opinion has formed an independent end of the pop tort reform movement, it also has been an instrumental means to successful legislation of tort reform measures. This campaign has generally been fought at three different levels of government. First, activists mounted campaigns for comprehensive federal tort reform in Congress beginning in the mid-1980s and finally passed legislation for "commonsense legal reform" in both houses in 1996, only to have it vetoed by President Clinton. Selective tort reform measures dealing with aviation, food donation, and volunteers were passed and signed by the president, who claimed to support "reasonable tort reform" (Greenlee 1997, 725 n. 65). The battle for congressional reform legislation continued during the late 1990s and was revived again in more particularized forms, especially medical malpractice reform, during the first term of President George W. Bush, who established a reputation as a tort reformer while governor of Texas.

Second, the tort reform crusade has made its biggest and most sustained legislative impact at the state level. Indeed, since the late 1970s nearly all of the states—forty-five by our count—have passed some type of tort reform measures. For example, the Ohio legislature in 1996 passed a comprehensive tort reform statute that limits punitive damages, caps noneconomic damages, eliminates in part joint and several liability, and more (see Greenlee 1997, 726). These reform statutes, and some occasional referenda or initiatives, were usually the result of coalition activity among business, insurance, and reform groups, often headed by CALAs. As of early 2003, the ATRA Web page reported that the tally of reform achievements at the state level looked like this:

- Thirty states have modified the legal standards for punitive damages;
- Thirty-three states have modified the law of joint and several liability;
- Twenty-one states have modified the collateral source rule;[7]
- Twenty-nine states have penalized parties who bring frivolous lawsuits;

---

7. The collateral source rule applies to evidence that may not be admitted at trial to show that plaintiffs' losses have been compensated from other sources, such as plaintiffs' insurance or worker compensation.

- Seven states have enacted comprehensive product liability reforms;
- Most states have enacted medical liability reforms in some form.

Third, reform advocates have been forced to defend these laws in the courts against opponents arguing that legal reform violates state constitutional provisions for separation of powers and judicial independence (see chapter 4). ATRA monitors these developments through its Judicial Observer program and works with various legal defense foundations and other legal teams to mount a defense of legislative achievements, including filing amicus briefs where appropriate (see Smith 1999; Schwartz, Behrens, and Taylor 1997). Lawyers have had to confront well more than a hundred legal challenges to state-level legal reform; in most but hardly all of these, the opponents of reform, led by teams of trial lawyers, have prevailed.

ADVANCEMENT OF KNOWLEDGE IN TORT REFORM CAMPAIGNS

Intellectuals, institutions, and interests identified and described above have made serious conceptual contributions to private and public debates about civil justice. But they have shaped common sense less by rigorous arguments and systematic measurements than by skillful rhetoric, alluring narratives, and consistent convictions. The rhetoric by which activists have tapped and reconstructed commonsense knowledge is ubiquitous in everyday politicking: statistics, slogans, and symbols. More remarkable encapsulizations of ideological and moral critiques of the modern tort regime persist in "tort tales," anecdotes and horror stories about civil litigation in the United States. While these rhetorical and narrative instrumentalities have imperfectly filled gaps in knowledge and understanding, they have powerfully diagnosed injustices in civil courts.

How Political Arithmetic Establishes the Plague of Lawsuits

One general pattern—that dubious numbers, yoked to indisputable concerns and spread by mass media, come to be taken as fact—has been common in public discourse for decades, not just in the area of torts. Nonetheless, the forces of pop tort reform have proved themselves remarkably adroit at establishing forceful figures in public discourse. When Vice President Dan Quayle asked whether the United States wouldn't be better off with less than 70 percent of the world's lawyers (Quayle 1994, 284), he exaggerated but thereby inserted into public discourse a dramatically rendered reminder that the United States was and is infested with too many lawyers for its own good. Quayle's "calculation" persists as a premise for public discourse and policy (e.g., Lebedoff 1997, 69) because, first, the number seizes the imagination of those who hear it and, second, counting lawyers across legal cultures has led to no definitive figures. Quayle's rough estimate and pop reformers' propagation of that estimate seem to have inadvertently begun a bidding war, as when the feature film *A Murder of Crows* included the pseudostatistic that "Do you realize that there are more people in law school right now than there are lawyers?" That the film glides past this absurd figure shows how diatribes against lawyers may perpetrate sheer nonsense in furtherance of "common sense." Iffy as such figures are, they are consistent with widespread concern that the United States hosts too many lawyers.

Common sense dictates that a surfeit of lawyers implies an abundance of lawsuits, so we should expect a useful but defensible count of lawsuits in the United States. When Vice President Quayle lamented the infliction of 18 million civil suits per year, his estimate was politically motivated but plausible and powerful. The United States had 18 million civil suits only if every hearing for divorce and child-support were lumped with the fender benders and other causes (Stefancic and Delgado 1996, 106–7). Whatever the valid measure, Quayle's number captured and thereby reproduced widespread perceptions of runaway litigiousness. From this instance we may infer that numbers that seem to follow from and lead to common-sense impressions of the legal system will be credible irrespective of their precision.

Some pop-tort calculations have proved instrumental and official. President Reagan's Tort Policy Working Group cited a 758% growth in products-liability filings, a figure that was arithmetically correct albeit an anomalous artifact of the reporting of federal filings. An unskeptical public would probably never learn that growth was closer to 400% when reporting practices were taken into account. A roughly fourfold increase in ten years would seem to establish a "litigation explosion" well enough, but citing the higher figure had the additional, perhaps unintended, benefit of diverting statisticians into assuring their few readers that products-liability cases had "only" grown by about 400% over ten years and that much of that growth was due to asbestos cases. *Wall Street Journal* editorialist Max Boot answered detractors of the original figure with the political facts of life—that numbers that comport with common sense will prevail: "Defenders of the system will offer a few other equivocations as to why no litigation explosion exists, but the jig is basically up. *The numbers we've examined confirm the evidence of our own eyes:* There are lots of suits, many of them frivolous, and the number is growing" (Boot 1998, 151 [emphasis added]).

In a similar manner, the Manhattan Institute's Peter Huber estimated the "tort tax"—a rough guess at aggregate costs to the U.S. economy of tort liability—carefully to establish its plausibility:

> The tax directly costs American individuals, businesses, municipalities, and other governmental bodies at least $80 billion a year, a figure that equals the total profits of the country's top 200 corporations. But many of the tax's costs are indirect and immeasurable, . . . *The extent of these indirect costs can only be guessed at.* . . . [T]he tax's hidden impact on the way we live and do business *may* amount to a $300 billion dollar [*sic*] annual levy on the American economy. (Huber 1989, 4 [emphasis added])

Of course, Huber's estimate was repeated more widely and more often than his qualifying remarks, making the "tort tax" available to citizens who read newspapers or journals. If most who use "tort tax" overestimate its magnitude,[8] the costs of the American system of liability to U.S. companies and the economy remain an issue crucial to readjusting the tort regime. Huber's widely recirculated guesstimate reminds citizens that liability and compensation are not cost-free and that liberties that American litigants take for granted may disadvantage American business. The "tax" image is especially effective in obscuring that tort litigation does not *create* costs to society but rather *shifts* payment for them from victims to injuring producers (Galanter 1996a). Like other examples of political arithmetic, the "tort tax" is an imprecise quantification of a constructed reality that, while often contested, resonates effectively: Americans sue each other freely, such suits are costly, and suits that are unnecessary or lead to injustice or individual irresponsibility should be discouraged.

How Tropes and Slogans Establish Frivolous Litigation

In a manner similar to political arithmetic, tropes and slogans distill commonsense objections to modern tort policies. For instance, lampooning the civil justice system as a "litigation lottery"—related terms include "jackpots," "roulettes," "casinos," "wheels of fortune," and "crap shoot"—draws attention to awards that strike many citizens as undeserved windfalls for lawyers and plaintiffs. The "litigation lottery" is a hopelessly inapt metaphor. It is also nearly ubiquitous because its moral and political critique may scarcely be improved on. Plaintiffs almost never prevail via a process

---

8. Others have set figures for direct costs higher than Huber did. On the other hand, it is not self-evident that transfer payments within an economy validly count as a levy on the economy.

that even approximates the randomness of a lottery, but equating prominent lawsuits to lotteries stresses the freakishness of plaintiffs' victories, the attenuated relationship between judgments and just deserts, and the vastness of awards.

Like tropes, slogans accentuate evils and perils in the systems pop reformers critique. Insurance industry advertisements have featured slogans—"Sue-icidal Impulse," "Sue City USA," "Justice for All?"—that seem both memorable and effective. The very title of a book by Manhattan Institute Senior Fellow Walter Olson exemplifies the potential of metaphorical sloganeering: *The Litigation Explosion.* We have already examined some of the arithmetic underlying "explosions" of litigation. Whether one might more properly state that litigation has "skyrocketed" or "mushroomed" or "ballooned" seems quite beside the point to all but academics. The moral of each metaphor is as unmistakable as the conditions at which Mr. Olson points.

Senator Mitch McConnell demonstrated standard sloganeering when he observed that "everyone is suing everyone, and most are getting big money" (Saks 1992, 1157, n. 23). Taken literally, Senator McConnell's generalization is nonsense. But it would be nonsensical to take the senator's remark literally. McConnell was bemoaning excessive, unnecessary litigation. Pop tort reformers do not themselves believe that Americans sue "at the drop of a hat." Rather, like other public speakers, they deploy hyperbole in service of defining problems and suggesting solutions. When such hyperbole matches conventional beliefs about civil justice, hype piques comprehension. This explains why President Bush's routinely exaggerated recitations that "everyone's suing, it seems like" by 2003 gave so few observers reason for pause (Bush 2003).

Some pop slogans are supported by extensive research and argumentation. Peter Huber introduced *Galileo's Revenge* with the following well-chosen words: "Junk science verdicts, once rare, are now common. Never before have so many lawyers grown so wealthy peddling such ambitious reports of the science of things that aren't so" (Huber 1991, 4). The second sentence makes it clear that by "common" in the first sentence Huber need only have meant "not rare." Huber repaid the confidence of the Manhattan Institute by popularizing a slogan into a cliché assumed to describe an endemic and epidemic problem in American justice. He then deepened the political significance of the slogan by summarizing disputes with which ordinary audiences for news were then familiar, such as silicone implants and uncontrollably accelerating Audis.

Putting punctiliousness to the side, we see that sloganeering and other instruments of popularization reflect the genius of caricature—exaggeration of commonly recognized features to advance moral and political judgments.[9] Neither slogans nor statistics are science. They are suasion. Suasion and science, however, share at least one characteristic: either they provide insight or they are ineffective. Pop reformers' slogans are undeniably effective in reflecting and reinforcing dissatisfaction with the modern tort regime.

How Sermonizing about Individual Responsibility Establishes Moral Authority

Catchy sloganeering and cavalier statistical citation cited in previous pages have reflected sophisticated public relations gambits exploiting two primary normative logics of harm allegedly caused by exploding tort litigation: a market-based logic of economic costs and inefficiencies, and a legal discourse about the increasingly arbitrary, unfair, and tyrannical interventions of tort law into civil society. These characterizations are often cast in the gloomy mode of doomsday prognostication. Consider, for example, an article by Michael Freedman in *Forbes.* A "tort crisis . . . could easily, in the space of a few years, crush important parts of the economy," he admonished.

> [W]ide swaths of the country . . . soon will be without medical specialists. . . . Drug companies will elect to stop producing vital but less profitable drugs. Construction companies will give up building the condos and high density projects necessary to affordable living. . . . When the payments (for lawsuit awards) lose any tether to the harm caused or the culpability of the defendant, they create economic havoc. (Freedman, 2002, 91–92)

Equally important has been the reformers' propensity for protracted, almost puritanical, and most likely quite sincere sermonizing about declining moral character in America that recalls old-time religion.[10] Indeed, most of the official articulations of the reform message are thoroughly infused with moralistic understandings—as opposed to, say, understandings that promote questions of relative power, of complex relational forces, of "social justice," even of arbitrary fate—focusing on the themes of individ-

---

9. That these claims are highly exaggerated is demonstrated in chapter 3.

10. The economic and legal logics of tort reform are often associated more broadly with "neoliberal" ideologies, while the moralistic focus on individual responsibility is more characteristic of "neoconservative" commitments. Narratives about the lawsuit crisis derive their power from the fusion of these two powerful currents in American political culture.

ual responsibility and personal virtue. Moreover, the very style and content of much reform discourse far more resembles jeremiads lamenting the decline of American society and homilies prescribing the arduous journey back to redemptive grace than systematic blueprints for formal rewriting of legal doctrine. We can see these tendencies most prominently, for example, in the newspaper advertisements that circulated in 1980s and in the spate of books by pop reform supporters in the 1990s. This material has the cumulative effect of a jackhammer endlessly pounding a simple, unmistakable message about the failure of moral character and the harmful effects on civic virtue wrought by the lawsuit crisis. Indeed, such steady repetition of a familiar, accessible ethical theme arguably provides the reform cause much of its undeniable power and authority.

Consider a classic newspaper advertisement from the late 1980s, one of many sponsored by Aetna Life and Casualty featuring a personal appeal from Vice-Chairman William O. Bailey, who is portrayed in the earnest, dark-suited pose of a midcentury evangelist (see fig. 1, p. 47). We learn that, once upon a time, all was well and harmonious in America: "In years past, I saw this system play a very valuable role in deterring careless and irresponsible behavior. The system once protected the careful and responsible from legal harassment, but not anymore." At least half of the text focuses on the subsequent fall from grace. Following the headline "Responsibility Repealed," the homily begins: "In order for someone to haul you into court today, the product you make doesn't have to be defective or shoddily made. It just has to have some kind of inherent risk." Mr. Bailey's sermon underlines that those who abdicate personal responsibility and exploit tort law for gain threaten the lives of us all by their unoriginal sins. "The constant threat of liability and the astronomical costs associated with litigation have stopped many manufacturers from producing life-saving vaccines." That the problem at its core is ethical in character is beyond doubt. "Our civil justice system has lost the ability to distinguish between the good guys and the bad guys."

Other ads echoed the same theme. The "lawsuit crisis," various headlines revealed, "is penalizing school sports," "is bad for babies," and even is undermining "the clergy" who are afraid of "religious malpractice" suits questioning their moral counsel.[11] There is, however, a promise of redemption, of a return to grace. "We can have a liability system that recognizes responsible behavior. Let's restore the notion of fault to the system. . . . The American people are ready for reforms like these. . . . I hope you will join

11. Notice that the most vulnerable and innocent—youth, babies, clergy—are claimed to be most victimized, not the huge corporations who pay for the ad.

me in working for meaningful reform of our civil justice system." Or, as the ad "Sue-icidal Impulse" concludes: "It's time to restore the principles of self-reliance and personal responsibility to our civil justice system."

Charles Sykes's 1992 book, *A Nation of Victims: The Decay of the American Character,* played out a similar moralistic drama. "American life is increasingly characterized by the plaintive insistence, *I am a victim. . . .* Americans act as if they had received a lifelong indemnification from misfortune and a contractual release from responsibility," he begins (11, 15). Sykes actually labels the "triumph of the therapeutic" ethos of "total justice" as a "substitute faith" for "The God That Failed" (49). By contrast, "self-restraint," the value that once guided free Americans, has come "to be looked upon as the scourge—if not *the* original sin—of modern life," directly reversing the old ethos of God's children (243). The heart of the problem is clear. Too many people at some point came to believe that if they don't get what they want to secure their lives by hard work, "there were always lawyers and courts" (125). Sykes cites Mary Ann Glendon's parallel polemic about "rights talk" (1991), highlighting the basic shifts in our culture from viewing rights as limits on government to "entitlements" obliging affirmative government action, and from viewing lawsuits as a "necessary evil" to hailing them as "an acceptable and even desirable weapon in the protection and extension of basic rights" (125). The culture of "instant gratification" is "the world made for the litigator, a figure who was to become dominant in our own time," writes Sykes (1992, 49). These trends are destroying our very society: "America's obsession with litigation has proven an onerous burden on the nation's enterprise" (248). Again, though, there is redemption available to us by a return to "common sense," which is the title of the book's last chapter, and to "a politics of personal responsibility"(244). This includes, of course, a plea that "substantial reform of tort liability could begin to roll back the tide of briefs, injunctions, and writs that has flooded the culture of victimization" (245). As Jesus instructed the lame to stand and walk, Sykes preaches "It is time to drop the crutch" (253).

This religiously infused moralistic language regarding the legal fall and possible moral redemption is common in Glendon's *Rights Talk* (1991), Howard's *The Death of Common Sense* (1994), and Olson's *The Litigation Explosion* (1991). They all trumpet "a call for personal responsibility," as a review on the opening pages of Howard's book proclaims. Most of these volumes, and Sykes's specifically, attack the growing tendencies of American citizens to avoid responsibility for the failings of personal behavior by blaming a catalog of diseases, addictions, biological disorders, or even a malignant social order that overwhelm individual choice (see 1992, 136). At the same time, however, most of these works themselves draw on the secular, therapeutic, or medical language they disavow. Sykes's rhetoric repeatedly likens the penchant for rights claiming, blaming, and litigation to a disease—to an "emotional influenza," a "poison," and an "onerous burden" that "debilitates," "suffocates," and infantilizes, reducing the body politic to "wreckage." Railing against the "quackery" of victimization science, he argues that "a diagnosis that a man ravaged by cancer is really the victim of witchcraft is not merely ignorant, it is deadly as well" (233). Mr. Howard likewise likens excessive legalism to a "poison," a "disease," or even "termites eating their way through our home" (1994, 124), producing a veritable "death" of common sense. Walter Olson informs us that, like a cancer, "litigation and its threat have begun to metastasize to virtually every sector of the economy" (1991, 7). On a single page, we learn that it is "invasive and coercive" and "painful;" it "sunders," "clogs and jams," "seizes," "exploits," torments," and "devours." "The unleashing of litigation in its full fury has done cruel, grave harm and little lasting good" (all on 2). Even justifiable litigation is like "other personal disasters, such as cirrhosis of the liver" (343).[12]

This combination of secular and religious language is fraught with conceptual tensions but fused into a powerful and coherent moral vocabulary. In short, individuals who control their bodily passions, care for their physical beings, avoid material harm to themselves, rely on their own resolve, and insure themselves against accidents and unexpected maladies both constitute the moral community and sustain the health of the larger "body politic." They ensure public order by adhering to common values, taking responsibility, respecting others, and refraining from overwhelming the legal system with unreasonable demands. By contrast, those opportunistic plaintiffs who evade personal responsibility by carelessly misusing products, performing dangerous practices, showing bad judgment at odds with common sense, and then selfishly resorting to unjustified legal blaming and claiming of remedies against virtuous others—these irresponsible beings undermine the bonds of moral community and eat away at the healthy social body. Those who attempt to pin responsibility on powerful organizations and to claim financial redress for material diseases, cancers, maimed limbs, singed skin, and the like are the source and carriers of the devastating social disease. To quote another moralistic reformer, Bayless Manning, "hyperlexis is not a nuisance. It is a heartworm that has a literally fatal potential for the body politic of this country" (1977, 77). And it is

12. Somewhat ironically, Olson elsewhere likens the lawsuit crisis to an epidemic of legal malpractice. "Like the cutting of flesh in surgery," litigation can be a necessary harm, but it "become(s) a horror in the hands of the truly bad, of those who never acquired, or had thrown away, a moral compass" (340).

only by following the evangelists' and moral doctors' prescription for healing ourselves that a whole, pure body, for both individuals and society collectively, can be restored.

The *political* strategy of reformers clearly follows this logic. Legislative reform of official tort law is intended to remove the opportunities and incentives for irresponsible, unhealthy, inefficient litigation. Meanwhile, steady doses of public moralizing sustain a disciplinary pressure within the body politic directly stigmatizing frivolous legal action while offering positive, empowering images of self-reliant, responsible citizen practice. The explicit targets of wrath in these sermons are to a large degree ordinary citizens who displace blame through litigation and undisciplined "Santa Claus juries" who reward them for their naughty behavior. But special attention is also reserved for greedy attorneys who, like Satans in suits, urge opportunistic claimants on and execute their destructive, unfair designs. The most obvious charge against lawyers, of course, is obsessive greed, which leads attorneys to litigate frivolous or dubious claims. "Contingency-fee law has made more overnight millionaires than just about any business one could name," proclaims Walter Olson, implying by the unsubstantiated allegation an ethical line between acceptable profit motives and the excessive rapacity of attorneys (1991, 45). Moreover, personal injury lawyers have the audacity to dress up their selfishness as serving the public good and helping "the little guy" stand up against the powerful. "There is a funny thing about this brand of lawyering: the more opulent it becomes, the more cloying an odor of sanctity it becomes," Olson adds (46). In truth, the moralists insist, lawyers mostly damage society. They breed dishonesty and distrust throughout society, fostering a world like Charles Dickens assailed in *Bleak House*—"a cynical, manipulative world of procedural intrigue, of lawyers manipulating court rules to guarantee, after decades of litigation, that the truth never emerges," laments Philip Howard (1994, 85–87). Charles Sykes is even more melodramatic in his assault: "The proliferation of lawyers . . . threatens to strangle the economy while further fraying our already tattered social fabric" (1992, 248). These sober assessments, typically cast in snatches of resentful assault, are like lawyer jokes without the humor, pithy lamentations about the destructive demons that we all bemoan around us.

It is tempting to dismiss all this as merely instrumental, even cynical, manipulation of loaded language by self-interested elites concerned only with corporate profits and profitability.[13] However, to do so discounts the

13. This is the tendency of opponents, especially social scientists in the realist legal tradition. See chapter 4.

power of ideology at stake in the discursive practices we identify. There is every reason to believe that pop reformers, no matter how instrumentally savvy, themselves are thoroughly enmeshed in the webs of meaning that they spin to persuade the public. More important, we urge appreciation of the ideological power conveyed by the values they invoke as a constitutive force binding them to their audience. After all, the discourse of individual responsibility (and, we would add, the related norm of antipaternalistic suspicion of government redistribution) is what Robert Bellah and his colleagues famously called the "first language of American moral life" (1985, 154). The norm was invoked by our nation's founders, was verified long ago by the incomparable French visitor Tocqueville, and has been resuscitated in new forms repeatedly through our history, most recently by both neoconservative and neoliberal activists (Rose 1999). It is hardly surprising that, as self-appointed guardians of our moral heritage, tort reformers, and their conservative moralistic kin, invoke a particular version of these familiar values—celebrating self-reliance and embracing an older conception of rights against the purportedly obsessive, destructive entitlement-claiming of perpetual victims—as the centerpiece of their campaign. Moreover, their capacity to invoke these specific normative constructions and their narrative expressions confidently, uncritically, and even dogmatically is yet another key to the considerable power of their familiar message about law. As Philip Howard concludes his book, "Relying on ourselves is not, after all, a new ideology. It's just common sense" (1994, 187).

How Tort Tales Establish Moral Illustrations

Pop tort reform has developed other tactics with which to feed mass media and attentive citizens ideas and impressions favorable to both reforms and civil defendants and unfavorable to civil plaintiffs and the modern tort regime. Such knowledge construction succeeds or fails to the extent that pop reform induces media personnel and conversationalists to propagate credible information that will reinforce the definitions of problems and the formulations of solutions around which tort reform has coalesced. One defining mode of tort reform public relations derives anecdotes from news media, condenses the anecdotes for optimal impact, then reflects the anecdotes back at media. These are what we, following others, label "tort tales"—moralistic parables that refocus general dissatisfaction with civil justice into particularized outrages or injustices. To judge from their prominence in pop tort appeals and from their circulation among the pundits and throughout the populace, tort tales are a potent source of information about civil justice in the United States.

How do tort tales construct commonsense knowledge of the legal system out of aberrations made apocryphal? Consider an example alluded to above:

A truck without brake lights is hit from behind. For "psychic damages" to the driver, because his pride was hurt when his wife had to work, *a jury awards $480,000 above and beyond his medical bills and wage losses.* . . . Then there's the one . . . but *you* can probably provide the next example. Most of us know hair-raising stories of windfall awards won in court. (Aetna Life and Casualty Ad, 1988; emphasis in original)

The primary element, evident in this example, is *elegance.* These parables communicate powerful moral lessons in a manner instantly understandable. A typical tort tale consumes only three to five sentences, a concision that makes tort tales widely available through retelling. Taglines such as "Then there's the one . . ." and "Did you hear the one about . . . ?" ready the listener for a stripped-down story that reveals anew the necessity of reforming civil justice.

Such concision accentuates *stereotypic characterization.* Tort tales almost always define disputes by characterizing disputants as morally if not legally blameworthy individuals (usually plaintiffs) who beset blameless, responsible, or hardworking individuals or entities (often defendants). In the example above, readers will tend to blame the driver for driving without standard equipment despite telling omissions. Why did the truck have no brake lights? Was the absence of brake lights important, or was the driver sitting at a red light or parked in a load zone when hit? Had the brake lights blinked out the previous day, or two years before? Skipping context essential to understanding the case, the advertisement encloses "psychic damages" in quotation marks and reduces the damages to macho vanity. This redirects and perhaps misdirects attention from the accident to familiar "villains" and victims. Stock characters in tort tales may include greedy plaintiffs, avaricious ambulance chasers, Robin Hoods, mendacious witnesses, scientists for hire, and witless judges and juries, *dramatis personae* who abound in modern American culture and politics.

High stakes intensify such characterizations via the "*holler of the dollar.*" The more that an undeserving, self-styled victim tries to take from the faultless party whom the tale shows to be the true victim (along with the economy, society, and sanity), the more egregious will the plaintiff's lack of character and decency be seen to be. At a minimum, a well-spun tort yarn emphasizes the price that immoral litigants, obtuse factfinders, and unjust enrichment exact from society and especially consumers, so one should expect monetary awards to be highlighted, even exaggerated. That a driver too heedless to have working brake lights should recover at all will offend many readers of the advertisement excerpted above. That the morally deficient plaintiff got nearly half a million dollars because his wife's employment harmed his machismo furthers the insult to justice and integrity.

A final element of a well-told tort tale lies in how *extraordinary occurrences symbolize ordinary outcomes*. Sometimes, the atypical incident becomes routine via a tag line, as when the ad above states, ". . . *you* can probably provide the next example. Most of us know hair-raising stories of windfall awards won in court." ATRA's Web page claimed that its horror stories show a legal system out of control, inviting the inference that miscarriages of justice were mundane. Of course, deploying stereotypes (element two above) and hollering the dollar (element three) facilitate such implications by presenting the tale as a particularly egregious example of a common trend.

Considered together, the four elements sketched above show how advocates have taken stories presented by and in mass media and added utility by subtracting complications or qualifications. They pitch tales so that the audience will attach norms and derive from the tales political and moral lessons adduced as much by audience members as by storytellers. Members of the audience, supplied with violations of common sense, personal responsibility, and decency, are enticed to complete tactically truncated tales with predictable moral lessons themselves. Once a deft taleteller has articulated an outrage, the audience will construct the dispute as an egregious violation of common sense, thereby reinforcing both the priority of everyday equities and the apparently routine failures of civil courts to satisfy those equities.[14]

To understand tort tales in terms of the four elements that audience members "complete" on their own is to understand immediately why those who defend the modern tort regime will be severely disadvantaged in story telling (a matter we cover at length in chapters 3 and 4). Even if members of the audience can and will fill in the details of tort tales that might redound to a defense of the current system, the status quo gains less credit for fulfilling its presumed function than it acquires censure for failing to fulfill that function—and rightly so. In addition, details that dramatize virtues of the current system must be spelled out because the audience cannot or likely will not fill in details as they can with tort tales told by pop reformers. Pop tort reformers rely on the audience's access to common

---

14. Of course, just how targeted subjects actually construct these tales and their implications is likely to be highly diverse, although we offer some selective evidence later in the book that the taletellers' intended message has had a demonstrable impact in various settings.

sense and mundane mores. Defense of the modern tort regime depends on the audience's access to knowledge that is far less common and norms that result from intricate balances and evolving doctrines and policies.

The foregoing discussion of how tort tales narrate tiny morality plays that testify to the wackiness of the civil justice system is evident from examples that have attained visibility through mass media, usually completing a circuit from (1) a small item in the news transformed into (2) a discrete, decontextualized object of ridicule that then becomes (3) a notorious epitome of injustice, ineptitude, or perfidy. Consider how a frivolous filing that was quickly dismissed became publicized into a tort tale through commercial television and the ATRA Web site:

Addicted to Milk

A self-described milk-a-holic is suing the dairy industry, claiming that a lifetime of drinking whole milk contributed to his clogged arteries and a minor stroke. Norman Mayo, 61, believe [*sic*] he might have avoided his health problems if he had been warned on milk cartons about fat and cholesterol. "I drank milk like some people drink beer or water," he said. "I've always loved a nice cold glass of milk, and I've drank a lot of it." (www.atra.org/hstories.f1ml?sid=106 [last visited July 25, 2001])

These four sentences defined the suit almost entirely by characterizing Mayo as a pathetic protagonist who proclaimed an imaginary addiction to escape blame for his own high-fat, high-cholesterol diet. The monetary damages he sought were not reported, so this succinct characterization features the "holler of the dollar" only by implication.

Perhaps the most fascinating aspect of this tort tale is how this bizarre story came to public notice as a normalized anomaly (the fourth element of tort tales). Late-night comedian Jay Leno noted in his monologue on June 10, 1997:

Here's another reason why Americans hate lawyers. A man in suburban Seattle is suing the dairy industry because he's become addicted to milk and it has raised his cholesterol to dangerous levels. It's just as dangerous as tobacco. The government should have warning labels on milk. In fact this is the proposed warning label: WARNING: TOO MUCH MILK CAN MAKE YOU A FRIVOLOUS-LAWSUIT-FILING MORON.

Leno swiftly normalized his tort tale by mentioning Norman Mayo's contention that milk can be as addictive and threatening to health as tobacco and by connecting the filing to widespread loathing of lawyers, a feat made all the more remarkable since Mayo had engaged no lawyer. From a snippet relayed by the Associated Press, an NBC late-night comedian reiterated on national television a broadside that ATRA publicized as a general affliction of the body politic. At each step, the tale gained different emphases and lost different details.

Such tales reveal anew the availability of filings to reinforce the claim that the nation is awash in silly suits. Loopy litigation that will never reach a courtroom or a settlement negotiation raises the specter of disputants who deviate from common sense, responsibility, and respectability. Newspaper filler, radio capsules, and humorous calendars will routinely find space for absurd complaints, most of which are actual and accurately reported to some extent but are open to being "completed" by storytellers or by their audiences at some expense to facts.

Beyond its Web site, ATRA has hosted tort tales narrated by newsworthy speakers. In 1986 President Ronald Reagan told an ATRA audience of a man who lost a leg when a car driven by a drunk driver smashed through the phone booth he was using. The man sued the telephone company that maintained the booth. As told, this tale exemplified the fleecing of a faultless corporation by a victim who squandered sympathy by heeding the holler of the big dollar rather than suing the blameworthy driver. Plaintiff Bigbee protested in a congressional hearing that Reagan had overlooked the malfunctioning door of the phone booth, which had not been repaired adequately after other automobiles had careened into it. Selective as Reagan's telling was, he was making the point that the drunk driver was more responsible for Bigbee's injuries than was the phone company, if indeed the latter was at fault at all.

The prominent tort tale with which we began chapter 1 similarly evolved from a malpractice case to a suit misreported and ridiculed in the press to a brief joke in a presidential speech. In only three sentences (element one), President Reagan retold the story about Judith Haimes's reaction to the dye injection in preparation for a CAT scan, and drew laughter from his immediate audience when he characterized the plaintiff as a psychic (element two). Even before jurors awarded nearly $1 million in compensatory damages and pre-trial interest (element three—"the holler of the dollar"), Philadelphia media had ridiculed Haimes's claims. *Haimes v. Temple University Hospital and Hart* (1986) came to symbolize a modern legal affliction even worse than silly lawsuits: successful silly lawsuits. "The Psychic CAT Scan" tale displaced what happened in the courtroom with moralizing about abuses of litigation, junk science in civil courts, and jurors' ineptitude owing to the tort tale's capacity to record everyday departures from common sense.

Many Americans have heard this story about the psychic, but perhaps even more know of the burglar who fell through a skylight and success-fully sued for his injuries. Few ever knew the details of *Bodine v. Enterprise High School,* the dispute from which the tort tale evolved (Strasser 1987, 39). Rick Bodine, a California teenager, sneaked onto the roof of a high school to snatch a floodlight (on some accounts, to light a basketball court). He fell through a tarred-over skylight and landed on the floor of the gym-nasium many feet below. He sued the school district for the resulting quadriplegia. The district settled with Mr. Bodine, in part because a simi-lar incident a few months earlier had alerted the district to dangers posed by the hard-to-discern skylights. A California legislator then proposed a law to prevent felons from suing for injuries sustained in commission of a felony. Amid resultant publicity and retellings of the story, Bodine was transformed from a trespassing prankster who had no desire to break and enter into a burglar who bilked a blameless innocent.

Those who recall the movie *Liar Liar* may find this tort tale somewhat familiar. The script of *Liar Liar* (Guay and Mazur 1997) "authenticated" a tort tale far removed from the facts of *Bodine:*

[S]everal years ago a friend of mine had a burglar on her roof, a burglar. He fell through the kitchen skylight, landing on a cutting board on a butcher's knife, cutting his leg. The burglar sued my friend! He sued my friend! And because of guys like you, he won. My friend had to pay the burglar $6,000. Is that justice?

In the movie, the lawyer replies, "No—I'd have got him ten!" because the lawyer has been compelled by a magic wish to tell the truth for the day. The filmmakers not only satirize attorneys as people whose lives would be upended if they had to stop lying even for a day but also get laughs by adding moral obtuseness to the outrageous miscarriage of justice. The now "twice-told" tale of a burglar profiting from his fall through a skylight dif-fers significantly from the actual incident, but only in details to which moviegoers were probably never exposed. This legend has separated from the real events that inspired it through retellings that succinctly and selec-tively alter the identities of the plaintiff and the defendant and that strate-gically alter the circumstances (e.g., settlement of the original case versus an award—even a jury award—in retellings) and consequences (e.g., paral-ysis versus a cut leg) of the incident and its processing.

Although most tort tales selectively recount actual disputes, an epi-graph at the beginning of this chapter memorializes an advertisement thought to be purely apocryphal (Brunvand 2001, 236; 1999, 163–64). Aetna Insurance showcased a tale of a winning litigant who made a lawn-mower manufacturer pay for his own recklessness in pulling wet grass from a power mower that was still running. A variant on this legend described two men who lost sixteen fingers, but no thumbs, while hoisting a power mower to trim hedges (Brunvand 1999, 163). Each version of this story seems utterly implausible, which reiterates the reservoir of distrust of and disgust with the civil justice system necessary for tort tales to "work." The version that features misuse of the power mower to trim hedges has the additional advantage of depicting the common complaint that too many consumers use machines in an inappropriate or downright foolhardy manner, then sue manufacturers for failing to warn consumers against their own stupidity. We show in chapter 6 how the spilling of the hot McDonald's coffee became the quintessential tort tale, and note here only that we shall show how that tale manifested the elements above and how its decontextualization facilitated distortions inadvertent and tactical.

Lengthy as our list of tort tales may seem, it is minuscule relative to anthologies of anecdotes that corporate leaders, tort reform authors, politicians, wags, and pundits have loosed on the polity. Other well-known tort tales include

- a man who sued Sears because he pulled so hard trying to start a Sears mower that he had a heart attack;
- people who fall in front of, leap in front of, or make love in front of speeding subway cars and sue subway companies over injuries;
- the drunken man whose survivors sued the transit authority after he electrocuted himself urinating on a subway rail;
- the worker who placed his ladder in manure and sued over a lack of warnings when the ladder slipped; and
- the weightlifter who sued when the refrigerator he was toting as part of a contest caused him back injuries.

Advocates of reform of the civil justice system have wielded such "stories" unabashedly and unapologetically. Although often assailed by scholars for reliance on such insubstantial narratives, tort reformers often praise the inherent commonsense value of tort tales, even analogizing such anecdotes to the case method of lawyers (Boot 1998, 149; Brakel 1996, 92–93). Indeed, Manhattan Institute policy advocate Walter Olson has been quoted as saying that such stories matter more to most people than statistical data or other types of evidence (Cox 1992). Olson has challenged this account of his words, but his affection for anecdotes and tort tales is quite evident. A content analysis of *The Litigation Explosion* found the following distribution of evidence marshaled to support his argument: 272 short anecdotes; 1 case study; 6 statistical citations. The literature generated by tort reformers generally—in newspaper and magazine ads, pamphlets, research reports, published books and articles, press releases, and the like—likewise abounds with tort tales. Readers curious about the variety and ubiquity of tort tales will find hours of entertainment at www.lawslore.info, the Web site associated with this volume. The legal legends there and those that we have analyzed above account for the potency of tort tales as a reinforcement of commonsense impressions of civil injustices in modern America.

ADVANTAGES OF POP TORT INFORMATION

We shall see in the next chapter that those beset and bested by pop reformers claim that their opponents have created knowledge by means of groundless anecdotes and bogus numbers, but they should not underestimate how ideas and narratives construct and confirm commonsense preconceptions that also explain pop reform's successes at setting agendas and shaping debates. Proper appreciation of reformers' aims and achievements requires attention to this dovetailing of moral content and dramatic form in mass-mediated cultural forums. Reformers' words and images are not mere pretexts for ulterior designs. They are depictions of the modern tort regime as its detractors view it. They are a constitutive force that must be understood rather than dismissed as epiphenomenal or unworthy. Two academics on different sides of debates about tort reform characterized the contributions of pop torts well:

> Regardless of the reasons for the uproar, it now comes more from potential tort defendants—the nation's professional and business elite—than from the scholars and occasional judges whose voices once dominated tort law protest. This opens up the debate. There is nothing like the prospect of real change to energize even the most hermetic legal scholar. As a result, the spotlights brought to bear by would-be reformers have illuminated many of the concerns about tort law that have long troubled thoughtful observers. (Bell and O'Connell 1997, 48)

Pop tort appeals manifest at least four advantages for knowledge production in mass-mediated culture. First, tort reformers convey information that is widely and readily *available*. Targeted audiences have everyday reminders of common sense, a construct that helps tort reform and undermines the modern tort regime. Whatever the empirical or intellectual imperfections of tort tropes, most viewers, listeners, and readers learn about litigation lotteries and ballooning civil awards if they learn anything about civil justice in America. We have seen above how reformers' statistics match common impressions (and in chapter 5 we shall see how mass media abet such impressions), so the tendency of ordinary observers to presume the lessons behind such figures cannot surprise us. Tort tales draw the attention of the public as well as of scholars precisely because they pop up in news capsules as details and nuances of disputing do not. The omnipresence of common knowledge and common sense endows popularizations with instant credibility.

Moreover, rhetorical and numerical figures are far more *accessible* than reliable, balanced presentations. Accessibility and availability are closely related: information that is comprehensible and memorable will tend to be circulated; perspectives that are easy to find will be easy to believe and to recall. Pop tort reformers tend to outdo not only defenders of the civil justice regime but also serious tort reformers because clever slogans, crafted numbers, cunning anecdotes, and common moral invocations of familiar values are instantly understandable in ways that "superior," more complex descriptions and data are elusive.

Tropes, slogans, statistics, and tales also tend to be more *adaptable* than opposing information. The fewer the empirical checks on information, the easier it is to free-wheel and to embellish. As complexities and contradictions are pared away, pop tort advocates readily suit appeals to different circumstances and contexts, defend their verities against necessarily complex challenges, and rebound from opponents' assaults by asserting a modified version of "what everybody knows." We have noted earlier in this chapter instances in which apparently devastating counterattacks have been seemingly effortlessly deflected through slightly restated reiterations of the moral vision and individualistic presumptions of popular tort reform. In particular, as tort tales prompt outrage while short-circuiting the intellect, their incredible lightness of being enables rapid circulation throughout society as familiar, routinely confirmed wisdom. One notable example is the reconstruction of the lawsuit crisis in the period following the deadly terrorist attack on September 11, 2001. One might expect that such horrific events might mute or modify the hyperbolic rhetoric about the litigation crisis that was ruining America. Quite the contrary. Conservative pundit Dennis Prager published in June 2003 an article in "town hall.com" entitled "The legal system is now our enemy," which includes the following lines of classic legal reform rhetoric:

> I was raised to believe that law is the glory of decent society. . . . I have come to fear almost everything having to do with law. . . . I now fear the legal profession more than I do Islamic terror. I am far from alone. I believe that more Americans rightly fear being ruined by the American legal system more than being killed by a terrorist. . . . The deprivation of freedoms in America because of laws and litigation has made this coun-

try less free than any time in its history. . . . It is a weapon in the hands of the indecent. . . . The Florida lawyer who brought the new legal terror of "class action suit" against tobacco companies rejected over 800 potential jurors before he could find 6 people who do not believe that anyone who smokes has freely chose to do so. . . . If America is destroyed, it will be done legally.

Pop information tends also to be *affirmative.* Jeremiads against the irresponsible, unjust modern tort regime may be quite negative but tend to yield rosy retrospectives and optimistic prospects. Tales of legal degeneration are matched by visions of moral regeneration. Romantic reconstructions of less adversarial, more civil good-old-days affirm virtues and advantages that Americans once again might relish if only a few common-sense reforms were adopted. If practitioners of pop torts seem dyspeptic about modern developments, they usually are bullish on an American civil justice system reformed. They support an agenda of manageable, realizable solutions. They call for action. Each figure of speech, catchphrase, gee-whiz number, and yarn that excoriates the present sets the stage for innovation and improvement. "Clearly, it is time for change. I hope you will join me in working for meaningful reform of our civil justice system. . . . We can work together to restore fairness and balance to this system," concluded the typical insurance-sponsored ad in the 1980s.

Available, accessible, adaptable, and affirmatively actionable appeals are undeniably powerful in mass culture. Popularized reform of civil justice has constructed an agenda for action, fitted agenda items to perceptions and beliefs (and vice versa), marshaled evidence and arguments in forms that are instantly grasped, and thereby suffused the polity with pop tort portraits and proposals. Americans who have never heard of joint and several liability become outraged that a deep-pocketed phone company may have to compensate a caller trapped in a phone booth into which an automobile careens. Citizens who had never heard or seen the word "litigious" bandy about Americans as the most litigious people on earth. Those who routinely watch, read, or listen to the news learn of narratives and notions that are neither precisely right nor exactly wrong, and such common learning reinforces various proposals for reforming the tort regime.

The more available, accessible, adaptable, and affirmative that proposals and arguments supporting proposals are, the more that reform popularizers persuade themselves anew. This dialectic is common. Advocates sign on to tort reform efforts because they come to believe that reforms will address problems. They marshal arguments and information that reinforce their beliefs and their exertions. The tort reform ideas they sell are ones they themselves have already bought, but those ideas become more compelling as advocates discover confirming evidence everywhere and see how clearly the evidence justifies this or that reform. Beyond defining tort problems and espousing tort solutions, tort reform rhetoric contributes to a holistic critique of civil justice and sociopolitical culture in the United States. Stories, sermons, slogans, and statistics mutually reinforce one another. The result is a coherence so factually elusive and morally resonant that is difficult to rebut.

Finally, one of the central contentions of this book is that the tort reform campaign, and its message about the lawsuit crisis, has derived considerable power from its fundamental, if little recognized, relationship to the broader "culture wars" raging throughout the United States since the middle of the twentieth century.[15] By this, we mean the broad-based reaction by diverse conservative groups, first, to newly triumphant New Deal national policies and, then in the post–World War II era, to challenges to traditional moral authority posed in part by new legal rights claims and claimants. The linkage of tort reform to the culture wars has many dimensions. For one thing, pop tort reformers echo culture warriors in believing and acting on the premise that "ideas count, that they can materially change the tenor of public discourse," that modern politics necessarily entails efforts to win the hearts and minds of citizens by capturing mass-mediated knowledge production (Kristol 1995). Second, many of the leading tort reform organizations also take strong stands against affirmative action, welfare, illicit drugs, street crime, extramarital sex, and other issues at the heart of the culture wars. Most conservative groups identified with the culture wars likewise extend at least soft support for legal reform advocates. Equally important, the campaign to remedy the lawsuit crisis has pinned the blame on the same types of individual moral failure that have produced other aspects of our purported cultural crisis. Indeed, frivolous litigants displacing responsibility for self-inflicted harm and greedy lawyers abusing the legal system have joined the growing catalog of Others—welfare queens, the chronically unemployed, street criminals, disorderly dissenters, amoral liberals and secular humanists, slackers of all kinds dependent on government help—stigmatized by neoconservative and neoliberal proponents as undeserving and dangerous (Lofquist 2002).

These general assaults on excessive litigation have worked undeniably to preserve or reestablish traditional hierarchies in American society. In fact, the culture wars to a large extent reflect a direct effort of dominant groups to redefine and triumph over the imagined "class wars" initiated by

15. There is much popular writing but little systematic academic analysis of the "culture wars." For different views, see Hunter 1991; Morone 2003; Lakoff 2002. For a useful list of primary resources, see www.jkalb.freeshell.org/web/culture_wars.html.

working class, minority, feminist, consumer, and liberal intellectual advocates earlier in the twentieth century (Dionne 2003). Perhaps the most notable specific contribution of tort reform advocates and accounts is the delegitimation of dangerous, reckless litigants and their lawyers in abstract, categorical moral terms that obscure the particular targets and unequal power relations at stake in the contest. This is a moralistic politics of resentment that big business can embrace. All in all, the instrumental campaign for addressing the lawsuit crisis has both drawn power from and contributed to the broader fault lines of contemporary American politics.

CHAPTER THREE

In Retort: Narratives versus Numbers

A lack of evidence, which might seem like an insuperable barrier, has barely slowed many policy-makers, scholars, and other commentators. Their discussions about the behavior of the tort liability system often have proceeded without even assembling the fragments that do exist, much less pausing to figure out how they fit together. The result is a picture of the litigation system built of little more than imagination.

MICHAEL SAKS, "DO WE REALLY KNOW ANYTHING ABOUT THE BEHAVIOR OF THE TORT LITIGATION SYSTEM—AND WHY NOT?"

Improving the civil justice system requires thoughtful, objective analysis based on sound empirical data. The lack of systematic, cumulative data in this area makes it possible for far-reaching policy proposals to be advanced on the basis of tendentious anecdotes and numbers.

MARC GALANTER, BRYANT GARTH, DEBORAH HENSLER, AND FRANCES KAHN ZEMANS, "HOW TO IMPROVE CIVIL JUSTICE POLICY"

Academics write mostly for one another and for others in their profession. Seldom do we seek a mass audience, and rarely do we find one.

DEBORAH RHODE, "A BAD PRESS ON BAD LAWYERS"

Pop tort reform went neither unnoticed nor unopposed. Rapid and robust responses from leading sociolegal scholars challenged the narratives, numbers, and notions about reform. Partly in response to pop reformers, these scholars have amassed and broadcast alternative forms of knowledge about civil courts and the litigation system, knowledge that the scholars assert reform activists have neglected or ignored in favor of tort tales and other questionable evidence.

This chapter recounts much of the knowledge that sociolegal scholars have mobilized to challenge the pop reform vision. We emphasize two dimensions of this knowledge. First, in opposition to tort reformers' reliance on simple narratives of isolated but morally illustrative legal actions, social scientists have labored to identify broad patterns of accumulated facts about aggregate civil disputing practices at state and federal levels. In other words, academic experts have offered and honored *statistical representations* of aggregate tort law activity as antidotes to tort reformer anecdotes (Galanter 1996b). Second, most scholars have invoked and contributed to a distinctive conceptual model, what is often labeled the sociolegal "Disputing Framework," to make sense of these general empirical patterns.[1] We use that framework in this chapter both to organize the presentation of abundant scholarly studies and to illustrate the conceptual logic that has structured much of the enterprise. This conceptual framework disaggregates disputes into a sequence of discrete moments or successive stages, from the earliest experience of injury through, at least potentially, various stages of dispute claiming, formal action, and resolution. The general framework provides a useful way to measure comparatively the changing frequencies of different disputing practices and trajectories across time, place, and domains of doctrine. These conceptual and empirical endeavors have demonstrated that actual tort law activity has been far more complex and varied than simplistic rhetoric suggests, have significantly qualified if not refuted claims about mushrooming litigation and exploding damages awards, have exposed the systemic obstacles to successful pursuit of frivolous lawsuits, and have provided a far more reasonable portrait of our civil legal system and its workings.

We conclude our discussion by assessing the scholars' massive empirical contributions to the contest over representing legal reality. The qualitative and quantitative information that scholars have accumulated has been demonstrably more reliable, representative, and reproducible than that of pop tort reformers, we argue. Any fair-minded reader, we would think, should find these data and their scholarly interpretations far more illuminating about how our civil legal system works and be convinced there is sufficient reason for skepticism about pop reform rants. At the same time, however, we question the effectiveness of scholars' statistical representations as forms of common knowledge and political discourse. Scholarly data are not as available, accessible, adaptable, or actionable as the reformers' commonsense narratives. Not only are social science studies more esoteric in form and remote in placement, but they tend neither to engage critically nor to offer compelling substantive alternatives to the

---

1. Professor Marc Galanter's work (1996b) reinforced our inclination to proceed in terms of the pyramidal representation of disputing.

deeply rooted vision celebrating individual responsibility at the heart of the tort reform enterprise. Scholars aspire to alter citizens' *empirical knowledge* about law while leaving largely uncontested prevailing *moral frameworks* for assessing law in modern society. Our general point is less to critique the intellectuals' endeavors, however, than to identify the substantial gap between the rigorous enterprise of scholarship and ordinary political discourse in our mass-mediated culture.

THE SCHOLARS

The scholarship to which we refer in this chapter emanates from a diverse group of intellectuals who form no official organization or clique, although they share certain characteristics.[2] All or almost all are well-recognized faculty members in law schools or social science departments at major U.S. universities or trained researchers working in leading think tanks (Rand) or foundations (American Bar Foundation). In addition, all these scholars openly embrace sophisticated social science methods—including especially techniques for computing and analyzing aggregate statistical data—for their capacity to produce rigorous, reliable, reproducible, and hence verifiable ways of knowing. Virtually all of these scholars have been associated with, and many have been leaders in, the widely respected Law and Society Association, whose members form an international coterie of interdisciplinary sociolegal scholars. As such, many of them have interacted over time by sharing research at professional meetings and intellectual conferences as well as through processes by which research is proposed, funded, and reviewed for publication. In short, most of these scholars are familiar with each other's research. They also share a propensity for seeing the world through values and attitudes that range from moderate liberal to social welfare liberal to quasi-socialist. Almost all of these scholars have provided empirical and normative grounds for critiquing specific problems in, or failures of, our civil law system through their academic research. Some have even selectively endorsed various reform measures that intersect with pop tort reform, although most identify with agendas rather

---

2. We take some pains in the text to emphasize that not all scholars oppose tort reform or "commonsense" proposals. We further acknowledge that we skimp on the contributions of journalists who specialize in legal matters, contributions that have advanced our learning and the learning of the scholars on whom we focus in this chapter. Moreover, our list of scholars is hardly exhaustive. We have focused on those who, in our judgment, have been recognized most widely as debunking claims advanced by incautious supporters of tort reform.

different from the neoliberal, business-supported agenda that has dominated discussion since the late 1970s in the United States.[3] These analysts
of legal processes are not mere apologists for the status quo (contrary to
Brakel 1996).

Given these shared characteristics, why do we designate these debunkers as "instrumental" actors in the tort reform debate? In this context as
in others, scholarship has some instrumental dimensions. The work of
these scholars has, at the least, routinely been invoked to call into question
pop versions of tort reform. Moreover, many of these scholars have continued, expanded, or refashioned their research agenda to advance premises in developing public debates. Indeed, some scholars—especially Marc
Galanter, Stephen Daniels, Theodore Eisenberg, and James Henderson,
to name just a few—are public intellectuals who have made it into the
Rolodexes of prominent journalists and routinely debate the issues in
mass-mediated forums. Nevertheless, this scholarship is far from merely
instrumental, ideological, or partisan. As first-rate scholars who are faithful to principles of social scientific rigor in their empirical research, almost
all of these critics of pop torts had researched civil litigation, disputing, juries, and the like before they entered the tort reform debate. As academic
experts who care about principled intellectual judgment and especially
about the assessments of fellow academics, these scholars must continually guard their credibility. If they overreached the evidence or made excessive claims, their academic standings would tumble, their capacity to
win research grants would wither, and their prospects for professional success would decline just as surely as their political voices would diminish
in influence. All in all, for these intellectuals, rigorous research standards
and instrumental political influence in most instances do not clash but
mutually reinforce.

At the same time, we do analyze interpretive implications and meanings of the empirical research that these scholars have projected into the
tort reform debate. Facts do not speak for themselves, after all. The cultural
and political significance of facts turns on the ways in which they have
been integrated into coherent, compelling accounts that make sense of the
world around us, its basic organizational logic, and the ways in which we
can act to preserve or change it. While the bulk of discussion in this chapter summarizes the empirical scholarship marshaled to challenge simplistic tort tales and reform rhetoric, we conclude by addressing the limiting
effect of social science conventions themselves on the presentations of such

3. We do suggest later, however, that the scholars' defensive reaction against tort reform
has deemphasized these often subtle, complex critical perspectives, thus nudging their public positions closer to an apology for the status quo.

data by their authors and their implications for relative influence in political contests to interpret legal reality. Precisely those qualities that make for good social science, we suggest, also make for ineffective political discourse and ordinary commonsense knowledge in mass-mediated society.

THE DISPUTING FRAMEWORK

We begin with the logic of the Disputing Framework for organizing and making sense of data about disputing practices. The framework initially was developed to address concerns more typical of the sociology of law than tort reform. Nevertheless, the accumulation of scholarship that the Disputing Framework informed, and was informed by, has called into question and often into disrepute the common knowledge on which reformers have relied.

In general, as we already noted, the Disputing Framework describes and analyzes disputing in a sequence from earliest stages before a dispute has formed to final stages when a dispute resolves or dissolves. Among the framework's most significant revelations are how few disputes escalate to successive adversarial stages and how many disputes come to a decision or dismissal before reaching public venues or formal litigation. All thoughtful observers knew, of course, that more people were injured than sued and that more people sued than saw the suit through to a courtroom or a verdict. However, the far greater visibility of later stages led many observers to focus on courts rather than on other settings in which the vast majority of legal "action" took place. The Disputing Framework redirected attention to normal disputing and, through accumulation of information, redefined and refined knowledge of legal practice.

Moreover, increased attention to disputing processes underlined for scholars the indeterminate, intersubjective, socially constructed dimensions of disputing practices. After all, the shifts involved in defining an injury as a grievance, a grievance as a claim, a claim as a legal right, and so on involve "naming, blaming, and claming" (Felstiner, Abel, Sarat 1980–81). To name an injury, to blame another for the injury, and to claim recompense each varies with the legal knowledge, skill, or "consciousness" of the namer, the blamer, and the claimer. Whether one makes a grievance of an injury depends on at least some rudimentary understanding of legal principles of liability, some knowledge about how legal disputes can develop into more formal stages, and the implications for parties in terms of potential financial cost, delay, anguish, and awards. The stages of disputing are not self-evident and predetermined, but rather are products of ongoing, interactive interpretive engagement and discretionary judgments among parties (Mather and Yngvesson 1980–81).

Disputing Pyramids

Conceiving of disputes in terms of "pyramids" is an idea familiar to all who study disputing.[4] Pyramids direct attention to stages that precede formal litigation, which corrects the tendency of the uninformed to concentrate on the courtroom and, at that, on how courts deal with the most publicized cases. In addition, the pyramid highlights ready escapes from and alternatives to formal resolutions. "Throughout the pyramid, bargaining is pervasive and authoritative adjudication is relatively rare" (Galanter 1993c, 4), leading more than nine out of ten disputes to an end other than a verdict or judgment.

Figure 2 represents two pyramids that Miller and Sarat (1980–81, 544) derived from the pioneering Civil Litigation Research Project (CLRP) data set at the University of Wisconsin during the late 1970s. One pyramid (marked by diamonds) enumerates civil disputes in general. The other pyramid (with dots instead of diamonds) counts tort disputes only. Each pyramid partitions disputing activity into five progressively public, formal, and adversarial stages. At the base of the pyramid lies the first stage, *grievance,* defined as one's belief that another owes one something, such as recompense for an injury, return of property for fraud, or acknowledgment of fault. The next stage of disputing, *claiming,* occurs when the injured party states that grievance to the one who is believed to owe something. If the party believed to owe something denies that she or he owes the claimant, the disagreement becomes a *dispute.* If one or more parties seek counsel, the dispute has reached the stage of *resort to lawyers.* Only after these four stages have been reached and passed will the dispute become a matter of litigation by some *filing* of the dispute in court.[5]

To represent these five stages of disputing as a face of a pyramid, Miller and Sarat set the base at one thousand grievances and centered successive stages above the base. We have set the base equal to one thousand on each side of the bisecting, dotted arrow in the middle of the diagram. The width at each successive stage represents the proportion of grievances that reached that stage in the CLRP data. Because the base was set at a thousand, the number of cases that survived to a successive stage could be interpreted easily as a percentage of all grievances (for example, 718 claims

---

4. In using "pyramid," we adopt settled usage while recognizing that the term is literally inaccurate. The disputing model diagrams employ stacked stages that narrow as they ascend; the diagram is two-dimensional rather than three-dimensional, and the displayed face is irregular rather than triangular.

5. We acknowledge that small claims and a few other matters are exceptions to this pattern.

FIGURE 2 Tort and civil disputing pyramids

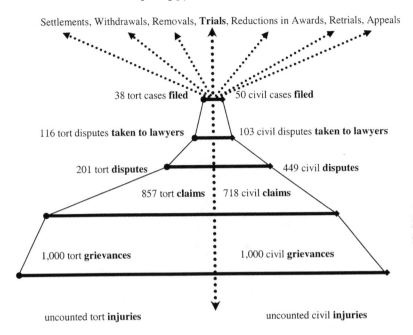

Settlements, Withdrawals, Removals, **Trials**, Reductions in Awards, Retrials, Appeals

38 tort cases **filed**   50 civil cases **filed**

116 tort disputes **taken to lawyers**   103 civil disputes **taken to lawyers**

201 tort **disputes**   449 civil **disputes**

857 tort **claims**   718 civil **claims**

1,000 tort **grievances**   1,000 civil **grievances**

uncounted tort **injuries**   uncounted civil **injuries**

Source of statistics: The Civil Litigation Research Project (Miller and Sarat 1980–81, 544)

in the general pattern represented 71.8 percent of all civil grievances). Each side of figure 2 must impress on an observer how few occasions for disputing persist from earliest stages (at the base of the figure) to latest stages (at the top). For example, the CLRP (Miller and Sarat 1980–81, 544) found that, for every 1,000 civil grievances, 718 became claims and 449 became disputes, of which 103 were brought to a lawyer and 50 were filed. The opposite side of the pyramid (for torts alone) differs slightly but reveals a *winnowing* of conflicts similar to civil conflicts in general. For every 1,000 tort grievances, the CLRP found, 857 would become claims, only 201 would become disputes, 116 would lead to a lawyer's being solicited, and 38 would result in court filings. Impressive reduction in the number of disputes from prior to later stages has been reinforced by many studies (Curran 1977, 145; Hensler et al. 1991, 122).

Winnowing may seem obvious, but the degree of *attrition* between perceptions of injuries and litigation may be surprising to many casual observers. If a grievance on average has about one chance in twenty of being filed as a case, as Miller and Sarat found for civil disputes in general and for tort disputes in particular, then the observer's attention might be redirected from the atypical "top" of the pyramid toward the more typical stages at which might-have-been lawsuits were resolved or abandoned. Attrition of conflicts from one disputing tier to the next implies *selection:* each successive tier is an unrepresentative sample of each preceding tier (Galanter 1996b, 1100). This implication of the Disputing Framework, too, is obvious but often overlooked.

The characteristics of injuries, accidents, and disputants, among other factors, will affect the composition of each tier of the pyramid.[6] If victims do not name serious wrongs, they may never blame another and claim recompense. In that instance, grievances never come to pass, let alone disputes or filings. The overwhelming majority of conflicts will never reach a lawyer, so curiosity prompted by this framework might direct observers to ask what happened to them. Among the answers that researchers have given is that lawyers who would prefer to win their suits are agents of selection, vetting disputes to find the few most likely to be winning cases.[7] Thus, the Disputing Framework bolsters the long-understood point that winnowing and selection work against frivolous lawsuits: the more frivolous or fraudulent the injuries, the less likely those injuries will lead to litigation (see Vidmar 1999, 184–85).

The narrowing of the pyramid as the eye moves from its bottom to its top also reminds observers of *bottlenecks* that constrain litigiousness. Despite complaints about the role of lawyers in modern American society, lawyers act as gatekeepers who restrict the flow of cases and discourage some litigation (Saks 1992, 1190–93). Movements from one stage to another may be retraced; not only may a potential litigant change her or his mind (e.g., positions that will be entrenched by trial are more fluid before filing), but she or he also may shift tactics based on the tactics or perceptions of others (Felstiner, Abel, and Sarat 1980–81, 637–38). As a result, complaints that go up often come down before attorneys and filings reach courtrooms.

---

6. A more complete picture than the one provided by the classic pyramid would add a large tier *below* grievances including all those injured persons who do not recognize a grievance and an enormous tier of all those users of a product or service who are not injured. Conversely, a more nuanced model would recognize the many settlements, withdrawals, and dismissals of claims at trial as well as the many post-trial reductions in awards, retrials, and appeals *above* the trial tier. We recognize these with arrows above and below the pyramid in the diagram. Their relevance will be demonstrated at many points throughout the book, but we stick here mostly with the classic model.

7. This point holds better for plaintiffs' attorneys working under contingency agreements than for lawyers for civil defendants, who are paid whether they win or lose and who may satisfy clients by losing less than expected.

SPECIALIZED KNOWLEDGE ABOUT TORT PRACTICE

Scholars have been building on the Disputing Framework, usually focusing on discrete elements of disputing rather than the whole. As a result of such specialized attention, knowledge about disputing and civil justice has expanded and evolved. Scholars insist that one may continue to embrace this or that reform of civil justice once one has updated one's commonsense presumptions with uncommonly appreciated information. They insist, however, that one may not in good faith traffic in canards that have been exposed by empirical research once one is no longer oblivious to the research. When convenient or expedient assumptions clash with products of disciplined observation and inference, common sense becomes nonsense to all who master better information. In the view of many scholars, too many Americans have yet to avail themselves of this information, relying instead on presumptions and information that have been disputed if not refuted.

Naming Injuries

In general, empirical studies have shown that, for the vast majority of injuries, the injured demand no compensation—legal or other.[8] Most injured parties do not even feint toward lawyers or courts or litigation. This reluctance to take claims to the courts at a minimum qualifies the assertion that Americans are hyperlitigious victims who turn to courts precipitously and needlessly (Quayle 1994; Sykes 1992). To be sure, a few Americans participate in the courts energetically, even ruthlessly. Far more Americans assiduously avoid participation in the third branch of government. In this regard, everyday discourse takes for granted what students of disputing practices deem problematic.

Because upward transitions in any pyramid lead from a larger class to a selection from that class, *grievances* (the relatively observable "ground floor" of the earliest pyramids) as a class will differ from *injuries* (the often unobservable "basement" beneath the earliest pyramids) as a class. Reliable information about injuries is thus essential if one is to understand

---

8. If one asserts that too many people sue, one should explicitly presume approximately how many people in which situations ought to sue. Those who observe how few injuries or grievances become lawsuits do not presume that every injury should see a courtroom. In fact, scholars presume that the gatekeeping functions of courts are prerequisites for the status quo. That two such astute observers as Samuel Jan Brakel (2000, 831 n. 40; 1996, 103–4) and Max Boot (1998, 150) should so misunderstand this obvious point leads us to rehearse it here.

disputing. In the absence of data to remind observers that nearly all injuries go unnamed and unclaimed, a crucial step in disputing goes unnoticed: "Though hard to study empirically, naming may be the critical transformation; the level and kind of disputing in a society may turn more on what is initially perceived as an injury than on any later decision" (Felstiner, Abel, and Sarat 1980–81, 635).

Those who do not perceive themselves to have been injured or do not associate injury with setting or causation are difficult to locate or to study for obvious reasons. Injuries too subtle to be perceived or harms latent for long periods may never reveal themselves to potential disputants or to scholars. Perceived injuries must be linked to some preconditions if they are to lead potential grievants to *name* afflictions as injuries. One study declared that in most cases injuries at or related to work led to no action because the injured did not connect injuries to, for example, how injuries might reasonably have been predicted and prevented (Hensler et al. 1991, 156–57). In addition, if the injured perceive their injuries but do little about them, inactions are hard to document or count. Numbers related to injuries exist (especially for accidents that insurance companies track) but are often inadequate due to gaps in data (e.g., afflictions of the uninsured); poor matches between injuries and legal categories (e.g., injuries that are clearly actionable in a court versus injuries that are clearly not); legal cultures (e.g., what customs trump which rules when); and legal authority (e.g., jurisdictions state, local, or national) (Saks 1992, 1175–76).

While one may not be able to prove a negative—that is, how many disputants might have entered the observable pyramid but did not—scholars and allied specialists have amassed data consistent with the presumption that many injured parties do not sue or see a lawyer but "lump" injuries due to ample disincentives to litigate (Baumgartner 1984; Engel 1984; Greenhouse 1982; Merry 1979). Professor Richard Abel drew attention to injuries that were never reported because employers discouraged workers from filing or because the injuries did not seem serious enough to justify expense and bother (1987, 448–52). At least two empirical propositions regarding injury rates are available in scholarship but usually go unacknowledged in everyday discourse. First, Americans' modal response to injury is to do little or nothing. Second, many common estimates of rates of litigating are based on very little observation of how many or how few candidates for grieving, disputing, and litigating exist. As a result, *the denominator for assertions about litigiousness is unknown or unavailable, which often means that it is conveniently or expediently presumed.*

Blaming Grievances and Claiming Remedies

Research shows that modern Americans formulate far fewer grievances (that is, requests for a remedy from another party) and generate far fewer formal claims than everyday knowledge pretends or the stereotype of U.S. litigiousness insists. Perhaps the largest national study of serious injuries—that is, injuries more likely to yield naming, blaming, and claiming than injuries or wrongs that are easily overlooked—found that those injured lodged claims in about 44 percent of automobile injuries, 7 percent of injuries at work, and about 3 percent of other injuries (Hensler et al. 1991, 19). This Institute for Civil Justice/RAND study further found that out of every 100 who suffered a disabling injury, 81 took no action while 19 considered a claim. Of these 19, 6 did not follow up, bringing the total of inactives to 87 out of 100. Two grievants dealt directly with the person whom they blamed, four consulted with an insurer, which left only seven who consulted a lawyer. Of the seven, four employed the attorney and two filed suit (Hensler et al. 1991). These data concerning serious injuries confirm a central lesson of disputing pyramids.

The much-cited Harvard Medical Practice Study found that every hundred injuries caused by negligent medical treatment or examination generated perhaps a dozen claims and that only one out of six patients who suffered major, permanent injuries that resulted in at least partial disability filed claims (Saks 1993, 10).[9] RAND economist Patricia Danzon (1985) estimated from data collected by the National Association of Insurance Commissioners that injuries caused by medical attention outnumbered malpractice claims by a ratio of ten to one. May and Stengel (1990) found that, of 175 respondents who felt that they had received unsatisfactory medical care, 46 percent changed physicians and 25 percent complained to the unsatisfactory caregiver. Only 9 percent of these disgruntled patients contacted lawyers. Not one of the 175 sued (see Studdert and Brennan 2000, 1647–48).

Of course, patients are more likely to sue when injuries are most serious (Saks 1993, 10–11; 1992, 1186–87). However, scholars have gone beyond that obvious point to advance some nonobvious findings. The propensity to claim correlates *positively* with surgery, personal income, ur-

9. Professor Saks (1993, 11) also noted two observations of greater importance to understanding malpractice disputes. First, perhaps five times as many claims of malpractice are unfounded as are justified, according to the Harvard Study (Brennan et al. 1991; but see Brakel 1996, 104 n. 60). Second, physicians drastically overestimate the probability of a demand for compensation in the event of negligence resulting in injury.

banization, and accommodating state laws; *negatively* with lawyers' earnings; and *not at all* with the number of lawyers, the age of the population, or recent tort reforms (Danzon 1985, 74–75, 82–83). Potential disputants are unlikely to become claimants if they know little about legal processes, about consulting lawyers, or about the possibilities of recovery (Saks 1992, 1188).[10] Saks (1992) accounted for the mismatch between highly publicized litigiousness and widely underappreciated reluctance to sue by a misleading asymmetry in cases. "False positives" (that is, cases in which civil defendants are wrongly hauled into court) are more likely to be discovered and publicized, especially by anxious might-be defendants, than are "false negatives" (that is, deserving cases that are not pursued). When the wronged choose to lump injuries, compensation or atonement forgone is almost always a very *private* decision. When grievants take action, in contrast, even informal complaints or reconciliations are more noticeable than decisions not to pursue a grievance. Securing a lawyer or filing suit is a still more *public* action, about which the press and reformers are even more likely to hear.

In sum, the findings of scholars who have looked into matters most intensively nearly invert widespread perceptions of litigiousness among Americans: "The real puzzle is to explain why, in the face of such a reasonable expectation of a doctrinally expanded pool of actionable injuries, the actual growth is so modest" (Saks 1992, 1175 n. 71).

Reaching Disputes

Most specialists accept as true still another generalization that those who lament a "litigation explosion" ignore: *a majority of would-be disputes terminates before blaming and claiming are rejected or even focused, not just before lawyers are consulted and litigation begun.* Common sense informed by experience with disputes explains why many conflicts end before a grievance is formulated as a claim and rejected. Confrontation costs money, time, and energy even when it does not take reputation and dignity from the one complaining or the one complained against or both. Would-be plaintiffs and would-be defendants alike have many reasons to avert a dispute, especially when the would-be disputants expect to interact with each other repeatedly or daily. Even in the supposedly litigious United States many citizens resent people who cannot solve "their own" problems

10. So imposing are obstacles to litigation that Abel (1987, 447) deduced a "crisis of underclaiming" and Felstiner, Abel, and Sarat (1980–81, 636) detected "grievance apathy," the unwillingness of harmed persons to lodge complaints when a grievance would seem legitimate.

but blame them on others (Engel 1984). Ordinary insurance practices suggest a third explanation for resolution of disputes outside courtrooms: companies compete by emphasizing how many routine claims will be neither disputed nor delayed. These countervailing considerations are seldom brought to the attention of ordinary readers or viewers, so most Americans are unaware how much naming, blaming, and claiming stops far short of lawyering, let alone litigation.

Enter the Suits—Legal Counsel

Many of the studies already discussed in this chapter vitiate the claim that Americans instantly, fervently seek legal representation and litigation upon perceiving a slight or injury. This research has reiterated what the Disputing Pyramid displayed: *transitions between injuries and the seeking of counsel wear down might-have-been disputants and encourage them to end if not to resolve their grievances.* Disputants move down the Disputing Pyramid more often than they ascend.

Scholars have deepened and expanded this portrait of resort to lawyers as rare and variable at some cost in complexity. Abel (1987, 457–58) likened securing an attorney to other forms of participation: grievants with higher incomes, greater education, and a stronger sense of legal efficacy are more likely to engage than those with less confidence in their ability to achieve objectives and less resources on which to draw. In contrast, the poor, women, and minorities were more likely to seek representation in matters of personal injury, Abel claimed, attributing such countertendencies to insurance undercoverage: those with more and better insurance need not engage lawyers as often as those without insurance. Abel concluded that a profit-seeking entrepreneur should discount tort liability severely because few injured people will even pursue grievances and disputes (Abel 1987, 460), let alone consult an attorney and sue (see Campbell and Talarico 1983, 315–16; Curran 1977).

Saks reviewed the other side of attrition at this stage—lawyers' agreeing to represent disputants. What he found was consistent with common sense but contrary to caricatures of greedy shysters. Saks cited studies that showed anew that lawyers were gatekeepers likely to reject far more cases than they undertook (1992, 1190): "At an extreme is a report of one New York City law firm that earns 15% of its business from personal injury cases against the city. The firm rejects any case that is expected to yield awards of less than $50,000. Of 2,500 medical malpractice complaints offered to the firm in one year, it accepted only forty." Lawyers preferred cases with the greatest prospects at settlement or, far less often, trial; cases that promised the greatest return for the least expenditure of money, time, and resources; and cases in which the plaintiff was sympathetic and the facts clear-cut and easily established (Saks 1992, 1190–91). If lawyers are the relentless score-seekers of stereotype, Saks concluded, then they filter out the least "worthy" disputes and send away litigationally "unworthy" disputants:

> Ironically, the solution sometimes suggested to solve the liability "explosion"—that plaintiffs' attorneys commit themselves to taking only the most meritorious cases deserving the greatest compensation—may be exactly what they have been doing. This solution tends to produce precisely the results critics have taken to indicate the existence of the "explosion" in the first place. (1192)

Kritzer (1997) found that plaintiffs' attorneys refused perhaps 90 percent of malpractice disputes brought to them. Other scholars have reported that even litigants who eventually won overcame obstacles to get a lawyer to present them (Sloan et al. 1993; Sloan and Hsieh 1990).

Filing in Court and the Three Worlds of Torts

Scholars have repeatedly demonstrated what *a minuscule proportion of disputes even approaches a courthouse, let alone a courtroom.* Precisely because so many disputes will never surface in a courtroom, however, citizens, lobbyists, and legislators easily overlook them. Information about disputing that is neither public nor formal is readily available only to those who read specialized studies, so common knowledge generally includes little about cases that never were. Because filings data are hardly self-interpreting, scholars have contextualized unwieldy data via the "three worlds" thesis (Hensler et al. 1987, 30–34). This thesis groups filed cases into three very different classes. The most common world of torts consists of routine litigation of which, paradoxically, the public has the most experience yet is least aware. A high volume of personal injury lawsuits with small stakes, stable law, and little emphasis on deterrence reaches settlement or, occasionally, trial. Slip-and-fall and especially automotive accidents exemplify this first "world" of civil litigation in which costs and outcomes change gradually if at all. First-world cases are ubiquitous in courts, but a second world of products liability, malpractice, and business torts looms larger in news media and public consciousness. This minority of lawsuits involves evolving yet somewhat stable law but larger stakes and greater emphasis on deterrence than the first world of torts. The third world of torts combines deterrence that primarily concerns some plaintiffs, monetary stakes that can be stupendous, procedures that may be innovative, and law that is not yet settled. This is the realm of class actions, mass torts, and latent injuries: asbestos, tobacco, Bhopal, silicone implants, and the Dalkon Shield. These cases involve so much of society that they may reverberate up the pyramid from widespread perceptions of harms to extensive awareness of putative causation to denials of responsibility or liability that lead to lawyering and many filings. Injuries, grievances, disputes, and even retention of counsel tend to be far more public in this third world than in the first two.

Filings in U.S. Federal Courts

From tort reform testimony in the Congress, one would never guess that *national* courts are targets of less than one in twenty tort filings. Nonetheless, many products liability and mass tort cases file in U.S. courts. Products liability filings in national courts nearly doubled between 1984 and 1995 (Galanter 1996b, 1107), but such data are "lumpy." That is, filings have tended since the 1970s to collect around celebrated products and companies: asbestos, breast implants, airplanes, and so on (Dunworth 1988, 49; Galanter 1996b, 1107–8).

When Professor Saks reviewed data from the Administrative Office of the United States Courts (AOUSC) for 1975–85, a period immediately prior to the "insurance crisis" of 1986, he discovered that tort filings in U.S. courts, far from powering some litigation explosion, had increased far more gradually than, for example, Social Security cases and filings for recovery of overpayments (the majority of them to veterans) (Saks 1992, 1197–1201). In 1985 the AOUSC reported 62 percent more tort cases than in 1975, but cases other than torts had increased by more than twice as much, 153 percent. To put the same statistics in a different manner: torts constituted 22 percent of civil filings in 1975, but 15 percent of far more U.S. filings in 1985 (Saks 1992, 1198–1200). Prior to 1986, tort filings in U.S. courts increased in number, but their numbers *decreased* relative to other civil filings.

Despite this relative decrease in *tort* cases, *products liability* filings expanded by almost four times between 1975 and 1985, just over half the 758 percent increase between 1974 and 1985 that the Reagan administration's Tort Policy Working Group claimed. Products liability filings account for most of the growth and flux in U.S. tort filings but, as scholars repeatedly point out, one-third of all U.S. products liability filings in that era concerned the unique product asbestos (Saks 1992, 1204). The pattern of personal injury and products liability cases has tended to be wavelike: certain products lead to swells of cases that crest and then wane as the system deals with those kinds of disputes and products (see Hensler et al. 1987,

10–11; Galanter 1996b, 1107–8). An implication of such waves of filings is that products liability and personal injury caseloads vary across times and subjects. At any point the U.S. courts will hear many lawsuits against a few corporate or commercial defendants—now asbestos manufacturers, then drug companies, then automakers, and so on—but one or two suits against individuals or smaller concerns. Even if an explosion of federal filings were attributable to products liability or personal injury, scholars have found, such an eruption would consist more of specific upsurges than some general upwelling. Reforms targeted to such waves might make sense, but cures for classes of cases that were declining in number made little sense to the scholars.

Filings in State Courts

Perhaps 98 percent of tort cases file in state courts, the data for which are spottier and less detailed than in U.S. courts. Saks found that, immediately prior to the alleged explosion of litigation, tort filings (the National Center for State Courts did not differentiate torts into subsets such as products liability) roughly grew with population, tort filings increasing 9 percent between 1978 and 1984 while population increased 8 percent (Saks 1992, 1207). Even that generalization was tricky, however, because an increase during 1978–81 had been followed by a decline during 1981–84, and the advent of state tort reforms may have spooked many litigants *into* courts in 1986. A rough estimate is that state cases grew less than 4 percent per year, even less with population growth taken into account.[11] Saks hazarded another generalization: tort cases tend to make up less than 10 percent of civil filings in states for which we have data, which means that, to an even greater extent than national courts, tort filings are far outnumbered in states by cases concerning property, contracts, divorce, and small claims (1208).[12]

Summarizing data on trends since the "insurance crisis," Galanter (1996b, 1104–5) has noted that tort filings between 1991 and 1993 (in twenty-seven states with available data) declined by 6 percent; that dispositions of state cases had been more numerous than filings since 1988; and that state caseloads had grown mostly due to criminal cases and domestic

11. We do not presume that population or population growth is anything other than a crude surrogate for the kinds of information that we should need but do not have. See Saks 1992, 1211.

12. Saks speculated (1208 n. 202) that this consistency in the makeup of state caseloads does not reach the public because defendants in property or divorce or small claims suits tend not to be well organized, well-heeled insurers, businesspeople, or professionals, while plaintiffs in such cases are often businesses.

relations cases (the latter experienced a 37 percent growth in filings in courts of general jurisdiction during 1988–93). In state courts, Galanter also noted, automobile-related tort filings had greatly increased while filings unrelated to automobiles had not increased dramatically—an expansion of litigation dominated by first-world torts.

Naturally, such summary statistics disguise various specific trends. A study of one month in 1988 found that filings ranged from 2.5 per 100,000 population to 164.8, depending on which of thirty-eight urban courts was under scrutiny (Rottman 1990, 4), and that rates varied over time. Overall, however, these data showed that products liability accounted for about 2 percent of the caseload and malpractice for about 6 percent. A consistent finding is that state civil caseloads abound with automobile accident cases, almost half of the filings in the 1988 data.

Resolutions Outside Trials

Not only are litigants and especially tort litigants far fewer than stereotypes and shibboleths presume, but they are far more transitory. About seven civil filings will be resolved before the conclusion of a trial for every one resolved in a courtroom. Far more cases will settle than will be tried, so most would-have-been plaintiffs will never stand before a judge or jury as formal plaintiffs. Specialized observers have concluded that *concentration on trials rather than other resolutions may be the most misleading aspect of common sense about courts.*

Herbert Kritzer, drawing on data collected for the CLRP, discovered that tort disputes were markedly more likely to settle than disputes concerning contracts, commercial dealings, real property, domestic relations, regulation of business, or discrimination in five U.S. and seven state courts. Kritzer found that only 7 percent of filed cases reached a verdict, an additional 15 percent terminated through some formal processes, and 9 percent more settled following one or more judicial rulings on a substantial motion (Kritzer 1986). This is why two observers suggested that "litigotiation" best describes the complexities of informal resolutions amid formal disputing: negotiations at each stage in disputing—even after verdicts and awards have been announced—may remove disputants from formal litigation and induce them to bargain less formally (Galanter and Cahill 1994, 1341–42).

A few knowledgeable tort reformers have noted that settlements are reached "in the shadow of" verdicts and awards made nearer the top of the Disputing Pyramid. They have not acknowledged that, systematically, shadowy resolutions consist in cutting losses that experienced civil defendants and their lawyers would expect any judge or jury to inflict. In an extraordinary study, Taragin and his co-authors examined thousands of insurance files to find what physicians to whom the insurer referred the files had concluded (Taragin et al. 1992). The insurers' own experts found negligence to be difficult or impossible to deny in about a quarter of the disputes (some of which had not yet been filed as cases), leading the insurer to offer some recompense in more than 90 percent of those disputes. In the 62 percent in which the insurers' referees discovered no negligence, on the other hand, payments were made only 21 percent of the time. The rest of the disputes were too close for the physicians to call. The insurer made payments in 59 percent of these cases. The median payment across cases was under $50,000. Payments correlated with the severity of injuries. This signal study reinforced similar findings in studies from hospital insurers (Sloan and Hsieh 1990) and was itself bolstered by interviews with other insurers (Vidmar 1995). Not surprisingly, awards offered in lieu of formal proceedings discount the actual economic losses of the grievant (Danzon 1985), often recompensing less than half of losses and discounting larger losses to a far greater degree than smaller claims (Sloan et al. 1993).

Outcomes of Civil Trials

Trials and outcomes—a focus of journalists and mass entertainment—transpire "above" the usual Disputing Pyramid. Specialized studies of cases after filings concern public disputing, which tends to make data more available. However, interpretation of those data introduces complications and subtleties likely to task even the patient and well schooled. For instance, wins and losses might seem among the easiest figures to come by, as important for practitioners as for policymakers. In reality, the rates at which plaintiffs or defendants prevail vary across time, locations, jurisdictions, and issues. This variability impedes generalizations even in malpractice cases, which, we have seen above, are a particularly well-researched area of tort law (Daniels 1990). As a result, summary numbers are as likely to mislead as to inform common sense and rhetoric. Our survey of sources in table 1 shows why news media, tort reformers, and even scholars are often unable to sort through the ranges of data available. Even if certain figures or creative trends did not benefit this side or that side of the tort reform wars, statistics on win rates alone would merit little confidence.[13]

Table 1 reveals ranges of victory statistics across the most authoritative sources we could find. Medical malpractice plaintiffs almost always lose more than they win, in part due to insurers' careful vetting of cases,

---

13. Moreover, statistics about victories or losses need not include post-trial developments.

TABLE 1 Plaintiffs' rates of victory in five sorts of cases

Study	Sample(s)	Plaintiffs' overall rates of victory				
		Civil cases	Tort cases	Medical malpractice	Products liability	Automobile cases
Litras et al. 2000, 4 (tab. 5); DeFrances and Litras 1999, 1	National Center for State Courts (NCSC) and Bureau of Justice Statistics (BJS) report on trials in state courts in 75 largest counties in 1996	52%	48%	23%	45%	58%
Litras and DeFrancis 1999, 5 (tab. 8)	Administrative Office of the United States Courts (AOUSC) reports on cases terminated in U.S. district courts for fiscal 1996–97		45%	34%	29%	
Vidmar, Gross and Rose 1998, 282	New York Jury Verdict Reporter data for jury trials concerning medical malpractice 1985–97		52%			
Eisenberg et al. 1996	NCSC and BJS reports for state courts for fiscal 1991–92	49%		30%	40%	
	AOUSC reports for U.S. district courts for fiscal 1991–92	55%		26%	37%	
Moller 1996,16	Jury verdict reports for state courts in California, Chicago, St. Louis, New York, Houston, and Seattle in 1985–94	57%		33%	44%	66%
Ostrom et al.1996, 235 (fig. 4)	NCSC and BJS report on trials in 45 urban state courts among 75 largest counties in 1992		49%	30%	40%	60%
DeFrances et al. 1995	BJS report on trials in state courts of general jurisdiction in 75 largest counties in 1992	52%	50%	30%	40%	
Daniels and Martin 1995, 66–81	Commercial jury verdicts reporters in 100 counties in 16 states from 1988 to 1990			30%	39%	62%
Daniels and Martin 1993, 7 (tab. 1)	Six Counties in California 1970–90	55%		41%		
Peterson 1987, 29 (tab. 3,7, 4,3)	*Cook County Jury Verdict Reporter* (Cook Co., Illinois) for civil trials —ranges for all civil cases are for 1960–84; rates for jury malpractice, products liability, and automobile are for 1980 84	49–64%		49%	52%	64%
	Jury Verdicts Weekly for selected Californial jury trials 1960 84 —ranges for all civil cases are for 1960–84; rates for malpractice, products liability, and automobile are for 1980–84	51–61%		40%	48%	
Danzon 1985	National surveys of claims closed in 1974 or 1976			28%		
Ranges of rates across studies		**49–64%**	**45–50%**	**26–52%**	**29–52%**	**58–66%**

discussed earlier in this chapter. Only in one study did win rates of products liability range above 50 percent. Civil cases in general frequently result in a majority of plaintiffs' verdicts, but table 1 shows that the lion's share of those wins favor plaintiffs in automotive cases. As we illustrate in table 2, data concerning products liability in six counties in California over about twenty years may be broken down according to the character of the injury and the setting in which the injury occurred to reveal even greater variability.

Professors Theodore Eisenberg and James A. Henderson Jr. of Cornell Law School undertook an even more daunting statistical analysis in two studies of trends for national and state courts. The first study found that plaintiffs' rates of winning products liability cases had *declined* in the 1980s, *before* many states' tort reforms had been considered, let alone passed (Henderson and Eisenberg 1990). Critics at the Manhattan Institute assailed those results (see Eisenberg and Henderson 1992 *passim,* but esp. 733 n. 4), which led Henderson and Eisenberg to follow up with an expanded survey.[14] In that follow-up, Eisenberg and Henderson confirmed that plaintiffs' success rates in products liability cases had declined since 1985. Moreover, they found that the pro-defendant turn in products liability had been geographically widespread, *not* a matter of a few jurisdictions, and pertained to almost all lines of products other than asbestos. Based on opinions published in the *Products Liability Reporter,* plaintiffs won 56 percent of cases in 1979, but 39 percent in 1989 (the last year covered in the second study) (Eisenberg and Henderson 1992, 741). Based on data collected by the Administrative Office of the U.S. Courts on all federal district court cases,[15] plaintiffs' success rates in U.S. courts fell from 41 percent in 1979 (the first year for which they had complete data) to 31 percent in 1989 (Eisenberg and Henderson 1992, 741). Most of the decline in plaintiffs' successes in U.S. district courts, Eisenberg and Henderson found (1992, 741), could be explained by developments during pretrial proceedings, for which the plaintiffs' win rate went from 50 percent in 1978 to about 26 percent in 1989. In addition, products liability filings (aside from asbestos filings) in U.S. courts declined by about 35 percent between 1985 and 1991 and by perhaps 44 percent if one controlled for rates of consumers' interactions with products (742–43).

14. We find at least two ironies in this episode. First, the Manhattan Institute loosed an agricultural economist on Henderson and Eisenberg despite the fact that studies by senior researchers at that institute would wither under far less exacting scrutiny (see Chesebro 1993). Second, when Eisenberg and Henderson demonstrated anew that their figures stood up to statistical critique, this supposedly lethal "shot in the head" of tort reform was ignored as far as we have been able to tell.

15. Recall how very few tort cases are entertained in U.S. courts.

Judges and Juries

Many critics of the civil justice system presume that neglectful judges and lawless juries account for some civil justice problems (Boot 1998, 146–75; Daniels and Martin 1995, 1–28), but studies have shown that most criticisms about juries are founded in apocrypha, anecdotes, exaggerations, rationalizations, and slanders—but not in data (Casper 1993; Daniels and Martin 1995; Galanter 1993a; Hans 2000; Lempert 1993). Perhaps those attacking the civil jury often lost sight of these verities due to mass media's emphasis on unusual or seemingly absurd decisions by juries and due to the differences between the cases jurors typically decide and cases that are settled, abandoned, dismissed, or argued to judges or arbiters (MacCoun 1993, 138–40). Because civil juries are routinely asked to decide the 10–20 percent of civil cases that are thorniest—the "easier" cases and disputes, as any pyramid would show, mostly disappear long before trial—those uninitiated into the workings of courts may underestimate jurors (Saks 1992, 1236–37). Getting beyond anomalies and anecdotes that create the common sense on which pop reformers rely is challenging. Like almost all data on win rates (supra) and awards (infra), the decisions and decisionmaking of juries vary across time and space, litigants, injuries, theories, and issues.[16] Amid the variations, however, these generalizations contradict pop reformers' claims:

- Defendants tend to win more often than plaintiffs in jury trials that concern medical malpractice or products liability issues.
- Jurors seldom award punitive damages.
- Jurors tend to come to personal injury or products liability cases skeptical of claims and suspicious of plaintiffs.
- Jurors do about as well as judges at untangling evidence and argument.
- Juries tended to reach malpractice decisions with which physicians who examined the files generally agreed.

To be sure, jurors often treat deep-pocketed civil defendants differently from defendants who have little money (Chin and Peterson 1985, 42–44). However, such relative generosity with awards when underdogs sue well-endowed defendants is less some "Robin Hood" penalizing the rich and more a matter of restraint toward defendants who cannot afford to pay, reflecting at the same time higher expectations of commercial enti-

16. Moller (1996, 15–16) states that civil jury verdicts in general vary much more according to the kind of case than according to jurisdictions or periods. However, within case types, verdicts vary across jurisdictions.

ties with extensive experience (and, sometimes, employed specialists) in avoiding risk and liability (Hamilton and Sanders 1996; Hans 2000, 1996; MacCoun 1993).

Awards

Civil awards are notoriously difficult to describe carefully and completely, a challenge that impairs cavalier characterizations by proponents of pop torts (e.g., exploding damages and ballooning awards) far less than it impairs good-faith efforts to determine what is happening and what, if anything, social policy should do about it (Saks 1992, 1242). The least controversial sorts of awards are *compensatory* damages, which are designed to "make whole" a grievant who proves by a preponderance of evidence her or his victimization. Of course, victims vary, as do the means of making victims whole. As medicine's capabilities and costs increase, courts have greater opportunities to make prevailing plaintiffs closer to wholeness than ever, but compensatory damages must increase if such wholeness is to be approached in personal injury or medical malpractice cases. Plaintiffs who may expect to live for many more years, plaintiffs who were making great money in careers that they must now forgo, and plaintiffs who discern injuries that were not even perceived decades ago may all insist that more money is necessary to compensate them for the liabilities that they have proved in court (Bell and O'Connell 1997; Galanter 1996b, 1114–15).

Saks (1993, 16) estimated that the liability system paid through settlements or trial awards 4.4 percent of the earnings lost, the medical expenses borne, and other direct costs of nonfatal accidental injuries. If the purpose of compensatory damages is to restore the prevailing grievant to his or her conditions had liability not arisen, then the system undercompensates injuries, just as the Disputing Framework would indicate. However, absent an accepted standard for how much compensation the system should churn out, Saks's figure is useless except to debunk the widespread notion that "everybody but me" is cashing in by proclaiming himself or herself a victim (e.g., Sykes 1992, 123–24).

Scholars, finding most summary statistics unenlightening, have disaggregated their study of the matter, which has debunked common misconceptions but complicated matters. Of the 1–2 million claimants who receive compensation for torts each year, almost 60 percent are compensated for claims from automotive accidents and about 20 percent more are compensated for injuries incurred at work (Hensler et al. 1991, 99), about the figures that we should expect from scholars' findings on the mix of filings.

Tort complaints in areas other than automobile and work-related accidents—products liability and medical malpractice, for examples—make up but a part of the roughly 20 percent of cases remaining. About 40 percent of all claimants who received payments had the help of a lawyer. Of the majority who achieved compensation without a lawyer's help, about 70 percent received payment from an insurer and the remainder from a party whom they blamed (Hensler et al. 1991, 100). Aside from automobile accidents and workplace injuries, 29 percent of those who gained compensation had legal assistance, while 34 percent dealt directly with the party or parties whom they held responsible and 49 percent dealt directly with insurers (Hensler et al. 1991, 100).

Dividing compensation into more subsets further undermines characterizations of greedy plaintiffs and expropriating trial lawyers, but at the price of additional complexity. For example, disaggregating data on accidents reveals (Hensler et al. 1991, 101 table 4.20) that for accidents not involving work or automobiles, less than 10 percent of compensation is eroded by attorneys' fees or awards for pain and suffering! Opinion leaders and legislators may demonize compensation for losses due to defective products or malpractice all that they please, but these figures show that perhaps 5 percent of attorneys' fees and about 2 percent of payments for pain and suffering may be attributed to all claims other than those occasioned by injuries in automobiles or at work.

Beyond cross-sections of data on compensation, scholars have researched trends in awards to rebut common sense. Table 2 (drawn from Daniels and Martin 1995, 78–87) reiterates those complications for an extensive sample of products liability cases. The table shows how awards vary according to the degree of injury and the setting in which injuries occur (as well as with the age of the plaintiffs, which is not capsulated in the table). "Any trends over time toward increasing award structure followed changes in the severity of the injuries and the age of plaintiffs" (Daniels and Martin 1995, 94). Examining medical malpractice awards, Sloan and Hsieh concluded that a large part of the increase in awards reflected changes in the mix of cases brought to verdict (1990, 1025). In contrast, Eisenberg and Henderson (1992) suggested that there was about as much evidence that real-dollar awards in products liability cases had declined as that they had grown. The gaudy awards that alarmed most observers were far fewer and harder to win than those observers appreciated (Eisenberg and Henderson 1992, 769 fig. 7, app. A table A-7).[17]

17. Statistical relationships that are neither commonly known nor easily understood complicate matters still further. Awards correlate directly with the *number* of jury trials in some jurisdictions (Peterson 1987, 29–31). As the number of cases in a jurisdiction increases, the

TABLE 2 Products liability verdicts in six California counties, 1970–90

Setting	Minor injury	Major injury	Death
Work			
Win rate	37.5%	48.6%	39.2%
Median award	$301,105	$345,000	$483,940
Mean award	$529,208	$1,020,838	$690,445
Vehicle			
Win rate	31.6%	45.6%	44.4%
Median award	$217,789	$1,636,744	$897,600
Mean award	$701,551	$3,796,221	$1,071,838
Home			
Win rate	28.6%	36.4%	50.0%
Median award	$49,296	$245,948	$456,960
Mean award	$240,253	$739,277	$577,506

Awards for "Pain and Suffering"

Awards for "pain and suffering" are particular targets for many critics of the civil justice system for reasons that make more sense the less one knows about the awards. Awarding money to compensate "nonpecuniary losses" seems to critics to follow no norms, legal or accounting, because remuneration for severe pain or long suffering must be at least somewhat arbitrary and any payment for minor discomfort seems unwarranted. Nonetheless, *awards for pain and suffering tend to be systematically predictable according to the severity of injuries* (Sloan and Hsieh 1990, 1025; Viscusi 1989, 217–19) and have been growing more slowly than compensation for lost wages or medical expenses (Galanter 1996b, 1123–24 fig. 5). Once again, scholars have found that common understandings are wrong, but these findings are hard to disseminate in a manner that would inform public discourse.

Punitive Damages

Tort reform advocates have publicized and exaggerated awards of punitive damages to induce unwary citizens to generalize from publicized anom-

median damages may be expected to decrease because the increased caseload brings more small cases into court alongside the large-ticket cases that would be there in any case. The same statistical relationship makes sense in reverse: as fewer cases are heard, the median award should be expected to increase because the cases abandoned or screened out will tend to be those with modest stakes. This tendency is fraught with policy implications but difficult to explain and thus unlikely to become widely known.

alies to the whole system. Scholars have verified just how unusual such punitive awards are and suggested that the very rarity of hefty punitive damages, if anything, argues for their not being a major problem in the U.S. system. Of course, the political logic of punitive damages may work in precisely the opposite direction: the rarity of huge punitive damages may, in a curious irony, make them more alarming when awarded and less acceptable to ordinary observers. It is easy to see why information about punitive damages is so malleable.

The Disputing Framework alone indicates how rare punitive damages must be. Punitive damages are awarded at the very end of an arduous process only if the plaintiff prevails. In states that permit punitive damages, a judge or jury may award them only if the decisionmaker declares that the defendant's actions exceeded mere negligence and veered into reckless or egregious misconduct. That is why finding after finding has revealed that *punitive damages have rarely been awarded and even more rarely collected* (Daniels and Martin 1995, 214; DeFrances et al. 1995; GAO 1989; Landes and Posner 1986; Moller 1996, 35–36; Peterson 1987, 10–12; Rustad 1992, 23). Scholars have long acknowledged that punitive damages tend to be awarded for financial harm increasingly more often than for products liability or medical malpractice (Daniels and Martin 1995, 217–21; DeFrances et al. 1995; Moller 1996; Peterson 1987, 22–25), but ordinary folk do not know that.

Even scholars, however, were startled by Michael Rustad's findings. Professor Rustad could find but 355 instances of punitive damages (about fourteen per year on average) in products liability cases in the United States during 1965–90 (1992). Studies across the years had turned up very few punitive damages in products liability cases (Rustad and Koenig 1993, 130 table 1), but to find relatively few cases in a twenty-five-year period that included the reform agitations of the 1980s was dramatic. Rustad further determined that, aside from asbestos awards, punitive damages in products liability had *decreased* since the mid-1980s (Rustad 1992, 38). Rustad also compiled (with Thomas Koenig) a database of all the punitive awards in medical malpractice cases in the United States from 1963 to 1993, finding 270 awards—perhaps 1 percent of all medical malpractice verdicts during those thirty years (Rustad and Koenig 1995, 1006). Contrary to stereotype, about 70 percent of those punitive damages were assessed against corporate entities rather than physicians. Scholars have also found that punitive damages correlated with or were rationally related to compensatory damages (Galanter 1998b; Koenig 1998; Eisenberg et al. 1995).

Proportionality of Damages

Although it is common knowledge that civil plaintiffs routinely reap wind-falls utterly unwarranted by law or facts, scholars have consistently found matters to be far more complicated. They have divided compensation into three parts (Saks 1993, 14; Saks 1992, 1218). When stakes are lowest, plaintiffs who win trials or settlements tend to be *over*compensated be-cause insurers would just as soon compensate, even for pain and suffering, to avoid administrative and litigative costs (Viscusi 1989, 95–97). Natu-rally, losers are more likely to pay such modest awards than larger awards. When stakes are highest, plaintiffs tend to be *under*compensated because what plaintiffs stand to win is many times administrative and litigative costs and because incentives are greater for losing parties to delay payment or to avoid payment. In the middle—at approximately the level of many caps on damages—awards just about match alleged costs. Saks (1992, 1218) declared that "[t]his pattern of overcompensation at the lower end of the range and undercompensation at the higher end is so well replicated that it qualifies as one of the major empirical phenomena of tort litigation ready for theoretical attention."

One remarkable implication of this confirmed pattern is that *the stu-pendous awards that draw attention tend to compensate plaintiffs for less than their losses, while the actual "windfalls" are much smaller and concern fender-benders and other small-scale disputes and so do not attract much notice* (Saks 1992, 1221). A second implication is that those who argue for caps on damages to prevent undeserved enrichment of high-stakes plain-tiffs very nearly invert empirical findings (see Peterson 1984; Sloan and Hsieh 1990). Professor Viscusi showed a particular manifestation of this inversion (1991, 216–17): caps will not affect most awards for "pain and suffering" because most awards are so small that caps will not kick in, but caps will truncate awards for the most serious injuries (e.g., cancer, brain damage, quadriplegia) because such awards track (albeit *under*compen-sate) the severity of injuries. However, amid most policy debates, the sus-ceptibility of evidence to manipulation or misinterpretation may not be obvious.

After Verdicts

Although scholars have made attrition obvious as disputes "ascend" the pyramid, they have also shown that attrition does not stop above the pyra-mid's apex (Galanter 1996b, 1115–16). Their findings are easily summa-rized if not commonly appreciated. One evident but overlooked point is that verdicts may be overturned or awards reduced after trials, on appeal, or both, so wins and losses are even murkier than they appeared above. *The greater the award, the more likely that it will be reduced by the trial judge or by an appeals judge or by each.* Perhaps the most unappreciated verity is that awards go partially or completely unpaid and uncollected far more often than most people would guess. The greater the award, the greater the probability that the awarded party will collect only part of it. Even a modestly attentive citizen should understand that appeals delay payment to encourage post-award settlements, but we know of no evidence that audiences receptive to pop reform keep that fact in mind.

Findings are so variegated that some of them may be argued to support tort reformers and their critics alike:

- Post-trial proceedings left about 80 percent of jury verdicts undisturbed and awards or other payments were increased in 2 percent of defendant verdicts and 3 percent of plaintiff verdicts (Shanley and Peterson 1987, vii–viii), which might benefit those who argue for tort reform.
- In a quarter of plaintiffs' verdicts, post-trial processes reduced payments due plaintiffs, predictably reducing larger awards much more than small ones (Shanley and Peterson 1987, viii), so critics of reformers may cite evidence that punitive damages were frequently reduced.
- In the aggregate, defendants were ordered to pay 93 percent of original awards under $100,000, 82 percent of awards between $100,000 and $1,000,000, but 67 percent of awards greater than $1,000,000 (Shanley and Peterson 1987, 29 table 4.2; see also Broder 1986; GAO 1989), which means that pop reformers and their critics may draw attention to different sorts of cases.
- Nearly twice as many changes in punitive awards followed from settlements between the litigants as post-verdict acts by courts (Peterson, Sarma, and Shanley 1987, 28), so critics of tort reforms may note that defendants presumably got the best deals they could, while reformers could argue that defendants acceded to litigational extortion.
- A nontrivial portion of reductions in punitive awards follow from defendants' difficulties in paying (Shanley and Peterson 1987, 46 table 4.8), which for reformers might evince the onerousness of awards and for critics might show the reasonable flexibility of the system.
- In three of five product liability cases, punitive damages were only partially paid or not at all (Rustad 1992, 56).

THE EXPERTS STRIKE BACK—OR OUT?

All in all, Professor Neil Vidmar probably too politely characterized tort reformers' evidence as "questionable" (1999, 177). The evidence is mixed on some matters and inconclusive on others, to be sure. But legal studies specialists have effectively discredited most of the shaky numbers, glib generalizations, misleading metaphors, and demonstrable insults against lawyers, judges, jurors, witnesses, and plaintiffs, showing that most popularized arguments for tort reform lack grounding in evidence. Moreover, scholars have made a strong case that tort tales are reductionist when they are not overtly distorted or mendacious. By the standards of empirical rigor, factual accuracy, and analytical acumen, pop tort propagandists have not matched the sober retorts of academic specialists.

Nevertheless, scholars' considerable intellectual achievements have been relatively inconsequential in challenging the common sense about law that reigns in contemporary mass culture and politics. One important reason, quite simply, is that the very qualities that distinguish rigorous social scientific knowledge significantly limit its potential for influencing mass knowledge and commonsense meaning. Vidmar himself noted that "sociolegal scholars had little initial impact on the highly charged political and policy debates," largely because "there were few systematic empirical studies of the tort system" and those studies were "published in relatively obscure scholarly journals" (1999, 177). We agree with Vidmar in this regard, but we develop a more expansive case outlining why the eventual proliferation of scholarly antidotes still has translated into little cultural impact on the tort reform campaign and the anecdotal lore that it disseminates. In step with our discussion at the conclusion of chapter 2, we focus on four criteria by which scholars' contributions, in following academic convention, can be understood to remain remote from common knowledge.

Availability

Expert knowledge about legal practice lacks influence because it remains relatively unknown to journalists and citizens, virtually ceding the contest for influence to proponents of the familiar common sense. Whereas tort reformers routinely lobby journalists, jump at the chance to spin mainstream news, write for editorial and opinion pages, sponsor mass advertisements, and distribute simplistic position papers for the uninformed, scholars produce mostly in specialized academic outlets for other scholarly specialists. Such esoteric placement means that few academics, let alone citizens and policymakers, will master the abundant literature from which we have sampled above, with the predictable result that reform of the civil system and scholarship about that system too often seem to occupy different universes. Demonstrably inaccurate information or misleading judgments about legal practice thus are likely to persist or prevail because they are available to ordinary and even well-read people while demonstrations of their inadequacies are not.[18]

These results reflect less the scholars' deficient strategic logic than the institutional realities of their situation. Whereas many pop tort reformers are paid to be full-time advocates and propagandists who regularly saturate the public sphere with their message, academics can engage in such activities only piecemeal after attending to their primary obligations of teaching, grading, mentoring, administering, researching, and writing for publication. Scholars have little discretionary time available in their academic schedules to wage effective battles over knowledge with reformers in the mass public sphere and even fewer financial resources to amplify that knowledge through public relations channels. Academics cannot afford to flood newspapers with advertisements, travel nonstop for performances, be available for print and electronic media outlets, consult television and movie produces, and the like on a scale that meaningfully approaches that of paid publicists. At the same time, the reward system in academic life—employment, promotion, tenure, salary rate, status—provides few incentives for scholars to sacrifice conventional scholarly routines for increased "practical" impact. Indeed, public intellectuals in the modern academy who attempt to engage broad nonacademic audiences often incur major sacrifices in professional standing and reward. Most scholars thus opt to publish their research in scholarly journals and related forums, and then hope that the message travels further into public life, taking advantage of scarce opportunities for direct communication in the press when they can. A few law professors, like the tireless Marc Galanter, have managed to make it occasionally into mass news outlets, where he has performed effectively. But he is an exception, and the frequency of his performances is quite limited.[19]

The resulting esoteric placement of the debunking literature has made it unnecessary, and perhaps unwise, for tort reformers even to acknowledge the existence of the studies and perspectives that we have surveyed

18. By the 1990s, an extraordinary public intellectual like Marc Galanter could manage occasionally to get words into coverage by the *New York Times* or *Newsweek,* while Theodore Eisenberg and James Henderson projected their voices on National Public Radio. But these commentaries were rare relative to those of opponents.

19. Scholars Stephen Daniels and Joanne Martin deserve note here, for their American Bar Foundation sponsorship does afford them more time for publicizing their message, although they are constrained in other ways noted below.

above. Why alert people to empirical flaws in one's case that otherwise would go unseen? On rare occasions, popularizers may respond to academic refutations, but even then placement and availability weigh decisively in favor of reformers. When, to continue an example we cited already, Professors Eisenberg and Henderson demonstrated that plaintiffs' success rates declined in the 1980s, they threatened proponents of tort reform enough to elicit critiques and to induce a tort reform lobbyist to pronounce their findings to be "a shot in the head of products liability reform" (1992, 733). They then followed up the 1990 publication with thirty-six thousand words demonstrating that their original conclusions were valid and reliable and that criticisms were mistaken. Any fair observer would be compelled to award the engagement to Eisenberg and Henderson on its merits. Nonetheless, these scholars demonstrated their empirical virtuosity in two articles in the *UCLA Law Review*, while, for example, Peter Huber of the Manhattan Institute challenged their numbers in his column in *Forbes* magazine and, to the best of our knowledge, let the matter go after the second law review article. Citizens, business leaders, and political decisionmakers were more likely to have read Huber's critique than Eisenberg and Henderson's original article, unlikely to have noticed the follow-up article, and less likely to have given the figures careful scrutiny than the few academic readers who were driven by specialized research interests.

In sum, even when scholars pushed their findings into a public arena, the superior placement of reformers' publications and the wider availability of their information have tended to outshine splendid work and dependable findings. Two scholars labeled the changes in legal knowledge and practice wrought by tort reformers during the 1980s a "quiet revolution." Though Henderson and Eisenberg won more publicity for their findings than most publications reviewed above, any counterrevolution in common understanding that they worked was indeed quiet.

Accessibility

When available, the primary forms of knowledge circulated by social scientists tend to be relatively inaccessible to even well-educated journalists, policy elites, and citizens. To state the matter simply, every step toward sophistication is a step away from ease of understanding; the same rigor to which the social scientist proudly aspires generally produces tedious impediments for the nonexpert. Scholarly articles are typically long, intricately attuned to the fine details of research design, presented in rigid conformity to formal methodologies, articulated in dry, often arcane language, and typically filled with myriad statistics rendered in a variety of challenging formats. We know from experience that even our favorites among the authors' articles cited above tend to be considered deadly by most undergraduates, not to mention by journalists of all sorts. Readers of previous pages in this chapter no doubt already have experienced our point (and our students' pain). Scholars cannot match the accessibility that reform advocates routinely achieve. Scholarly articles offering detailed, balanced, complex case studies, large-N longitudinal studies, or multivariate regression analysis make far greater demands on the reader than does the three-sentence tort tale, the broadside quip ridiculing greedy attorneys, or the singular dramatic statistic unattended by methodological baggage.[20]

Moreover, scholarly retorts generally follow recognized conventions of good scholarship. Even the best study must be attended by acknowledgments of what the data do not confirm, what the study did not include, what questions remain unanswered. If compelled to make shaky inferences, scholars are expected to draw readers' attention to the infirmities of their best guesses. Some scholars have even endeavored to show what is not presently known and may never be knowable about tort law practice (Saks 1992). Indeed, nearly all the articles we cited in previous pages end by recognizing how little we know about the vast world of legal practice, about the huge landscape that remains unexplored and the vast amount of work yet to be done, about how little confidence we can have in our assertions about what "really" is going on. The problem is that this empirical skepticism informing scholarship hardly offers a match to the snappy certitude that tort reformers and polemicists are all too quick to provide to journalists, policymakers, business leaders, and the general public. If scholarship costs much and yields few clear answers, anecdotal knowledge costs little and reaffirms common sense.

This is not to deny that rigorous statistical studies can be powerful in some public settings outside of academic circles. Substantial studies with robust findings can make a difference to the programmatic work of technical policy elites who advise officials, and even directly in public hearings before politicians and other powerful actors. Sometimes, sophisticated social science empirical studies are very potent in speaking "truth to power" (see Songer 1988). Moreover, we should not discount the influence of such studies within circles of intellectuals who educate future elites. But such forums of influence for the most part remain relatively separate from public discourse that dominates the mass media and visible political performance.

We illustrate accessibility by continuing an example from the previous

---

20. RAND researcher Deborah Hensler admitted to a *National Law Journal* staff reporter: "I talk numbers because that's what I do . . . [but] people's eyes glaze over when one tries to reason by way of statistics. And lobbyists know that" (Cox 1992).

section. When Professors Eisenberg and Henderson clarified whence their data came and how they had taken into account various economic and legal contingencies that might affect their results, they made their results far more difficult to convey to mass audiences than the misbegotten numbers and misleading horror stories wielded by tort reformers. Eisenberg and Henderson took care to explain that their data began and ended with fiscal years for which they were able to accumulate reasonably complete data. They did not begin with the most convenient year from which to manufacture spectacular statistics, which is what the Reagan administration's Tort Policy Working Group did. The scholars showed that, if one excluded asbestos cases or other products that led to "waves" of mass tort actions, products filings had declined greatly. Max Boot dismissed their precision, caution, and sensitivity to context with an absurdly comic simile: "That's sort of like saying 'with the exception of Ted Bundy and Jeffrey Dahmer, the number of serial killers in America has declined'" (Boot 1998, 236). Decisionmakers were not likely to read or hear about this dust-up, but were much more likely to learn of Mr. Boot's response (on the editorial pages of the *Wall Street Journal,* if not in Boot's book) than to learn of Eisenberg and Henderson's research. Beyond the placement/availability of Mr. Boot's dismissals, decisionmakers were and are much more likely to grasp sophomoric humor than to ponder systematic study. When the scholars made their evidence less assailable, they also made it less accessible.

Adaptability

Even when available and accessible, the academic virtues (such as reliability and validity) reduce flexibility for reshaping accounts in different contexts and for different audiences. Elaboration of methodology leaves little room for mystery and post-hoc manipulation of the message, and explicit standards of assessment provide plenty for critics to assail and little room for refuge. This is the opposite of the vague but morally loaded criteria that pop reformers prefer to peddle. Take, for example, the common claim that "there are too many frivolous lawsuits." A reformer cannot go wrong with this claim; while implying that frivolous lawsuits have increased dramatically in number, the proponent can always retreat to the simple commitment that any unwarranted lawsuit is undesirable. "I have never gone along with citing numbers about exploding litigation. As I see it, the very fact that some lawsuits are winning that should never have been allowed into court defines an injustice demanding attention, and reform as necessary," one leading reform spokesperson told us. Loaded phrases like "excessive litigation," "greedy lawyers," "Santa Claus jurors," and "irresponsible plaintiffs" similarly allow maximum flexibility for reformers to render moral judgments without offering convincing evidence about frequency. By contrast, a social scientist would insist on coding some representative sample of lawsuits, specifying criteria of evaluation, distinguishing a continuum of performances, and determining a threshold of acceptability—all enmeshed in various caveats about inadequate data, imperfect variables, limiting analytical techniques, and the like. We hardly need point out which type of account is far more adaptable to a reporter's story or a policymaker's speech.

Consider the following classic example. When the Tort Policy Working Group at the Reagan administration's Department of Justice estimated that filings of products liability cases in U.S. courts during 1974–85 had grown by 758 percent, it overstated growth by a factor of between two and three.[21] The group had selected a starting year in which products liability filings had been drastically undercounted (Galanter 1992). Had Attorney General Meese's group selected the first year with complete data (1976), the growth would have been 267 percent between 1976 and 1985. Nearly a tripling would have seemed significant enough, at least until scholars showed that removal of mass torts—asbestos, Dalkon Shield, and Bendectin cases— would reduce the rate of "explosion" to 104 percent over those ten years. Nevertheless, the inflated statistic could be claimed to be based on official data—a tactic merely cunning by political standards but clearly cheating by academic norms. When social scientists reduced the figure radically, they ended up certifying that lawsuit growth still had doubled, thus reaffirming the reformers' bigger claim about an "explosion."

A similar dilemma undermines the social scientists' extensive reliance on statistics to shape public knowledge. No matter how imperfect or ungrounded, all the pop advocates must do is wave a report, toss out their own numbers, question select (and often acknowledged) weak points in opponents' statistics that scholars themselves highlight, and declare a standoff. (It is ironic that critics of U.S. courts assail a similar process in courtrooms when scientific witnesses are undermined by hired-gun witnesses.) At the least, the polemicists can neutralize the experts, and at best they might discredit statistical knowledge itself. This is one reason why Peter Huber's work on "junk science" has been so important to the tort reform campaign—to make a case that numbers can be unreliable, that experts and statistics can be mobilized arbitrarily for all sides, and that experts and studies do not resolve anything. With social science experts either matched, de-authorized, or ignored, populist common sense again

21. Under "Filings in U.S. Federal Courts" earlier in this chapter, we cited Professor Galanter's evidence from filing data between 1975 and 1985 to "split the differences" between the Tort Policy Working Group and critics.

might have an easy time prevailing as the default standard that reformers can invoke effectively.

An Affirmative, Actionable Agenda

We noted in the previous chapter that the pop tort platform meets the key criteria—a well-defined social problem, a simple diagnosis of causes, culturally resonant moral claims, and a remedial plan—that policy experts identify as effective to the "framing" of issues and to setting the agenda for policy (Entman 1993; Gamson 1992; Neuman, Just, and Crigler 1992). It strikes us, by contrast, that the social scientists' predilections for empirically cautious, rigorous, and testable truths and conventions celebrating value-neutral study impede development of a similarly affirmative, actionable agenda on at least three counts.

Count One: Scholars have been almost entirely reactive (see Lempert 2001). Their primary gambit has been to debunk reformers' broad allegations and to demonstrate the unrepresentativeness of anecdotes. Because the aim has been far more to show that tort reformers are inaccurate in their portrayals of existing tort law practice than to develop clear alternative accounts of the legal system or actionable reform programs, the scholars have been more concerned with refuting the reformers' agenda than resetting the agenda on new terms. In fact, the experts' primary message has been that existing tort law practice is too diverse and complex to characterize confidently; we do not know enough to formulate sensible reform.[22] This studied agnosticism leads critics to allege that scholars by default become apologists for the existing system.[23] This is notable, on the one hand, in that it provides the scholars no claim to which they can appeal for support. Defensive positions claiming that "the system ain't broke," or "problems are neither systemic nor systematic," or "we don't know enough to act" are unlikely to mobilize commitments from anyone, much less to ring true to citizens who every day hear stories that *seem* to reinforce the rants of polemicists and who experience the personal frustrations of a legally complex society.

On the other hand, this implicit defense of the status quo ironically runs counter to most of these scholars' actual critical assessments, many of which are well published. Indeed, many of the scholarly experts who contest pop reform have long identified with the public interest law reform and "access to justice" movements. Their early writings, either ex-

---

22. The quote by Galanter et al. (1994, 185) that serves as one of this chapter's epigraphs is a good example of this cautious perspective.

23. We see matters in different light. See note 3 supra this chapter and the text around it.

plicitly or implicitly, were committed to a dualistic vision of law that powerfully rivals tort reformers. In short, scholars contended that law presently fails its mission by overserving the "haves" and underserving the many "have nots," while at the same time exalting the rule of law, legal procedures and processes, legal professionals, litigation, and rights talk as the best resources for advancing justice in democratic society (Galanter 1974; McCann 1986). Traces of these positions can be found amid debunkings of reform rhetoric, but one must read carefully to discern any consistent, clear counteragenda among all the numbers, tables, and reactive charges.[24]

Count Two: Realist scholars' statistical debunkings repeatedly evade what is perhaps the most palpable, if bewildering, transformation in tort law itself for journalists, pundits, and ordinary citizens over recent decades—namely, the rapid rise of the "third world" of social policy torts regarding asbestos, tobacco, Dalkon Shield, breast implants, and other allegedly harmful products. Tort reformers have cleverly focused on the alleged explosion of *individual* lawsuits along with the huge awards from class actions and mass torts, which diverts attention from the dangerous products and their manufacturers, who heavily fund tort reform politics.[25] But, as we have seen, social scientific debunkers have repeatedly treated mass torts, involving billions of dollars in awards and court costs, as outliers in broader statistical patterns, as "different" or "unique" legal actions that should not be confused with typical torts, and the like. Mass torts *are* anomalous, as noted earlier, but they are hardly irrelevant. That is precisely why we might expect scholars to educate the public about the character and implications of social policy torts, shaping the lenses through which they are understood and appreciated. Why is litigation regarding asbestos and tobacco in particular—two long-proven deadly products that corporations knowingly, deceptively continued to produce—not worth highlighting as a positive, affirmative story about the value of civil litigation, especially given failures of Congress to legislate adequate health insurance and regulatory guarantees?[26] Again, reactive debunking and unmasking complexity have produced good social science but a decidedly evasive popular discourse and political rhetoric.

Count Three is the most general: Realist scholars have systematically evaded direct engagement with the moral ethos at the heart of the com-

24. A notable exception to this claim has been Rick Abel, who has continuously parsed the theoretical, ideological, and normative aspects of tort reform rhetoric from a clear, neo-Left perspective. See also Galanter et al. 1994.

25. This was true at least until the late phases of the "tobacco wars," after the Master Settlement Agreement was struck. See chapter 7.

26. For one example of what we have in mind, see Rustad and Koenig 2002. On the larger question at stake, see chapter 7.

monsense lore embraced by reformers. In fact, the primary logic of most debunking studies has been to challenge normatively oriented thinking itself—routinely derided as "moral rhetoric," "the politics of ideas," "symbolic politics," and so on—as inherently flawed and inferior to "objective," "empirically based" evidence. While consistent with the positivist premises that scholars invoke as authority, such empiricism is impolitic in a variety of ways. Most important, this faith in facts leaves unanalyzed and uncontested what arguably is the core of the reformers' popular appeal—their unabashed defense of core American values of individual responsibility and moral discipline (Rose 1999). If we are correct that the reformers' assault on excessive litigation represents a moral crusade as much or more than an empirical challenge, then normative arguments about justice, democracy, and social responsibility define the terrain on which the primary political battle must be waged. Scholarly dismissals of the "politics of ideas"—as if this politics were somehow impure or dishonest—retreats from the challenge of demonstrating how individualistic moral frames obscure key issues, how such frames displace concerns about power, how norms of responsibility might be applied differently, and a host of other possible challenges to neoliberal and neoconservative values. Realist social scientists and other critics of pop torts have routinely hit the opponents' wildest pitches but usually laid off tort reformers' moralistic offerings that cross the heart of the political strike zone.

Moreover, it follows that what is lacking in the social scientists' campaign is a larger social vision that reworks core values for new ends and taps alternative values deeply embedded in American society. Indeed, we recall that tort reform arose precisely to challenge earlier modes of "liberal" reform that hailed law, courts, legal processes, juries, rights, and the like as the very foundations of justice, freedom, and other basic ideals revered in American society. Once again, however, scholarly experts have contested what Americans know about tort law while ceding to opponents the more basic endeavor of tapping and shaping citizens' normative beliefs about law. Although at times every bit as righteous in tone as their adversaries, the scholars have skimped on actual moral content, while trumpeting powerful empirical information that has been barely heard amidst the din of mass-mediated discourse about civil law.

CONCLUSION

Our discussion in this chapter has been decidedly Janus-faced. Looking toward scholarship, we have summarized the impressive array of data that social scientists have marshaled to discredit the legal lore disseminated by tort reform polemicists. In this regard, social scientists have used the tools of their academic craft to correct the record with more accurate, informed, and sophisticated understandings about tort law practices over recent decades. By academic standards of rigor and exactitude, the scholars have prevailed hands-down in the clash of ideas.

Looking toward public discourse, we have argued that sophisticated studies alone are not the stuff of common knowledge and transformative political discourse. They no doubt do command some attention and sometimes provide a resource for effectively "speaking truth to power" in the world of policy elites and lawmakers (Lempert 2001), although later parts of this book might question even that assumption. Our primary point, though, is that the studies we have recounted here are, by standards of ordinary discourse, unfamiliar and difficult, and, by standards of opinion leaders, esoteric and tedious. Such sophisticated forms of knowledge simply do not translate into modern mass communication. The features identified as most important by analysts of framing, agenda setting, and common knowledge—simple narrative forms; clear causal stories; linkages of personal experiences to deeply rooted moral values; attention to human impact—are in short supply in the scholars' systematic studies.

This latter face of our argument is not intended as a critique of social scientific endeavors. We, as social scientists, profoundly respect the intrinsic merits and important contributions of this scholarship. In fact, we could not have written this book without such research. And we realize that our own academic product suffers from many of the same professional liabilities that we identify in the work of others. But that is our point. While scholars deserve credit for responsibly contributing to the public record the fruits of their labors, their greatest virtues as producers of knowledge are little appreciated in the prevailing modes of mass knowledge production and political discourse.

We do not intend to suggest, finally, that social scientists *cannot* contribute effectively to mass cultural knowledge. Sophisticated research can be used in the service of mass influence, but to do so it must transcend narrow academic conventions. Richard Lempert, a scholar cited in previous pages, made the point recently. Research has been largely "reactive," aiming mostly to "correct false impressions," he noted. "To move policy, activist scholarship must tell a convincing story. Where scholarship conflicts, we have a contest between stories, the resolution of which does not necessarily depend on the relative soundness of the competing work. . . . The general public, too, best understands and is moved by specific examples and narrative explanation" (2001, 29, 31). Austin Sarat, also a pioneer in disputing research, has concluded similarly that "there is little reason to believe . . . that social science prevails over popular culture representations. . . . If there is to be a persuasive alternative story, it must be constructed or identified within popular culture" (2001, 428). That is, scholars need to connect their powerful debunking efforts to more artful narratives that illustrate the complexities of tort law practice, highlight its implications in experiential terms, link tort law remedies to our nation's deepest values, and yet nurture the aspiration of rendering these legal processes ever more accessible, just, and democratic.[27] In short, the critical empirical project must be more thoroughly balanced by the interpretive, constructive normative project. But that work yet remains to be done; its relative absence to date has left pop reform advocates and publicizers of legal lore only very modestly challenged in contemporary mass culture. And given the resource disadvantages at stake, it is hardly likely that scholars alone, however skillful in presenting their message, will make a huge impact in the future.

27. We find that the interesting book by Carl T. Bogus, *Why Lawsuits Are Good for America* (2001), has many virtues along these lines. While a university press book written for law school audiences, it is accessible, affirmative, visionary, and full of moral fervor in defending our inherited tort system on grounds of democracy and social justice. Curiously, this recent work by a law professor cites little of the research by the leading sociolegal scholars cited above. It also seems to have generated little attention from academics.

CHAPTER FOUR

ATLA Shrugged: Plaintiffs' Lawyers Play Defense

ATLA is an international non-profit professional association of lawyers who preserve and protect the rights of those who have been harmed. The Association serves the public, the legal profession, and the justice system by representing lawyers and the public in the public debate of reforming the civil justice system; preserving, promoting, and improving the common law in courts and legislatures; advancing the principles of constitutional law; and providing the tools and environment for its members, to serve their clients better.

ATLA MISSION STATEMENT

I think lawyers undersell themselves. I think lawyers so believe their own bad press and believe in the inability of lay people to appreciate what they do, that they are scared of public exposure.

STEVEN BRILL, "ADDRESS TO TEXAS LAW REVIEW ASSOCIATION"

The downside of ATLA's strategy [is] that the lawyers seemed to be losing the battle of public opinion, and with it the hearts and minds of juries and judges.

THOMAS BURKE, "LITIGATION AND ITS DISCONTENTS"

Our conclusion in the preceding chapter that academic social scientists, however impressive their empirical and analytical challenges, have proved to be little political match for well-funded, business-backed tort reformers probably surprises few readers. But what of more formidable interest group opponents of tort reform? At least two types of organizations have, often in alliance, pitted themselves against pop tort reformers and polemicists. One is the broad array of consumer and liberal public-interest groups, including the Consumer Federation of America, Consumers Union, and various organizations in the constellation of Ralph Nader's Public Citizen. These groups have often challenged tort reform legislation and initiatives at both the state and national level. While they have exhibited considerable political savvy and public authority in these contests, however, such consumer groups tend to possess relatively limited resources that must be allocated to a broad array of issue campaigns, often at the same time. Consequently, tort reform has constituted more of an episodic and low-profile adversary rather than sustained, high-profile target for most of these groups.

By contrast, the tort reform campaign has stimulated a persistent challenge from one of the very best funded and most powerful lobbying establishments in the nation, the Association of Trial Lawyers of America. Plaintiffs' lawyers have rallied massive resources behind the cause of defending the existing civil justice system, their own role as counsel for injured consumers in that system, and their very financial interests in preserving legal market share and jurisdictional power.[1] This campaign by trial lawyers, and its loose alliance with consumer groups, is the primary focus of this chapter. Our primary argument is that, *while the trial lawyers have committed considerable resources toward a "stealth" policy of insider legislative and judicial influence to block legal reform policies, they have virtually conceded the public domain of popular discourse about civil law practices to their moralistic, business-supported critics.* In this chapter we develop and illustrate this thesis, identify a number of interrelated institutional and professional factors to make sense of why trial lawyers have evaded the ideological contest, and conclude with some reflections regarding the implications of these strategic choices for the continued vitality of lore about the lawsuit crisis.

TRIAL LAWYERS: A PROFILE

The Plaintiffs' Bar

We begin with a brief sketch of the trial lawyers and their unique institutional sector of the legal profession in the United States. An influential series of studies sponsored by the American Bar Foundation (ABF) (Heinz and Laumann 1982; Heinz et al. 1997) identified three general spheres of influence in the bar, each with distinct social networks, personal characteristics, and religious or political orientations: liberal politics, the corporate establishment, and trial lawyers. The last group represents injured plaintiffs in civil disputes. These attorneys perform a small part, perhaps

---

1. On the complex relationship among financial interests, client interests, market share, and jurisdictional control by various strata of the legal profession, see Shamir 1995.

about 6 percent, of the total legal activity of the bar (Heinz et al. 1998). In 1995, 8 percent of practicing Chicago attorneys spent a quarter or more of their time representing plaintiffs in personal injury cases, while only 6 percent spent more than half their time on such representation (Parikh 2001).

Overall, personal injury practice has evolved in recent decades from an enterprise conducted primarily by generalists to one of increasing specialization. The personal injury bar today features a number of well-known expert subfields: products liability, medical malpractice, workers' compensation, premise liability, auto accidents, and the like. Tort lawyers who represent consumers injured by various products and services are probably the most high profile of such lawyers. Moreover, many of the latter attorneys specialize quite narrowly—on hot liquids, asbestos, aviation, pharmaceuticals, and so forth. Personal injury lawyers also tend to be organized primarily in small firms or solo practices. The 1995 ABF study of the Chicago Bar found that 90 percent of personal injury lawyers for plaintiffs practiced in small firms or solo practice, with 29 percent as solo practitioners (Heinz et al. 1998).

Sara Parikh's well-documented study (2001) demonstrates that the personal injury bar is quite cohesive in its goals and identity but quite stratified in character. A few wealthy lawyers specializing in complex, high-stakes class actions and mass tort cases receive much of the press attention, while most personal injury attorneys specialize in routine auto accident claims and generate relatively modest incomes. Because so many lawyers depend on contingency fees from mostly one-shot clients (Galanter 1974), their practices are inherently unstable, uncertain, and risky; ordinary practices oscillate between feast and famine, often precariously (see Daniels and Martin 2000, 2002). Indeed, such attorneys must work hard to generate a routine flow of clients. While good reputations arguably are the more important resources for success, the pressure to "manufacture" clients in various ways, including through commercial advertising and a host of less savory methods, is common among the lower strata of the profession. It is this feature that has provoked the most negative images of personal injury lawyers as crass "ambulance chasers," images reserved mostly for ethnic immigrants excluded from the elite corporate bar in earlier generations (Auerbach 1976). While the anti-Semitic and other elitist residue has faded somewhat, the plaintiffs' personal injury bar remains one of the least prestigious in the legal profession (Abel 1989; Parikh 2001). The assaults on personal injury lawyers by tort reformers and in popular culture have made their practice at once more precarious and less profitable for many of them.

Professional Organization and Political Representation

Trial lawyers for plaintiffs in personal injury cases are represented by a variety of organizations. The largest and most important organ of representation, and hence the focus of this chapter, is the Association of Trial Lawyers of America (ATLA). ATLA grew out of the National Association of Claimants' Attorneys, an organization of attorneys who wanted to redress the lack of institutional representation for injured workers under the developing workers' compensation system in the 1940s.[2] The organization eventually changed its name and took up the cause of personal injury lawyers, who were seriously lacking in professional respect and effective organization. The key mission of ATLA in its formative years was the dissemination of technical information about tort advocacy among plaintiffs' lawyers around the country. ATLA's membership size, identity, and power grew dramatically in response to the tort reform movement and other assaults on trial lawyers that began to percolate in the late 1970s. As the epigraph that introduces this chapter reads, ATLA's mission statement includes unabashedly "representing lawyers and the public in the public debate of reforming the civil justice system." Today, ATLA represents fifty-six thousand members nationwide—about 7.5 percent of the eight hundred thousand members of the American Bar Association (ABA)—and boasts a substantial operating budget for advancing its instrumental causes. State-level associations of trial lawyers work both independently and in tandem with the national organization on a variety of related issues.

Liberal public-interest and consumer groups with more specific political missions have allied with ATLA in defending the cause of personal injury lawyers for plaintiffs. This constellation of liberal public-interest groups includes most prominently Ralph Nader and his spin-off groups such as Public Citizen and Congress Watch. Nader and his allies have been tireless opponents of the many reform proposals that undermine citizens' rights to sue for justice—no-fault insurance, alternative dispute resolution, tort reform, and the like. Perhaps no single person in the second half of the twentieth century was more influential than Nader in advocating a litigation-centered vision of citizen politics and judicialized democratic institutional change in the United States. Nader's staunch defense of civil justice, dogged opposition to unaccountable corporate power, suspicion of bureaucratic regulatory mechanisms, and personal inspiration for many trial lawyers have provided considerable ground for alliance with ATLA and the plaintiffs' bar generally (McCann 1986). However, Nader's financial resource base has always been small and has depended heavily on individ-

---

2. The classic study of the evolution of the plaintiffs' bar is Speiser 1993.

ual trial lawyers. Nader's prickly style also has excited tensions on occasion, and his ill-fated run for the presidency in 2000 turned many longtime admirers and allies into bitter critics who have shunned all residue of common cause.

One significant public-interest law firm that was inspired by Nader but deserves special attention here is Trial Lawyers for Public Justice (TLPJ), which is the largest public-interest law firm in the nation.[3] It focuses on precedent-setting, socially significant tort litigation and has played an important, if controversial, leadership role among trial lawyers. One of the organization's most important and contentious activities is its Class Action Prevention Abuse Project, whereby TLPJ attorneys routinely "police" class actions in mass torts that could be considered as selling injured consumers short.

ATLA has also been joined on many occasions by a host of consumer groups in defending against critics the civil justice system and plaintiffs' attorneys. Key organizations include Consumer Federation of America, Consumers Union, Citizen Action, National Insurance Consumer Organization, and other more specialized public-interest and research groups. One especially important group established in the late 1990s specifically to educate the public about the importance of civil justice and the damage done by tort reform is the Citizens for Corporate Accountability and Individual Rights (CCAIR), later renamed the Center for Justice and Democracy (CJD), in both incarnations led by the indefatigable Joanne Doroshow. The alliance between ATLA and these groups against tort reform has been fairly strong, but there also have been many points of discord as well, such as on no-fault insurance proposals (see Burke 2002).

While recognizing that all of these groups work together, often in a stable division of labor, it is important to emphasize that ATLA is the key organization for our inquiry. That association manifests by far the largest and most stable constituent network of trial lawyers, the clearest motives in linking plaintiffs' lawyers' interests and principles, and the greatest resource base for taking on the business-supported forces of tort reform.

THE STEALTH STRATEGY OF INSIDE LEGISLATIVE INFLUENCE

From its origins ATLA has pursued a very simple, clearly defined political strategy—what we characterize as a "stealth" strategy[4]—in defense of its

---

3. See www.tlpj.org/search.cfm.

4. By "stealth" strategy, we intend several different but related meanings offered by the *New Oxford American Dictionary*. First, the strategy is a relatively surreptitious, furtive, "behind-the-scenes" approach. The ATLA campaign is designed primarily to fly under the

members, the plaintiffs' bar generally, and their larger causes of legal justice. This strategy has a number of tactical components, but one commitment has dominated by far all others. ATLA has focused the overwhelming bulk of its financial, organizational, and personal resources on cultivating support in Congress and state legislatures in order to block proposals that its members find unacceptable.

"Insider" Legislative Politics

The logic of the legislative approach was initially credited to Thomas Bendorf, a former lobbyist seasoned in California politics, in the early years of ATLA. It developed over several decades until the early 1990s, when it was described by Alan A. Parker, the senior director of public affairs, as a "very successful formula." The approach "consistently rejected," in Parker's words, the idea that media-oriented and grassroots mobilization tactics were worthwhile for ATLA. "Part of the strategy of the trial lawyers was to be quiet, to be invisible. . . . I think it was [tort reformer] Victor Schwartz who always called us 'no-see-ums.'"[5]

A number of assumptions supported ATLA's stealth strategy. For one thing, it removed trial lawyers from the line of fire in political disputes. "My theory always was, if the lawyers got out front, everyone beats them up," Parker explained. As such, lawyers could wield influence without themselves becoming targets of attention that diverted attention from their issues. This is a key reason we label ATLA's strategy a "stealth" approach. Moreover, by remaining largely behind the scenes, the advocates for the plaintiffs' bar could portray many conflicts as being between the corporate "special interests" and ordinary citizens, injured victims, consumers, and the like. Conversely, the "insider" strategy took advantage of the fact that trial lawyers tend to be skilled advocates who are well-connected politically, at both state and federal levels. Given that lawyers' professional power derives from both skilled tactical maneuvering in disputing and developed organizational contacts (Sarat and Felstiner 1995),

---

radar of popular attention and to leave its mark quietly on specific elite legislative targets. Second, we want to suggest that this tactical logic, while undeniably successful in some key regards, is very cautious, cagey, and conservative in character. Third, the term's likely origins in the Middle English word "steal" are indicative of how the contemporary public tends to view such strategies of unseen "insider influence." This is discussed in later sections of this chapter.

5. The 1994 interview with Alan Parker referred to here was conducted and graciously provided to us by Thomas Burke. Every point was corroborated by other key actors whom we directly interviewed.

the insider strategy thus took advantage of the lawyers' strengths to cultivate ties with legislators. Finally, the trial lawyers, and especially the elite
group of high rollers in class-action mass torts, could raise huge amounts
of money to fund their pressure tactics in legislatures. This was especially
true in the wake of huge awards generated by class-action social policy
torts like asbestos and, later, tobacco, which provided enormous funds for
both subsequent legal campaigns and political influence.

This general strategy also fit the overall ethical, legal, and policy inclinations of ATLA leadership. In short, ATLA has been fundamentally opposed to all federal efforts to pass uniform tort legislation that preempts
state law, and for the most part to state legislative intervention as well.[6] As
the trial lawyers see it, the most reliably informed and desirable changes
in tort law should be initiated through the common law by judges, who are
closest to the action and, of course, in regular interaction with the lawyers.
Courts are better situated, a leading ATLA strategist told us, because the legal issues "get more seriously considered, over a longer time. The changes
are incremental and the changes adapt to the exigencies of what's happening in the world. When you legislate you freeze at that millisecond whatever it is you've legislated on and you can't change it until you go back to
the legislature."[7] All in all, ATLA would prefer to take its chances with the
courts on most issues of reform; if legislation must be passed, they would
prefer to fight it out at the state rather than the federal level.

This legislatively focused obstructionist strategy has entailed two key
interrelated components. First, trial lawyers have contributed generously
to campaigns by elected officials, including especially legislators, but also
judges and governors or presidents. Trial lawyers have given large amounts
of money to PACs at the federal and state levels. In 1999–2000, ATLA was
the second largest PAC contributor to federal candidates, just behind the
National Association of Realtors; 86 percent of the $2,661,000 it con-
tributed went to Democrats. This mirrored almost exactly the same pattern
the previous year. In 2001–2, trial lawyers were the largest PAC contributor to federal candidates, although the actual amount dropped in the electoral off-year. Moreover, trial lawyers, individually and through PACs, were
the seventh largest group of contributors (over $200 apiece) overall in fed-

---

6. "At the national level, what tort lawyers are mainly seeking from the government . . . is
inaction," notes Martha Derthick (2002, 187).

7. By contrast, tort reformers argue that legislatures are far more accountable and democratic in nature, that common law tort awards lack consistent, general standards, and that legislatures historically always had primary responsibility for tort principles. See Schwartz,
Behrens, and Taylor 1997.

eral elections in 1999–2000, roughly the same as the American Medical Association and just behind the Teamsters and United Auto Workers.[8] Almost 90 percent of these contributions went to Democratic candidates. Trial lawyers contribute even more aggressively at the state and local level. For example, California trial lawyers contributed a total of $9.8 million to California candidates and another half million to political parties statewide in the 1997–78 election cycle (Civil Justice Association of California 1999). Tort lawyer contributions to electoral candidates for state judges likewise have been quite significant (Derthick 2002, 188).

These numbers can be misleading, of course. While contributions from plaintiffs' lawyers rank high next to those of discrete industries, they are dwarfed by the aggregate of corporate groups—insurance, pharmaceuticals, manufacturers, tobacco, and so on—that they challenge. For example, lawyer groups (not just ATLA) gave $21.3 million to House members during 2002 elections in an effort to influence legislation limiting medical malpractice awards and venue shifting of class-action lawsuits to federal courts, among others. This is a large amount, but it is far less than the $276.7 million that business groups as a whole contributed to House members (Salant 2003). Moreover, trial lawyers exhibit little of the structural economic power inherent in generating jobs, tax revenues, and overall productivity that renders corporations so indirectly influential in government policymaking.

Second, trial lawyers have invested strategically in lobbying legislators and other elected officials. ATLA has relied on professional lobbyists, led by chief consultant Thomas Hale Boggs Jr. of Patton, Boggs, LLP, for virtually all of their lobbying in Congress. The relationship is contracted for a fee on a quarterly basis. Comparatively, though, ATLA spends rather less on lobbying than on electoral contributions. The ATLA lobbying budget in 1999 was only $2.4 million (Burke 2002, 46), compared to nearly $200 million by the health care industry and $86 million by the insurance industry. The expenditures in the states generally parallel this same modest amount. However, the conventional focus on the amounts of money spent overlooks two important facts. One is that the trial lawyers' agenda is far narrower and more focused—namely, to stop tort reform, no-fault insurance, and the like—than that of their corporate competitors. Even more important is the fact that plaintiffs' lawyers, and especially the high rolling elite, have labored successfully to cultivate strong personal ties to many elected officials at both the federal and state levels. Indeed, several leaders in ATLA

---

8. All figures on individual and PAC contributions as well as lobbying expenditures were taken from the Center for Responsive Government Web site: www.opensecrets.org.

and other organizations stressed in interviews that this was probably the most effective tactical source of influence developed by trial lawyers. Overall, a *Reader's Digest* article surely exaggerated when it claimed that ATLA was "America's Most Powerful Lobby" (Evans and Novak 1994), but trial lawyers have proved to be a potent force in legislative policymaking arenas.

These interrelated components of the trial lawyers' insider strategy are regularly urged among state-level organizations by ATLA. Coordination is led by a special committee on federal/state relations and a committee of state trial lawyers' executives in the national organization, both of which share strategic political information as well as technical advocacy information on litigation with members. ATLA clearly is proud of its achievements on these matters. A former ATLA president boasted to members in his *Trial* column that they had topped the list of PACs and that *Fortune* magazine had ranked ATLA as the fifth most influential lobbying organization in Congress. "We will continue to fulfill our responsibilities as the principal lobbyist for open access to justice in America" (July 2001, p. 9). At the same time, trial lawyers have drawn much fire for their aggressive courting of politicians. For example, Republicans during the 2000 presidential campaign effectively challenged Al Gore by publicly linking a 1995 dinner hosted by wealthy Texas trial lawyers, over $4 millions in campaign contributions that followed, and President Clinton's veto of a federal tort reform bill passed by the Republican-led Congress in the following year. A Democratic Party aide purportedly wrote the script for the Democratic national chairman to present to Walter Umphrey, the famously wealthy Texas trial attorney: "Sorry you missed the vice president. . . . I know (you) will give $100k when the president vetoes tort reform, but we really need it now. Please send ASAP if possible" (Van Natta and Oppel 2000, A1).

Despite frequent criticism from opponents, it is difficult to deny the success of the general strategy. ATLA has blocked federal no-fault and tort reform legislation for twenty-five years. Indeed, ATLA has been so effective at frustrating tort reform advocates that the latter's proposed bills were watered down increasingly during the 1990s to the point that they were almost meaningless. One ATLA strategist actually considered recommending support for one bill. "It gets a lot harder to oppose it because there's not a hell of a lot left there." By supporting a toothless bill, he surmised, trial lawyers could look responsive, co-opt the corporate opposition, and yet suffer little actual impact on their practices. ATLA chose not to do so, however, for it would violate their basic principle that the federal government should not at all involve itself in the common law of tort. Trial lawyer organizations have been more uneven in their success diverting or derailing reform at the state level, but overall their obstructionist influence in the legislatures has been felt strongly in many states such as California, Ohio, Texas, and Florida.

Perhaps the ultimate compliment to this approach comes from leading tort reform advocate and ATRA spokesperson Victor Schwartz. "I think ATLA is far more organized than the people on the other side. They are brilliant in how they spend their money. It's targeted money," he told us. At the federal level, "they can give $10,000 (in contributions) to a chairman of a committee, or a speaker, or a president. They go to the leadership, they go to the top of the bottle." Moreover, for trial lawyers "there is a very limited menu" that focuses on tort reform and related issues, whereas the business group "menu is watered down with ten things, and they are not cohesive in focusing on liability reform. So most of the time the plaintiffs' bar wins it. They are focused." If the lawyers tried to pass new legislation increasing liability in courts, business interests would find it easy to mobilize as a cohesive force of opposition. However, the fact that ATLA and its allies mostly fight defensive battles to stop all affirmative legislation in tort matters gives them an advantage. Finally, Schwartz argued, in the aftermath of huge windfall returns from asbestos and tobacco litigation, trial lawyers should be able to improve their lobbying position in legislative contests long into the future (see Derthick 2002, 186–89).

Litigating to Disarm Tort Reform at the State Level

A second, parallel strategy has been developed to undo legislative reforms in the states where they have passed in spite of political opposition from trial lawyers. This strategy has enabled personal injury trial lawyers to do what they do best—to litigate against specific parts or entire packages of legislated civil justice reform. The key legal argument in nearly all these cases is that legislated tort reform violates separation of powers principles of state constitutions by infringing on judicial discretion. As the Ohio Supreme Court stated in a landmark decision in 1999 striking down a series of tort reform laws capping damages and modifying the collateral source rule, the latter were "openly subversive of the separation of powers and, in particular, of the judicial system."[9] Alice Robie Resnick wrote for the narrow court majority, "The general assembly has circumvented our mandates. . . . It has boldly seized the power of constitutional adjudication" that rightly belongs to the courts. Moreover, other legislation establishing statutes of repose (statute of temporal limitations) in products liability and re-

9. State ex rel. Ohio Academy of Trial Lawyers v. Sheward, 86 Ohio St. 3d 451 (1990).

lated tort issues also have been struck down in many states as violating basic principles of due process and equal protection. Overall, between 1986 and 2000 at least ninety-one court decisions overturned parts or all of tort reform legislation in specific states nationwide (Smith 1999; Brakel 2000; Schwartz, Behrens, and Taylor 1997). Along with Ohio, major victories in Oregon, Illinois, Florida, and Indiana during the late 1990s demonstrated the expansive reach of the strategy by trial lawyers in gutting tort reform (Glaberson 1999). Indeed, only a handful of states have passed tort reform that was not subsequently limited by judicial rulings.

This overall strategy of state-level constitutional litigation has largely been guided by Robert S. Peck, ATLA's senior director for legal affairs and policy research. By the 1990s, coordination and leadership was focused in the Center for Constitutional Litigation, a public-interest law firm designed specifically to provide direct assistance to lawyers challenging tort reform enactments at the state level. Again the primary logic of the campaigns has been that tort reform laws limiting damages, liability, and repose "constitute an improper legislative usurpation of judicial power, and an intrusion into the exclusive authority of the judiciary."[10] Tort reformers have vigorously challenged this argument in court, contending that historically courts derived their common law authority from legislatures and that the latter should act to render trial decisions consistent with general rules (Schwartz, Behrens, and Taylor 1997; Brakel 2000). But for the most part these arguments have fared poorly (Smith 1999).

What we find most noteworthy about this litigation strategy is its similarity to the primary stealth strategy of insider legislative influence. Like the former, constitutional litigation in the states takes place in relatively insular official settings, largely removed from mass attention; it is carefully targeted to influence elite judges rather than the general public; it takes advantage of lawyers' specialized skills and professional connections; and it is entirely reactive, defensive, and obstructionist in character. Moreover, the strategy does not require attorneys to address the merits of the pop reformers' claims about a lawsuit crisis, the epidemic of frivolous litigation, the excesses of plaintiff and lawyer greed, and the erosion of moral responsibility. All in all, while generally quite effective in stopping or limiting official tort reform enactments, the strategy is likely to have little effect on public perceptions of trial lawyers and the civil litigation process. In this regard, the savvy and pervasive assaults on lawyers projected throughout mass culture by business-supported polemicists thus have remained

10. Cited in "Constitutional Challenges: An Antidote to Tort 'Reform,'" *ATLA Advocate* 25, no. 9 (1999): 1. See also Peck's article in the November 1999 issue of *Trial*.

relatively uncontested beyond the courts. As ATLA director of public relations in the late 1990s, Carlton Carl, related to us, "For years, the philosophy of ATLA was 'don't make any noise,' even though the other side has
spent billions to change public attitudes, to change views on personal
responsibility."

Public Relations: Token Efforts to Share the Load

The fact that the two-pronged strategy outlined above has dominated ATLA
responses to tort reform assaults should not obscure the many voices in
the organization advocating greater efforts on other fronts. Beginning in
the mid-1980s, the insider, obstructionist strategy of ATLA was paralleled
by strategies oriented more toward public advocacy. Led by Ralph Nader,
liberal public-interest groups, and consumer groups, these strategies were
intended to challenge tort reform at both the national and state levels. As
Pam Gilbert, director of Public Citizen, put it in an interview in the early
1990s, "What we (initially) failed to do, and we're now waking up to the
fact, is it's not enough to fight these defensive battles. We have to do our
own campaign affirmatively expanding citizens' rights. Because there is a
lot of good [done by] the civil liability system, there's a lot of flaws or problems with people being shut out." Nader not only co-authored a book *(No
Contest: Corporate Lawyers and the Perversion of Justice in America)* challenging the corporate assault on trial lawyers and the civil justice system,
but he led campaigns in many states against tort reform.[11] Moreover,
Nader, Gilbert, Joan Claybrook, and other liberal public-interest leaders
constantly chided ATLA for not joining in the effort to shape public opinion of both the general population and targeted groups—jurors, judges,
politicians—around civil justice issues in the 1980s. "We wish that they
[ATLA] would use their resources less in giving PAC money and more for
public education," confided one high-profile activist. However, the traditional strategists and their approach generally won out among the trial
lawyers. As one former ATLA strategist put it, consumer groups

> have to bring in victims and have them crawl through the halls of Con-
> gress in their wheelchairs and stuff. . . . I don't think you need that to
> win—or it's part of the equation, but it isn't the whole thing and not
> everybody should be doing that. Actually I think if Ralph (Nader) and
> Joan (Claybrook) would stop and think about it, the way we've done it
> for all this time has been a great system. You do your thing, we'll do
> ours, and it all adds up to we can beat 'em.

11. Burke's (2002) study of "no-fault" in California is a classic example.

However, the argument of Nader and others both without and within ATLA developed momentum by the early 1990s. This resulted in and reflected a change of personnel in the public relations leadership within ATLA and the emergence of a series of presidents who placed somewhat greater emphasis on public education about trial lawyers and the civil justice system. Believing that "we cannot expect the public to sympathize with our positions unless they are understood and supported by strong arguments," ATLA's public education staff began to formulate initiatives during the remainder of the decade (*Trial*, January 2001, p. 9).

In the first relatively uncoordinated phase, trial lawyers made some efforts to challenge the anecdotal "horror stories" and "tort tales" propagated by conservative critics. This practice had its roots in the mid-1980s, when allies of trial lawyers began to publish "counterstories" supplying missing facts and adding positive perspectives to correct the typically apocryphal accounts of their business-supported adversaries. Sometimes these corrective accounts were full-fledged case studies—complex, thorough, and multidimensional (see Yin 1994)—but typically they instead were merely elaborated versions of previously circulated anecdotes. One early example was "The Not-So Simple Crisis" by (editor) Steven Brill and James Lyons in the *American Lawyer* (1986). This much-cited article set the template for future accounts. For one thing, it reflected lawyers' inclinations for "getting the facts" behind the spin: "Myths about the litigation explosion that never happened shouldn't substitute for real debate." This paralleled the realist response of social scientists, but it leaned toward far more accessible forms of "narrative correctives" than statistics. Also like the scholars, the corrective account of Brill and Lyons was generally defensive in character rather than hortatory or idealistic. "What the reforms we prefer have in common . . . is that they're based on the idea that lawyers and the legal system aren't solely responsible for the 'crisis.'" In yet another parallel to the response of scholars, the article was published in a relatively esoteric professional journal that was highly unlikely reading for anyone but a small group of lawyers and jurists.

Other essays from this period (Strasser 1987; Cox 1992) became classics among a relatively small group of trial attorneys and scholarly allies. But they were similarly reactive, defensive, and realist in their orientation, answering their critics in often defiant terms but hardly aiming to redefine the agenda of debate. Cox's article, for example, noted that tort tales were "a game that two can play. There's been time enough for the plaintiffs' bar to start collecting anecdotes of a different stripe: the wronged plaintiff." This was followed by the statement of a California lobbyist for trial lawyers, who claimed that "I've got a drawer full of horror stories." On the opposite page was a large picture of the lobbyist with a large bold-letter title:

"Trial Bar Aims Horror Stories at Tort Reform." A few such counternarratives follow. But again, the article was published in a relatively esoteric professional journal with very limited mass readership.

Not surprisingly, perhaps, ATLA's efforts to challenge tort reformists' horror stories in the 1990s followed in much the same mold. A memo from ATLA publicity planners in 1994 read:

> We could greatly benefit from in-depth, impeccably researched, and scrupulously accurate exposes of various myths and folk tales that the tort "reformers" have invented and propagated in order to sell judges, jurors, scholars, and legislators on the necessity for and the virtues of tort "reforms." The articles, could, as appropriate, put the lie to specific anecdotes, e.g. Peter Huber's tall tales about cerebral palsy or CAT scans.

Before long, ATLA's Web site featured a section titled "Civil Justice Facts" and subtitled "The Other Side of the Story: What They *Don't* Want You to Know." One-page accounts added little-known facts and interpretive spin concerning a number of the stories told by tort reformers that needed to be set right. ATLA began to send such corrective accounts to state organizations and journalists. At the same time, ATLA strategists prepared a litany of "fact sheets" for their members and for reporters in an effort to offset two decades of misinformation from tort "deformers."

Such efforts appear to have been of limited value, however. Trial lawyers' accounts not only have been reactive or defensive in character and esoteric in placement, but these "real story" materials typically have lacked a compelling normative angle or political vision. Such diffuse, often complex, fact-laden accounts can hardly hope to match the simple moralistic appeal of tales told by critics, of jeremiads that effectively tap common sense about cultural decline at the hands of greedy lawyers and irresponsible plaintiffs. To debunk specific tales as inaccurate or simplistic hardly does damage to the cumulative cultural logic of odes to individual responsibility and paeans to a more harmonious communal past. That such reactive counternarratives have not circulated throughout popular culture to any significant degree is hardly surprising. Moreover, the labels developed by trial lawyers and their allies to shift the focus of responsibility to corporate opponents tend to be equally defensive (Nader and Smith's phrase "tort deformers" is perhaps the best, while allegations of "corporate propaganda" and the "wrongdoers lobby" never stuck) and even whiny (as when assailing critics of lawyers as looking for "tar babies," "whipping boys," and "scapegoats") (Greenlee 1997, 711).

In the mid-1990s, ATLA began to develop a more systematic, multidimensional approach to public education. The key initiative that facilitated this effort was the formation of the ATLA Endowment—contributions from trial lawyers used to fund research that challenges "with authority, the flawed data and unfounded conclusions foisted on the public by the organized tortfeasors. . . . Endowment funded work is under way to help refine the message that will combat our enemies' attempts to tarnish the image of trial lawyers" (Fred Baron, "President's Page," *Trial*, July 2001, p. 9). Spearheaded by two past presidents of ATLA, Bob Habush and Larry Stewart, and taken to new levels by Fred Baron in his 2001 presidential term, the endowment reflected the conviction that ATLA "must have a long-term strategy to combat the poisonous propaganda constantly emanating from those who seek to destroy the efficacy of the civil justice system" (Baron in *Trial*, February 2001, p. 9). The tax-exempt endowment mobilized $16.5 million in pledges by 1998, with $5.7 million collected by early 2001, thus producing over $300,000 a year for public education.

A comprehensive Public Education Strategic Plan developed earlier in the decade outlined the multidimensional approach to education funded by the endowment, which included:

- The Public Education Institute, which is responsible for developing curricula, including mock trial exercises, for primary and high schools that impart better information about the civil justice system to America's youth, "who will be voters and jurors" one day.
- The Law School Institute, which funds scholarship and research on the advancement of individual rights through the civil justice system.
- The Judicial Institute, which supports programs on judicial independence and provides members of the judiciary with "balanced" research.
- The Research Institute, which funds research to inform and shape public policy and dispute resolution efforts.

Special projects aligned with these working institutes included a systematic plan for developing Web-based curricula to educate journalists about what lawyers do and how the civil litigation system works, as well as funding for coordinated focus group and mass survey studies probing how well the public understands the legal system. The underlying goal of these proposals is essentially the same, according to an internal memo proposal in the mid 1990s: "enabling ATLA to develop strategic approaches—up to and including specific messages and language—to public education, which also contributes to public policy and, of course, winning back the jury pool."

In addition, ATLA has worked closely with and through the Roscoe Pound Institute. Drawing inspiration from Dean Pound's legal realist philosophy of sociological jurisprudence, the institute works, according to an official pamphlet, to "facilitate positive change where outdated political abstractions have fallen short." The institute has supported numerous outreach efforts that parallel those of ATLA in recent years, including a Pound Fellows program that encourages dialogue about change in American jurisprudence; an annual Forum for State Court Judges; publications of related writings in the *Civil Justice Digest;* annual awards to outstanding law professors and law students, in an effort to offset the influx of "law and economics" support in law schools; and grants to legal scholars, including tort reform opponents Michael Rustad and Ken Chesebro, for research on civil justice.

All the new counternarratives, approaches, and programs initiated by ATLA, however, seem to add up to too little, too late. The present ATLA Endowment investment in all of its programs, after all, is only around $300,000, which is tiny relative to the sums still invested in the insider legislative and litigation strategies. Most of the institutes listed above presently are engaged in small-scale pilot projects. Even when all the existing pledges are collected and return becomes available in a few years, the total budget for public education will be under $1 million. Moreover, nearly all of this funding has gone to programs directed at legal elites (lawyers, judges, law school students, law professors, and the like), while only a small part has targeted mass media or the mass public; it is as much another expression of the targeted insider strategy as an investment in public education. It is relevant here that even Fred Baron, the ATLA president often credited with leading the charge for more public outreach, told us that the overall strategy of ATLA remains essentially the same as before. "ATLA has always focused on legislative policy, on a legislative strategy. We do a little bit of publicity, but what's the point? We can't even begin to match the funding by the corporations. They spend as much on a single ad as our entire public relations budget in a year."

We also again question whether the realist-inspired, "get out the real facts" logic of the lawyer campaigns, no matter how well funded, available, and accessible, is likely to provide a powerful answer to the moralistic appeals of conservatives to traditional values. The instrumental strategy simply lacks powerful ideological bite. This is as true for individual lawyers as for the collective. We were consistently surprised to find that very few high-profile personal lawyers we interviewed actively worked to "spin" their successful cases as successful campaigns for social justice. "Well, I figured the jury decision to grant such an award pretty much spoke for itself," one attorney told us. We have been impressed with the capacity of Nader-affiliated organizations and consumer groups to make a more positive pitch for access to justice, for legal representation, and for consumer rights. These groups match reform spirit with a powerful message about law and justice. Beginning in the 1960s, they effectively mobilized the prevailing ethos of "responsibility" to challenge the harmful practices of corporate institutions. But the bottom line is that tort reformers began their campaigns in earnest during the late 1970s and altered the public agenda, leaving a lasting mark on American popular culture. The challenge for trial lawyers has involved not just answering that message, but contending with the residue of its nearly uncontested influence for several decades. And this challenge is unlikely to be met by liberal public-interest groups who have traditionally taken on responsibility for public relations and media communication. Given the fallout over Ralph Nader's bid for the presidency in 2000, which many trial lawyers blamed as the cause of Democrat Al Gore's defeat, Nader's popular authority and alliance with ATLA have been severely damaged.

THE POLITICAL CONTEXT OF ATLA'S STRATEGIC (NON)INVESTMENT

The preceding summary suggested some reasons for the trial lawyers' insider, "stealth" strategy in responding to the tort reformers' assault on the existing civil justice system. This strategy has many obvious virtues. It takes advantage of trial lawyers' ample financial resources and professional connections; it targets key venues of policy change in focused ways; it requires far less funding than would be required in trying to match the massive corporate investment in public relations; and it has been quite successful in blocking or neutralizing tort reform legislation. However, this strategy also has left largely uncontested the public images widely circulated by conservatives portraying greedy trial lawyers and a civil litigation system gone awry. The instrumental strategy avoids an institutional plan for mass media amplification and ideological appeal.

The aversion to public advocacy does not stem from lack of a normative commitment, it would seem. Individually, scores of personal injury lawyers whom we have met, and in many cases interviewed, see themselves as lawyering for the good in both particular and general senses. Consider this quote from a lawyer who litigated a well-known case for an individual client and later was angry about simplistic, ill-founded criticism:

> What really drives most trial lawyers that are successful in this business, and who are winning cases, is that they really have some underlying philosophy of good—and of outrage, disgust about what's going on with corporate indifference and abuse. . . . I always had a real strong

background in blue collar culture. And I was very aggravated at the way there's a lot of injustice in all phases of life. The way people abuse people. The way corporations abuse people. . . . I have always had this sense that if you really worked something real, real hard and get to the truth and win, that's the right thing to do. That's what keeps me going.

Many trial lawyers similarly define their practices as committed to representing "the little person" against large corporations and faceless bureaucracies, to being the great "equalizers" in a hierarchical corporate society (see Burke 2002).

In fact, trial lawyers often boast that they have a "silver bullet" position that can win the argument with corporate-sponsored, pro-business opponents every time. For one thing, counterstories of lawyers as champions who fight for the "little guy" and the underdog against the powerful, for the "Davids versus the Goliaths," for making the powerful responsible for harms they impose—all were ascendant in the post–World War II era and retain some currency in contemporary American culture (Speiser 1993). Moreover, as one strategist told us, "People believe their right to trial by jury is sacrosanct, just as fundamental as the First Amendment. If you tell people 'they are taking away your rights,' you can always win. . . . They've won almost every time on ballot propositions. Deep down, people agree with the position" of trial lawyers on the importance of this right. But this strategist nevertheless opposed massive investment in public relations campaigns. His reasoning was grounded in the trial lawyers' common complaint that they are radically outspent by corporations. As a 2000 ATLA education committee report concluded, "Public education is all about message development, message delivery, and audience. Unfortunately, America's public opinion about the civil justice and tort law changes that would radically limit people's legal rights have been influenced by decades and billions of dollars worth of propaganda from corporate America." Tort reform advocates, however, sincerely voice the same sentiments about the huge sums spent by rival trial lawyers. While business groups do have greater financial resources, the major difference is in *how* the adversaries spend their respective funds.

Understanding why the personal injury bar has largely forfeited the struggle for public opinion, citizen understanding, and moral conviction thus invites attention to several other factors beyond those of strategy alone. We briefly suggest four additional factors that have contributed to trial lawyers' relative reticence in the dispute about torts and more broadly in the "culture wars" of which tort reform is one generally underrecognized component.

The Constraints of Legalized Corporate Secrecy

We begin by identifying a very important exogenous constraint of legally mandated secrecy, which has the effect of preventing trial lawyers from publicly telling their stories about legal action to right wrongs committed by unaccountable corporate producers and professionals. This constraint is a primary subject of Ralph Nader and Wesley Smith's well-known book on corporate legal advantage *No Contest* (1996), and many articles by members of the plaintiffs' bar (see Zitrin 1999; Zitrin and Langford 1999; Ramsey, Durrell, and Ahearn 1998). At its heart are the insistent efforts of corporate defense attorneys to conceal or obfuscate basic data about corporate responsibility for injuries that emerge from legal proceedings. There are three primary legal maneuvers by which corporate interests can undertake this concealment. The defense may (1) obtain a protective order preventing the disclosure of discovery materials to third parties or the general public; (2) obtain a post-trial vacature of the judgment, making the case legally nonexistent; or (3) obtain a confidentiality agreement as a condition of settlement, prohibiting the plaintiff and the plaintiff's attorney from disclosing information regarding the facts of the case or the amount of the settlement. In short, from discovery through settlement, businesses and government can prevent the disclosure of information regarding harms to particular individuals, even if such harms might pose continued dangers.

Such practices often thwart those who are concerned with promoting safety and democratic accountability in modern society. But most critical to our concern in this chapter are the significant restraints imposed on lawyers' capacities to expose corporate wrongdoing and to defend legal action that challenges such harmful practices. *Attorneys who are best situated to tell powerful stories about the valuable role of cause-oriented personal injury litigation typically are forbidden to do so by law.* Such proscriptions can be enforced either by fines imposed by judges or by forfeiture of monetary awards to plaintiffs—costs that in both cases target attorneys' well-defined professional obligations and reputations.

Such constraints on public disclosure of legal findings by attorneys are common. In 1988, one study reported that "the system [of court ordered secrecy] has become pervasive. In local and federal courthouses across the country, there are confidentiality orders in hundreds of cases that allege safety problems with widely used products and facilities. Every day, someone gets into a car, sees a doctor or wakes up near a toxic site that has been the subject of a confidentiality order." At that time, in the District of Columbia alone, there were twelve cases on the federal court docket that bore the case name *"Sealed v. Sealed"* (Walsh and Weiser 1988). Judges have been particularly willing to seal records or otherwise prohibit disclosure where the parties have agreed, and, as noted above, there are strong incentives for plaintiffs to give their assent to such constraints. The judiciary has powerful incentives to sign broad secrecy orders, since this avoids the need for a time-consuming review of large numbers of documents to determine which are appropriately protected. A judge interviewed by the *Washington Post* remarked that "I may be busy enough so that I may approve four or five or six such things before I say 'wait a minute'" (Walsh and Weiser 1988). More recent reports indicate that trial court secrecy is still fairly pervasive (Gibeat 1998).

Many examples evidence the widespread use of the above techniques, and its efficacy in concealing cases of potential corporate wrongdoing. From the standpoint of our particular interest regarding compulsory silence on the part of plaintiffs' lawyers, perhaps the most compelling example involved breast implant litigation against Dow Corning. Following a successful trial against Dow Corning alleging health problems as a result of defective implants, Dow and the plaintiff reached a settlement under which the adverse judgment was vacated and the records sealed. Plaintiff's attorney Dan Bolton, who had made the agreement on the instructions of his client, attempted to alert the Food and Drug Administration (FDA) to the risks of silicone implants revealed by materials obtained in discovery, but he was unable to provide any details due to the secrecy agreement and order. Bolton actually appeared before an FDA panel and alluded to the case in testimony, although he could provide no substantive evidence in support of his allegation because of the vacature and secrecy agreement. The FDA finally obtained the documents eight years after Bolton had first seen them, following their disclosure in another case argued by Bolton (Kennedy 1992, 53; Kolata 1992). Dow claimed that the agency already had "much of the material" (Nader and Smith 1996, 80; Kennedy 1992, 53).

Other examples of litigation secrecy include General Motors' enforcement actions, including a large fine, against a plaintiffs' attorney who talked to newspapers about risks of ill-placed gas tanks; litigation against Pfizer Laboratories in which a plaintiffs' attorney, who was alleging that Pfizer had withheld information from the FDA, was ordered by the court not to disclose information obtained in litigation to any government agency, including the FDA (Kolata 1992); litigation against Ford in which information concerning possible tire defects was protected from disclosure over a period of ten years prior to the recall of the tires (Walsh and Weiser 1998); and litigation against A. H. Robins, maker of the Dalkon Shield, in which secret settlements were concluded before the device was taken off the market (Zitrin 1999). We found as well in many of our own interviews that plaintiffs' attorneys were remarkably restrained in talking about the harms that were exposed in particular cases they litigated, even when clearly off the record. As we suggest below, confidentiality constraints provide one important reason why spokespersons for defendants as well as tort reform generally are cited in newspaper articles far more often than are plaintiffs' attorneys.

Political and legal contests over these types of secrecy mandates have provided an important but little-recognized sideshow to the larger battles over tort reform. ATLA, TLPJ, and other plaintiffs' bar allies have repeatedly argued in courts and lobbied in state legislatures for restrictions on secrecy agreements, while ATRA and business interests have supported secrecy in the name of "privacy." A debate apparently tracked this division between the plaintiffs' and defendants' bars at an ABA Conference on Professional Responsibility. A dispute over California legislation regarding secrecy agreements pitted corporations and the defense bar directly against the plaintiffs' bar in similar fashion. The bill passed twice, but was vetoed by the governor both times. A few states have actually passed legislation limiting confidentiality agreements; Florida's Sunshine in Litigation Act and a parallel act in Washington state are the most expansive, while at least eight other states have passed more limited acts (Ramsey, Durrell, and Ahearn 1998). The several attempts to pass federal anti-secrecy legislation, by contrast, have been unsuccessful. Finally, despite a good deal of appellate case law disfavoring court secrecy, courts continue to range widely on the issue. Trial courts routinely find themselves under pressure to agree to protective orders in the interest of dispatching the litigation (Gibeat 1998). Even when particular plaintiffs' lawyers do want to preach their message, they thus remain muzzled to a large extent by existing legal restrictions.

Mission Impossible: Changing the Public Image of Trial Lawyers

Trial lawyers are further constrained from publicly preaching their cause by a variety of less formal but very real endogenous factors as well. The most obvious of these reasons for reticence is the widespread skepticism that major improvement in the image of lawyers is possible. Even if the well-funded charges of conservative tort reformers could be matched effectively in words and dollars, overturning the long-established, deeply rooted public cynicism about lawyers generally, and especially about personal injury lawyers, seems Sisyphean to many trial lawyers. Such is the conventional wisdom found among plaintiffs' attorneys themselves, and they may draw much support from scholars. As legal scholar Robert Post wrote in the mid-1980s, just as tort reform was gaining momentum, "The most striking aspect of the image of the lawyer in popular culture is the intense hostility with which it is invested" (1987, 1). While the topic is enormous, we review just a few relevant factors that support this perception.

For one thing, attorneys to whom we have talked echo that "lawyers have always been demonized throughout history." Legal historian Max Radin (1946) long ago identified the "ancient grudge" against lawyers that is traceable to early Greek and Roman cultures. His study documented that lawyers were routinely vilified thousands of years ago in terms similar to today—as hypocritical, rapacious, and inclined to esoteric, arcane language. The biblical invective in Luke 11:46 is also frequently recalled: "Woe until you also, ye lawyers; for he lade men with burdens grievous to be borne . . . ." Indeed, virtually every lawyer learns as part of her cultural education the familiar and deep literary cuts into the legal profession, from Shakespeare's "kill all the lawyers first" to lawyer Thomas More's banishment of lawyers from his Utopia to Dickens' unflattering portrait in *Bleak House* (see Post 1987). Other historians have provided ample supporting evidence, such as Arthur Bryant's summary of fourteenth-century English opinion: "Of all who enforced the lord's rights, the lawyer was the most hated" (cited in Mindes and Acock 1982, 172). And American antipathy to lawyers has been a common theme from the colonial era to the present (Post 1987; Mindes and Acock 1982; Galanter 1998a). If Americans' attitudes traditionally have thus been ambivalent toward the legal profession, most attorneys we interviewed view the dark side as most salient in our historical legacy.

Attorneys cannot, moreover, help but be overwhelmed with the negative images of their profession that surround them in contemporary popular culture. As Marc Galanter (1998a) and others (Cramton 1996) have powerfully demonstrated, the pervasive practice of telling lawyer jokes has at once expressed and deepened the profound distrust that citizens have for attorneys, and especially for personal injury lawyers. The fact that lawyers are among the most active tellers of such jokes only underlines the degree to which they share reservations or guilt about their own professional activity. Moreover, an enormous amount of scholarly literature has documented the generally very negative images of lawyers—and especially noncriminal attorneys—in movies, in popular literature, and on television (see Chase 1986a; Sherwin 2000; Asimow 2000a; Galanter 1998a). In fact, an entire journal—*Picturing Justice: The Online Journal of Law and Popular Culture* (www.usfca.edu/pj/index.html)—is dedicated to scholarly documentation and assessment of the saturation of popular culture with images of attorneys and the legal system. The common conclusion in most such scholarship is that, while a relatively benign and even heroic image of lawyers balanced the dark stereotype in the 1950s and 1960s, that was a momentary blip in an otherwise continuous and increasingly negative portrayal of lawyers in American mass society.

Images of the personal injury lawyers as Satans in suits *(The Devil's Advocate)*, as amoral chiselers and con artists *(The Rainmaker)*, as chronic liars *(Liar, Liar)*, as apt appetizers for hungry dinosaurs *(Jurassic Park)*, as elite narcissists *(A Civil Action)*, or as myopic, feckless, unprincipled hacks *(Erin Brockovich)*—all flood American movie and television screens, novels, music, and other artifacts of mass culture. All in all, as law has "gone pop," it has been shorn of much of its complexity, and what remains is the familiar trope of the villainous, sleazy, or greedy lawyer whom everyone loves to hate (Sherwin 2000).

There are both institutional and instrumental reasons for these developments, of course. Ambivalent attitudes toward lawyers have become increasingly pertinent to policy debates as law and courts have become more salient to policymaking (Friedman 1989, 1598). Because litigation has become a more public (or at least more publicized) means of affecting or effecting policies, litigators have been held more responsible for policies; they are praised if policy changes are welcomed but damned by those for whom the changes are unwanted. Mobilization of citizen rights to challenge established power can be seen, after all, as both increased democratic participation (Zemans 1983) and costly excess, depending on whether one is more sympathetic to those who have previously borne costs of "business as usual" silently or to those who must now adjust "business as usual" to account for more of the costs that they had previously shirked. Moreover, as class-action suits concerning high-profile public issues like automobile safety, prescription drugs, and asbestos and tobacco poisoning have increased, so have the financial and political stakes risen in portraying lawyers as heroes or villains. The simple fact is that detractors in the established corporate world have more at stake, more resources, and more access to mass media than the legal profession's fearless admirers. Public pundits and intellectuals (Glendon 1991; Howard 1994) who identify increasing lawyers' power as the source of myriad social ills, reformers who liken lawyers to insects and parasites to embellish simplistic narratives (Huber 1990; Olson 1991), and popular jokes stooping ever lower to poke fun at plaintiffs' lawyers and their profession—all have taken their toll over recent decades. Meanwhile, defense counsel for established producers labor in far greater obscurity while wielding even greater power for handsome return, insulated from blame for the rising court costs, delays, and obscurantism to which they contribute. We recount later, for example, how the decision of tobacco defenders to exhaust the resources of plaintiffs—by spending more than $50 million in one lawsuit by a widower—

was an economic and legal calculation for which the defendants bore individual and collective responsibility. "Stop commercial defendants before they spend again" is not very a plausible critique of civil litigation, however, while blaming the newly arrived, highly visible plaintiffs' attorneys draws blood almost every time. And all these developments have taken place against the backdrop of escalating neoliberal discourse that celebrates business freedom and extols market competition while expressing skepticism about state policies to improve social welfare.

Regardless of causes, the impact of increasingly mixed, if not outright negative, images in mass culture can be measured in public opinion polls. Three widely cited summaries of national polls conducted on the topic between 1986 and 1993—two by the *National Law Journal* (Kaplan 1986; Samborn 1993) and one by the ABA (Hengstler 1993; see also Galanter 1998a)—provided discouraging findings that greatly influenced trial lawyers. While most respondents in all three polls reported that they had retained lawyers and were mostly quite satisfied with their particular performances, lawyers in the aggregate were given quite low marks. Respondents judged lawyers' ethical behavior to be lacking, with seven times as many people rating lawyers as poor (21 percent) than as excellent (3 percent) (Galanter 1998a, 808–9). Samborn (1993) found that the public's assessment of the ethical status of attorneys declined notably from 1986 to 1993, with those who thought lawyers were less honest than most people nearly doubling from 17 percent to 31 percent. He also noted that 36 percent of those polled agreed that the general image of lawyers had "gotten worse" while only 8 percent said it had "improved" (1). In comparative rankings of trust in the professions, lawyers also ranked very poorly; they were at the bottom of a 1991 poll, well below car salesmen and politicians, just as they had been forty years earlier (Galanter 1998a, 809).

The polls just cited all confirm that the image of lawyers is still relatively mixed, with some bright as well as many dark areas. But the leading attorneys in ATLA whom we interviewed seemed only to see the dark side. After all, the plaintiffs' bar generally is regarded as the very low end of the legal profession itself in terms of trust and respect. Hence, while tort reformers' messages may be simplistic and misleading, they are perceived to be playing with the "stacked deck" of highly negative popular images and an ascendant neoliberal political consensus supporting them. As a 1998 ATLA memo put it, "The sad truth is not simply that these charges are false, but that they are believed by a majority of Americans, including judges, jurors, judges, and academics." A longtime public relations director expressed the matter well: "I don't buy into that worry that we're losing the public relations battle. We've always lost the public relations battle," Alan Parker told an interviewer. "I certainly think it's a waste of time to spend millions of dollars a month trying to change the public relations image of lawyers. You might as well throw the money into the Potomac." A more recent public relations director, Carlton Carl, echoed this sentiment. It is all "very depressing, but what can we do about it, except make it worse by spending money?"

Perhaps the best summary of the perspective comes from longtime advocate for trial lawyers and editor of *American Lawyer,* Steven Brill. He had this to say in an address to the Texas Law Review Association in 1996:

> We all know how much people hate lawyers—a trend that rightly or wrongly, a lot of notorious lawyers here in Texas have lately contributed to. . . . I have a theory about lawyers. I think lawyers undersell themselves. I think lawyers so believe their own bad press and believe in the inability of lay people to appreciate what they do, that they are scared of public exposure. And instead of going out and telling people about what they do—instead of, for example, wanting the public to see for themselves the best legal system the world has ever created—lots of lawyers and judges [leave] it to Hollywood and tabloid writers and pundits to tell the American people and the world what the world's greatest legal system is all about. . . . And instead of speaking out against a few bad apples in the profession . . . most of you in this room prefer that discipline of unworthy lawyers be painstaking and relatively secret. . . . So the profession allegedly celebrated for its ability to articulate and persuade, and vilified for its power, finds today that its agenda and public persona is [sic] being set by the *Wall Street Journal* editorial page, by Hollywood and by anyone else with an apocryphal and usually false lawyer story.

Professional Paradoxes and the Problem of Image

Many analysts connect the negative popular image of attorneys, especially for personal injury lawyers, with the paradoxes intrinsic to their very professional status. We note two paradoxes—the first a problem for lawyers generally, and the second one especially problematic for more cause-oriented trial lawyers.

The first paradox derives from the fact that the public tends to criticize lawyers as a group for doing well what individual clients most value about lawyers and what professional ethics define as the core obligation of attorneys—namely, representing clients aggressively, skillfully, and even ruthlessly. The core image of the legal professional pictures the lawyer as a value-neutral, technically competent "hired gun" whose competence and zealous commitment are critical to the adversary process (Luban 1988).

This is what individual clients want from an attorney: zealous and skillful representation that maximizes their chances of winning a dispute, whether it goes to trial or not. Hence, it almost seems counterproductive to promote an image of lawyers as affable, altruistic, and publicly spirited. As an ATLA leader put it, "Nobody wants a friendly, sweet, lovable, loving lawyer. They want a junkyard dog. Your lawyer you want to be tough. So I don't understand the ABA and everybody else saying 'Oh, we want everybody to love lawyers.' I don't want them to love lawyers; I don't even care."

The problem is that it is just these same characteristics for which lawyers in general are distrusted and disrespected. Public opinions polls cited in the *National Law Journal* study (Kaplan 1986) suggest that the principal reason why the public dislikes lawyers is that they are "too interested in money."[12] The contingency fee basis of compensation and increased exposure through commercial advertising has meant that the pecuniary interests of lawyers are difficult to escape (Daniels and Martin 2000). This focus on what is perceived to be greed on the part of lawyers has occupied much of the internal discussion about their poor public reputation (Daniels 1986). However, a public image that includes financial self-interest hardly separates tort lawyers from business persons, stock traders, and almost any other powerful figure in American society. The unique complaints about lawyers instead focus on two other important negative traits—that they "manipulate the legal system without any concern for right and wrong" and that they "file too many unnecessary lawsuits" (Post 1987). In short, the public assessment is contradictory; lawyers are respected and distrusted for the very same traits of aggressive client representation. As Robert Post deftly concludes in an article on this paradox, "Lawyers, it seems, can't win for trying. They are simultaneously praised and blamed for the same actions" (1987, 4; see also Galanter 1998a). And no doubt, this dilemma is exaggerated for attorneys in the plaintiffs' bar, who are among the least trusted. Like Machiavelli's prince, trial attorneys want to be both feared and loved, though being feared arguably is more important for the success of their practice.

Marvin Mindes and Alan Acock (1982) have argued further that attorneys' own reading of this apparent paradox makes the problem more acute. These scholars contend that the public long has viewed attorneys in terms of three prevailing images. In order of salience, they are "hero," "helper," and "trickster." However, lawyers tend to reverse the order of perceived salience in the public mind. That is, attorneys themselves interpret the "good lawyer" as that professional who can best combine the hero and trickster traits. In short, Mindes and Acock conclude that lawyers tend to

12. This is mirrored in our study of news articles critical of lawyers. See chapter 5.

embrace as critical to success that very characteristic that the public finds most problematic and troubling. If these authors are correct, then lawyers' own social constructions of their professional identity perpetuate both their negative public image and their fatalism that such an image can be improved.

All in all, it seems, trial lawyers for personal injury plaintiffs have concluded that they just cannot win in the public relations arena. Whatever public image they project is likely to be loaded with negative implications for their professional status. For this reason, trial lawyers have concluded that it makes sense for them to remain off the public stage as much as possible and to pursue their agendas through stealth-oriented insider politics.

Divisions among Trial Lawyers

A final factor that has weighed heavily in the political strategies of trial lawyers is the manifold divisions among themselves. We already noted that trial lawyers are united in their opposition to tort reform, but otherwise are a rather stratified and contentious group in a variety of ways. The first obvious dimension of differentiation that generates tensions is simply along the lines of wealth. We pointed out that ATLA includes a small stratum of extraordinarily affluent lawyers, most of whom focus on complex class actions such as mass torts; a large lower stratum of modest income attorneys who handle routine cases such as auto accidents; and a wide array of lawyers who handle diverse types of cases and generate quite variable incomes (see Parikh 2001). These disparities in the types of practice and the income they produce not surprisingly have lead to different perceptions of interest and identity, and more than a little resentment, among personal injury lawyers. Those attorneys most likely to envision their practices as within the more virtuous domains of ordinary lawyering in particular have resented other types of attorneys at both the ends of the spectrum.

On the one hand, we have encountered many attorneys who are quite proud of their own practices but harbor some disdain for other personal injury attorneys, mostly in the lower income end, who rely on mass advertising to generate business. The former view advertising as a tawdry practice that both demeans those who do it and tarnishes the image of other lawyers who view themselves as motivated by ideals of justice as well as by a comfortable income. As one attorney who specializes in cases for low income plaintiffs told us,

> I think lawyer advertising is deadly. It's comical. These guys on TV with a big smile on their face holding up a check. "I got this guy $400,000.

I'll come to your hospital. I'll make house calls." All this kind of thing. I think the average person that sees that—they don't see a caring lawyer that wants to do good. They see a lawyer out hustling business. And they see it a lot. They see it in phone books. It's on TV all day long. It's on the radio. So, you know, you go to a courtroom, what's their initial impression? Here's another one of those greedy advertising lawyers representing somebody who says they're [*sic*] hurt. Makes us all look like frauds.

On the other hand, many lawyers across the income spectrum seem to be offended by the ostentatious displays of their wealth and power by some of the most wealthy products liability attorneys. One quite affluent but humble and decidedly idealistic attorney put the sentiment in these words:

The trial lawyers in many ways, you know, have been their own worst enemies. . . . It's hardly complicated. It's ego. It's ego and arrogance and bragging, and unfortunately lawyers have a tendency with their war stories and—ego and arrogance. For example, sometimes I just look in disbelief. You see a lawyer goes on *20/20*, goes on *60 Minutes*, and even though a high school kid would understand where they are coming from, they want to show that the lawyer lives in a mansion, and he's very rich. And the lawyer cooperates, and says "Here's my Rolls Royce" and "Here's my mansion" and "Here's my staff." What world are these guys living in? There's a lot of jealousy, there's a lot of envy out there. And this is not wonderful. If the lawyer's done well, and he's made a lot of money—if that is the focus of an interview or a program, you get the hell out of my office. I don't want to talk to you. What's the point? Where is that going? And you see a lot of that and it creates a lot of resentment. . . . You and I both know that there are many, many lawyers who are very dedicated and who work very hard and don't make a lot of money. There's a tiny percentage of rich lawyers, but you know, this is where the focus is. And it doesn't really help when lawyers get on television and they get arrogant and they start bragging about how many cases they've won and how much money they've made.

Given that greed is the vice attributed to lawyers most commonly in public opinion polls, this complaint is understandable.

Other divisions matter as well, especially within that stratum of lawyers who deal with complex, high-stakes litigation involving many plaintiffs— such as asbestos, diet pills, and tobacco—and who wield considerable influence in ATLA or the legal community generally. One group of such lawyers largely came up through the ranks of tort lawyers handling cases of individuals, and then began to connect diverse plaintiffs who were injured by the same product. These attorneys tend to adhere to a basic "right to sue" philosophy that places a premium on individualized or specialized group cases and awards. These attorneys are often allied to some degree, at least in philosophy, with Ralph Nader, Gerry Spence, and other legal populists. Another group of attorneys in this stratum often developed their experience through litigation involving securities, consumers, and other large groups. They specialize in consolidating large numbers of complaints and developing negotiated class-wide settlements.

These two groups of lawyers have often found themselves in "rather nasty disputes," which in part are, again, "rooted in money" (Rheingold 2000). The populist lawyers take individual cases on fee contract, and thus want to maximize the recovery for each case. They often resist paying a portion of their fees to groups of lawyer "consolidators" who represent mega-classes of plaintiffs. The latter group, by contrast, tends either to amass huge amounts of billable hours for their aggregative work or take their fees—sometimes up to 25 percent—from the recoveries of plaintiffs and their individual attorneys. This clash often prompts the former attorneys, more oriented toward individual case work, to take on roles as "objectors" to large class actions.

But money is not always, or necessarily, the core issue making these lawyer groups "natural born enemies, unable to cooperate effectively" (Rheingold 2000). Populist attorneys often challenge class actions as muting the diversity of facts in cases, failing to disaggregate plaintiffs into subclasses, privileging some plaintiff groups represented by the consolidators over other plaintiff groups, and selling out future plaintiffs whose harm has not yet become evident from any award for damages at all. In short, the conflicts often stem from different perceptions of fair representation, effective advocacy, the proper means to ensure corporate accountability, and just outcomes. Most dramatic, populist trial attorneys often charge class-action consolidators with willingness to negotiate pernicious deals that secure their own large incomes and the future security of corporate defendants at the expense of many or most plaintiffs, and even the general collective interest in safety (Coffee 1995; Koniak 1995).

These clashes were especially acute in asbestos litigation, which produced two landmark Supreme Court cases supporting the objectors' challenge to class actions.[13] One activist lawyer was admirably branded a "traitor to his class" for his old-fashioned populist challenges that cost him both money and "the brotherhood that had bound the plaintiffs lawyers" for de-

---

13. Amchem Products, Inc. v. Windsor, 521 U.S. 591 (1997); Ortiz v. Fireboard Corp., 527 U.S. 815 (1999).

cades in the "clubby asbestos bar" (Frankel and Morris 2000). The ongoing "Stop Class Action Abuse" project led by Trial Lawyers for Public Justice and animated by the same populist vision has made this conflict among elite personal injury attorneys an enduring feature of the plaintiffs bar. As we shall see in chapter 7, a similar clash among ATLA populists and the private lawyers who negotiated the initial global tobacco settlement became a key factor in the congressional rejection and reformulation of the plan.

Finally, these latter divisions have been related to splits among leaders in ATLA over the strategy of stepping up public challenges to tort reform critics. For one thing, some of the elite attorneys who prefer class-action approaches have actually allied with business interests to promote some types of tort reform legislation that restrict only traditional individual actions, most notably in Texas and Florida[14] (Daniels and Martin 2000). By contrast, many of the high-profile populist attorneys have become leaders of drives to invest more heavily, widely, and creatively in challenging the tort reform assault in law schools, among jurists, and in the mass media. After a period of some struggle, the latter group seemed to have ascended to control of ATLA in the 1990s, although their commitment to the cause hardly was a radical break. At the same time, we again noted earlier, this apparent emergence of populist, public-interest-oriented leadership in ATLA seems to have been seriously compromised or undermined by the traumatic split with Ralph Nader after the 2000 election. The possibility of an outsider–insider coalition successfully pushing for a more dramatic public challenge to business-supported tort reformers thus seems as meager now as in previous years.

CONCLUSION

We have aimed in this chapter to develop several lines of argument. First, we sought to explain and document the response of ATLA and its allies to the pervasive public assault on personal injury lawyers and the civil legal system waged by pro-business tort reformers. Citing both the volunteered reflections by ATLA leaders and the organization's policy practices, we charted the stealth logic of insider influence at the core of this strategic response on the part of the plaintiffs' bar. The long-standing focus of this ap-

---

14. One Public Citizen leader confided on this matter: "We fight tort reform efforts when the trial lawyers have abandoned the fight, most recently in Texas. We held a press conference accusing them of abandoning consumers because they signed off on tort reform and we would never sign off on it. We are much more hard core on protecting consumers' access to the courts than the trial lawyers ever have been."

proach has been to cultivate support from public officials, and especially from legislators, at the federal and state level by spending large amounts of money in electoral contests and developing close personal alliances. A more recent part of the strategy has been to use litigation to challenge state tort reform measures on constitutional grounds. Together, these tactics have proved quite successful in reducing the influence of tort reformers on official policy at both the state and federal levels. At the same time, organized investments in mass media and public relations to challenge the negative stories, arguments, and images of tort lawyers and tort law practice propagated by conservative critics have been minimal. Both the elected leadership and staff strategists for ATLA have long believed that staying out of the public debate was the best policy, for lawyers are more likely to compromise their cause by drawing increased attention to themselves. During the 1990s, a new wave of organizational leaders did envision more aggressive campaigns to influence the views of targeted publics such as judges, legal scholars, and juries, but this investment so far has been very little and very late.

Our second aim has been to outline some larger institutional factors that have encouraged or rendered sensible this chosen instrumental strategy by the plaintiffs' bar. Perhaps the most important factor has been the perceived success of the insider strategy itself that was inherited from early organizational leaders. If one focuses on the battle over official public policy, it is difficult to deny that ATLA's defensive insider campaign has been victorious to a large extent. Moreover, we identified four additional factors that help to explain why trial lawyers have not extended their campaign further into the arenas of public debate: the legal restraints imposed by settlement agreements with defendants that constrain plaintiff attorneys' capacity to reveal their knowledge about corporate harm; resignation about the deeply embedded public cynicism regarding lawyers, and especially attorneys for injured plaintiffs; the paradoxes of professional commitment to aggressive client representation; and the substantial divisions within the plaintiffs' bar, especially among its wealthiest and most influential members. When one adds to these factors the trauma caused by Ralph Nader's presidential campaign in 2000, it seems unlikely that ATLA will become in the near future a more prominent public defender of its members, their role in the civil legal system, and their loftiest social causes of consumer justice.

Third, we have questioned the substantive character and logic of the specific educational efforts that have been pursued, questions that parallel closely our argument in chapter 3 concerning the limitations of social scientists. On the one hand, the trial lawyers' focus on correcting and retelling tort tale narratives, on challenging myths and adding relevant factors for reconsideration, is a clear advance for the *accessibility* of their message over that of scholars' statistical data. On the other hand, the public appeal of trial lawyers has been similarly reactive and defensive, aimed at challenging and correcting the distortions of legal lore rather than offering a coherent, ideologically resonant alternative to it. Publications by trial lawyers offer few stories about the benefits of tort law, about the empowerment of ordinary citizens, or about the increases in safety and democratic accountability. As such, the remedial approach scores relatively low on the criteria of *adaptability* and, especially, *affirmative agenda* advancement discussed in previous chapters. Finally, most of the trial lawyers' investments have targeted the elite legal community—judges, lawyers, law professors, law students—rather than the general public or their mass mediators in institutionalized news production. As such, the scheme scores low on our *availability* indicator, much as do the efforts of scholars. In all these regards, we might add, the trial lawyers have proved less creative and effective than the much less well-funded consumer groups with which they often ally. Even if trial lawyers invested more resources, we thus are not sure that they would make a huge difference.

Finally, while our goal has not been to challenge or to criticize ATLA's political strategy, we have underlined some potentially costly implications of its insider stealth tactics. For one thing, new federal campaign laws might significantly impede ATLA's traditional reliance on financial contributions to secure political influence in the future. More fundamental, ATLA's public reticence and reluctance to answer tort reform critics—their public "shrug" to the continual barrage of attacks—have virtually ceded the public relations contest to their critics, who already were arguably at an advantage. The primary instrumental politics of ATLA evades direct ideological engagement with their moralistic detractors in the leading institutional forums of mass media. Indeed, we contend that this virtual silence of plaintiffs' lawyers is as important as the steady chants of tort reformers in shaping public knowledge about the civil legal system. The relative reticence of plaintiffs' lawyers has left unchallenged media propensities for reporting pop reformers' horror stories of frivolous lawsuits and, even more, for representing serious lawsuits in ways that parallel these trivialized tort tales. And this has meant as well that the individualistic logic of legal lore and conservative moralistic spin has prevailed with hardly an articulated challenge from advocates of more complex structural accounts. As Thomas Burke concluded in his study of political contests over litigation, "The downside of ATLA's strategy . . . was that the lawyers seemed to be losing the battle of public opinion, and with it the hearts and minds of juries and judges" (2002, 49). While trial lawyers have spent a bundle to make sure they will not lose the fight, the mass public has been exposed to a radical mismatch in which one side routinely refuses to raise its gloves in either defense or offense (see Eisenberg and Henderson 1992).

In this regard, of course, the problem is not just the reluctance of the plaintiffs' bar to aggressively voice its core political and moral vision, but the basic commitments to and interests in litigation-based approaches at the heart of that cause-oriented vision. Indeed, there is much reason to believe that even the most cause-oriented, populist-minded plaintiffs' attorneys are as voluntaristic, individualistic, and suspicious of state authority as are their corporate adversaries (McCann 1986; Burke 1998).[15] It is noteworthy in this regard that trial lawyers have extended little positive support to public calls for more expansive policies regarding social insurance, health care benefits, regulation of products and practices, and the like. All in all, there thus is little reason to think that the plaintiffs' bar is likely to be a prominent public force for either advancing new substantive policy agendas or new forms of democratic politics in contemporary U.S. society.

15. Populist attorneys tend to favor litigation as an alternative to statist regulatory and social welfare policies. This was repeatedly affirmed in our interview with ATLA leaders, including those on the political Left. When asked about national health insurance, one leading populist attorney responded, "I don't think that ATLA has much stake in that." What about increased state regulation? "I used to have great faith in OSHA, EPA, all those agencies in the 1960s, but that turned out to be a really lousy deal. The same old thing, disarmed and captured by big business." The liberal "private attorney general" logic of regulatory litigation and the individual's "right to sue" thus formed his primary faith.

PART TWO

Reporting Legal Realities

CHAPTER FIVE

Full Tort Press: Media Coverage of Civil Litigation

A striking feature of legal systems is that they have no systematic mechanism for the dissemination of information about law. . . . Virtually all non-lawyers and, under many circumstance, lawyers as well learn about the law not from original sources but rather from professional and popular news sources.

LAUREN EDELMAN, STEVEN ABRAHAM, AND HOWARD ERLANGER, "PROFESSIONAL CONSTRUCTION OF LAW"

For even the most responsible journalists, various constraints of craft work against responsible journalism. Coverage of the legal profession is subject to the same pressures of time, resources, expertise, and balance that limit reporting on most topics.

DEBORAH RHODE, "A BAD PRESS ON BAD LAWYERS"

[T]he power of the media lies not only (and not even primarily) in its power to declare things to be true, but in its power to provide the forms in which the declarations appear. News in a newspaper or on television has a relationship to the "real world," not only in content but in form; that is, in the way the world is incorporated into unquestioned and unnoticed conventions of narration, and then transfigured, no longer a subject for discussion but a premise of any conversation at all.

MICHAEL SCHUDSON, THE POWER OF NEWS

The previous three chapters surveyed the ways in which pop reformists, scholarly experts, and plaintiffs' attorneys have competed to produce common knowledge about civil justice in the United States. Tort reform polemicists have launched anecdotal tort tales, memorable soundbites, bold sermons, and stunning (if unsupported and suspect) statistics to fortify their position. Scholarly experts have debunked tort tales, pseudostatistics, and shibboleths by means of abundant data that is more reliable, more representative, more rigorous, and more reproducible than reformists' truncated tales and polemical jeremiads. In some instances, the scholars have frankly acknowledged that some useful information is simply unknown or even unknowable. Trial lawyers, while focusing their efforts on "insider" legislative and litigation battles, have provided additional public correctives to misleading narratives and slanderous representations from pop reformers.

By virtually all accounts, the resulting contest has been a mismatch heavily favoring the scholars on intellectual grounds, but a veritable triumph for the reform proponents in the broader cultural terrains of American mass society. "[D]espite the demonstrated flaws in its evidence, the products liability reform lobby's major points have gained wide acceptance—to the frustration of its opponents," notes observer Kenneth Jost (1992, 46). Scholars Theodore Eisenberg and James Henderson (1992, 770) labeled the outcome more dramatically: it has been a "slaughter." Journalistic and scholarly observers alike thus have recognized that the "commonsense" legal lore about the lawsuit crisis has easily survived academic beatings; indeed, they note how "what everyone knows" about a legal system run amok has even have flourished amid the debates.

Scholars, trial lawyers, and their allies have been virtually unanimous in explaining this paradoxical debacle by which "sophistry," "propaganda," and inflammatory "rhetoric" have trumped good sense, enlightened study, and solid evidence in mass society. First, the advocates of reform have been accused of deliberately using market-oriented public relations techniques to manipulate ideas, images, and icons for the purpose of subverting public policy discussion and short-circuiting rational deliberation.[1] Second, opponents have insisted that the reformers have been greatly advantaged by the abundant financial backing and influence of powerful business corporations, including especially the insurance industry, tobacco producers, drug manufacturers, and health care providers. In short, this emphasis on the unequally funded and devious "politics of ideas" posits a classic instrumentalist explanation of the sort that we might expect from realist-oriented behavioral social scientists, law professors, and legal practitioners.

By contrast, in the first part of this book we offered a more complex account of the contest. We acknowledged real resource inequalities among

---

1. The position of scholars in resisting the tort reformers is ambiguous in this regard. On the one hand, they seem to accuse tort reformers of playing politics in unfair—deceptive, dishonest, manipulative—ways. The battle seems to be between those true to facts and those who dissemble. On the other hand, scholars and lawyers alike are realists who acknowledge that this "politics of ideas" is "what politics is all about—who gets what, when, and how" (Daniels and Martin 1992, 245).

the players but contended that these factors are easily exaggerated. Our social constructionist account analyzed the form and content of the knowledge advanced by these various actors as relevant variables in the contest as well. On the one hand, we argued that reform polemicists have crafted available, accessible, adaptable information into an affirmative agenda supporting tort reform. However shaky their empirical groundings, the reformers have proved both savvy political advocates and compelling ministers of a culturally salient individualistic moral ethos. On the other hand, scholars have waged their intellectual battles within intellectual venues unavailable to most citizens, through largely inaccessible, highly technical forms of knowledge, and for mostly defensive, reactive, debunking purposes. This response, we argued, reflects both the habitual routines of deeply ingrained academic conventions and a reasoned conviction that the scholar's primary authority emanates from fidelity to such conventional practices. Therefore, the public seldom sees or understands what scholars know; what scholars do not know or profess reformists have been only too happy to fill in. For their part, trial lawyers have forfeited the public debate almost altogether, while mimicking the scholars' defensive, reactive posture in similarly esoteric professional venues on those occasions when they have made their voices heard. In sum, we contend that both the paucity of culturally resonant, inspiring presentations by reform opponents and the political proficiency and moral credibility of well-funded pop reform advocates have facilitated the latter's successful mobilization of commonsense lore.

Our interpretive argument does not end there, however. Specifically, we emphasize in the next four chapters the powerful role of the mass media in the production of common legal knowledge. Scholars, plaintiffs' lawyers, and other opponents of reform have often acknowledged the role of the media in supporting the conventional wisdom. However, the character and motivations of that alleged media role generally have been left unexplored or explained only vaguely in terms of the reformers' instrumental, quasi-conspiratorial access and influence among reporters. We present in the following pages some evidence supporting this *instrumental* impact of business-supported reformers on news reporting and media production generally. However, we advance as well a more ambitious argument about the relatively independent *institutional* impetus and impact of the mass media in manufacturing legal knowledge. That is, we demonstrate how routinized conventions of news reporting have contributed to scripted representations of civil disputing and tort litigation that closely parallel and support the narrative constructions advanced by pop reformers. We evidence these homologous elements through both a large data set of news articles regarding civil litigation and specific examples selected to illustrate key features. The cumulative media output is not seamless, unitary, or lacking in counternarratives, but the patterns of knowledge production and their parallels to the narratives of tort polemicists are striking.

Our point in this analysis is not to "blame" the media for complicity in constructing and supporting common knowledge about law and lawyers so much as to illustrate how the practical constraints, conventions, and codes of journalists re-present the world of tort law practice in partial and problematic ways for public consumption. When the instrumental and institutional linkages between pop reform narratives and mainstream news production are joined, we can appreciate more fully the power of legal lore as manufactured conventional wisdom in our society. Moreover, we begin in this chapter to develop yet further the ideological dimensions of media representations as well, a topic that will be addressed more fully in chapters 6–8.

AN INSTRUMENTAL ACCOUNT: REFORMERS SATURATE THE NEWS

The instrumental account attributes the triumph of common legal lore almost entirely to strategic efforts by advocates to publicize information in support of reforms. In this regard, realists assume that reformers have successfully executed their agenda-setting designs. As we noted in chapter 2, the media have been viewed by reform strategists as largely passive, porous, and reactive; journalists simply reflect and reproduce the views of those who supply them with content. As tort reformers have disseminated messages that politicians, pundits, and others have accepted as reliable, therefore, journalists have been complicitous in conveying those messages to the public—whether by narratives, propositions, or anecdotes—with minimal or no investigation and criticism. The press has essentially provided a high-gain amplifier for tort reform communications distorting the law, according to this account.

There is some evidence for these allegations. Reformers have successfully injected their stories and messages directly into mass media, often without apparent resistance or revision. For example, we noted earlier that business and reform groups—including Aetna Life and Casualty, the Insurance Information Institute, Citizens against Lawsuit Abuse, and the American Tort Reform Association (ATRA)—sponsored a major advertising campaign in prominent national newspapers and on the radio during the 1980s. These ads typically featured bold headlines and titles ("Sue City USA," "Sue-icidal Impulse," "Life without Risk," "Responsibility Repealed," "The Lawsuit Crisis is Penalizing School Sports," "The Lawsuit Crisis is Bad for Babies," "Justice for All?") followed by one or more tort tales illustrating the woes of a legal system gone awry. Consider this example, which recalls those cited in chapter 2:

> Since 1961, the number of all U.S. companies making measles vaccine dropped from six to one; those making oral polio vaccine, from three to one. Their reason for withdrawing? Fear of being sued. One manufacturer alone faces $3 billion in liability claims. . . . We need to crack down on frivolous, harassing lawsuits [and] to accept some risk and responsibility for ourselves. (Aetna Life and Casualty ad, 1987)

Other paid ads featured staged pictures (of empty swimming pools; defunded sports teams or children's organizations; a bumper sticker reading "Go Ahead. Hit me. I need the money.") followed by catchy headlines, statements decrying lawsuit abuse, and an address where pamphlets could be requested.

Reform spokespersons also have enjoyed ample opportunity for communicating their message in solicited "expert" commentary as part of news reports. As we shall see in coming pages, reformers and critics of the existing system are cited widely in news articles. At the same time, tort reform spokespersons and their allies—Max Boot in the *Wall Street Journal*, Peter Huber in *Forbes*, John Leo in *U.S. News and World Report*, George Will in *Newsweek* and the *Washington Post*, Daniel J. Popeo in the *New York Times*, to mention but a few—have regularly filled the print media with editorials and opinion pieces that confirm the lawsuit crisis narrative, its lamentable consequences, and the need for change. Such essays are replete with the very same types of anecdotes, grand charges, and shaky evidence that are at the core of legal lore. Consider, for example, an "Outlook" essay in *U.S. News and World Report* by John Leo (1995, 24) entitled "The World's Most Litigious Nation." The article begins with the author's lament about increased insurance costs for the parks where his summer softball games are played. This is followed by a litany of other examples and tort reform clichés: the increasing trend is to think that "everything that happens to us is someone else's fault"; "tort taxes" raise prices for consumers; doctors have stopped delivering babies because "of the cost of litigation"; "litigation in America is a lucrative, lawyer-driven enterprise" protected by the powerful trial lawyers' association at a cost to clients and defendants; legislation is necessary to achieve a "saner system"; and so forth. Unsupported numbers are tossed in almost randomly. The article is classic pop reform pap.

Most such essays appear on the opinion and editorial pages, but they also show up in more prominent places as thematic articles mixed in with the spot news. One example is an article by then staff reporter Robert Lindsey (1985) that appeared on the front page of the *New York Times* and was entitled "Businesses Change Ways in Fear of Lawsuits." Once again, the article teems with anecdotes—of *Peanuts* creator Charles Schultz closing an ice skating rink due to rising liability costs, of architects overdesigning buildings at extra cost to preempt lawsuits, of a restaurant owner training employees to avoid liability for intoxicated customers, and other stories. The subsequent rhetoric runs thick as it recounts tales of "a rising tide of litigation that is swamping the nation's courts," "higher liability insurance rates," the "medical malpractice crisis," "the growing population of lawyers," and "unjust lawsuits" that are destroying the economy and civic bonds of trust. This is followed by more anecdotes, dramatic numbers, and a wrap-up about the dangerous illusions of creating a "risk-free society."

Such obvious plants from the reformist camp, masquerading as news, branch into broadcast media. Perhaps the most familiar are the episodic *ABC News Special* television shows skewering lawyers, litigation, and the politics of risk hosted by correspondent John Stossel, who is well connected to corporate causes (Dowie 2002). We note here one classic example—"The Trouble with Lawyers," in January 1996, as congressional debates over tort reform were about to resume—whose debt to pop reformers is unmistakable. Indeed, there is ample evidence that Manhattan Institute cronies Peter Huber and Walter Olson provided extensive advice for the show (Lieberman 2000). The program itself is a virtual nonstop review of arrogant, affluent, and in some cases seemingly unstable lawyers who utilize civil litigation as a form of "extortion" to line their own pockets at consumers' expense. "Like armies, lawyers can be horribly destructive, harmful to innovation, to our good will toward one another, our freedom to make choices. I haven't even mentioned what they cost . . . ," the correspondent admonishes. Our legal system is a "laughingstock," Stossel concludes, one that is tearing apart American society with 90 million lawsuits a year with no clear benefit beyond the incomes of lawyers. The rhetorical tricks used by Stossel—leading questions, commonsense appeals to what "Some say . . . ," non sequiturs, slick editing to decontextualize segments, and treatment of outrageous anecdotal examples as "typical"—exemplify all that scholars and trial lawyers condemn about reform propaganda. Moreover, the shows are effective. It is nearly impossible to watch such a program and not view lawyers, the legal system, and civil litigation in more negative terms, even if one knows better and is repulsed by the manipulative presentation. Similar offerings by Stossel on later shows entitled "Junk Science," "The Blame Game," and "Are We Scaring Ourselves to Death?" reinforced related themes.

In addition to such direct interventions of tort reformers and their allies in news production, there are many indirect impacts as well. Most of the newspaper journalists we interviewed affirmed that they had received abundant reading material from tort reform groups and often had contacted such advocates for information or commentary on articles. Several reporters from major national newspapers even reported attending seminars, retreats, or presentations hosted by the Manhattan Institute and other organizations. While most journalists denied that these encounters influenced their thinking or reporting, most also acknowledged that they had become far more aware of civil litigation, large awards in personal injury cases, and tort reform politics in the 1980s and 1990s. "Well, of course, this stuff was in the air. You could hardly ignore the buzz about the litigation crisis, which seemed to be coming from everywhere. I was never sure whether to believe this stuff, what to make of it all, but I sure heard a lot about it. . . . It stayed on the radar," reported one journalist at a prominent national newspaper.

It thus should not be surprising that uncommitted reporters and editorialists alike very often come to view civil justice outrages as routine. "There is probably one in the paper today, if you take the time to look. There usually is: A numbing tale of a citizen hauling someone into court over something absurd," lamented one typical 1995 editorial in the *Oakland Tribune*, echoing a reform mantra. Such tendencies reveal a self-fulfilling "availability heuristic."[2] Newspapers report the spinning of tort reformers and, having thereby made tort tales widely available, cite that very availability as evidence of frequency. As pundits remake tort reform fabrications into accurate representations of civil justice, so does this common knowledge find its way into commentary, reporting, and even headlines. One need only recall, for example, the derisive treatment of Judith Haimes's personal injury lawsuit with which we began the introduction to this book; we will encounter more of the same in the next chapter. One further example will suffice here. An excerpt from a *New York Times* article shows how journalists may make anomalous events seem typical, even predictable, just as tort tales do:

> One contender for valedictorian of the class of 1996 at Bayside High School in Queens was shy, studious, a soprano in the chorus; the other, the popular senior class president and captain of the tennis team. But their grade point averages were practically identical, separated by just 0.05 points. And at different times, each girl was told that she, and she alone, would address more than 600 graduating seniors on June 25.

2. The availability heuristic is the cognitive tendency to estimate frequency or probability according to ease of recall (Tversky and Kahneman 1973, 220–21). Compare Iyengar 1992.

Both students have already been accepted to Ivy League colleges, so the choice of valedictorian has strictly symbolic importance. But in what seems to be a case of academic competition run wild, the fight has pitted two Queens families against each other and left one girl a "wreck" and the other "devastated," according to family and friends. *And, inevitably, it has ended up in court.*

The Board of Education had ruled that the two girls should be co-valedictorians, prompting the senior class president to sue to have the honor to herself. Yesterday, a State Appellate Court judge in Brooklyn upheld the school board's decision, but that ruling could change when a panel of judges hears the case next Wednesday, said Frank Sobrino, a spokesman for Chancellor Rudy Crew. (Onishi 1996; emphasis added)

This vignette makes an unusual dispute seem familiar by means of a short sentence: "And, inevitably, it has ended up in court." That editorializing hook pronounces as inevitable a development that is unusual if not unique.[3] The reporter's comment implied a claim about rampant litigiousness that tort reformers have tirelessly sought to circulate. Such examples clearly support the thesis that tort reformers have had both indirect and direct impacts on the manufacturing of legal knowledge by the conventional mass media.

TOWARD AN INSTITUTIONAL ANALYSIS

This instrumental focus on the impact of tort reformers captures only a part of the larger picture, however. For one thing, the evidence for the instrumental thesis itself is selective and anecdotal. Such claims would only be meaningful if reform interventions were demonstrated to constitute a large proportion of media content about civil litigation, including routine news, and to be bereft of contrary narratives or positions. Moreover, examples like those above prompt questions about the likely influence of reformers' explicit appeals to mass audiences. After all, advertisements, editorials, and opinion articles all clearly announce—by their placement, tone, style, authors—some overtly partisan motivation. It is unlikely that most readers of such materials would fail to realize that the perspectives they represent are partial and propagandistic. This does not mean that such knowledge forms have no influence; no doubt they often confirm preexisting views for some readers, offend other readers, and momentarily slant perspectives of yet other readers (see Loftus 1979). One must take

---

3. It may be worth noting that the reporter adduced no evidence about the inevitability of recourse to adjudication nor specified exactly what made the trip to court unavoidable.

a fairly dim view of readers, though, to assume that they are greatly in-fluenced by exposure to such simplistically slanted forms of knowledge production alone. Indeed, it is relevant to note that, as several sources told us, insurance companies pulled their ads dramatizing the lawsuit crisis in the 1980s because their own data showed that the public was annoyed by simplistic slander from sources that were no more trusted than the lawyers under assault.

Tort Tales and Real News

More important still, the *great majority of anecdotal tort tales cited by re-formers originate in the mass media, and especially in the print news.* The story of the "CAT-scanned psychic" (who did not claim lost psychic powers and was not actually scanned), the litany of tales reviewed in chapter 2, the infamous McDonald's hot coffee case that we will review in the next chap-ter—all were first reported in the mainstream press. In fact, the American Tort Reform Association nowadays documents its "horror stories" by citing the news outlets in which ATRA located the scary suits. Pop reform polemi-cists have been vigilant about picking up such stories, further trimming details and adding spin to fit their designs, and then recycling them in both specialized and general media. This was illustrated earlier, in chap-ter 2 (page 64), by the story of the litigious milk-oholic, which began as an Associated Press story, quickly appeared on the ATRA Web site, received a boost from Jay Leno, and evolved into a modestly familiar tort tale. This blurred convergence of serious news, mass entertainment, and pop reform propaganda means that the mass media are both the primary sources and most powerful disseminators of skewed narratives about civil litigation.

The fact that the media produce narratives that so easily translate into tort tales raises important questions about the form and content of ordi-nary news production. This is important to the extent that ordinary news production is more influential than editorials and opinion essays. Social science research suggests that readers are far more likely to take news re-ports, especially spot news reports but also thematic features, as accurate, trustworthy, and "real" accounts of actual events (Neuman, Just, and Crig-ler 1992; Salomon 1984). As Michael Schudson (1982, 98) has put it, both the contents and the conventions of news reporting in mass media tend to become common sense about the "real world." The emphasis both on basic "facts" and, especially, on "objectivity" in citing expert judgment—which means printing perspectives from different sides of disputes—in particular contributes to the naturalization of news reporting as reliable representations of reality (Bennett 1996, 141–67). Readers thus may be amused by television comedy and provoked by partisan pap presenting legal lore, but it is the routine repetition of narrative scripts in everyday news that provides such knowledge a commonsense foundation as practical or ethical truth (Neuman, Just, and Crigler 1992).

Routine News Practices and News Worth

The observation that routine news stories of civil litigation resemble, and are easily translated into, anecdotal tort tales is relatively unsurprising in light of the conventions and practices of ordinary news production. News stories conform to standards and stereotypes that reporters acquire through apprenticeship and professionalization and that editors apply throughout the newsroom (Darnton 1975, 188–92). These standards and stereotypes ensure that reports make good stories—stories that are interesting or entertaining or titillating, accessible, and concise (Chibnall 1977, 23; Davis 1994, 22; Paletz and Entman 1981, 16–18). Standardized and stereotypical, simplified and succinct, reports must be written on short deadlines if the news is to have immediacy. This in turn puts a premium not only on speed but also on efficiency, driving reporters to information readily available and to sources that are informative but pithy. Reporting in depth, critical analysis, and extended reflection are luxuries that reporters and editors routinely cannot afford in an era in which the commercial bottom line is ever more important (Serrin 2000; Squires 1994; Underwood 1993). Were such extravagances more affordable, they would not be lavished on spot news.

Due to these realities of their profession, journalists rely on conventions and formulas to guide them toward what their superiors and peers believe to be newsworthy. Formulas are acquired, for example, through journalistic beats and other bureaucratized settings as well as from sources and even objects of coverage (Drechsel 1983; Fishman 1980; Paletz and Entman 1981, 19–22; Sigal 1973). The inevitable result is that certain aspects and interpretations of events will habitually be deemed worthy of reporting while others are judged less newsworthy. In practice, news is packaged according to standard storylines, scripts, and strategies of representation so that regularities promote the consistency and credibility of established expectations (Paletz 1999, 63).

Political scientist W. Lance Bennett has identified four interrelated proclivities that define workaday news worth: personalization, dramatization, fragmentation, and normalization.[4] *Personalized* coverage emphasizes individual actors, acts, and moral judgments that usually are easily

---

4. In a later edition of his book (2001), Bennett rechristened "normalization" the "authority-disorder bias" and argued that news media often communicated the insufficiency of

and efficiently characterized, to the exclusion or detriment of case-specific institutional, historical, or social relationships that would demand that reporters devote time, resources, and reflection to researching a story or compromise their "objectivity" in favor of analysis and interpretation. Because reports that personalize exclude so many aspects of a would-be story, personalization leads to fragmentation. *Fragmented* reporting treats happenings as immediate and self-contained. Broader contexts, systemic relations, and institutional power tend to be slighted to emphasize discrete vignettes that are easier to document and to relate in accessible, inexpensive morsels that hold the audience. In short, news tends to be selectively decontextualized.

To further hold the interest of the audience in an age of "infotainment," news tends to be *dramatized.* To ensure circulation or ratings, news media play up the sensational, surprising, or titillating: violence ("If it bleeds it leads"), scandal (tabloidization), and money ("dollars holler") are among the usual inducements to watch or read. Not every story will bear dramatization, but potential stories that can be hyped will tend to be covered more than stories that cannot, and parts of the story that can be made vivid or affecting will be emphasized more than less exciting parts.

Normalization complements the other three proclivities formulated by Bennett. The process of normalizing news elaborates what is new by reference to what is familiar. Audiences need common referents and accessible scenarios if they are to grasp news effortlessly and efficiently, so news organizations presume that consumers will be attracted to coverage that matches ordinary norms and patterns even when events do not. As routine events are dramatized and personalized into fragmentary newsbites, reporters regularly are informed by and reproduce conventional explanations and expectations to frame "news" in terms of "olds."

Neither Bennett nor we assert that the press always suffuses articles with all or any of the four qualities that make up a working definition of what is newsworthy. Articles missing one or more of these qualities appear every day. Rather, we take Bennett's perspective to be that the press is more likely to provide coverage—and likely to provide more coverage—to those stories in which news worth is to be found or into which it may be injected.

The four practices that Bennett found generally to characterize news and journalists' sense of news worth seem well suited to coverage of civil

---

authorities to control, stabilize, or normalize threatening situations. We have used Bennett's former term to capture the tendency of news media to contextualize some immediate development so that much or most of a reported situation seems familiar, thus ignoring other potentially relevant contextual factors.

disputes in particular. In an adversarial legal culture, disputes tend to be personalized for observers in a courtroom or gallery by the preeminence of disputants, who tailor presentations to their claimed interests. Because disputes almost always come in discrete cases, we should expect disputes to be not only personalized but also fragmented and decontextualized. That is, crafty parties arrange details of evidence or testimony to bear directly on the problem or solution as seen by each party—a fragmentation of experience into socially or legally prescribed categories to suit forensic exigencies. Each disputant knows that a preferred outcome (judgment in one's favor, damages, and the like) may turn on sympathy or emotion, so advocates will often dramatize their cases. Of course, disputing consists largely in fitting grievances under conventions and norms, so normalization of disputes is nearly axiomatic.

Nonetheless, this fourfold definition of news worth is likely to apply or to be applied to only a few disputes rather than to most of them. Disputes that can be presented by disputants or reporters as more newsworthy—that is, as embodying each of the four proclivities of the press or all four taken together—will draw more coverage than disputes that do not meet these criteria for news worth as routinely applied in modern journalism. Journalists will refine raw news worth in its re-presentation to enhance the appeal of the article to readers, editors, and publishers. Understood this way, news worth explains why news narratives about civil litigation so often provide the makings of tort tales. Qualities that make cases more likely to be reported (and likely to be reported more) make for better stories, so tort tales and news narratives alike appeal to their respective producers and to those producers' notions of what audiences for stories expect or demand. News reporters, like tort reform publicists, will often reshape potentially newsworthy cases to secure interest and attention. It cannot surprise us that the construction of stories is so similar in reporters' publications and reformers' public relations outreach. As in the examples we analyzed above, news media all too often skimp on details that complicate a case, just as tellers of tales drop details and emphasize the newsworthy elements that the media often uses to headline and lead their stories.

In sum, parallels or convergences between tort tales and news narratives follow at least in part from the elements of constructing stories that satisfy mass audiences. If they had to, tort reformers might be willing to distort news narratives.[5] We suspect that has rarely been necessary to any

5. We are not eager to presume tort reformers to be dishonest or ruthless, so we are not prepared to assert that they knowingly distort—as opposed to spin—news narratives in the creation of tort tales. Samuel Jan Brakel (2000, 833) asserts that anecdotal (as well as other) evidence that supports tort reform abounds.

great degree because many news narratives readily suit dissemination for tort reformers' purposes. The elements, common to politics and to journalism, of interesting, understandable stories will usually guarantee that reformers may act in good faith when they modestly repackage news narratives for recycling. News narratives supply the raw materials of tort tales because reporting, which may be the first draft of history but for most people assuredly is the first (and perhaps only) draft of case law, supplies all or almost all of the elements of an arresting story, which tort reformers may then encapsulate further into tort tales. Although tort tales, twice removed and twice distilled (once by reporters and then by reformers), may be more elliptical and more tendentious than most news narratives, the two sorts of stories aim for similar audiences and hence share style and substance.

TWO DECADES OF COVERAGE IN FIVE NEWSPAPERS

Many previous studies have traced the circulation of select tort tales in the mass media (Galanter 1993a, 1998b; Cox 1992; Strasser 1987). Other studies have alluded to or identified various elements that tort tales and ordinary news reporting generally share.[6] Very little scholarship, however, has offered systematic empirical and conceptual investigation regarding this latter linkage (but see McCann, Haltom, Bloom 2001). Two statistical studies have reiterated some matches between print coverage and tort reform allegations about civil justice. Bailis and MacCoun (1996) found that reporting in *Time, Newsweek, Forbes, Fortune,* and *Business Week* was highly selective and unrepresentative in ways that paralleled the message of tort reformers. Their examination of news coverage found gross exaggeration when compared to actual data concerning litigation rates, products liability and medical malpractice disputes, disputes resolved by trials rather than by settlements, plaintiff victory rates, and jury awards. Such magazines presented readers a picture of the world in which, far out of proportion to actual rates, plaintiffs won huge jury judgments against corporations. Garber and Bower (1999), examining newspapers' reports of products liability verdicts concerning automobiles between 1983 and 1996, found that verdicts in favor of automobile manufacturers were seldom covered by even one of the dozens of newspapers in their sample while plaintiffs' victories, far rarer events, were covered by one or more papers in roughly half of the instances. They also discovered that the best predictors of press coverage were large awards (especially awards greater than

---

6. See Abel 1987, 445; Cox 1992; Daniels 1989; Galanter 1993a, 1998b; Glaberson and Farrell 1986; Haltom 1998, 238–43; Hayden 1991; Jost 1992; Saks 1992; Strasser 1987.

$1 million, which threshold predicted coverage after the raw damages were controlled statistically), the existence and severity of punitive damages (both in concert with and independently of overall damages), and injuries resulting in fatality (but not survivors' burns or paralysis).

Our own empirical study, cued by these previous inquiries, directly explored the correspondence between the knowledge conveyed through tort tales and news narratives in leading newspapers. We derived data from reports, features, and commentaries in the *New York Times, Wall Street Journal, Washington Post, Los Angeles Times,* and *Christian Science Monitor* between January 1, 1980, and June 30, 1999. We identified 3,300 articles from these newspapers by use of the National Newspaper Index (NNI), an aggregated independent index for all five papers dating before 1980. These we divided into a "case-specific" subset of 2,347 stories that focused on one or several instant disputes, and a "general" subset that consisted of 953 articles that addressed general trends and multiple cases in tort litigation. We retained editorials or commentaries in the sample. Specifically, we examined the output of journalists in these articles to ascertain whether news coverage of civil litigation represents a highly selective, skewed sample of events presented in ways that parallel or converge with the simplistic, dramatic, decontextualized,[7] individualized morality tales of tort reformers. We anticipated that the general message and specific words of tort reformers would be reproduced or at least supported in many news reports owing to the energetic efforts of tort reformers. Beyond that instrumental influence and, we have argued, far more significant than the suasion of tort reform, routine practices of gathering and rendering stories about civil justice will generate a body of coverage that conforms to premises and perspectives of tort reform. For instrumental and institutional reasons, we expected news coverage and tort reform to conform to, and confirm, each other.

Because institutional and instrumental influences intermingle, we did not expect to be able to tease out the influence of each except under the rare circumstance that one or the other may be assumed to be minimal. Rather, our point in analyzing these data is to reveal the extent to which news narratives suit tort reform messages about as well as tort tales do. Thus, we here demonstrate quantitatively the *homologies* between tort tales and news narratives that we have discussed qualitatively above.

7. In this chapter, we use "decontextualized" to signal that cultural productions have been stripped of various elements from real-world settings in a manner that likely alters the interpretation of the productions. As we strive to make clear, tort tales and news narratives do supply contexts. Those contexts, we maintain, tactically shortchange aspects of civil disputing that might complicate interpretation.

Products Liability Cases Are Greatly Overcovered

Table 3 shows that the general subset (that is, thematic articles not about a specific case) overwhelmingly raised products liability or personal injury as issues when coders could discern cases and issues at all. The frequencies of references and row percentages reading across table 3 show that out of 953 opportunities to raise each sort of issue (that is, 953 articles of the general subset in which coders assessed issues) articles referred explicitly to products liability more often and far more extensively than other types of personal injury. Medical malpractice, another target of tort reformers, came up in less than 5 percent of general articles. Of all references that consumed more than 30 percent of an article (our rough operationalization of "extensive" coverage), more than two out of five concerned either products liability or other personal injury cases. If we exclude references that coders could not categorize due to insufficient information in the articles, almost 91 percent of extensively covered disputes in the general subset were products liability disputes.

Table 3 reveals that citizens who routinely read the newspaper will be exposed to far more information and stories—that is to say, legal knowledge—about products liability and personal injury litigation than about other types of civil litigation that are far more common (e.g., automobile or contractual cases). As previous studies (Bailis and MacCoun 1996; Garber and Bower 1999) had led us to expect, *reports greatly overrepresent products liability amid personal injury cases, much as the publicity surrounding tort reform does.* Even if we presumed that tort reform's emphasis on products liability stories had influenced reporters' views of law over time, we might not have presumed such stark disparities of emphasis. An institutional consideration—ready-made personalized, decontextualized, and dramatized conflicts over products and injuries familiar to readers—at least complements the instrumental exertions of tort reformers. Products liability suits will tend to incorporate wider social and economic ramifications, larger awards, and more striking injuries than more typical disputes do. On the other hand, those very elements of news worth may interfere with the caricature of plaintiffs as self-aggrandizing pseudovictims and with the exculpation of manufacturers, so news narratives may not do as much for tort reform as caustic tort tales might do.

These quantitative findings dovetail with qualitative characteristics of news reporting about civil litigation. Like tort tales, these stories almost always spotlight the clash of adversaries in a formal contest. Plaintiffs are described almost exclusively by the claims that they make, their challenges to defendants, and the fate of their claims in judgments and awards. The

TABLE 3 Civil issues to which articles in general subset referred

Mentions in 953 articles of the general subset	No references to issue in article		Reference(s) to issue take up less than 10% of the article		Reference(s) to issue take up between 10% and 30% of the article		Reference(s) to issue take up more than 30% of the article	
Issue	n	row%	n	row%	n	row%	n	row%
Products liablity	390	41	135	14	167	18	260	27
Other personal injury	883	93	27	3	29	3	12	1
Medical malpractice	905	95	34	3	8	1	4	0
Auto accidents	943	99	5	1	2	0	1	0
Discrimination	945	99	4	0	1	0	2	0
Breach of contract	949	100	0	0	1	0	1	0
Worker's compensation	945	99	2	0	3	0	1	0
Libel	945	99	1	0	0	0	5	1
Issue reference unclear	562	59	13	1	41	4	335	35
Mean number of references	829.6		24.6		28.0		69.1	
Median number of references	945		5		3		4	

focus on their roles as legal adversaries effaces in most cases their status as victims of harm—the character, degree, impact, and suffering associated with the harm. Articles often use such generic terms as "were injured" or "suffered injuries" or pain, or refer to specific harms such as scalding, maiming, loss of limbs, paralysis, and the like. But nearly all spot news articles and most thematic or general articles focus on the roles of plaintiffs in the legal contest rather than the experienced suffering or hardship that preceded the claim. Like tort tales, news narratives tend to shortchange elements of stories that might induce sympathy for injured parties and instead play up formal claims, outcomes, and questions of liability. Explicit or implicit attention to the personal traits and relative responsibility of the plaintiff typically supplants broader social implications of injuries and conflicts.

Civil Litigation Coverage Has Burgeoned

To judge from our sample, the efforts of tort reformers to call civil litigation to the attention of reporters and editors have succeeded over the last two decades (see fig. 3).[8] Increases in the number of disputes covered in the five news leaders are striking, to say the least. These increases are mirrored in data we derived from Westlaw, so we have some external validation of the trend represented in figure 3.

Coverage increased dramatically in the five national newspapers from the mid-1980s (roughly at the time when campaigns, speeches, popular books and articles, and other publicization expanded the scope of tort reform beyond academia) through the 1990s, and particularly after 1994. Tort filings have been decreasing since they crested after moderate rises in the late 1980s, so real growth in rates of litigation does not well explain the data in figure 3. The vast majority of the stories that we retrieved concerned products liability, but trends in products liability do not track figure 3 either. Abundant coverage of tobacco suits came too late to account for the upswings in the 1980s, but may explain some increases in the 1990s. In contrast, proliferating publicity claiming an explosive growth in litigation roughly matches the upswing of coverage depicted in figure 3.[9] Publicization and politicization of tort reform (among other instrumental activities) may account for some of the trends we can discern in the figure. Interviews with activists and reporters confirmed that, in general and with regard to tort coverage in particular, reporters who had been alerted to alleged crises or patterns tended to notice and even to look for evidence consistent with the alarms. Indeed, several reporters for leading national newspapers told us that, once reformers put tort litigation on the agenda by directly lobbying both the press and Congress in the 1980s, reporters increasingly paid attention to particular, dramatic cases and the larger legal issues, including them whenever possible as part of the daily news coverage.

We suspect that institutional factors played an important role as well. In particular, the elements of civil litigation—personalized conflict, dramatic spectacle, large sums of money, reducibility to simple decontextualized scripts, and the like—fit extremely well with those features attractive to news reporters. In short, civil litigation involving bitter conflict and large consequences is potentially newsworthy. As reporters developed scripts that could be routinely reproduced, and as dramatic, high-stakes, "third world" (see chapter 3) mass tort cases increased during the 1980s, the newsworthiness of civil litigation only increased. All in all, responding

8. We omit 126 articles from the first part of 1999 so that figure 3 reflects only complete years.

9. One might speculate that the "Contract with America" contributed to the ascent in the number of cases covered. Of course, tort reformers were prime movers in that process as well.

FIGURE 3 Disputes in national newspaper index and articles in Westlaw

both to instrumental lobbying of reformers and the intrinsic pull as "good news," the volume of reporting increased dramatically.

Whatever the mix of instrumental and institutional influences, the likely impact of burgeoning coverage is to reinforce reformist depictions of rampant litigiousness. *Routine readers of these five newspapers and of the print and broadcast media that rely on them would have every reason to believe claims about exploding rates of tort litigation over the last two decades due to reportage, which greatly increased, rather than to actual rates, which were not exploding.* News narratives, we find, have substantiated a key proposition of the tort reform campaign and have done so far more often at the end of the twentieth century than they had twenty years previously.

Plaintiffs' Victories Are Overreported

In our case-specific subset, more than three times as many reports concerned winning plaintiffs than victories by the defense. We found identifiable winners or losers in 1,249 reports of specific cases. Of those reports, 972 (77.8 percent) identified victorious plaintiff(s), a figure close to the 85 percent plaintiffs' win rate in the five magazines that Bailis and Mac-Coun studied (1996, 425). This figure is also obviously far greater than the percentage of plaintiffs' wins across tort cases, which ranged between 46 percent and 52 percent, if not far less (ibid.).[10] What Garber and Bower (1999) found in a sample of up to fifty-eight newspapers we found for five national papers: plaintiffs' victories are far more newsworthy than those of defendants.

   Thus, ordinary news coverage has supported and encouraged another basic premise of tort reform: *plaintiffs seem to be litigating, especially against business, not only with great frequency (fig. 3) but also with inordinate success.* News narratives thus chronically and systematically exacerbate the tendency to overestimate the probability of victory in civil litigation due to the frequency with which one hears about victories—again exemplifying Tversky and Kahneman's availability heuristic (see note 2 supra). Moreover, news narratives seem to bear out the familiar lore that plaintiffs routinely win suits that they should lose or should never file: "[P]unitive damages are out of control, plaintiffs are winning huge awards without proving that the defendants caused their injuries, and various class-action scams are proliferating. . . . There are lots of suits, many of them frivolous, and the number is growing" (Boot 1998, 149, 151). The regularity with which plaintiffs are seen to win may even be mistaken as evidence for the "litigation lottery" against which tort reformers rail routinely, an ironic confusion given the infrequency with which actual lotteries pay off.

Settlements and Awards Are Exaggerated

Of course, one major reason why newspapers have tended to overreport wins by plaintiffs and underreport those by defendants is that the former may result in large monetary awards while the latter almost never do. Tort reform's lobbyists and publicists have exaggerated the number of winners and the jackpots in "litigation lotteries," so agenda setting may have dis-

10. Studies of the products liability cases, which dominate our case-specific subset, report that plaintiffs win between 30 percent and 55 percent of trials, depending on venue and era.

posed reporters to emphasize large payouts at the expense of normal outcomes. At the same time, large transfers of money are the type of dramatic or sensational factors that make for newsworthiness. Just as what "bleeds" leads in newspapers, the big dollar will holler in reports of civil disputes. Just as those who relate tort tales delight in "upping the stakes" of their yarns, those who construct news narratives will tend to report stories of major transfers in preference to stories in which little is at stake. Table 4 bears out that our findings in the five newspapers approximate what others have found for other print media (Garber and Bower 1999; Bailis and MacCoun 1996).

To assess how much the newspapers hyped awards, we employ in table 4 a measure of central tendency, the median,[11] which we have overestimated to create a forgiving standard. Setting medians at $100,000 for settlements and at $1 million for awards (denoted by boldfaced segments in the table), we find that more than nine out of ten reported settlements and about seven out of ten reported awards surpass even those generous thresholds. The "holler of the dollar" is especially marked regarding settlements, concerning which 275 (65 percent) reported figures exceeding $100 million.[12] We readily acknowledge that secret settlements and negotiations that never reach the press both make estimates of settlements less reliable than amounts awarded in open court, but nearly two out of three reports of amounts involved in settlements overshoot the best estimate extant by a factor greater than 1,000. *Anyone who relies on these five papers or on media that count on these five will be barraged by extravagant numbers out of line with routine real-world amounts.*

The dollar hollers almost as loudly when punitive damages are imposed. In tort trials in 1996, for example, the median amount of punitive damages awarded was $38,000 in the 3 percent of plaintiffs' victories in which punitive damages were awarded at all (Litras et al. 2000). How

11. Statisticians prefer medians to means as indicators of central tendency when distributions are skewed because the mean follows extreme values to a greater extent than the median does. Means and medians at the bottom of table 3, for example, demonstrate this statistical verity. Reported medians vary but do not approach the thresholds used in table 4. The Bureau of Justice Statistics reported medians in tort cases in general to range from $30,500 to $51,000 in surveys of state courts in the seventy-five largest counties in the United States (DeFrances and Litras 1999; DeFrances et al. 1995; Litras et al. 2000). The median in tort cases in U.S. courts during 1979–83 was appreciably higher, $136,000 (Eisenberg et al. 1995), but had grown to $141,000 by 1996–97. The products liability cases that dominate our sample featured awards greater than those in tort cases in general, but estimates for state and federal cases were less than $400,000. Eisenberg and Henderson (1992, 763) estimated the median settlement to be $75,000.

12. Nearly 86 percent of reported settlements exceed $75,000, the median settlement estimated by Eisenberg and Henderson 1992.

TABLE 4 Identified winnings in case-specific stories

Amounts identified ($$)	Reports of settlements		Reports of compensatory punitive, and/or un-identified awards		Reports of compensatory awards only		Reports of punitive awards only		Reports of awards not identified as compensatory or punitive	
	n	Col%	n	Col%	n	Col%	n	Col%	n	Col%
$$ ≤ 100,000	28	7	9	2	21	13	4	2	9	2
100,000 < $$ ≤ 1 million	24	6	138	25	31	19	36	21	131	31
1 million < $$ ≤ 10 million	54	13	177	33	78	47	60	35	124	29
10 million < $$ ≤ 100 million	46	11	153	28	36	22	50	29	115	27
100 million < $$ ≤ 1 billion	123	29	60	11	1	1	22	13	42	10
1 billion < $$ ≤ 10 billion	111	26	5	1	0	0	1	1	5	1
10 billion < $$ ≤ 100 billion	17	4	3	1	0	0	0	0	2	1
$$ > 100 billion	21	5	0	0	0	0	0	0	0	0
Amounts > generous medians ($100,000 for settlements; $1 million for awards)	93%		73%		69%		77%		67%	
Number of awards identified	424	101	545	101	167	102	173	101	428	100

many journalists, let alone ordinary citizens, would guess that from coverage of punitive amounts disclosed by table 4?[13]

As above, the proclivities of mass media point in the same direction as the contentions of tort reformers, making it difficult to distinguish instrumental from institutional proclivities. Clearly, big bucks make for sensational stories—multimillion-dollar winners of state lotteries are covered far more than those who win only thousands. Beyond such advantages for dramatization, big-money awards make for big winners about whose struggles readers are likely to want to read. That is, such results are easily personalized not merely *by* the press but often *for* the press. This insight provides an institutional explanation not only for why civil actions have been represented in dramatic form, but also for why they have been increasingly selected as significant news items for reporting during the last two decades of the twentieth century. A small number of lawsuits made large claims and occasionally won huge awards for serious harms—as-

13. The National Newspaper Index led us to twelve reports of punitive damages in 1996, the least of which equaled $1.1 million (almost 29 times the "real world" figure) and the median of which equaled $10 million.

bestos poisoning was the most important in the 1980s, followed by injuries from the Dalkon Shield, breast implants, Agent Orange, and auto defects; since 1989 tobacco has been the focus of large claims of injury—to which the rest of the political system remained deaf or deadlocked. The large stakes and serious harms clearly provided the money and misery on which news thrives. However, one notable effect of this reporting was that proliferation of thin, morselized, decontextualized, dramatized stories that supported perceptions of rapidly increasing rates of litigation hindered rather than helped readers to understand the exceptional legal, political, and social developments at stake in mass tort claims.

Case-Specific Commentary Slightly Favors Plaintiffs—or Does It?

Reporters must quickly and efficiently collect reactions to disputes or decisions from authorities, parties, and others who might increase readers' understanding or interest. Reporters and editors strive for fair and balanced coverage but lack time, resources, and background to assess many sources, especially in spot coverage of formal legal conflicts (Rhode 1999, 152–53; Slotnick and Segal 1998, 58–75). For these reasons, we expected only a rough balance between pro-plaintiff and pro-defendant quotations and paraphrases. What we gleaned from the data was more complicated. We found that our case-specific subset of coverage featured more remarks that favored plaintiffs than remarks that supported civil defendants. Of 15,357 quotations or paraphrases detected, 43 percent (6,546) redounded to the benefit of the party or parties that originally brought suit, while 35 percent of remarks (5,450) inclined toward the party originally sued. The remaining 22 percent of remarks (3,361) impressed coders as neither pro-plaintiff nor pro-defendant.[14]

This ratio of 1.2 remarks from pro-plaintiff sources for every pro-defendant remark seems to compromise the pro-reform coverage that we find elsewhere. But such an interpretation is misleading in two related ways. First, we reiterate that the commentary on each side is in response to stories that grossly overrepresent plaintiff wins. Balanced commentary does nothing to correct the radically imbalanced attention to plaintiffs' victories relative to defense victories. Second, it follows that nearly balanced commentary about a radically skewed selection of legal cases underreports *those comments (by plaintiffs and their lawyers) most likely to explain or justify the victories.* In other words, the institutional imperative for balance

---

14. Although pro-plaintiff, pro-defendant, and neutral remarks varied over time, our analyses found the relationship between eras and remarks to be statistically significant but substantively trivial.

between contending parties may have unwittingly led the papers to slight attention to legal arguments, principles, and evidentiary proceedings that shaped the winning legal outcomes. As Deborah Rhode has noted, "Balanced positions do not necessarily make for balanced messages if the reporter declines to fill in gaps or to add any critical analysis" (1999, 157; see also Bennett 1996).

We cannot justly rebuke journalists for pursuing impartiality, and we do not mean to damn journalists if they are in a way both impartial *and* partial. Rather, we seek to understand reporting that is balanced as well as imbalanced. If journalistic canons dictate balance story by story, then journalists will adduce sources and quote remarks to fulfill the canonical mandate rather than to advance understanding of causes or disputes. If so, adherence to journalistic standards should not be expected to make up for significant imbalances elsewhere.

Reform Spokespersons and Themes Predominate in Thematic Articles

Although coders of our five newspapers found 45 percent of all quotations and paraphrases in 953 general subset articles to be mixed, neutral, or unclear, they were able to code a majority. Of this majority (2,931 remarks), the press cited proponents of reform of civil justice 1,861 times (35 percent of all remarks and 63 percent of identifiable proponents or opponents), but opponents of reform efforts or supporters of the status quo were cited 1,070 times (20 percent of all remarks and, of course, 37 percent of remarks from identifiable sources).[15] For each remark opposed to tort reform, these papers cited 1.7 in favor of tort reform. In the general subset, then, we find journalists favoring critics of the status quo and favoring reform, just as the Manhattan Institute memorandum we excerpted in chapter 2 strategized.

The efforts of lobbyists, public intellectuals, and other champions of civil justice reform would seem to have paid off in features, analyses, and other interpretive journalism that provide a platform and perhaps some

15. In general articles that concerned tobacco, about seven out of ten of the sources invoked were *not* demonstrably pro-reform or anti-reform. This contrasts with the roughly one-third of sources in general subset articles that concerned litigation other than tobacco cases. As we discuss in chapter 7, the advantage of tort reformers in coverage overall appears attenuated in tobacco coverage.

Other than that tobacco-related pattern, differences between pro-reform and anti-reform remarks peaked in 1985, 1988, 1991, and 1994–5 and plunged after each peak. This pattern is consistent with some mobilizations on behalf of tort reform followed by dormancies, but we lack data from which to infer more. Remarks that favored tort reform and remarks that were mixed or neutral varied far more year to year than remarks opposing tort reform.

credibility for tort reformers. Of course, the proficiency of tort reform spokespeople at bite-sized comments and spin may account for the media's greater attention to tort reform sources. This interpretation of our findings matches our conclusion from interviews with reporters: instrumental efforts to "prime" journalists have been very successful. Still, one must not overlook institutional factors. The challenge of contextualizing and characterizing civil justice accurately will weed out sources unwilling to simplify their remarks, so many scholarly specialists and dispassionate analysts have probably removed themselves from reporters' Rolodexes inadvertently. Others will be muted again, either wholly or in part, by legally mandated secrecy. In addition, anomalies and absurdities jazz up articles in ways that regularities cannot, which imparts to those who brandish arresting anecdotes a worthiness to be quoted or cited that cannot be matched by those who would draw attention to laws or legal procedures that shape disputes or to decisions and developments that are hundreds of times more common.

What sort of remarks do pro-reformists make? Table 5 lists the specific contentions of tort reform that have circulated most in the press. Since claims totaled 1,001, percentages are easily computed from the reported frequencies. As we saw earlier, the finding here is that the dollar hollers. The three most frequent claims in table 5 (58 percent of all claims coded) characterize modern civil justice in pecuniary terms familiar from tort reform efforts.[16] Soaring costs of litigation (the most frequent claim listed) and skyrocketing civil awards (the third most frequent claim) provide descriptions at once economic and empirical. The second most frequent claim concerns the greed of lawyers, an economic and empirical depiction fraught with moral connotations and common in tort reform arguments and advertisements.

Claims 4–7 of table 5 reflect that mix of the economic, the empirical, and the moral that, as we saw in chapter 2, constitutes the tort-reform litany. Lawsuits are said to victimize society and civil defendants (the fourth and seventh most frequent contentions) while lawyers and plaintiffs who pursue such suits invent liability (claim five) and concoct victimization (claim six) for profit. Claims 4–7 together account for almost 30 percent of the claims coded.

The remaining six claims in table 5 are less frequent. To some degree, the relative infrequency may be attributed to the difficulty of conveying succinctly and clearly ideas such as how many lawyers are too many, how much litigation is litigiousness, and what a tort tax might be. Perhaps com-

---

16. Although claims 7, 11, and 13 have economic connotations or implications, they are far less frequent contentions.

TABLE 5 Claims about legal system mentioned in general articles

Claims about legal system in 952 articles	Frequency
1. Litigation costs U.S. too much.	256
2. Lawyers are greedy.	193
3. Civil damages have soared.	134
4. Too much litigation injures society.	105
5. Civil suits tend to be frivolous.	78
6. Citizens too often act like victims.	67
7. Defendants are often ripped off.	49
8. Too many lawyers bedevil U.S.	27
9. Jurors tend to be incompetent or biased.	27
10. Americans are too litigious.	22
11. Litigants are greedy.	17
12. Judges tend to be incompetent or biased.	16
13. An irrational "tort tax" burdens U.S.	10
Total mentions of claims	1001

mentators and other journalists resist generalizing about the competence of judges or jurors and about the motives of particular plaintiffs or Americans on the whole. We cannot be certain.

What we are certain of, however, is that *these national newspapers have widely circulated tort reform themes.* Whether journalists have succumbed to tort reformists' blandishments or have shaped their descriptions and opinions according to commonsense presumptions (or, as we suspect, both), the themes of tort reform have been evident over the decades.[17]

Sensationalistic Claiming and Blaming: What's Law Got to Do with It?

Reporters habitually cover pre-trial and post-trial pronouncements far more than statements about law, testimony, and evidence that make up trials (Haltom 1998, 212). Discrete events such as the filing of a case or the announcement of an outcome are far easier and less costly for journalists

---

17. The four most common themes vary in frequency over the years. The claim that litigation costs the U.S. too much constitutes a quarter of all claims detected but fluctuates widely, dominating in 1985, 1989, 1992, and 1994, but appearing less prominently in other years. In contrast, the "greedy lawyers" theme was never absolutely prominent and seldom relatively prominent; it had the least variance year to year. The claim that civil damages had soared was most obvious during 1984–87, but quite minor thereafter. Fears of too much litigation peaked in newspapers in 1982, 1990, and 1994, but was not much in evidence otherwise. For more, see www.lawslore.info, the Web site associated with this volume.

to cover "objectively" than are protracted exchanges over contested evidence, technical testimony, and juridical nuances. For this reason, reporting will tend to give more coverage to disputing before and after than it does to what takes place during formal proceedings. To be certain, some happenings during adversarial procedures can be readily dramatized and personalized into news bites.[18] For the most part, however, the press tends to cover and even to witness courtroom occurrences far less than utterances designed to be reported. *In the context of civil disputing, this pattern of coverage betokens that newspapers pay attention to frivolous filings, wild charges and countercharges, and interpretations redolent of propaganda and spin.* Such filings, charges, and interpretations may be decisively debunked during the trial, but their discrediting usually takes a back seat to reporting that focuses on the informal, emotionally laden expressions of claiming and blaming, used by partisan reformers to overwhelm reports of what actually is transpiring in the formal legal arena.

To test these patterns of greater and lesser coverage in our five national newspapers, we divided stories in the case-specific subset according to the phases at which the dispute drew coverage. Coders discerned the stage at which a specific dispute was covered in 2,385 instances.[19] Of these instances, only 85 (3.6 percent) concerned disputes without a formal filing. We noted in chapter 3 that contests without formal action or even consultation with a lawyer far outnumber formal litigation (Miller and Sarat 1980–81), so our finding may suggest that news narratives, like tort tales, usually neglect conflicts that involve no litigation. However, we must qualify that suggestion because the headings available in the NNI make it more likely that we would retrieve formal litigation than informal squabbling. Nonetheless, undercoverage of disputing outside formal arenas must accentuate disputing in formal arenas, with the result that news coverage constructs "litigiousness" to some degree.

Restricting our survey to cases that had reached a formal procedural phase, press coverage of developments *during* trials was a fraction of the coverage given to developments before or after trials. We found 351 instances of coverage during trial (14.7 percent of disputes that could be coded for phase). Filings alone constituted 270 of the trials we found (11.3 percent), and another 584 items concerned pre-trial maneuvering

---

18. In chapter 7 we note examples of such "newsworthy" courtroom events from tobacco litigation.

19. Coders could not discern the stage of proceedings for only about 16 percent of the case-specific subset. The newspapers are thus very effective in conveying the phase at which an action takes place, perhaps because the procedural stage answers the "When?" that reporters are supposed to ask.

(24.5 percent). Taken together, then, the five national newspapers covered trials prior to opening statements about 2.5 times more often than they conveyed events during trials. Conclusions of civil suits accounted for almost 30 percent of the coverage (707 instances), so events at or after the ends of trials were covered twice as often as events during trials.[20]

In the light of the sociolegal research considered in chapter 3, it is somewhat predictable that newspapers in our study would be found to cover events and assertions before and after trials more often (about four-and-a-half times more often) than they covered events and assertions during trials. After all, formal trials of civil suits consume far less time than preparations for the courtroom do, and journalists will often be unable to predict how newsworthy a trial will be before its conclusion. However understandable the tendencies of these newspapers, their coverage during 1980–1999 gave shorter shrift to happenings inside the courtroom than to objects of coverage outside the courtroom.[21] Relatively scant attention to contested interpretations of causation or fault, to presentations of evidence, to testimony from experts, and to argument about principle combined with relatively abundant attention to adversarial argumentation unsupervised by judges and undisciplined by dispassionate factfinders to some extent "de-legalizes" disputes. News narratives, we find, tend to play down the rational processes of civil disputing and play up the rhetorical excesses of arguing cases in the press, just as tort tales accentuate caprice or injustice in "litigation lotteries."

Overall, phases at which disputes elicit coverage seem more easily explicable by journalistic imperatives than by agenda-setting or spin.[22] Pretrial coverage is festooned with conflict as plaintiffs' allegations clash with defendants' responses or evasions of responses. Formulations before trials,

20. Coders found that news items covered appeals at or after decisions in another 388 instances.

21. As we shall see in chapter 7, coverage during tobacco trials nearly doubles the midtrial coverage in other cases in the case-specific subset. Thus, we should qualify any generalizations that legal proceedings in the courtroom tend to be less newsworthy than events before or after the trial. Midtrial developments can be newsworthy even though they are often or usually less newsworthy than beginnings or endings of cases. Evidence that dramatizes allegations of wrongdoing by defendants and testimony that personalizes allegations of suffering of plaintiffs better meets the needs and wants of the press. We suspect that the superior news worth of evidence and testimony in tobacco suits accounts for coverage during tobacco trials that nearly doubles the midtrial coverage in other cases in the subset.

22. These patterns would seem to follow more from press proclivities than from spin for at least three reasons. First, coverage before and after trials overwhelms coverage during trials fairly consistently across the years of our study. Second, interrelations between official phases and coverage were explained long ago (Fishman 1980, 55–78): formalities and routines that divide streams of activity into manageable, discrete phases often shape coverage,

at the start of trials, and in closing arguments may reduce complexities in a manner that makes reporting easier, while adversarial relationships tend to personalize and sensationalize claims and counterclaims. Once we realize that the conclusions of trials pose fewer uncertainties than their origins, we scarcely wonder that so much coverage attends trials' endings. Indeed, given that the conclusions of trials tend to yield perishable spot news rather than colloquy with a longer shelf life, the extent to which coverage focuses on conclusions is not surprising.

Whatever the instrumental or institutional provenance of patterns of coverage of phases, the implication for homologies between news narratives and tort tales is clear: like tort tales, news narratives will almost always report less about what transpires legally, formally, or officially in trials and more that is sensationalized, personalized, and unreliable.

SUMMARY: HOMOLOGIES OF COVERAGE AND NONCOVERAGE

The foregoing findings illustrate how newspaper coverage over decades has resembled the everyday knowledge constructed by tort reformers and has diverged, at least implicitly, from the esoteric knowledge about general patterns of civil litigation amassed by scholars. These parallel narrative forms both highlight and omit specific features of tort practice in a remarkably homologous manner that we now briefly review.

First, *newspaper headlines, spot coverage, and features about tort litigation have rapidly increased as recycled tort tales have proliferated over the last two decades.* It thus stands to reason that attentive citizens would find in the daily news considerable support for the commonly alleged but empirically dubious conclusion that actual rates of litigation have grown radically or "exploded." The fact that our empirical study identified abundant commentary within spot news, features, and opinion pieces articulating tort reform themes criticizing that imagined explosion of litigiousness only further highlights the degree to which increased attention has likely been critical, even cynical, attention as well.

Second, *news reporting and tort tales alike select and neglect certain legal actions.* We have seen, for instance, that radical overcoverage of plain-

---

especially coverage organized around beat reporters who adapt to the phases prevalent on their beats. Formalities and routines constrain journalistic interpretations and direct journalists' attention to phases at which events are accessible and so well defined as to be predigested. Third, the patterns of coverage for civil and criminal trials are similar (Haltom 1998, 177, 212). Indeed, the pattern has been likened to a submarine, which is clearly seen at the beginning and end of voyages but seldom during them (ibid., 210–17). Since tort reformers should not be supposed to affect coverage of criminal proceedings, this trend should be seen as mostly a product of the interplay between journalism and the judiciary.

tiffs' victories and undercoverage of defense wins in news capsules have provided attentive readers much reason to accept uncritically the message of tellers of tort tales that plaintiffs typically prevail against corporations and professionals, despite reliable but remote evidence to the contrary. Likewise, the faithful reader of news might come to surmise that products liability cases overwhelm civil courts just as they suffuse tort tales, when in fact cases concerning auto insurance claims, contracts, divorce contests, and other issues are far more prevalent. Moreover, newspaper coverage to a great degree has justified the metaphor of the "litigation lottery" that tort reformers broadcast and legal specialists disparage. If headlines and lead paragraphs are to be trusted, huge amounts of money routinely change hands, just as they are said to do in reformists' tort tales, nurturing popular suppositions that legal rights claiming pays off rather more frequently than, and at least as handsomely as, the local Lotto game. At the same time, routine legal actions—for example, reductions in large awards, small and proportionate awards, reversals of trial outcomes on appeal, post-verdict settlements, and outcomes in which neither party wins any award—all receive barely more attention in the news than in reformers' anecdotes and broadside commentary.

Third, *the choices about what factors to highlight and to omit in the representation of selected legal events are notably similar as well.* This includes, most obviously, the tendency for key criteria guiding selection of events—especially large damage awards for successful plaintiffs—to be reinforced in the dramatic narrative depictions of those events in news stories and tort tales alike. The dollar hollers very loudly in both types of narratives. Equally important but less obvious, news narratives and tort tales both tend to be extremely thin and devoid of details about the histories of disputes, short on analysis of institutional and relational contexts in which disputes develop, and evasive about the representativeness of cases or outcomes, relying more on normalizing conventions than on evidence that might betray the lack of ordinariness for most news.

Even more significant, we think, *news narratives are inclined to echo tort tales in their tendency to discount the role of legal principles and processes in formal resolutions of most covered disputes.* Our data demonstrated that newspapers encourage readers to judge the civil justice process on the basis of assertions and events either prior to or subsequent to trials, thus largely ignoring the legal arguments and evidentiary proceedings in formal courtroom settings that shaped eventual judgments. As in tort tales, law is virtually eviscerated by news accounts of legal disputes, having been displaced by a focus on adversarial contests waged by narrowly self-interested parties and by outcomes seemingly as arbitrary as any lottery. Thus does news reporting unwittingly exhibit a version of legal realism more extreme, simplistic, perhaps even cynical than any found in the academy. This is further advanced by the tendency of news articles, like tort tales, to focus on persons almost exclusively in their roles as adversarial disputants. Such a tendency artificially "equalizes" relationships between parties that are often highly unequal in material resources and social power, especially when consumers challenge corporate producers. Also important is that claimants are rarely portrayed as injured, suffering victims. In fact, in most spot news reports, the damage, pain, anguish, and costs of injuries suffered by ordinary people are significantly deemphasized or ignored. This effacement of injury both reduces potential sympathy for plaintiffs and obscures the moral foundation of their claims, facilitating the common reversal of narrative logics whereby the defendant is portrayed as the "real" victim of plaintiff or lawyer greed.

We note two more complex and subtle but equally important omissions in news coverage. For one thing, news stories provide readers little means for distinguishing among radically different types of legal cases. We saw earlier that the specific legal claims of plaintiffs are often obscured in news reports. More fundamental, news reports rarely address directly the unique, highly atypical features of legal cases that most account for increased reporting since the 1980s—the legally rare but high-profile incidents of class-action social policy torts concerning asbestos, Dalkon Shield, tobacco, and the like. Attentive readers would witness such cases in ever-increasing coverage but have little idea about the unique, problematic status of these "third world" cases in the universe of tort litigation. Again, anomalies—whether the seeming trivial disputes of individuals such as the valedictorians, milk-oholic, and supposedly CAT-scanned psychic or the mega-class-action challenges to asbestos and tobacco—dominate the news and tort tales alike. Our point is not that social policy torts do not deserve coverage, but rather that informative coverage would help readers to distinguish such new, distinctive, consequential forms of legal action from the broader landscape of civil litigation.[23]

As if this were not enough, we find it highly significant that news reports, much like reform anecdotes, are generally reticent about alternative institutional processes for resolving disputes over claims of harm and responsibility, processes that might improve on or complement the civil tort litigation system. In our analysis of the 952 general articles on tort litigation, we found only sixteen mentions of cross-national comparisons among different types of tort systems, principles, or remedies; only

---

23. Recall our point in earlier chapters that neither social scientists nor trial lawyers have been very helpful in this regard either, which spreads responsibility for the problem quite broadly.

twenty-nine mentions of alternative institutional processes for determining liability or reducing risk were identified! In sum, news narratives and tort tales do not merely contradict expert knowledge but also overlook learned debates about civil justice that would directly contradict or at least call into question tort reformers' pronouncements.

Together, these homologies between the news and tort reform narratives indicate why the prevailing common sense in America seems so at odds with what scholarly experts demonstrate. Citizens know so much lore about law because reporters' stories and reformers' tales blend selected facts about highly unusual events with propagandistic fictions into familiar reference points about ordinary legal practice. These narrative accounts in the news, just as in tort tales, are as important for what they omit as for what atypical features they include and emphasize. Disputes and cases too sweeping to be personalized or morselized and too intricate to be sensationalized or normalized lack appeal, and thus often are filtered out of newspapers and press releases. Recognition of the infrequency of punitive damage awards and the unusual purposes for which judges or juries authorize them routinely goes unmentioned in the pursuit of accessibility and zest, while the more newsworthy payout and payee of the latest litigation lottery is moved to the head of the story.

This is not to say that typical news accounts are as palpably skewed as are typical tort tales. The ordinary reader might fail to notice the homologous reinforcement of selective knowledge linking the two types of narrative, especially when individual examples of each narrative are directly compared with one another. We have presumed that most readers are skeptical and perceptive enough to trace the partisan origins of tort tales and to see the narrowness and unfairness of the derision and sarcastic humor with which tort tales often drip. By contrast, news accounts appear more neutral, less biased, less consciously selective about their representations—an impression that no doubt is reinforced by the familiarity of daily exposure over long periods. Citizens and scholars alike know that news is not reality but cannot avoid relying on the news as a reflection of reality, often moderating the critical attitudes that they bring to self-evident propaganda. Presumed knowledge embedded in the news seeps into readers' consciousness subtly and steadily. In fact, news media cultivate credibility precisely to make their service go down easily, thereby encountering fewer challenges from less critical minds than editorials likely meet. That such narratives fit easily with pervasive ideological commitments to the fragile norm of individual responsibility and discipline—a theme developed in subsequent chapters—further underlines their power. And therein lies the great constructive power of the print media (Neuman, Just, and Crigler 1992). We suspect that in the aggregate, given regular repetition as news, reporting over time works to naturalize and normalize highly unusual features of law more compellingly than do tort tales, whose partisan motivations, exaggerated claims, and reliance on sarcasm are more transparent.

Our account of mainstream news reporting assumes yet greater significance when placed in the broader context of trends in the entertainment-oriented domains of mass culture. When one recalls the routine circulation of lawyer jokes and the pervasively suspect images of lawyers and civil litigation on television and in novels and movies (see chapter 4), the congruities of ordinary knowledge about law are striking. While hardly a seamlessly unitary portrait, the aggregated, manufactured media portrait of civil law surely makes the work of its detractors fairly simple.

PARALLEL, CONVERGENT, AND INTERACTIVE: INSTRUMENTAL AND INSTITUTIONAL FACTORS RECONSIDERED

Our emphasis on the homologies, in form and content, between tort tales and news narratives as modes of knowledge in modern mass culture also underlines our argument about the relative independence of their respective origins and means of production. Tort tales largely derive from the self-conscious, strategically motivated, *instrumental* actions of political activists aiming to alter public opinion and terms of discourse. By contrast, news narratives of civil litigation betray far less the instrumental or partisan designs of reporters and editors than the *institutional* pressures of news reporting practice. We have speculated that it is precisely the subtler, more familiar, normalized and naturalized character of the latter narratives that over time has contributed most to the development of the conventional wisdom in recent years about explosions of civil litigation, assertions of rights, punitive damages, and civil sweepstakes.

At the same time, we do not want to slight interactions between policy elites and news practices, and thus between instrumental and institutional forces, in the production of legal knowledge. Tort reform advocates seem to have derived most of their tales from accounts that began as print news stories. If our analysis is sound, the transformation required to make news stories into tort tales is often quite modest. Moreover, reform advocates and critics of the legal system no doubt derive some credibility by citing news sources as the foundation for their anecdotal portrayals. Conversely, respun news narratives, recycled tort tales, and attention-grabbing statistics in advertisements, editorials, features, and books endow tort reform publicists with presumptive expertise and credibility to the extent that their views come to create or reiterate common knowledge. Their reputed authority equips them to serve as sources for journalists and as commentators in print and broadcast media. Many tort reformers advertise their availability for comment in other settings as well. We cannot ascertain how much the proselytizing and publicizing efforts of tort reformers have familiarized journalists with their agenda, but interviews suggest that routine interactions—through phone calls, selective mailings, social events, business-supported conferences and weekend retreats—enable tort reformers to shape conventional understandings on which reporters rely and to which reporters in turn contribute. In any case, we expect that the symbiosis that communication scholars have found to characterize the interrelations of political elites and mass media extends to tort reformers who set out, we have shown, to commandeer mass media. This hardly adds up to a conspiracy, but collusive interaction surely plays some role in reinforcing the homologies and convergences in the process of constructing legal knowledge.

Two final examples illustrate the interplay of the instrumental and institutional. In the summer of 2002, Caesar Barber, age fifty-six, a maintenance worker whose 5-foot-10-inch frame carries 270 pounds, filed a class-action lawsuit claiming that McDonald's, Burger King, Wendy's, and KFC failed to properly disclose the fatty and salty ingredients in their fast food and the health risks they impose. The lawsuit was covered gleefully in hundreds of print and electronic news venues. The articles that we surveyed were in the mold of standard lore—focusing on the outrageous claim and seemingly undisciplined claimants, then decrying the lawsuit as "ridiculous," "senseless," baseless," "irresponsible," of "frivolous." Headlines were replete with parody: "Whopper of a Lawsuit" *(ABC NEWS.com);* "Want a Class-Action with That Burger? *(FOXNEWS);* "Lawsuit: Hold the Fat" *(Newsday);* "Fast Food Junkies Sue Eateries over Fatty Food *(Boston Herald);* "Would You Like Fries with That Lawsuit? *(CNN).* Opinion essays quickly followed, with such titles as "Fat Police Are Here," "Sue Your Way to Fame and Fortune," "In War on Fat, It's the Food's Fault," and "Burger Fans View Lawsuit as Bum Steer," which wraps up with "We sue too much in this country" (Michael Stetz, *San Diego Union-Tribune,* August 4, 2002). In the *Time Online* commentary, entitled "A Lawsuit to Choke On," the editorialist concluded that "Americans are going to have to decide if they want to be treated like adults." "It's not your fault. And there's money to be made," noted columnist Kathleen Parker. An *Online News* alternative Web site went even further: "Big Fat Man Sues Self for Being Such a Dumbass."

Even the careful reader might miss, amid such jocular condescension, that the primary goal of plaintiffs in most such cases is to draw public attention to the issue of fast food vendors' pervasive deceptions and the huge profits they provide. Only a few stories noted as well the fact that doctors, nutrition experts, consumer groups, and even FDA officials praised the

FIGURE 4 Ad published in *Newsweek* magazine and other news sources in 2002

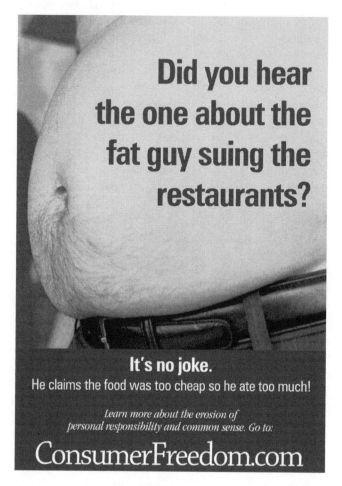

Reproduced at www.consumerfreedom.com/images/ads/lawsuit_fat.jpg. Reprinted by permission of Consumer Freedom.

lawsuit for amplifying an important public issue (see www.banzhaf.net/ obesity links). Meanwhile, tort reformers displayed their art by quickly making the story another memorable, if quite distorted, horror story. One group ran a prominent full-page ad in major magazines showing a huge naked belly falling over belted pants and bearing the caption "Did you hear the one about the fat guy suing the restaurants? It's no joke. He claims the food was too cheap so he ate too much! Learn more about the erosion of personal responsibility and common sense. Go to: ConsumerFreedom .com" (fig. 4). One need not agree with either the ends or the means of the lawsuit to recognize that these routine characterizations by the press and partisans alike encourages derision rather than intelligent debate over serious public issues.

This conventional wisdom has become so powerful that even hard-boiled, realistic gatekeepers of the press seem beguiled by its fanciful logic (see Galanter 1998b). On June 16, 2003, *U.S. News and World Report* editor-in-chief Mort Zuckerman offered dual anecdotes about allegedly frivolous lawsuits to show that one "can haul anybody into court for just about anything these days." The tort system, he contended, is rewarding cynical opportunists. However, as *Washington Post* media reporter Howard Kurtz soon revealed, drawing on the debunking Web sites Snopes.com and StellaAwards.com (the latter named in "honor" of the women who claimed to be burned by McDonald's coffee), the anecdotes cited by the editor were fabrications or urban legends derived from Internet spam (Kurtz 2003). Contrary to journalistic norms, *U.S. News* did not deny that the cases were fabrications or offer a correction for its conflation of fiction and opinion in "Welcome to Sue City, U.S.A." A spokesperson for the editor responded to the *Post* with remarkable bootstrapping: "These cases were reported in a variety of other reputable publications, such as the *Fort Worth Star-Telegram* and the *London Telegraph,* and Mr. Zuckerman could have cited dozens of other cases. . . . Few Americans would disagree with the proposition that there are far too many frivolous lawsuits filed" (Kurtz 2003, C1). In other words, if everyone believes it, then the conventional wisdom must be true, or at least true enough to thrive in the juridico-entertainment complex. That a respected editor so readily adapted tort tales in a commentary and his newsmagazine was unabashed by his reliance on Internet fiction (provided that it had been reprinted in newspapers and conformed to a truism) illustrates how instrumental concoctions and the journalistic conclusions merge to reproduce common sense.

CHAPTER SIX

Java Jive: Genealogy of a Juridical Icon

Woman Burned by Hot McDonald's Coffee Gets $2.9 Million

AP WIRE HEADLINE

When Stella Liebeck fumbled her coffee cup . . . she might as well have bought a winning lottery ticket. . . . This absurd judgment is a stunning illustration of what is wrong with America's civil justice system.

SAN DIEGO TRIBUNE

Oh, I can be quite litigious.

SEINFELD'S COSMO KRAMER, SUING FOR HOT COFFEE BURNS

Top Ten List—Blizzard Safety Tips . . . 8. Clear snow off driveway with just one scalding hot cup of McDonald's coffee.

THE LATE SHOW WITH DAVID LETTERMAN

"Dude!"

TELEVISION AUTO AD SHOWING YOUTHS HOLDING CUPS OF HOT COFFEE IN A VEHICLE TRAVERSING BUMPS

On Sunday, January 2, 2000, the front page of the *New York Times* "Arts and Leisure" section featured a long article in which comic Steve Martin ruminated about his dilemma of just "exactly what to celebrate on December 31, 1999." Martin's witty meditation, titled "The Third Millennium: So Far, So Good," began with a "A Short History of Thought," in which the author urged readers to "think of poor Socrates, with his simple answer to the question 'What is justice?' There was no way for him to have foreseen a jury's $3 million payout to a McDonald's customer who spilled a cup of too-hot coffee in her lap" (Martin 2000). Martin's joke turned on the absurdity that the legal damages awarded to octogenarian Stella Liebeck in 1994 for injuries resulting from an everyday occurrence represented twenty-five hundred years of human progress in thinking about justice. The wry juxtaposition worked, of course, only to the extent that Martin's reference to the jury verdict over five years earlier still resonated clearly among readers of the newspaper.[1]

Martin had a sure bet. The case involving burns from McDonald's coffee is likely responsible for more of the everyday knowledge about the U.S. justice system than any other lawsuit. This chapter addresses how constructions in the courtroom, the press, and mass culture transformed the complaint of a badly burned plaintiff into a personification of runaway litigiousness. We illustrate in particular the institutional propensities and power of the media, which almost single-handedly made this story into a mass cultural symbol of the lawsuit crisis. Initial media reports of the coffee case were not merely homologous in form and content to tort tales, as discussed in the preceding chapter; news coverage from the start was ready-made, needing little trim and spin, to launch the most infamous of all tort tales. We recognize as well the instrumental role of tort reformers in the larger process, although they were more the beneficiaries of the media phenomenon than its agents. Finally, we develop further the ideological dimensions of the story that focused on the suspect character and motives of plaintiff Stella Liebeck and her attorney. Our analysis makes clear how the travails of a low-income retired woman were rendered as a pithy homily condemning individual recklessness, blame avoidance, and greed.[2]

The aim of our inquiry is not to argue that the trial judgment, award, or even settlement were, in fact, more just than the conventional media wisdom dictated. Rather, our point is that media coverage and analysis made any rational discussion of the dispute and the policy issues it raises virtually impossible, while providing a powerful boost to the dubious general claims of a partisan political reform movement (see chapter 2). Our analysis begins with a detailed narrative outlining the facts, evidence, and arguments made available by reports of the trial. We then track the story's simplification and amplification in subsequent newspaper coverage, from initial spot news reporting of the award through coverage and commentary in subsequent phases, to show how journalism and jocularity made

1. Martin's assertion about a "$3 million payout" highlights the type of popular misinformation that has circulated about this case, as we document below.

2. There is no small irony in the fact that the same legal logic that individualizes responsibility and commodifies the mechanisms of relief for injury can be turned toward characterizing rights claimants as rapacious and irresponsible individuals. See Abel 1989.

Stella an icon and her lawsuit a tort tale. Along the way, we look at how initial print news coverage primed increasingly satirical editorials, television and radio news, television talk shows and late-night comedy shows, sitcoms, movies, corporate advertisements, and the like. The case study provides a fuller picture about how media constructions spread throughout mass culture and became available, accessible, adaptable, and actionable apocrypha.

THE DEVELOPMENT OF A LEGAL DISPUTE

The disputing framework outlined in chapter 3 is useful here for organizing our review of the actual legal dispute. We thus begin with the initial incident and then trace the evolution of the dispute through the stages of grievance, claiming, lawyer involvement, filed claims, trial, and post-trial settlement. Along the way, we emphasize the key facts and interpretive accounts by which the dispute was waged among the growing list of actors (see Miller and Sarat 1980–81; Mather and Yngvesson 1980–81).

A Grievant Becomes a Claimant: Stella Liebeck Seeks Recompense

On February 27, 1992, seventy-nine-year-old Stella Liebeck purchased a cup of coffee from a drive-through window at an Albuquerque McDonald's. She was sitting in the front passenger seat of a Ford Probe driven by her grandson, Chris Tiano, who had pulled away from the window and fully stopped by a curb in the parking lot. Liebeck tried to remove the cup's lid to add sugar and cream. Lacking a flat surface inside the small car, she placed the coffee between her legs to free up both her hands for prying off the lid. As the lid came off, the Styrofoam cup tipped, spilling all the coffee into her lap, where it was rapidly soaked up by her sweatpants.[3] Ms. Liebeck screamed in pain, but Mr. Tiano did not understand, later relating that it at first seemed to be "no big deal." "When it happened, I thought, well, you know, we spilled a cup of coffee; it's basically our fault. You know it was our clumsiness that spilled the coffee." After all, spilling coffee or some other hot liquid on oneself is a relatively common occurrence; "it was just a scald," he said repeatedly in his deposition.[4]

The grandson then proceeded to drive out of the parking lot, until a minute later when his grandmother became quite nauseous, and he suspected she was in shock. Now realizing that the incident was serious, he

---

3. Liebeck's letter to McDonald's estimated that the spill took place less than four minutes after the coffee was served to her. Authors' files.

4. Authors' files.

pulled over to the side of the road, helped her out of the car, aided her in removing the sweatpants, and covered her with a sheet from the car's trunk. Mr. Tiano headed for the nearest hospital, which was full, and then made his way to a second hospital, where Liebeck was admitted. Doctors determined that the hot coffee had caused third-degree burns on her thighs, buttocks, genitals, and groin area—about 6 percent of her body—and lesser burns that eventually left permanent scarring over 16 percent of her body. Third-degree burns are extreme injuries in that they penetrate through the full thickness of the skin to the fat, muscle, and bone. Stella Liebeck stayed in the hospital for over a week, where she was treated by a vascular surgeon and eventually subjected to a regimen of very painful skin grafts. The surgeon, Dr. Arredondo, reported that her injuries added up to one of the worst burn cases from hot liquids he had ever treated. Due to the mounting medical costs, Liebeck left the hospital earlier than recommended and had to be driven back to the doctor for medical treatment many days by her daughter, who was forced to take time off from work. Liebeck suffered great discomfort, lost over twenty pounds, was permanently disfigured, and was partially disabled for up to two years following the accident.

A recently retired department store salesclerk and member of a longtime Republican family, Stella Liebeck had never filed a lawsuit in her life and did not immediately seek relief with the aid of a lawyer, judge, or jury. But she also was aware that a simple coffee spill should not have caused such extensive injuries. Liebeck turned her *injury* into a *grievance* with a letter sent to the corporate offices of McDonald's Restaurants on March 13, 1992, two weeks after the incident. She wrote:

> It seems to me that no person would find it reasonable to have been given coffee so hot that it would do the severe damage it did to my skin. Obviously, it was undrinkable in that it would have burnt my mouth. It seems that the reasonable expectation for a spilling accident would be a mess and a reddening of the skin at worst. . . . Although I did the spilling, I had no warning that the coffee was that hot. It should never have been given to a customer at that temperature.

In terms familiar from our Disputing Pyramid in chapter 3, Liebeck acknowledged that she was responsible for the accident but translated her *grievance* into a *claim* about a dangerously defective product that caused severe injuries for which, she averred, the McDonald's Corporation was at least somewhat liable. Liebeck's initial letter made it clear that she had "no intention of suing or asking for unreasonable recompense." Instead, she asked the corporation (1) to check the coffee machine and coffee-making process to see if they were faulty; (2) to reevaluate the temperature standards for coffee served to customers, for others must have been severely injured as well; and (3) to cover medical, recuperation, and incidental costs related to her injuries that were not covered by Medicare, which initially were left unspecified because the medical treatment at that time was far from over. Later estimates for incurred costs have varied in different accounts, but they hovered around $10,000 to $15,000 for medical bills, plus other directly related expenditures, for a total of around $20,000. After six months of claiming without the counsel of a lawyer, however, Liebeck's request for a change in policy on McDonald's part was rejected, and the company offered only $800 for personal compensation. In terms of the Disputing Pyramid, Liebeck's *grievance* was now a *dispute.*

A Claimant Becomes a Litigant: Lawyers Attempt to Settle the Dispute

Frustrated by her inability to secure compensation for the physical and financial harm wrought by the scalding accident, Liebeck moved up the pyramid and sought counsel. In the fall of 1992, she retained Kenneth R. Wagner and Associates, an Albuquerque law firm. Through a legal assistant at the firm, Wagner learned of S. Reed Morgan, a Houston attorney who had settled a similar case against McDonald's involving scalding coffee (for $27,500) in the late 1980s. Morgan was contacted and agreed to take on Liebeck's cause, in part because he had been angered by what he saw as callous indifference displayed by the corporation in the previous dispute. Morgan quickly issued a formal request for $90,000 to cover Liebeck's medical expenses as well as pain and suffering. His amended claim fared no better than Stella's original claim, however, and was dismissed by McDonald's.

Morgan *filed a formal complaint* on behalf of Stella Liebeck in the Second Judicial District Court, County of Bernalillo, New Mexico. The complaint alleged that the coffee that Liebeck purchased form McDonald's in 1992 was excessively, dangerously hot and that inadequate warnings were provided regarding the risks posed by the hot coffee. The key legal claim was that the coffee breached warranties of fitness for its intended purpose of consumption under the Uniform Commercial Code. Along with the claim for compensatory damages, punitive damages were requested on the reasoning that McDonald's sold the coffee with reckless indifference to the safety and welfare of its customers. Once the trial date was set, Morgan offered to settle the case for $300,000, with no success. He later acknowledged that he would have settled for rather less, perhaps half as much.

Just a few days before the trial, Judge Robert H. Scott ordered the disputing parties to participate in a mediation session. Based on earlier cases and a projection of what a jury would likely award, the mediator recommended a settlement at $225,000.[5] Once again, however, the McDonald's mega-corporation refused the opportunity to negotiate a settlement. The trial commenced in the second week of August 1994.

A Litigant Becomes a Plaintiff: The Legal Contest to Define Reality

The trial produced relatively few important disagreements regarding the facts of the case. McDonald's did not contest that the coffee was very hot or that hot coffee can scald customers. For her part, Stella Liebeck did not contest that she spilled the coffee on herself or that she was responsible for the accident. While the adversaries disagreed about some details, those issues by themselves could not determine a just outcome. Rather, the case turned on contending interpretive arguments, or narratives, devised by each side to select, support, and make sense of the evidence in a coherent, compelling way. Indeed, civil disputes typically can be understood in terms of contending "causal stories" that attempt to identify different levels of responsibility or fault among different parties (Stone 1998; Conley and O'Barr 1990). The two interpretive accounts formulated by opposing counsel in Stella's lawsuit against McDonald's were as follows.

Attorneys for Liebeck systematically sought to present the jury with a coherent and compelling interpretation of the accident that focused on the inordinately hot coffee produced and sold by McDonald's. This *defective products liability narrative* combined basics of products liability law with supporting legal themes suitable to the circumstances surrounding the accident. The relevant products liability law came straight from the Uniform Commercial Code's implied warranties of merchantability and fitness. Attorney Morgan confirmed that the plaintiff had relied on fundamental business law: "The heart of the case [was that] the product was defectively designed. . . . It wasn't a negligence case. We didn't even plead negligence. Just products liability. . . . The individual responsibility is not the issue. The product is unreasonably dangerous."[6] Media coverage would consistently state that Liebeck contended that the spill was McDonald's fault. In fact, she claimed instead that McDonald's had failed to abide by standards that many or most businesses must meet.

To complement the implied warranties, plaintiff Liebeck marshaled supporting themes. The *first* theme acknowledged that, while coffee spills were routine events, Liebeck's injuries were extremely atypical due to Mc-

5. Morgan had provided evidence of a California woman scalded by coffee who was awarded $280,000.
6. Interview with S. Reed Morgan. Authors' files.

Donald's dangerously hot coffee. This factual contention challenged Mc-Donald's adherence to the implied warranties discussed above, a challenge that was established by several points. Liebeck's attorney presented as evidence a McDonald's manual specifying that coffee should be made at temperatures between 195 and 205 degrees, and served at temperatures between 180 and 190 degrees. Morgan then introduced testimony by two renowned experts—Dr. Kenneth Diller, chairman of the Department of Mechanical Engineering and Bio-Mechanical Engineering at the University of Texas, and Dr. Charles Baxter of Southwestern Medical School and the Baxter Wound Center—regarding the severe burns that such hot coffee inflicts. Specifically, they confirmed that liquids between 180 and 190 degrees cause full thickness, third-degree, highly painful and disfiguring burns in less than seven seconds, which in many cases is before spilled coffee can be wiped off or clothing can be removed. The time that it takes for liquids to burn skin with equal severity increases greatly as the temperature descends. Liebeck testified about the extent of her painful injuries to illustrate this point, and graphic pictures of her severely burned and scarred skin were introduced along with her doctor's statements to show the damage that the extremely hot coffee caused in only a few seconds—four minutes, Liebeck stated, after purchase. In addition to the testimony by the plaintiff and her experts, a McDonald's quality assurance supervisor admitted that McDonald's served coffee that would scald:

> REED MORGAN: [Y]ou know, as a matter of fact, that coffee is a hazard, selling it at 180 to 190 degrees, don't you?
> CHRISTOPHER APPELTON: I have testified before, the fact that this coffee can cause burns.
> MORGAN: It is hazardous at this temperature?
> APPELTON: At that high temperature the coffee is a hazard.
> MORGAN: If customers attempt to swallow that coffee, isn't it a fact that it will scald their throat or esophagus?
> APPELTON: Yes, under those conditions, if they could get the coffee in their throat, that could happen, yes.[7]

A *second* theme in the products liability frame was that most customers are not aware of the danger posed by coffee as hot as McDonald's serves. This theme was important to underscore the contention that McDonald's was vending an unfit product to customers who could not be presumed to know about or make provision for the coffee's extreme temperature. Morgan used two studies—one by a restaurant services consultant show-

7. Trial transcript, authors' files. See Nader and Smith 1996, 719.

ing that home coffeemakers brew coffee at 158–68 degrees and hold it at 150–57 degrees after three minutes; the other from his earlier case showing that McDonald's served their coffee at temperatures well above most other fast food restaurants—to demonstrate that McDonald's coffee was significantly hotter than most coffee that consumers make for themselves or purchase elsewhere. This was critical, for while Liebeck admitted to spilling the coffee on herself, she had no reasonable expectation that it would be so unusually hot and dangerous. Another expert for the plaintiff testified in support of this contention.[8]

The *third* critical theme used to complement plaintiff's interpretive account of the event was that McDonald's knew their customers were unaware of the dangers posed by its hot coffee. Evidence was submitted that McDonald's had received over seven hundred complaints about hot coffee in the previous decade and had paid out nearly three quarters of a million dollars to settle such claims, including some payments of up to $66,000. The case settled by Reed Morgan in the late 1980s, in which graphic evidence of third-degree burns was presented, was just one of such complaints. To rebut this contention, Dr. Robert Knaff, a safety consultant for McDonald's, testified that seven hundred complaints of burns were statistically tiny relative to the large number of customers served.

Finally, counsel for the plaintiff alleged that McDonald's displayed reckless indifference to their customers' safety by doing nothing either to reduce the heat of coffee known to be dangerous or to provide adequate warning to customers. Morgan noted that a message (CAUTION: CONTENTS HOT) appeared on the cup, but pointed out that it was difficult to read because it was the same color and size as the ornamental trim on the cup.[9] McDonald's admitted that the message was intended more as a "reminder" than as a warning. What is more, the plaintiff urged, the motive that trumped the corporation's concerns for safety was well documented: the desire to lure more customers, to sell more coffee, and to earn greater profits. By emphasizing this pecuniary motive, attorneys for the plaintiff thus sought to strip the mega-corporation of its family-friendly marketing hype and to expose a fearsome Goliath that the David-like plaintiff was challenging.

More than plaintiff's arguments alone supported this final theme.

---

8. The deposition by Chris Tiano, Stella's grandson, is evidence that most consumers do not know of the dangers at stake. He indicated he could not imagine the severity of injury suffered by his grandmother even while witnessing her screams of pain. Author's files.

9. Chris Tiano said in his deposition that there was no warning on the cup, underlining how difficult it was to see and read the words. Authors' files.

Christopher Appleton, having testified that McDonald's coffee was not "fit for consumption" when served, further admitted that he had been shown the injurious effects of hot coffee in the earlier case presented by Reed Morgan, but the company still did nothing.

> REED MORGAN: Isn't it a fact that back in 1988, when I showed you the pictures of the young lady that was burned in that situation, that you were appalled and surprised that coffee could cause that kind of burn?
>
> CHRISTOPHER APPLETON: Yes, I had never seen photographs like that before.
>
> MORGAN: All right. In those six years, you still have not attempted, yourself, or know of anyone within the corporation that has attempted to find out the rate of speed, the lack of margin of safety in serving coffee at this temperature right . . . .
>
> APPLETON: No, we have not.[10]

Appelton further acknowledged that the McDonald's corporation did not have a systematic mechanism for keeping track of the severity of injuries caused by its products or for determining when a sufficient number of people were injured to justify lowering the heat of the coffee they serve; most such information was only known by the company's insurance agency. He unabashedly acknowledged that "there are more serious dangers in restaurants" than hot coffee and "there is no current plan to change the procedure [for making coffee] that we're using in that regard now."

Reed Morgan presented all such testimony to support his request for punitive damages in light of McDonald's callous indifference to the safety of its customers. The closing argument by the plaintiff's lawyers noted that McDonald's sells over a billion cups of coffee a year, which generates daily revenues of $1.35 million; payment of two days' revenue from coffee might constitute a reasonable basis for punitive damages. As attorney Ken Wagner later summarized, "We said in order to send a message, you have to penalize them financially before the message will get to corporate headquarters in respect to serving coffee at this temperature."

Defendant McDonald's conceded many facts at the core of the plaintiff's products liability frame but countered by emphasizing different facts framed in an alternative interpretive story about the incident. The company responded that people spill coffee on themselves all the time but don't expect others to take responsibility for the outcomes, however ter-

10. Nader and Smith 1996, 720.

rible. In short, a commonplace event like a coffee spill merited a common-sense response, the same one Chris Tiano immediately had: the spill was the fault of his grandmother, not the McDonald's Corporation.

The defense organized its own evidence to support this narrative. *First,* the defense appealed to the ethic of individual responsibility deeply rooted in American culture. Stella Liebeck, not McDonald's, spilled the coffee that resulted in injuries; she must accept the blame. It was relevant that Liebeck's own letter of March 13 admitted that she had spilled the coffee on herself. Noting that the placement of a cup of hot coffee between her knees while sitting in the car and the failure to remove her clothes imme-diately were "unwise," defense attorneys insisted that Stella should accept responsibility for the lamentable accident.

A *second* theme was directly aimed at challenging the plaintiff's key scientific point regarding proximate cause of the injury. McDonald's pre-sented an affidavit from Turner M. Osler, a burn specialist, contending that Liebeck might have received the same burns if the coffee had been less hot, even as low as 130 degrees.[11] Major reasons for the bad burns in this case, the expert testified, included Liebeck's advanced age and her failure to re-move in a timely fashion her clothing soaked with the coffee.

A *third* theme turned on the question of "Why pick on us?" The attor-neys for McDonald's argued that systematic marketing studies, presented as evidence, showed that customers prefer their coffee very hot. In fact, this was one of the most appealing traits of McCoffee. Most customers don't drink the coffee immediately after purchase at drive-through win-dows, but typically wait until they arrive at the office or home. At the same time, it was shown that some other restaurants, and especially those lead-ing in coffee sales, tend to serve their coffee at nearly the same high tem-perature as McDonald's. Indeed, McDonald's provided evidence that their specifications followed industry standards. Experts for the defense also testified about the highly quality of insulation in their cups and the special plastic tab on the tops of coffee cups that reduce the chance of spilling. Far from being insensitive to customers, the defense contended, McDonald's hot coffee served in state-of-the-art containers was just what the public wanted.

Finally, the defense attorneys played on a theme at the heart of the tort reform campaign, implying that Stella Liebeck's claim was an example of a litigious plaintiff seeking damages for harms that she, however unfortu-

---

11. The plaintiff's attorney challenged Osler testimony, arguing that he left out of his ac-count the significantly varying amounts of exposure time required for extreme burns by liq-uids at different temperatures.

nately, caused to herself. Attorney Tracy McGee summarized this assessment of her lawsuit to *Newsweek* reporters. "The real question . . . is how far you want our society to go to restrict what most of us enjoy and accept." McGee fended off the plaintiff's attempt to introduce evidence from previous scalding litigation by deriding the claims: "First person accounts of sundry women whose nether regions have been scorched by McDonald's coffee might well be worthy of Oprah. . . . But they have no place in a court of law" (Gerlin 1994, A1, A4). Each theme of the defense's interpretive narrative used notions of fairness and common sense to support its key assertion of individual responsibility, as opposed to the strict letter of business law.

A Plaintiff Becomes a Victor: Jurors Accept Most of
Stella Liebeck's Account

After a tedious trial over seven days, the jurors took but four hours to reach their verdict: McDonald's Restaurants owed Ms. Liebeck $160,000 in compensatory damages and about $2.7 million in punitive damages. In calculating compensatory damages, the jury synthesized the contrasting claims and frames into a slightly mixed verdict. The jury agreed with the defense that Stella Liebeck was responsible for her accident, but only to a degree—namely, 20 percent. Assessing the expenses, pain and suffering, disfigurement, and immobility consequent to the accident, jurors awarded compensatory damages of $200,000 for the accident. Since they held Ms. Liebeck to be 20 percent responsible for her accident, the jury then discounted the compensatory award by $40,000 (one-fifth of $200,000), which left the plaintiff $160,000 in compensatory damages. Jurors had come to see McDonald's coffee as a product made hazardous by extreme heat, a dangerous brew for which the corporation had to bear primary liability even if Ms. Liebeck was partly responsible for her own injuries.

Beyond specific damages, jurors had come to see the Liebeck episode as an example of a stream of dangerously hot coffee flowing from drive-throughs and across counters. Jurors accepted the plaintiff's characterization: McDonald's and other outlets that serve steaming coffee were recklessly indifferent to consumers' safety. To dissuade McDonald's and others from continuing their willful indifference, the jury granted the punitive award—damages designed to deter a wrongdoer from continued wrongful conduct—that Liebeck's lawyers had recommended: $2.7 million, based on an estimate of two days' revenues from coffee sales at McDonald's restaurants nationwide. Remarkably, the award that would set off alarms among editorialists and other professional chatterers had been scaled back from several jurors' arguments for awarding a full week's coffee grosses at McDonald's, around $9.6 million (Gerlin 1994)!

As always, public indications of the logic behind the jurors' judgment were sparse. Still, we know that jurors were convinced by the key themes of the plaintiff's narrative about corporate liability for a defective product. Jurors who spoke to interviewers frankly admitted that they initially thought the case was a waste of their time. For example, jury foreman Jerry Goens told a reporter that he "wasn't convinced as to why I need to be there to settle a coffee spill," implying his predisposition toward the "individual responsibility" narrative of the defense before the trial (Gerlin 1994). Another juror felt insulted. "The whole thing sounded ridiculous to me" (Press 1995, 35).[12] But the plaintiff's attorneys' construction of the case changed their minds. Several jurors commented on the strength of the scientific evidence regarding how quickly 180-degree coffee burns skin as well as the graphic photos of Liebeck's injuries. Juror Jack Elliott concluded from the testimony by a McDonald's quality assurance executive that McDonald's was profoundly indifferent to burns and suffering (Gerlin 1994, A4). Juror Betty Farnham was so unimpressed by the defense's claim that seven hundred complaints were trivial relative to the millions of cups that McDonald's served that she began to doubt that the corporation could see the human suffering underlying the statistics. "The facts were so overwhelmingly against the company. They were not taking care of their customers" (Gerlin 1994, A1). Another juror justified the punitive damages as a way to "get McDonald's attention. Their callous disregard was very upsetting" (Nader and Smith 1996, 270). Indeed, the plaintiff won over the jury to such an extent that their judgment was meant to extend beyond the immediate defendant. Juror Richard Anglada stated that the punitive damages were aimed at all restaurants that served too-hot coffee: "The coffee's too hot out there. This happened to be McDonald's." Juror Roxanne Bell echoed the point, recalling "It was our way of saying, 'Hey, open your eyes. People are getting burned'" (Press 1995, 34).

Not surprisingly, the attorneys for McDonald's promised to appeal the case. There is evidence, however, that some in the corporation took the verdict to heart, at least initially. An Albuquerque news investigator reported that the temperature of coffee at a local McDonald's shortly after the trial fell to 158 degrees. Moreover, the lids of coffee cups began to carry the clear warning "HOT! HOT! HOT," and admonitions that "Coffee, tea, and hot chocolate are VERY HOT!" soon were routinely posted at most McDonald's drive-throughs.

12. Attorney Reed Morgan confirmed this in an interview. "The first thing they [the jury] had to get over was they thought it was a silly case." Authors' file.

A Victory Becomes Less Spectacular: Judge Reduces the Punitive Damages

Trial judge Robert H. Scott on September 14, 1994, reduced the punitive damages from nearly $2.7 million to $480,000, somewhat ironically using the tort reformers' own formula of "three times the awarded compensatory damages" as the upper limit. He did not set aside the verdict or adjust compensatory damages, however. Instead, he agreed with the jurors on key findings. Judge Scott concurred that testimony and evidence showed that McDonald's knew or should have known that its coffee was too hot and unfit for consumption, that McDonald's and its employees were indifferent to consumer safety, and that McDonald's undertook inadequate efforts to warn its customers. He stated that the punitive damages were an appropriate means to deter, punish, and warn McDonald's (Nader and Smith 1996, 272). Judge Scott then ordered another conference (as he had done before the trial) that produced a final confidential settlement for an undisclosed amount, after Morgan's appeal challenging the reduced damages was denied.

In sum, the legal narrative of Stella Liebeck's grievance and claim regarding a defective, dangerous coffee product won hands down in a court of law, even though the award she received was less than one-fifth of that initially authorized by the jury.

THE PRINT MEDIA CONSTRUCT A LEGAL LEGEND: INITIAL ACCOUNTS

Evidence presented in chapter 5 gives us reason to expect that newspapers would reconstruct the McDonald's coffee dispute to match standard understandings of *news worth:* easy-to-understand specifics, personalized conflict, and sensationalized results would garner far more coverage than insightful observations about the complexities of events, of disputing case history, of multicausal relations, and of the legal process. As a result, important facts and interpretations critical to the jury would be slighted or left out altogether. Moreover, we had reason to expect that less familiar story lines would receive little attention while well-known scripts would serve as defaults for journalists and readers alike. Specifically, we anticipated that the subtle elements of the plaintiff's legally successful but technically complex product liability narrative would take a back seat to the culturally pervasive narrative of individual responsibility that jurors largely rejected as less apt. Finally, we surmised that fragmentary accounts and misleading factoids would facilitate intercessions by reform-oriented and reform-influenced commentators to spin the case as another instance of frivolous litigation. If so, media constructions would make the Liebeck legend a principal source of skewed, misleading, and often inaccurate knowledge about the civil legal system routinely disseminated to ordinary Americans. With only a few exceptions, our expectations proved extremely well founded.

Phases of Newspaper Construction of the Coffee Case

The first point to note about the hot coffee case is that it was widely covered in the print media; the jury award was immediately reported in at least twenty-six leading newspapers, and many scores of articles followed in subsequent years. As we show below, the case was widely covered because of its easy fit into prevailing press conventions. Moreover, the McDonald's case affords the close observer valuable insights because it generated multiple waves of coverage (Haltom 1998, 201–4). Figure 5 shows how and why we separate *Liebeck* news coverage, gathered through a systematic search of "Academic Universe,"[13] into five discrete phases. The *initial* and largest spate of spot coverage followed the announcement of the jury verdict on August 18, 1994. After the first two days, the *Liebeck* case was in the public domain and the pundit domain, as we shall show. Two subsequent events might have elicited corrective coverage of the case around September 1, so we treated these events and their spotty coverage together as a *second* phase. When Judge Scott reduced the jury's punitive award by over 80 percent to three times the compensatory award, he inaugurated a *third* phase of coverage. This phase stretched from September 14 until December 1, when final case settlement piqued a brief *fourth* phase of coverage. These developments in the dispute occasioned spot coverage and commentaries throughout the final months of 1994. Together with a modestly covered but substantial article correcting initial reports, spot articles and opinion pieces in phases 1–4 reveal the process by which legally successful narratives and constructions of fact yielded to factoids and default "commonsense" frames, transforming Litigant Liebeck into Symbolic Stella. After spot reports of the settlement ended (December 2–3, 1994), an ongoing *fifth* phase reinforced dissemination of the symbolic case while ignoring the actual case the plaintiff and jurors decided.

13. In June of 2000, we searched Lexis-Nexis "Academic Universe" from August 1, 1994, until December 31, 1994. Under "News," we searched both in "General News" and in " U.S. News," the latter to pick up regional newspapers not accessible in the former. Our primary keywords included "court," "courts," "burn," "burns," "jury," "jurors," "coffee," "million," and "award." We then narrowed this far-flung search with the demand that all articles contain some spellings of both "McDonald's" and "Liebeck."

FIGURE 5 1994 newspaper articles related to *Liebeck v. McDonald's Restaurants* (wire reports excluded)

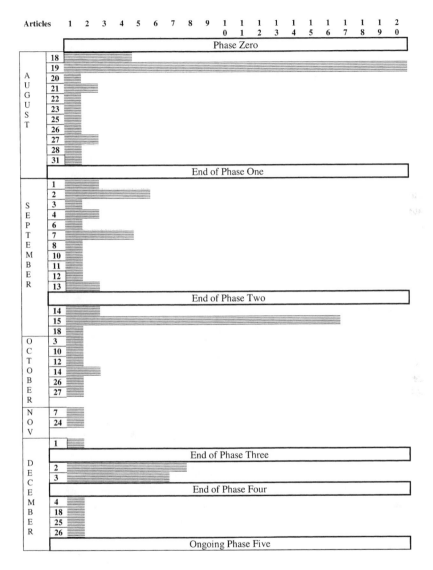

Phase 0: Omission of Coverage Prior to the Verdict

While much of our account turns on omissions in coverage during the five phases just identified, we first note a practically total absence of coverage before the jury verdict was announced. The dearth of coverage prior to the jury award made the results seem even more surprising than might otherwise have been the case. Had trial testimony and evidence been widely available—as has been the case in many instances of tobacco litigation, for example—Liebeck's victory might have seemed less inexplicable and the claims she actually advanced more understandable. In noting omitted coverage, we do not presume that the *Liebeck* case merited coverage before its denouement. We merely remind readers that, as we previously suggested, the scarcity of pre-verdict coverage left much of the evidence and testimony underdeveloped and unlikely to become developed, given demands on the press for alacrity and conciseness. The failure of reporters to witness the trial or scrutinize the trial record greatly increased the chances that a substantial judgment would generate sensational but incomplete, misleading, and even erroneous coverage shaped by media conventions and prevailing cultural norms. This first omission thus may have been as significant as any of the others considered below.

Phase 1: Newspapers Selectively Report the Verdict

Despite unavailability of the story prior to the verdict and concomitant omissions from coverage, print reports during phase 1 covered the verdict in a predictable, professional manner, repeating the standard emphases of mainstream media. Basics of the specific accident and particular judgment—the answers to "Who?" "What?" "Where?" and similar questions—were featured prominently in reportage. At the same time, consistent with our general findings, the most dramatic and personalized elements were reported simplistically in a way that would be familiar to readers, while subtle and complex dimensions of the trial record that did not fit prevailing formulas were left out. This reconstruction and fragmentation to suit newspapers' standards became accentuated when editorialists and commentators filled in the gaps in reporting with spin and factoids.

We begin with the Associated Press morning wire-service report for three related reasons: it was the longest and most detailed national account; it became a basis for coverage by most newspapers in our sample; and it reported major developments in later phases as well. The initial news account on August 18 is reprinted below in its entirety as replicated on "Academic Universe."

Woman Burned by Hot McDonald's Coffee Gets $2.9 Million

A woman who was scalded when her McDonald's coffee spilled was awarded nearly $2.9 million—or about two days' coffee sales for the fast-food chain—by a jury.

Lawyers for Stella Liebeck, who suffered third-degree burns in the 1992 incident, contended that McDonald's coffee was too hot.

A state district court jury imposed $2.7 million in punitive damages and $160,000 in compensatory damages Wednesday.

Ken Wagner, Liebeck's attorney, said that he had asked the jury for punitive damages equal to two days' worth of McDonald's coffee sales, which he estimated at $1.34 million a day.

Testimony indicated McDonald's coffee is served at 180–190 degrees, based on advice from a coffee consultant who has said it tastes best that hot, Wagner said Thursday.

The lawsuit contended Liebreck's [*sic*] coffee was 165–170 degrees when it spilled. In contrast, he said, coffee brewed at home is generally 135–140 degrees.

He said McDonald's expressed no willingness during the trial to turn down the heat or print a warning.

Defense attorney Tracy McGee already has said the company will appeal. McGee also said the jury was "concerned about an industrywide practice" of selling hot coffee.

Juror Richard Anglada confirmed the jury was trying to deliver a message to the industry. "The coffee's too hot out there [in the industry]. This happened to be McDonald's," Anglada said Wednesday.

Liebeck's lead counsel, Reed Morgan of Houston, said there have been several lawsuits nationally over the temperature of McDonald's coffee but that he believes the Liebeck case was the first to reach the verdict stage. A California case was settled out of court for $235,000, he said.

Morgan said Wednesday the woman's medical bills totaled nearly $10,000.

According to testimony, Liebeck was a passenger in a car driven by her grandson outside a McDonald's in southeast Albuquerque when she was burned by a cup of coffee purchased at a drive-through window. The jury found, among other things, that the coffee was defective and that McDonald's engaged in conduct justifying the punitive damages.

The astute reader immediately should notice two characteristics of this account. For one thing, it is very short, simple, and thin—already well suited to become an anecdote. Moreover, the characteristically fragmented, disjointed presentation of information is familiar. Virtually no signs of carefully constructed legal arguments presented by the disputing parties, of debate over the basic legal issues at stake, or of contrasting evidentiary claims in the trial survive the AP reconstruction. Readers hoping to find clearly demarcated themes or well-crafted legal positions are sure to be frustrated. The wire account offers few explicit cues to make sense of what principles were at stake, or even reason to believe that legal norms of right or justice mattered at all.

Beneath its surface randomness, however, the selection and prioritization of information in the AP story exhibit a logic that we have encountered before and will see repeated in news coverage of the hot coffee case. While little direct attention to substantive themes and arguments is apparent, the information presented in the wire report clearly displays the logic of news worth discussed above and the defendant's interpretive framing of the accident that stresses individual accountability.

The first and most extensively noted information in the article— namely, identifying the burn injury and the award—*dramatizes* the case. By far most prominent in the wire report are the monetary figures. The headline and the first, third, and fourth sentences each highlight either the $2.7 million punitive damages award or the cumulative $2.9 million award; the fourth mention (fourth sentence) disaggregates the total into two figures, followed by the calculus of two times $1.34 million in coffee sales to determine the punitive damages. This is important, for journalistic norms privilege placing the most important information first, after which repetition highlights the message. Near the end of the report, other lesser but still large sums—an earlier settlement of $234,000 and medical bills of $10,000—are mentioned. In short, as any reader of wire-service stories might have predicted, "dollars holler" from the headline through to the end of the brief report.

The news account also is highly *personalized.* Indeed, it is filled with mentions of individual actors: Stella Liebeck; her attorneys Reed Morgan and Kenneth Wagner; McDonald's; one defense attorney, Tracy McGee; and one juror, Richard Anglada. Some synecdoche seems expedient and even efficient, but personalization deprived client newspapers and readers of contextual elements. Recognition that the dispute, for one thing, was between a retired seventy-nine-year-old, working-class woman with inadequate Medicare benefits and a huge multinational corporation, and for another thing that the legal duel was largely between a solo personal injury attorney and a battalion of corporate lawyers [14] are almost entirely obscured by the individualized account, which casts each agent in his or her formal role. While "McDonald's" appears repeatedly, the AP report nowhere reminds readers of the vast size and wealth of the McDonald's cor-

---

14. While Morgan had handled a couple of hot liquid cases, he was hardly a "repeat player" (Galanter 1974).

poration; it is at most a "fast-food chain," one player in a larger "industry." Indeed, some readers might not have been certain that the corporation, rather than the Albuquerque franchise, was the defendant.

Moreover, the attention to the spill accident—although generally incomplete and misleading, and later often flatly erroneous—further tended to reconstruct the case to suit interpretations that stress individual responsibility far more than the plaintiff's case or the jury's rationale. Specifically, no mention is made that the car was parked motionless to the side rather than at the window or moving, or that there was little recklessness about the action leading to the accident, or that the injuries involved extreme pain, skin grafts, sustained disability, and large medical costs. In fact, the wire account notably omits the potentially sensationalistic details of the disfiguring injury that were prominent at trial; the language is antiseptic and unrevealing. That the accident was indeed ordinary but the injury extraordinary—Stella Liebeck's fundamental claim—is difficult, at best, to discern from the news account. Liebeck was portrayed only as a plaintiff who claimed, blamed, and won big. In sum, the slant of the AP wire story favored McDonald's interpretive narrative about consumer irresponsibility and disadvantaged Liebeck's story of a dangerous product.

Important items implicating the corporation in the accident were included in the AP report, but selective dramatization and personalization pared down details essential to the plaintiff's arguments and the jury's verdict. As we might expect, the wire service fragmented the coffee case by its inclusions and exclusions. The story notes that Liebeck, her lawyer, and a juror contended that the "coffee was too hot." But the links to the defective product claim are indirect and implicit rather than explicit. The news account also specifies that the coffee temperature of 165–70 degrees was about 30 degrees hotter than most home-brewed coffee, and that complaints and lawsuits had been filed previously against McDonald's. These points, however, which were pivotal for the jury, are included only at the end of the news report. Conspicuously absent are the most important elements of the plaintiff's defective products narrative that convinced the jury and judge: (1) the scientific evidence from two noted experts about the celerity at which skin burns at 170–80 degrees, without which mere mention of coffee temperatures means little; (2) the details about the plaintiff's immense pain and disability; (3) the fact that a documented seven hundred complaints had been filed against McDonald's in recent years; (4) the fact that McDonald's administrators admitted the company knew about and ignored the palpable dangers of extremely hot coffee; and (5) the facts about the early stages of the dispute, including Liebeck's initial request for meager compensation, the plaintiff's multiple efforts over two years to settle that McDonald's spurned, the mediator's recommended award, and the like. Our previous generalization about news coverage is evidenced here in wire reportage of *Liebeck v. McDonald's Restaurants*—large awards make news while crucial details are discarded to make stories concise and accessible.

Whether the discarded facts were unknown or regarded as irrelevant or too esoteric by journalists, we can only guess.[15] But the inclusion of some key facts and the exclusion of others emphasized the large award to the plaintiff for a seemingly inconsequential mishap—a key contention in the narratives of individual greed disseminated by tort reformers—while obscuring essential elements of the legal argument that led jurors to find the corporation responsible for the painful injury in question. Failure to mention the legal grounding for that judgment in the Uniform Commercial Code or the plaintiff's multiple, amply evidenced arguments leaves readers to question whether the jury acted on either law or reason, much less both. The enigmatic final statement of the report underlined this question. Albeit "the jury found . . . that the coffee was defective" and "punitive damages" were justified, readers would have little idea why jurors decided as they did. That this case represented another incident of the litigation lottery would be a reasonable conclusion.

On balance, the concise spot news offered by the Associated Press thus conveyed much relevant information about the case, but it decontextualized the accident in ways that analysts of the news have led us to expect. The omissions and underemphases of the wire report repeated in many newspapers tended to discount the plaintiff's defective product narrative far more than McDonald's commonsensical frame stressing individual responsibility, which readers and journalists arguably had long been primed to presume in making sense of public events. While nothing in the wire report explicitly linked Stella Liebeck's suit to the alleged epidemic of silly suits afflicting the nation, the AP story reconstructed the case in such a way that left open, even invited, that linkage. The "man bites dog" angle of a person's being awarded $3 million in a suit over spilled coffee made this item far more newsworthy and culturally resonant, but also far less accurate and informative.

---

15. We asked many journalists about this. Some confirmed that scientific evidence is often considered too esoteric or technical to print in spot news. We expect that there is a routine filtering bias at work in this regard, which is part of the newsworthiness framing process. However, the most obvious reason for the absence of such facts in the news reports of the case is that no journalists were present at the trial to hear such evidence or to obtain a clear version of it.

Initial Print Reports: More Concision, Less Precision

Reports in the twenty-four newspapers in our Lexis-Nexis "Academic Universe" sample emulated the AP report.[16] As we expected, the AP stories were more copiously detailed than almost all stories run by clients who edited the wire copy.[17] Thus, inclusions and exclusions by the wires prevailed in newspapers. As table 6 demonstrates, newspapers varied in the wire-service inclusions they printed, but they rarely added elements omitted by the wires.[18]

Three patterns in table 6 characterize what made it into reports of *Liebeck v. McDonald's* and what was filtered out. We can see that four elements of the Liebeck victory were included in reports in *every* newspaper in our sample: the severity of the injuries, the stupendous award, the claim that McDonald's coffee was too hot, and description of the coffee spill.

A second pattern consists in elements regularly excluded altogether. Scientific testimony about the swiftness with which very hot liquids inflict severe burns surfaced only in the tenth sentence of the *Bergen (N.J.) Record*, not in the AP stories and not in stories in larger papers. Details about the extent and severity of the burns or the infirmity they caused were almost completely absent from the accounts. The *Houston Chronicle* commented

16. The other wire services reprinted in "Academic Universe" tracked the AP story sometimes verbatim, sometimes more briefly. Because the newspapers in our sample cited the AP and because the AP story is expansive relative to the other wires, we used the AP's morning report.

17. Only the *Houston Chronicle* and *Albuquerque Journal* (the latter unavailable in "Academic Universe" and hence not in our sample)—ostensibly due to Reed Morgan's residence and local relevance respectively—ran articles that were longer and more detailed.

18. Table 6 gives an overview of relative emphases in both the AP reports and subsequent newspapers accounts. It breaks down reports of the *Liebeck* verdict according to the information mentioned in each sentence of each report. Rows feature every print report we were able to locate by "Academic Universe." The morning and evening AP reports are highlighted for easy contrast with two dozen reports in newspapers. We array fifteen categories of information in an order determined by coverage. Having coded located articles published on August 18 or 19 in 1994 for the fifteen categories of data, we rearranged vertical columns (defined by categories of facts) and horizontal rows (defined by the news organs that published the articles) to maximize reproducibility. The advantage of a reproducible table is that newspaper articles range from the ones that covered the greatest number of categories of information (at the top of the table) to the ones that covered the fewest ("lower" rows of table 6), while the categories of information are ordered from the categories mentioned in at least one sentence in every report (the leftmost columns) to categories mentioned in not even one sentence of one article (the four rightmost columns). The large gray area on the right represents information that jurors heard and considered important during the trial but which was not covered in the news articles.

TABLE 6 Patterns of information in spot coverage of *Liebeck v. McDonald's*, August 18–19, 1994

	Liebeck's burn injuries	Jury award for damages	Allegations that coffee was too hot	Liebeck's spill of coffee	Reactions of parties to spill or judgment	McDonald's conduct and past complaints	Location of spill	Jury's reasoning or message	Adequate warnings on coffee cups?	Science of burns	Place in broader civil justice system	Sympathy for plaintiff	Initial claim, desire to settle	Litigiousness of plaintiff or others	Uniform Commercial Code	Total sentences	Total words
Associated Press AM 8-18	0-2, 16-17	0-1,	2, 5-7, 10-13, 18	6	9	8, 14-15	17	10-11	8							18	341
Phoenix Gazette	0-2, 15-16, 19	0-1, 3-4,	2, 5-7, 10-12, 17	1,		8, 13-14	16	10-12	8							19	330
Charleston Daily Mail	0-2, 12	0-1, 3-4	2, 5-7, 10		9	8, 11	10	10	8							12	273
Houston Chronicle	0-1, 16	3, 26-28, 33, 29-30, 32-33	2, 5-12, 17-24, 26	1, 14-15	4, 29, 33-34	13	14	30-32, 36, 38			37, 39					39	621
Chicago Sun Times	0-2, 5-10, 14	0-1, 3-4	2, 11-13, 17-18, 20-22	1, 5	19	14-15	1	17-18								22	340
Bergen Record	1, 11, 20-21	0-2, 6	4-5, 9, 12-18	1, 3, 20	8	3	6-7			10						21	324
Associated Press PM 8-18	0-1, 6-7	0-1, 12-13	2-3, 9-10, 13	1, 5-6	11	3-4	5	8								13	205
Charleston Gazette	0-1, 6-7	0-1, 12-13	2-3, 9-10, 13	1, 5-6	11	3-4, 13	5	8								13	205

Greensboro News & Rec.	0–1, 6–7	0–1, 12–13	2–3, 9–11, 13	1, 5–6	11	3–4	5	8, 10							13	204
Memphis Com. Ap.	0–1, 6	0–1	2–3	1, 5–6	7	3–4	5								7	132
Atlanta Jo. & Const.	1, 6–7	1	2–3	1, 5		3–4	5–6								7	132
Louisville Cour. Jo.	1–2	1, 3–4	0, 2, 6–7	1											7	127
USA Today	2, 6–12	2–3, 20	0, 13–15, 17	2, 6	4, 16	18									20	256
Wall Street Journal	0–2, 5	0–1, 3	2, 6–8	1	4										8	151
Des Moines Register	1–2	0–1, 3–4	2, 6	1	5										6	116
New York Times	0–2	0–1, 3	2	1	4										4	67
Dayton Daily News	1–2	1	0, 3–4	1			2								4	78
The Columbian 8–18	1, 5–6	0–1	2–3	1, 4–5			4								6	186
St. Petersburg Times	0–1, 3	1–2	2, 4–6	0–1											6	117
Atlanta Jo. & Const.	0–2	0–1, 3–4	2, 5–7	1											7	161
Chicago Sun Times 8–18	1	1	2–3	1		3–4									4	85
Arkansas Dem. Gaz.	1	1	1–2	1				1							2	59
Denver Post	1–2	1, 3	2	1											3	71
Boston Herald	0–2	1, 3	2	1											3	69
Seattle Post Int.	1–2	1	2	1											2	49
Washington Post	1–2	1	2	1											2	48
Total headlines	14	14	3	2	0	0	0	0	0	0	0	0	0	0	—	—
Mean first mention	1.04	1.12	2.5	1.23	7.92	6.58	6.77	10.8	8	10	37	—	—	—	—	—
Total sentences	77	64	117	43	18	24	14	20	3	1	2	0	0	0	268	—

Note: All articles appeared August 19, 1994, unless otherwise noted. Entries in cells are the ordinal numbers of sentences, counting from the headline (0). Italicized column headings mark information that jurors reported to be crucial to their verdict but reporters seldom relayed.

on routine civil justice cases in its thirty-seventh and thirty-ninth sentences; no other source in table 6 so contextualized the Albuquerque anomaly. Not even one source mentioned the Uniform Commercial Code or the initial inclination of the plaintiff to settle without filing suit or, later, to settle without trial. All sources avoided characterizing the plaintiff as litigious or either party as sympathetic.

A third pattern involves selective inclusions. Some elements in table 6 correlated with the length (in sentences) of articles. Only three articles (including the AP morning report) raised the presence or adequacy of warnings about the temperature of the coffee. About one-third of the reports listed in table 6 devoted one or more sentences to the jurors' reasoning, despite the quotation from juror Richard Anglada in the AP report. Slightly more papers and both the AP morning and evening reports placed the car at the side of the lot or Liebeck in the passenger seat, and the same number of sources mentioned the intransigence of McDonald's concerning past complaints and lawsuits. More sources than not mentioned reactions to the verdict, if only in single sentences in all but two instances.

These three patterns and other data in table 6 reveal much about reporting during phase 1. The four elements invariably covered—the burns, the awards, the temperature of McDonald's coffee, and the spill—also led the other elements in the total number of sentences that made reference to the element, in the priority (that is, how low the number) of the first mention of the element in the article, and in being part of headlines. These four provided a succinct, simple sequence: a woman spills coffee in her lap, sues McDonald's for making coffee so hot it severely burned her, and gets millions. This sequence preserved the perceived irrationality, if not absurdity, of an extravagant award in a case making a novel claim about an everyday occurrence.

If those four elements are all that the reader may learn about the story—and in about half of the newspapers sampled they are all or almost all of the crucial elements of the story that we found—then newspapers' reports were not merely fragmentary, as the wire stories were, but reductionist. The patterns discussed above and the totals below table 6 testify to the elements missing from most or many articles and scanted in most or all: past complaints about and lawsuits against McDonald's; the impassivity and indifference evident in the testimony of McDonald's officials; the low-ball offer extended to Stella Liebeck for her crippling injuries, extensive rehabilitation, and onerous expenses; the contrasting mindsets of plaintiff and jurors; the location of the car in the lot and of Liebeck in the car; and the presence and usefulness of warnings on cups. Each element that, by itself, would have made the story less bizarre—the science of burns; Ms. Liebeck's initial request for $20,000 in expenses; and the Uniform Commercial Code—was filtered out of almost all reports.

In sum, table 6 shows how newspapers constructed the story of the McDonald's coffee case to suit news worth at considerable cost in precision and comprehensiveness. That the initial reports suited the defense's interpretive narrative stressing individual responsibility far better than the plaintiff's narrative of defective products liability or the jury's decision was an unintended boon for McDonald's and, as we shall see, for tort reform in the public relations battle that followed the case.

Phase 1 Features and Commentaries: Enter the Spin and Factoids

To be sure, pundits might have distorted the coffee case for partisan, ideological, policy, or satirical purposes no matter how well spot reports had conveyed the facts. Fragmentary or reductionist reportage, however, left editorialists and commentators free to fill in omissions with incorrect or misleading information. Even if the misinformation that saturated print media after August 18, 1994, were not a result of fragmentary coverage, the predominance of interpretations would probably still have assumed that Stella Liebeck was solely and personally responsible for the accident and that McDonald's was utterly blameless. Gaps in public knowledge about the specifics of the case simply made it easier to impute greater moral blame to Liebeck, the injured victim.

Features on reactions to the *Liebeck* verdict, editorials, and letters to the editor tended to gloss over the most technical information on which the plaintiff's case depended, thereby divorcing commentators' views ever further from the case the jurors actually heard. On the Web site accompanying this book (www.lawslore.info), we have systematically arrayed these data in a way that is similar to table 6, and here we just summarize and illustrate those findings. As with spot reports, burns and monetary awards drew widespread comment, albeit averaging only about two-and-a-half sentences per category. The heat of McDonald's coffee, Liebeck's allegation that its temperature was "too hot," and the specifics of the spill elicited even more sentences than information about the injury and award. That the car was parked to the side of the drive-through and was not moving remained matters for but passing comment. These differences are significant, for they display the alacrity with which the known facts and fact patterns were arrayed against the plaintiff. Most important, *information pertaining to the litigiousness of the plaintiff drew the most sentences of any category,* despite that category's having elicited not a single mention in spot coverage (see the column fourth from the right margin in table 6) and despite the defense's having presented no evidence that an octogenarian who had never before sued anyone was trifling with McDonald's or trying to pull a fast one.

Spotty coverage left commentators and editorialists free to adopt differing perspectives on the case's justifiability and significance and to marshal information to suit their presuppositions. Some articles required no embellishing of the story to assail the jury for failing to use common sense and value individual responsibility. Diana Griego Erwin's editorial for the *San Diego Union-Tribune* recounted the facts of the case accurately and without unfair spin, but imputed litigiousness to Stella Liebeck and unfairness to the jurors (Erwin 1994). Far more commentators, however, fell back on stereotypes and shibboleths to accentuate apparent absurdities that had made the case newsworthy. An earlier brief comment in the *San Diego Union-Tribune* (1994) immediately sounded the tort reform refrain with the headline "Java Hijack" and gave short shrift to Liebeck's injuries, to her repeatedly spurned efforts to settle for modest compensation, to the litany of complaints and lawsuits against McDonald's, and to inadequate warnings about the dangers of hot liquids. The editorial read in its entirety:

> When Stella Liebeck fumbled her coffee cup as she rode in the car with her grandson, she might as well have bought a winning lottery ticket. The spilled coffee netted her $2.9 million in the form of a jury award. Liebeck had sued McDonald's for serving take-out coffee that her lawyer claimed was too hot. This absurd judgment is a stunning illustration of what is wrong with America's civil justice system. Ironically, it also may become a powerful spur to the cause of tort reform. Our guess is that other greedy copycats in restaurants throughout America soon will be happily dumping coffee into their laps in a bid to make a similar killing in the courtroom.

Amid hyperbole and misstatements, the *Union-Tribune* mischaracterized the events of the accident. It is untrue that Liebeck fumbled her cup "as she rode," a fact that was known to jurors but mangled in several instances of print reportage. Editorial writers for the *Arizona Republic* (1994) veered into a statement that contradicted their own coverage of the spot news: Ms. Liebeck "tried to open the cup in a moving car . . . ." Just days after the verdict, in sum, misinformation began to alter the story in a manner that inaccurately highlighted the plaintiff's recklessness. The fact that commentators filled in often inaccurate details about the "reckless" nature of the accident underscores the inclination to focus on matters of individual responsibility and the opening left by fragmentary initial reports that emphasized the incongruities between coffee spilled and millions awarded.

Other commentaries were festooned with misleading factoids. Talk-show host Mike Rosen (1994) excoriated jurors' decisionmaking while minimizing the evidence on the basis of which the jurors had decided. Amid a welter of presumptions about lawsuit epidemics and what the economics of litigation would teach, Rosen acknowledged that Stella Liebeck was a passenger and did not say whether the car she was in was moving. Skipping over the multitude of complaints about McDonald's coffee and the science of burns and mentioning the issue of warnings in but one sentence, Rosen then attacked jurors who had issued "[t]he latest winner in the Stupid Lawsuit Sweepstakes."

> Our nation's suing epidemic may enrich some plaintiffs and their lawyers, but it all shows up as overhead on society. Perhaps prospective jurors should be required to attend a seminar on the economics of litigation. Maybe, then, they wouldn't be so generous. Or better yet: if a ridiculous award like this is reversed on appeal, how about letting the defendants sue the jury.[*sic*]

Jurors were not educated in the economics of litigation, but they did learn about pertinent law. Had news reports similarly instructed Rosen about the relevant official law, he might not have dismissed the suit out of hand. The same could be said regarding systematic patterns of personal injury litigation over recent decades. Regular readers of the news would find there precious little reason for complex, much less skeptical thinking, about the alleged epidemic of lawsuits and the "litigation lottery."

The champion at twisting the case and, to some extent, the harbinger of conventional beliefs to come was Dave Rossie (1994). His column in the *Denver Post* glossed over other lawsuits and complaints about McDonald's coffee, the science of burns, the degree of treatment those burns required, and adequate warnings, all of which were integral to the products liability case advanced by the plaintiff. He then compounded these sins of omission with others of commission. Rossie began his commentary with the hackneyed non sequitur that the *Liebeck* decision proved that the United States was the most litigious society on the planet, then accused the Associated Press of having excluded inconvenient details about the case. He followed those broadsides with speculative details (number of physicians involved) and convenient factoids, including dramatic mischaracterizations regarding the coffee's heat, Liebeck's status in the vehicle, and the jury's punitive justification (rather than "pain and suffering") for the bulk of the award—all inaccuracies that could not have been derived from the AP report.

After snidely jabbing lawyers for "their fees," Mr. Rossie then slandered civil jurors in general: "[M]ore often than not, when confronted by a giant, corporation of uncounted wealth on the one hand and the lone individual, especially a little old lady, on the other, the jury is going to come down on the side of the individual." Rossie adduced no evidence to show that the Albuquerque jurors had merely punished the deep-pocketed fast-food corporation.[19] Mr. Rossie concluded that the *Liebeck* case "should never have gone to trial. The judge should have tossed it before the first May it please the court.[*sic*]" Had the Associated Press provided a more complete account or had Dave Rossie researched the case, he might have discovered the latent truth of his first sentiment: the case should never have gone to trial because McDonald's had multiple opportunities to settle. His comment that the judge should have thrown the case out was based on profound ignorance of the facts and law at issue in the case, an ignorance aided and abetted by selective news coverage.

To summarize: spot coverage of phase 1 featured few outright errors, but commentators filled in omissions in reporting with faulty inference and invention. In such a manner did concise, fragmentary coverage foster a flood of factoids and derisive spin about the accident, which quickly morphed into a fashionable fable about a civil legal system gone awry and the triumph of a predatory plaintiff and litigious lawyer.

THE LEGEND GROWS: SUBSEQUENT PHASES OF COVERAGE

Subsequent phases of print news coverage of *Liebeck v. McDonald's* conjured a case increasingly distant from the one the jurors actually heard. Testimony the jurors had found significant was omitted, and misleading or inaccurate facts interjected. But there was more trenchant commentary berating the decline of individual responsibility in American society. We briefly summarize the trends.[20]

Phase 2 Coverage in Newspapers: Second Chances

On September 1, 1994, two developments might have changed the evolving story of Stella Liebeck. First, trial judge Robert Scott directed the parties toward a mediator. Second, a front-page article in the *Wall Street Journal* revealed much about the *Liebeck* case that had been obscured in or

---

19. Lest we assist Rossie in misinforming the citizenry, we note that abundant scholarship undermines his facile claim that juries tend to side with underdogs or against corporations. See Hans 2000.

20. Our summary here of phases 2–5 is presented in much greater detail in McCann, Haltom, and Bloom 2001.

omitted from earlier coverage. These two events constitute a second stage in the Liebeck litigation.

The directed mediation had little impact on the general knowledge about the *Liebeck* case because, as far as we could find, only the Associated Press and the *Chicago Sun Times* carried the story. These reports were, predictably, sketchy and perfunctory, making for an even more fragmentary, decontextualized public account. The AP also added an important error by stating that Stella Liebeck spilled the coffee at the drive-through window, rather than nearly four minutes later once parked. But what is more important is the lack of any post-trial coverage whatsoever by any of the other twenty-two papers that covered the verdict. This omission is not merely a matter of concern for scholars who expect more of the news. Noncoverage of post-trial events facilitated misconceptions. It not only failed to educate, but also misled. When editorialists argued as if the McDonald's coffee case ended in the Albuquerque courtroom on August 18 and letter writers seemed unaware that punitive damages are commonly reduced by trial judges and appellate judges, both may have been relying on spot reports that treated civil judgments as *faits accomplis.*

The other potential stimulus, Andrea Gerlin's investigation of the *Liebeck* case as jurors saw it, had enormous potential for broadening and deepening understanding of the lawsuit and verdict. Gerlin (1994) explained in the *Wall Street Journal* how jurors reasonably could have reached judgments that pundits had ridiculed and editorialists had pronounced absurd or stupid. She found it easier to understand, if not agree with, the jury once she learned about major facts and legal arguments that had shaped their reasoning. Gerlin recounted McDonald's long-standing and extensive record of scalding its customers. She reviewed testimony from McDonald's officials and experts that made the corporation appear nonchalant and even callous. She reported on the severity of the burns, on the impact that photographs of Liebeck's injuries had had on jurors, and on some scientific evidence regarding the celerity of burns. Gerlin uncovered reasons for sympathizing with Stella Liebeck, reasons that had hitherto received but the shortest shrift. To be sure, Gerlin's piece glossed over some aspects of the case. Nowhere did she inform readers that the grandson was driving or that the car was parked away from the window. She also skimped on how the science of burns suggested the urgency of reducing the temperature of hot liquids, on the legal basis for the judgment, and on the long history of the dispute prior to trial. But, overall, the account reflected the complexity of the trial and was well researched—but available and accessible nonetheless.

Despite the excellence of Andrea Gerlin's report, any potential for at least some increased understanding about the case was not impressively realized. Only seven additional news sources (of the twenty-four in table 6) produced articles that wholly or largely reprinted Gerlin's *Wall Street Journal* report. These articles generally repeated but supplemented phase 1 coverage by adding additional information about McDonald's record of past scaldings, complaints, and litigation; resistance and recalcitrance; and flaunting and flouting of standards for coffee in the fast-food industry. But even the slightly augmented and more balanced factual record did not inhibit editorialists from criticizing the case and chastising its prinicipal actors. For example, a version of Gerlin's report in the *Cincinnati Enquirer* (1994) added these judgments:

> Unfortunately, cases like these have destroyed the credibility of the justice system, giving Americans a picture of bone-headed jurors giving away millions for cuts and scrapes at the demand of greedy gold-diggers and their ambulance-chasing lawyers. . . . Personal responsibility has been scrapped for the notion that someone can be made to pay for any mistake—including opening a cup of hot coffee between your legs while driving.

Tort reformers could not have articulated the theme of individual responsibility at the heart of their moral crusade any better!

Why did Gerlin's correction appear to have made so little difference? Pundit Dave Rossie may be right that dailies choose not to recognize shortcomings and superficiality in their coverage.[21] Having missed crucial details in the first place, most papers may have been averse to revisiting a matter no longer timely. Absent the factual update, commentators were left to fill in missing details as suited their moralistic spin. When journalistic omissions and commissions mutually reinforce one another, erroneous factoids result and familiar story lines (here echoing tort reformers) find implicit support.

Phase 3 Coverage in Newspapers: More Omissions and More Factoids

When Judge Scott inaugurated phase 3 by reducing the punitive damages by over 80 percent to three times the compensatory damages, the press had an opportunity to correct its previous omissions of details about the case and to educate the public about how the civil legal system routinely works. Instead, crucial omissions persisted and errors of commission proliferated.

---

21. Our interviews with journalists confirmed this point quite emphatically, especially regarding trying to "make up" for earlier omissions.

We found two wire-service stories that announced Judge Scott's action but only fifteen spot reports in newspapers, two of them in the *Chicago Sun-Times*. The good news is that about 61 percent of the papers followed the reduction of punitive damages—the sort of development often under-reported. The bad news is that the 39 percent reduction in coverage exacerbated the original holler of the dollar. In many locales, even diligent readers would find no story of the decrease in their daily, making them more likely to remember only the original award but not its reduction. Indeed, attention to money increased in these accounts as attention to the original injury declined (see McCann, Haltom, and Bloom 2001). Little wonder that even well-informed commentators missed the reduction. This understandable omission conformed the story to *news* framing but deformed the *legal* frame that the jury had accepted.

Other omissions continued to track the original reports fairly closely. At the same time, errors of commission proliferated and distanced the case as reported even farther from the one the jury heard. For example, errors about the location and mobility of the Ford Probe dotted editorials and features during phrase 3. Six of the nine editorials and letters we found between September 15 and December 1 once again made some reference to the drive-through window. Some comments were wildly inaccurate. The *Greensboro News and Record* accurately placed the plaintiff in the passenger's seat but distorted the locale of the accident: "Liebeck, who had put the cup of coffee between her legs while riding through the drive-thru, spilled it on her lap when she tried to pry off the lid" (Pressley 1994). A *Cleveland Plain Dealer* editorial (written by a high school student) made a similar error (Vakil 1994). In addition, five of the nine articles linked the case to excessive litigiousness, with the *Providence Journal-Bulletin* devoting numerous sentences to the charge (Martin 1994); none of the commentaries expressed sympathy or support for Stella Liebeck.

Phase 4: The Case Settles and the Legend Is Set

On November 30, 1994, McDonald's settled with Stella Liebeck for an undisclosed sum. Spot coverage about the end of the formal dispute marked a fourth phase and completed the story for most reporters. We located sixteen spot reports in fourteen newspapers, most on December 2. After news of the settlement, the *Liebeck* case surfaced in only a few articles in the remainder of 1994. Phase 4, then, represents a resolution of reportage, after which the case largely yielded to widespread factoids.

In phase 4, omissions—especially involving evidence about the effects of hot coffee and the response of McDonald's to complaints—increased again as spot coverage crystallized for a last time. The dollar continued to holler even as Liebeck's "jackpot" actually shrank, perhaps because agreement on money resolved the dispute. Even coverage regarding the award was somewhat mixed: the only relevant headlines we found referred to injuries rather than money. Having hollered dollar awards to accentuate the absurdity of millions for an everyday mishap (and to increase the news value of the report), print media now alluded vaguely to how little Liebeck and her attorneys may have gotten, mainly because McDonald's made confidentiality legally binding. Papers lost the hype of the hollered dollar but could not provide an alternative to the gaudy figure of initial reports. As a result, editorialists and commentators continue to use wildly inflated figures for Stella's award. Other distortions, such as where Stella was when she spilled the coffee, ossified into accepted fact, further indicting the victim as responsible.

Phase 5 Begins: McDonald's Lost the Battle but Liebeck Lost the War

The end of 1994 formed a cusp between the first four phases of the story about Stella Liebeck and McDonald's and the extended fifth stage that began with the settlement and continues today. We located but four references to the *Liebeck* case during the remainder of 1994 after spot reports of the settlement. All four, in different newspapers,[22] were Scott Montgomery's discourse on blame-avoidance (Montgomery 1994). Approximately 114 of his 1,600 words pertained to the McDonald's case. Tracking earlier editorials, Montgomery emphasized Liebeck's responsibility for the spill and the lamentable litigiousness that her case represented.

As was the case in commentaries during the third phase, the *Liebeck* case had been distilled in editorials, features, and comments to a very shallow account. This account related briefly elements indispensable for identifying the case: hollering dollars, burned skin, spilt coffee, and reaction from McDonald's Corporation or counsel. The overwhelming focus of the treatment, however, was on Stella Liebeck's failure to take personal responsibility for her clumsiness and her litigious inclinations toward blaming her misfortune on a corporation with deep pockets. In short, by the start of phase 5, the interpretive narrative extolling individual responsibility had obliterated the narrative about defective products liability that had motivated the plaintiff and persuaded the jury. To be certain, given its ideological pull in our society, the invocation of "individual responsibility" against the plaintiff's greed, adversarialism, and rights obsession might

22. Our search in "Academic Universe" did not turn up all references. See, for example, Pelline 1994.

have triumphed anyway. Emphasis on elements and interpretations that redounded to the benefit of the defendant and, far more important, omission of information and arguments crucial to the plaintiff's case, certainly assisted that triumph, however. Omissions from otherwise solid spot coverage in effect disguised and distorted the actual claims made by Stella that were assessed favorably by the jury and trial judge. We should not wonder, then, that "the McDonald's Coffee Lady" became a symbol for undeserved victory in the "litigation lottery."

Indeed, over the subsequent years newspaper references to the incident were common if widely variable in type (editorial, letter to editor, advice column, humor column, and the like) and location. Not only was the *Liebeck* case often recalled, but disputes over hot liquids in other settings increasingly received attention in the news (see Greenlee 1997, 738 n. 57). Moreover, invocations of Stella's saga proliferated in commentaries, with inaccuracies increasing in relative proportion to self-righteous moralizing. Closing out the year, Jeff Pelline wrote in the *San Francisco Chronicle* (1994) that "America has a victim complex," as witnessed by "such surreal cases as the woman who recently won a $2.7 million verdict after spilling coffee on her leg in a McDonald's restaurant." A few months later, a *New York Times* editorial (1995) similarly invoked Stella Liebeck as a symbol for a society run off of its tracks. "Life used to be blissfully simple: the coffee hot, the drinker sitting and sipping. But now everyone's hither and yon, perching take-out coffee in mid-dash. And spilling it. And suing someone." Around the same time, an editorial in the *Oakland Tribune* (1995) began by making our own point quite concisely, but for a different purpose: "There is probably one in the paper today. . . . A numbing tale of a citizen hauling someone into court over something absurd." This rant continued:

> The poster woman for this sort of ludicrous lawsuit is an 81 year old [sic] New Mexico woman who sued McDonald's after she spilled her hot McDonald's coffee in her lap. . . .
>
> Is there any doubt in anyone's mind that our legal system is being badly abused? Greedy lawyers, victims out to make a buck, and a culture that encourages people to sue instead of accepting their own responsibility or working things out, have clogged with cases that don't belong there.

Humorist Dave Barry included inaccurate references to the hot coffee judgment on his list of major reasons for wonder about American society at the start of 1995; he titled his retrospective essay "A Great Year for Victims." Columnist Joseph Perkins of the *San Diego Union-Tribune* even named an annual award "The Stellas."[23] "The award is named for Stella Liebeck, the Albuquerque, N.M. woman who became an instant million-aire—and American icon—after spilling a cup of McDonald's coffee in her lap and winning a judgment against the fast-food chain" (Perkins 1997). Ann Landers added the dispute to her own columns regularly dispensing "common sense" about moral responsibility to the American public. An angry reader is quoted as saying about Stella Liebeck that "she was a ma-lingering old biddy who pumped up her alleged injuries to get more money. [F]ar from being a victory for the consumer, this case merely en-courages unethical, greedy lawyers and their greedy clients to continue to perpetuate such frauds on gullible juries."

The legend of Stella has lived on in newspapers until the present. Spot news coverage of lawsuits for excessively hot liquids or pickles on ham-burgers or a chicken head among the new fried chicken wings at McDon-ald's provide one form of enduring reference keeping alive memory of the original case and what it represented. In the high-profile article with which we began this chapter, heralded entertainer Steve Martin satirized the hot coffee case as the epitome of justice in advanced Western civiliza-tion. One feature of phase 5 coverage is especially notable if, by this point, unsurprising. Whereas quoted reactions regarding the judgment in the first four phases were dominated by those sympathetic to the winning plaintiff (Liebeck's attorney, juror, and so forth), by phase 5 cited authori-ties and experts were critical of the judgment and/or Stella by more than a two-to-one margin.[24]

BLAMING THE VICTIM: STELLA LIEBECK IN MASS CULTURE

The transformation of the scalding coffee case into a classic tort tale and Stella Liebeck into the poster lady for tort reform burgeoned outside news-papers. Indeed, the diffusion of the inverted, factoid-riddled morality tale throughout the electronic media, mass culture, and political discourse was so rapid, dramatic, and sustained that every reader of this sentence must be familiar with some invocation of the symbol that Stella Liebeck has become.[25] In this section we briefly catalogue just some of the venues in which the story was replicated, usually in derisively cartoonish terms. In doing so, we not only elaborate on the dissemination of the McDonald's

23. Compare "The True Stella Awards" available at www.stellaawards.com.

24. The data were derived from our data set of five top newspapers during 1995–98.

25. A quick Google search in December 2002, under the name "Stella Liebeck," produced 1,280 citations.

coffee chronicle, but demonstrate through the case study the ways that representations by print media and other media of popular culture are continuously interrelated in constructing knowledge and lore about the law.[26]

Television News Coverage

We found thirty-eight transcripts of spot news television broadcasts mentioning the verdict (fourteen national, twenty-four local) in the two days after the jury award was announced. For the most part, this coverage was similar to the newspaper coverage in what it did and did not provide for public consumption, although it was even less substantial and accurate in content than the print versions. Accounts were riddled with the same errors and, more important, omissions of critical elements heard at the trial, thus again emphasizing the recklessness of the accident over the dangerous product. One important difference from spot coverage in newspapers was that local television broadcasts often openly ridiculed the decision that they reported as news. One report joked with a pun about "burned buns" at McDonald's.[27] Another sardonically reported that Liebeck (after "she spilled coffee on herself in a McDonald's restaurant") said, "hot coffee is terrible on the groin and buttocks."[28] Yet another report quoted a customer and an attorney who both said they thought "the suit was stupid," offered no parallel defenses of the suit, and ended by pointing to Liebeck "explaining how to get rich after spilling a hot beverage on their [*sic*] crotch."[29]

Newsmagazines and Newsletters

Newsmagazines also expanded public knowledge of the hot coffee incident, usually in similarly abridged, misleading, often inaccurate tort tale-like versions. Indeed, a quick search of "Academic Universe" identified numerous mentions for "McDonald's and coffee and burn or scald" in *Newsweek, Time, Business Week, US News and World Report,* and *Forbes* between August 1994 and January 1, 2000.[30] Most such accounts echoed the

26. We take seriously the advice of media scholar Benjamin Page that "we need to pay attention to the totality of political information that is made available . . . to the public" (1996, 7).

27. See KABC 1994b.

28. See KABC 1994a.

29. See KTTV 1994.

30. One notable exception, providing balanced and sophisticated coverage, was Press 1995.

critical editorials in the newspapers—full of misleading errors, focused on the accident rather than the product, and again openly disdainful of what they saw as an irresponsible plaintiff and the capricious legal system.

TV News Features and Talk Shows

Stella Liebeck's saga played widely on television feature news and interview shows. For example, the case was mentioned, and Stella's daughter interviewed, shortly after the trial on *Larry King.* Perhaps the most incendiary treatment was on an ABC special, "The Blame Game: Are We a Country of Victims?" hosted by the controversial John Stossel (ABC John Stossel Special 1995). Like his later attack on the civil legal system, "The Trouble with Lawyers" (ABC John Stossel Special 1997), Stossel combined selected anecdotes, assorted facts, and a barrage of leading rhetorical questions into a mix of caustic casuistry and diverting entertainment. The show began provocatively by citing the McDonald's coffee case as one of several examples of business owners' complaints about "what's wrong with America?" In short, claims one interviewee, "everybody's a damn victim. . . . We have so much to give, and so many who take." The show later used a highly selective, simplified cartoon version of the story to illustrate what Stossel posed as a fundamental breakdown in Americans' individual responsibility, civil law, and culture. Roger Conner, of the American Alliance for Rights and Responsibilities, capped the sermon:

> The word of these lawsuits spills out into society, enters into the national conversation. And people start thinking that this is the appropriate way to live. . . . It makes people think, I'd be a chump if I did otherwise. If I take responsibility for what I do and for what happens to me, I'm a fool. Now, when that idea gets loose, America's in trouble. . . . This whole victimization, it's like a—it's like a disease that's weakening America's moral fiber.

A host of other shows on virtually every major channel offered up similar invocations for responsibility that ripped the hot coffee case, the plaintiff, and the judgment. In fall of 2002, we heard commentator Andy Rooney conclude a *60 Minutes* broadcast by recycling clichéd rants that "suing has become a popular American pastime," using Stella Liebeck— "the woman who spilled coffee in her lap in a car and got big bucks when she sued McDonald's because the coffee was too hot"—as a prime example, among other tortured tales (Rooney 2002). Rooney surmised that he perhaps he could quit work and get rich just by suing people, but his last gambit for a chuckle was that lawyers would receive 90 percent of the awards. With populist pundits like this, reformers barely need tell any tales.

Late-Night Television

Given the ridicule that permeated ostensibly serious news coverage, it is not surprising that late-night talk show hosts appropriated Stella Liebeck's saga for their own comic routines. Most prominent among these was Jay Leno, who on several occasions joked about the case. Attorney Reed Morgan told us that he wrote Leno in protest, and Leno actually called him in response.[31] However, Leno continued to make jokes about scalding spills of McDonald's coffee at least through February 9, 2001. David Letterman also made reference to the hot coffee liability issue a number of times over several years; one short, indirect, but very clear reference is included as one of the epigraphs to this chapter.

Prime-Time Television Comedy

Viewers who do not stay up to watch late-night television could catch a longer comic take on the dispute over spilled coffee on the wildly popular *Seinfeld* (1995) show. The specific episode, titled "The Maestro," initially ran October 5, 1995, and has been rerun many times. The show focuses on the aftermath of an incident in which the zany and socially inept Kramer spills coffee on himself when trying to sneak a cup of latte into a movie theater by stuffing it into his pants. After filing a lawsuit, he confronts his friend Jerry, who expresses surprise at Kramer's litigiousness. That prompts Kramer to reply "Oh, I can be quite litigious,"[32] another epigraph for this chapter.

The Movies

A bit to our surprise, we have found the coffee incident to be alluded to in only one major movie—*Good Bye Lover* (1999), starring Ellen DeGeneres. Discarding a newspaper, DeGeneris's character exclaims, "See, now this just makes me sick. A woman spills coffee on herself and gets three million dollars. I do that every day and what do I get? Coffee stains!"

Corporate Advertisements

It took a while, it seems, but eventually the advertising industry appropriated references and images of the case for humorous promotions as well. We found national magazine advertisements for a major hot choco-

31. Interview with Reed Morgan. Authors' files.
32. For extensive analysis of this show and its implications, see Greenlee 1997.

late product ("Change is bad" is the caption under a cup with warnings about heat on it) and television commercials for both a major phone company and several automobile manufacturers that made explicit references to the hot coffee case. A quotation from an automobile ad serves as yet another epigraph to this chapter. In a like advertisement, a little girl says, "Here's a scalding hot cup of tea, Grandma" in the back seat of a Mercedes-Benz careening over rough roads. The fact that corporations could so blithely appropriate the image to promote their products reflects both the dominant story line attached to the coffee case in mass-mediated culture and the privileged position of corporate producers in that culture.

The Tort Tale Endures

We have sampled merely a few of the many forums in which the McDonald's coffee case has become a prominent part of the prevailing legal lore in America. In fact, as one of us sat writing an early draft of this chapter on July 13, 2000, National Public Radio reported that a man had sued after being scalded by a coffee in a restaurant. He insisted that ceramic cups should have warning labels on them. The judge denied the claim, asking, "What next? Warnings on steak knives?" Such a report obviously was intended as humorous fluff amid the serious news. But it would not be funny without the lingering legacy of *Liebeck*. A few months later, readers were bombarded with similarly derisive reports about a woman suing McDonald's over a hot pickle (see *Seattle Times* 2000). Shortly thereafter, we saw a *Ziggy* cartoon showing a coffee machine with a sign reading WARNING: DO NOT POUR IN LAP! and Ziggy lamenting, "Everybody's so **litigious** these days!" (fig. 6), confirming the familiar usage of the "L" word to convey a bold moral message in contemporary mass discourse. Regarding references to the hot coffee case, the *Oakland Tribune* had it nearly right: "There is probably one in the paper today." But, again, the cultural references to the case far transcend the print news. In 2001, one of us learned that a Mexican restaurant in Burlington, Vermont, featured a sign in the women's restroom reading (in English and Spanish): CAUTION: WATER MAY BE HOTTER THAN A MCDONALD'S COFFEE (fig. 7).[33]

ANALYSIS: THE MEDIA CONSTRUCT A TALE,
RECONSTRUCT LEGALITY

The story of Stella Liebeck's being scalded by McDonald's coffee demonstrates in great detail how ordinary news reporting practices choose particular types of events and construct them for the reading public in highly

33. We have not altered the Spanish version to correct a solecism.

FIGURE 6 The litigation crisis becomes cartoon common sense

selective and problematic ways. But why did this atypical legal case come to be so typically newsworthy? While many factors were involved, the juxtaposition of a familiar accident with a seemingly astounding award provided a perfect mix of the personal, dramatic, and normal that the press loves, all bound together in a discrete incident. Aspects of the case fit almost perfectly the standard conventions of news worth for infotainment coverage. For one thing, the disputing parties fit very familiar images: an elderly female claimant and the most familiar, ubiquitous family restaurant chain in the world. That nearly everyone has taken out food and beverages from a McDonald's drive-through no doubt mattered also. Moreover, the fact that nearly all persons have spilled hot coffee, or hot chocolate or tea, on themselves likewise highlights the routine character of the case. What infotainment could *not* handle well—including those aspects of the defective products liability narrative that persuaded jurors—could be omitted from coverage without notice.

As a result of both news worth conventions and routine exposure to

FIGURE 7 Sign on bathroom wall at the Coyote Café, Burlington, Vermont, 2001

Photograph by Candace L. Smith

parallel tort tale narratives, the widespread coverage of this case (1) privileged certain facts that fit the predilections for personalized and dramatized stories while omitting other information, issues, and story lines in ways that left the account highly fragmented and routinized; (2) provided little attention to the key facts and narrative logic that proved successful in the official trial phase; (3) failed to provide perspective for this particular, atypical case relative to broader patterns in civil disputing; and (4) represented an event in ways that were open to, and even invited, interpretations consistent with the tort reform agenda by elite news spinners and the mass audience. Thin, selective initial coverage quickly gave way to a simplistic anecdotal version of the story that has become a staple of American conventional wisdom about law, a notable chapter of "law's lore."

This case study also reveals parallels and interconnections between newspaper coverage and that of other media that participate in cultural knowledge production—especially television daily news, news features, talk shows, and comedy shows as well as radio, movies, and public forums of official politics—in our infotainment-oriented society. Our evidence suggests that this broader complex of technologically mediated information production today may be even more conducive to legend production than that of newspapers alone. Moreover, attention to multiple media manifestations of the hot coffee story distinguishes its impact from familiar "big" stories in the news. The infamous story of Stella Liebeck did not hit the public over the head in one huge mass attack of front-page headlines. Rather, the repetition of short, thin accounts and brief allusions in multiple media over a sustained period of time quietly turned a real victim into a caricature familiar across the U.S. legal and political culture.

The argument in the previous section is not intended to suggest that sophisticated tort reformers contributed little instrumental influence in the rapid rise of Stella Liebeck as a symbol for a legal system gone awry. For one thing, the preceding fifteen or so years of concerted tort reform advocacy assaulting the legal system and personal injury lawyers conditioned the context of media reporting, elite discourse, and public understanding so that the McDonald's coffee case attained such symbolic significance so quickly (rather than being regarded as an aberration). The tort reform movement and corporate campaign to impugn the legal system and celebrate norms of individual responsibility provided a public appetite and familiar menu that the McDonald's case served very well (Galanter 1993b, 1998b; Daniels and Martin 1995). That the movement's standard charges against the legal system found, or generated, allies among newspaper editors and columnists and credibility among letter writers is clear.

Moreover, tort reformers contributed directly to accelerating and sustaining the continuing familiarity of the story in the ongoing fifth phase of the story's public life (since 1995). While the appointed spokespersons and spinners for tort reform did not influence the initial phases of the public interpretation, they subsequently had a field day with the McDonald's coffee case. "Tort reformers . . . gleefully seized on the case as the epitome of frivolity, " confirms one observer (Torry 1995, F7). The incident became a staple on the list of "horror stories" maintained by the American Tort Reform Association (ATRA) and others. ATRA bought radio ads invoking the coffee case as a prime example of litigation run amok (Press 1995, 35). Reporters have told us in interviews that the McDonald's coffee case quickly became a routine component in the standard tort reform literature regularly fed to the press. For example, Roberta Katz, a senior fellow at the Discovery Institute, made the case a lead item in a published and widely distributed address, "Is It Time to Reform the Adversarial Civil Justice System?" in late 1996. An ATRA press release decrying a lawsuit against toothbrush manufacturers as late as April 15, 1999, listed the McDonald's coffee case as the leading honoree in the "Crazy Lawsuit and Warning Label Hall of Fame."[34]

Corporations were also quick to get into the act of exploiting the high-profile case. Mobil Oil (1995) took out a substantial advertisement in the *New York Times* that cited the case, noting that "nearly $3 million was awarded to a customer who spilled hot coffee on herself." Echoing ATRA press releases and paid ads, the Chamber of Commerce sponsored its own ad on the radio: "Is it fair to get a couple of million dollars from a restaurant just because you spilled your hot coffee on yourself? Of course not. It's ridiculous. But it happened" (cited in Torry 1995).

Conversely, the wider community of trial lawyers was relatively slow to recast the story in positive ways. Their attempts to react to misrepresentations of the case were neither widely available nor readily accessible. Gordon E. Tabor, president of the Indiana Trial Lawyers Association, just weeks after the jury verdict wrote the excellent account "McFacts, McMedia, and McCoffee," which was not visible to the mainstream press and general public. As noted above, Ralph Nader attempted to present the overlooked facts and key issues to legislators in 1995, and he later wrote a detailed account of the case with Wesley Smith in their 1996 book *No Contest.* Likewise, the Association of Trial Lawyers of America Web site (www.atla.org) carried a defense of the case in the late 1990s, but that also came rather late and was aimed at specialized audiences. Again, this relatively tepid and delayed defense of the *Liebeck* case illustrates some of the general political limitations of the plaintiff's bar as an advocacy group (see chapter 4).

In sum, instrumental political gambits and institutional news practices were interrelated parts of the process that constructed legal knowledge emanating from the case against McDonald's, although practices of the media strike us as being far more important in producing the Liebeck legend.

Reconstructing Legality

Our case study of Stella Liebeck's saga demonstrates a more general theme of our larger project—that mass media have played a relatively independent institutional role in the specific social construction of law, or *legality,* itself. By legality, we refer to Ewick and Silbey's provocative, expansive concept regarding the "'ideas, problems, or situations of interest' to unofficial actors as they take account of, anticipate, or imagine 'legal acts and behaviors.'" Legality thus operates "as both an interpretative framework and a set of resources with which and through which the social world (in-

34. Authors' files.

cluding that part known as law) is constituted" (Ewick and Silbey 1998, 23, 273 n. 1). If our analysis is correct, routines of news worth largely defeated legal narratives that won at trial and constructed new legal knowledge for the citizenry to integrate into their reserve of "common sense."

These reconstructions of legality entailed serious implications. On an individual level, they generated yet another, far more enduring source of anguish for Stella Liebeck, who already had suffered profoundly from severe burns and an anxious dispute culminating in trial. They also had an impact on Liebeck's attorney, Reed Morgan, in emotional, financial, and professional ways. Both won in court, but lost to the prevailing consensus about civil law. In chapter 8 we take up the significant indirect influence of the hot coffee legend on countless other legal actors—injured victims, plaintiffs, attorneys, jurors, judges, to name a few—in subsequent years.

At a broader political level, the hot coffee case virtually jump-started the stalled movement to reform tort law in the mid-1990s. By 1994, the national tort reform movement seemed to be on the wane. A decade of failure to pass major national legislation in Congress had sapped reformists' energies and nurtured frustration. The easy victories at the state level had been exhausted, and even these were being undone or undercut through effective litigation campaigns by trial lawyers. In short, the tort reform movement was on its heels, locked into an increasingly defensive battle. Then, along came the McDonald's case—the perfect anecdotal antidote to the movement's maladies. No better case could have been fabricated by the movement to provide an effective "We told you so" to skeptics in the media, the political establishment, and the general public. Stella Liebeck's saga, reduced to factoids by ordinary news reporting routines and repeatedly respun by reformers, quickly hot-wired the currents of concern about our failing civil legal system and flagging ethos of individual discipline. It is hardly a coincidence that the next year the story circulated widely among congressional hearings and debates, leading to the first major national tort reform legislation passed by Congress. Although President Clinton vetoed that bill, it was clear that the movement had found new life in the aftermath of the scalding coffee story. Indeed, Clinton's successor in the White House made his name as a Texas governor successfully leading the tort reform charge; the leading party presidential and vice-presidential candidates in 2000 were all open supporters, in varying degrees, of national tort reform.

More generally yet, prevailing popular constructions of the hot coffee case have at once reflected and reinforced cultural tendencies to view relationships and events in terms of individual responsibility and blame. The moralistic, individualizing, disciplinary logics *of* law have been reinforced by popular representations *about* law. The hot coffee case also il-

lustrates the very social costs and constraining implications of these logics, however. Consider first the consequences for political debate about the
rationality of the existing tort law system. Specifically, the construction of
the McDonald's case as a lightning rod for concern about the alleged litigation crisis has inhibited the emergence of alternative constructions that
complicated issues of individual blame with attention to other integrally
related public concerns (see Abel 1989). For example, the injuries suffered
by Stella Liebeck and her frustrated resort to litigation could instead have
highlighted the need for better consumer protection standards or regulatory oversight, or the need for expanded medical benefits for the elderly, or the inadequate medical insurance options for most citizens in the
United States, or the lack of workplace leave compensation policies to deal
with family emergencies. After all, the high costs of medical treatment and
the loss of wages suffered by Stella's daughter, who had to take care of her,
prompted the reluctant plaintiff to sue. But virtually nowhere—in the media, among any of the major players on either side of the dispute, or among
the politicians and policy advocates who appropriated the symbolic case
for partisan ends—were any of these policy concerns raised in connection
to the incident. This is particularly striking, because just a short time
before the incident President Clinton had unveiled proposals for radical
transformation of health care and medical insurance in the United States.

Finally, the core challenge to the enormous discretionary power, pecuniary motives, and unaccountable practices of corporate producers identified by Liebeck's lawyers barely saw the light of media attention. Indeed,
what media coverage, popular legend, and political debate all obscured was
just how anomalous was Stella Liebeck's victory in court against a multinational mega-corporation. The motives of corporate-sponsored tort reformers in assailing this and many other cases are clear enough, of course.
Plaintiffs of small means and low status who win substantial awards for
challenging corporate recklessness destabilize the prevailing legal logic of
distributing economic costs widely and generally supporting the structures of inequality that are a part of capitalist society. Nevertheless, political activists, lawyers, scholars—including those on the ostensible political
Left—were drawn into defending the existing inadequate, inegalitarian,
inaccessible tort law system and contesting the case's significance in the
moralistic terms of "individual responsibility" and reckless rapacity
defined by tort reformers. The social construction of the McDonald's coffee case thus illustrates the ways in which prevailing norms, institutional
arrangements, and power relations reproduce themselves as law in mass
culture.

CHAPTER SEVEN

Smoke Signals from the Tobacco Wars

The antitobacco litigation constituted *a new problem definition and normative frame, new policy actors and alliances, and new rules of the game. At the same time the litigation* caused *an increase in media coverage, greater political opposition to tobacco, and legal uncertainty that hurt the tobacco industry.*

LYNN MATHER, "THEORIZING ABOUT TRIAL COURTS"

Current polling finds Americans quite unsympathetic to the plaintiffs' arguments in these cases, ruling that smokers—not tobacco companies—are to blame for the consequences of their decisions to smoke. . . . A 1998 NBC/Wall Street Journal *poll found practically no change in attitudes (from a decade earlier), with 16 percent indicting the companies and 72 percent the smokers.*

LYDIA SAAD, "A HALF-CENTURY OF POLLING ON TOBACCO"

The size of the tort lawyers' fees was perhaps the most publicized and controversial feature of the settlement.

MARTHA DERTHICK, UP IN SMOKE

If *Liebeck v. McDonald's* afforded snapshots of how tort reform tactics, journalistic habits, and individualistic values converged to transform an idiosyncratic lawsuit into a sensationalized symbol, episodic battles that are part of the long-running "Tobacco Wars" provide a more panoramic and complex serial of the construction of legal knowledge. This litigation from the "third world" of torts [1] has involved a much larger scale of harmed

---

1. Recall from chapter 3 that third-world torts are class-action lawsuits over mass torts and latent injuries, often in pursuit of policymaking through civil courts and usually concerning legal rules that are not yet settled. This world of torts features suits concerning such products as asbestos, tobacco, and silicone implants.

plaintiffs, corporate profits, and court-ordered awards than asbestos, breast implants, the Dalkon Shield, or Bendictin. Moreover, the campaign against tobacco enlisted state attorneys general who, while still working with private trial lawyers, redefined the terms of legal challenge, altered somewhat the unequal power relationships between plaintiffs and corporate defendants, and lent public authority to the cause. This alliance of public and private legal actors was rare at the time, but it may well have been a harbinger of future development of social policy torts involving gun manufacturers, fast food producers, and new categories of drug manufacture, among other targets.[2]

At the same time, tobacco litigation has maintained a curious place in the popular discourse about the lawsuit crisis. While tobacco companies have long been major financial supporters of the tort reform cause, neither they nor their opponents have made tobacco litigation a central public issue in the tort reform debate.[3] However, the Tobacco Wars have generated their own media-based politics with important connections to conventional legal lore. For at least fifty years, tobacco companies have waged an aggressive public relations campaign on their own behalf along with a more classic "insider" strategy of overwhelming opponents in court and narrowing the scope of conflict to legislative, executive, and bureaucratic arenas. At the same time, many plaintiffs in tobacco disputes have pursued exposure of tobacco producers, publicists, and lawyers as an important means or as an end in itself, a pursuit that further intensified the relevance of mass media. In this chapter we show that the themes dominating this media contest track closely and intersect with general discourse about the lawsuit crisis.

Given the scope of harms inflicted by tobacco companies, their well-documented practices of deception, their general unpopularity, and the minimal regulatory actions of other governmental institutions, one might expect that successful litigation for injured citizens against tobacco giants would come to be considered a heroic public story for the civil legal system. In the mid-1990s, once states' attorneys general joined hands with private trial lawyers in pursuing an innovative legal strategy, media coverage did seem to buck conventional wisdom somewhat and portray legal ac-

---

2. The Web site accompanying this volume—www.lawslore.info—lists new developments of this sort.

3. One major reason is that lawsuits posed little threat to tobacco companies during most of the first two decades of the tort reform movement. Tort reformers began to assail tobacco litigation more during the 1990s, but even then the relationship to pop tort reform was mostly indirect and complex.

tion in more positive ways. However, as we shall see, such praise had limited duration and depth in journalism and scholarship alike (see, for example, Derthick 2002). The media's mixed portrayals have echoed in public opinion polls. While Americans almost unanimously believe tobacco kills, by the late 1990s polled respondents—by consistent margins of three to one—blamed smokers rather than tobacco companies for the harm. Support for bans by the Food and Drug Administration (FDA) on tobacco sales were opposed by similar margins, while only about half the population applauded legal victories in court against tobacco companies during the 1990s. Why so few storytellers have crafted heroic tales of tobacco fights is, we believe, a fascinating puzzle, one that we explore in this chapter.

In keeping with the triangulation of instrumental, institutional, and ideological analyses undertaken in previous chapters, this chapter proceeds along three lines. First, we rehearse some strategies and tactics in the Tobacco Wars, paying special attention to an allegedly groundbreaking "third period" of litigation in the 1990s. Then we examine reportage of tobacco disputes in the five national newspapers whose spot coverage and features were our subject in chapter 5. That examination enables us to assess the degree to which the coverage of the Tobacco Wars changed with litigation outcomes and, conversely, the degree to which persisting patterns of coverage of civil disputing tempered responses to the dramatic developments in the 1990s. Our analysis of instrumental maneuvering and institutional news practices show again how inherited beliefs about individual responsibility, lawsuit avoidance, and parasitical lawyers have conditioned the public spectacle of tobacco litigation. By chapter's end, we shall have shown how long-standing skepticism concerning civil litigation and civil litigants, in concert with adversaries' tactics and journalists' practices, shaped the Tobacco Wars.

TOBACCO'S INSTRUMENTAL TRIUMPHS

Any accurate account about tobacco litigation must be in part a story about tobacco producers' instrumental dominance and in part, for those dependent on tobacco for their livelihoods as for those addicted to nicotine, a story of felt necessity. Tobacco has wreaked grave havoc but wrought great profits. Tobacco consumption has caused myriad health and social problems in America but also provided pleasures to consumers and treasures to corporations and taxing authorities. Because of their profitability and despite their peril, tobacco products have been subjected to remarkably little regulation or oversight, albeit far more scrutiny than manufacturers would have preferred.[4] On the other hand, injuries from tobacco products have imperiled profits to tobacco producers, so producers have acquired a profound if not mortal interest in managing action, knowledge, and opinion regarding tobacco (Rabin 1993, 112–18). The intense benefits of even small victories and the catastrophic consequences of even small defeats have mutually goaded tobacco's producers and protectors—labeled "tobacco's defenders" in this chapter whenever more specific identification is not warranted—to contend in arenas in which policies have been created (Fritschler and Hoefler 1996; Hilts 1996; Kagan and Vogel 1993; Kluger 1996; Mather 1998, 898; Pringle 1998). In routine politics inside legislatures, cigarette manufacturers have successfully narrowed issues, limited participation, and reduced adverse notice (Mather 1998, 898). Of course, public and private lobbying, contributions above and below the table, and helpful inside information coordinated with outside propaganda all provided tobacco's defenders in Congress with incentives, resources, and cover.[5]

The stupendous successes of tobacco's defenders inside courtrooms have been equally crucial to their dominance. Well-funded litigation waged by armies of defense counsel has facilitated containment-oriented "inside" politicking using a style that one challenger dubbed "Scorched Earth, Wall of Flesh" (Zegart 2000, 85).[6] Before and during trials, tobacco's defenders have used bare-knuckle tactics, have denied their product causes any harms, diseases, addiction, and death, and have invoked the ethics of personal choice and responsibility—all in the confidence that almost none of their misbehavior would "make the news." Because the coordinated de-

4. Kagan and Nelson (2001) show that cross-national comparisons defy easy characterization. In some respects—protecting nonsmokers from second-hand smoke, for example—the U.S. tobacco regime is stringent, while in other respects—taxation, for example—the United States lags behind comparable polities.

5. To cite obvious examples, decisions and nondecisions in Congress followed from relatively hidden control by representatives with the seniority to waylay or delay challenges, or from the cunning to craft regulations that were patent defeats but latent wins for the industry. Thus tobacco interests were shielded from stronger regulations, insurgent knowledge, and agitated demands for action in the states.

In a similar manner, routine politicking has superseded efforts of the Federal Trade Commission (Fritschler and Hoefler 1996) and the Food and Drug Administration (Kessler 2001). In each instance, technicalities and other tactics have thwarted administrative actions and strangled release of information to attentive publics. Groups that have reached the public, on the other hand, have been outwitted and outspent (Zegart 2000, 53–54).

6. The "scorched earth" refers to tobacco lawyers' willingness to contest every substantive and procedural issue over and over to delay and to attrite challengers' resources. The "wall of flesh" refers to the plenitude of attorneys representing tobacco in each deposition or courtroom venue.

fense among the tobacco companies eschewed the most private, most routine mode of resolving civil disputes (settlement);[7] because plaintiffs had to narrow issues to those that civil law accommodated; because most plaintiffs were individuals or small groups with too few personnel, resources, and expertise to overcome limited visibility; because most disputes never made it to trials; and because plaintiffs' losses were too predictable to be newsworthy—for all these reasons news outlets seldom reported much about most legal challenges to use of tobacco (Haltom 1998, 233).

To complement this insider strategy in courtrooms and legislatures, tobacco defenders have also pursued an aggressive and savvy public relations campaign. Tobacco's publicists have paid close attention to public image and opinion, using the commercial and political clout of tobacco defenders to cajole or coerce favorable coverage from news institutions.[8] Over nearly fifty years of disputing, public relations on behalf of tobacco interests has trumpeted the consumer's freedom to choose whether to consume tobacco and to accept responsibility for consequences of that freedom exercised. As a result of this combination of inside/private and outside/public virtuosity, plaintiffs made little headway with juries or public opinion until the 1990s. *Until that time, no tobacco company ever paid one cent to any plaintiff in lawsuits or settlements.* During the 1990s, however, innovative causes of civil actions, newly admissible evidence, novel coalitions of private and public plaintiffs that even tobacco's resources could not deplete, and the proliferation of fronts that tobacco's supporters had to defend against all portended novel deployments of instrumental forces.[9] Those instrumental forces we now survey.

Three periods of litigation and strategies distinctive to each have been characterized skillfully (Mather 1998; Pringle 1998, 5–6; Rabin 2001, 204 n. 1).[10] We have summarized this scholarship in table 7, which affords an overview of the strategic themes that have clashed in the Tobacco Wars.

7. Had tobacco defendants ever settled, reports of out-of-court resolutions would have provided the sort of official settlement of conflicts that journalists are accustomed to cover.

8. Telling examples include attacking reporter Morton Mintz over his coverage of the *Cipollone* case (Kluger 1996, 669), harassing whistleblower Jeffrey Wigand (Mollenkamp et al. 1998, 221–22). and filing suit against the network ABC over its *Day One* report on the manipulation by tobacco producers of levels of nicotine (Pringle 1998, 187).

9. Of course, tobacco's setbacks need not have translated to lasting defeats. Appeals to alternative arenas, shifts in laws and procedures, and public and private exploitation of the still-present theme of individual responsibility continue to loom as means by which tobacco and its defenders might return to dominance.

10. Chronicles and analyses of doctrinal and empirical issues and arguments in tobacco abound. Those curious about various issues will find recent analyses in Rabin and Sugarman 2001. The historical sweep of agitation and litigation against tobacco products is contained

TABLE 7 Themes in three periods of tobacco fights

Producers'/protectors' themes	Challengers' themes
1st period: 1954–65	
Medical/scientific interdeterminacy theme: Science cannot objectively prove that tobacco causes illnesses (especially various cancers).	*Medical/scientific evidence theme:* Scientific and medical evidence establishes that tobacco use leads to illnesses, including cancers.
2nd period: 1983–92 (roughly)	
Medical/scientific/indeterminacy theme: (as above)	*Medical/scientific consensus theme:* (as above, with more evidence of causation)
Individual responsibility/assumed risk theme: Consumers may use tobacco or not as they please; any harms that tobacco usage may foster (but not cause) are so well known that users can/may make an informed choice.	*Corporate liability theme:* Tobacco is "unreasonably dangerous" because, used as intended, it causes illness and addiction; the tobacco industry's public deceptions, frauds, and seductive advertising failed to warn consumers adequately.
3rd period: 1993–99 (roughly)	
Medical/scientific interdeterminacy theme: (as above, applied to addiction)	*Medical/scientific and corporate theme:* (as above with overwhelming evidence)
Individual responsibility/assumed risk theme: (as above)	*Corporate liability/recklessness/ willfulness theme:* (as above, with more evidence for deceptions, frauds, advertisement to teens, and addiction, with concomitant vulnerability to punitive damages)
Avaricious attorneys, insatiable states, and anti-tobacco zealots theme: Lawsuits are not about health but about extorting money from deep-pocketed manufacturers of a legal product; cases are means for high-living attorneys to pad their bank accounts, states to swell their coffers, and opponents of tobacco to savage tobacco companies.	*Addiction/youthful indiscretion theme:* Marketers addict new smokers by appealing to youths who are not yet fully responsible.
	Third-parties theme: Victims who did not choose to use did not assume risks of use of tobacco.
	Public costs theme: States did not choose to use tobacco but must pay medical bills for victims of tobacco advertising, deceptions, and frauds.

First Themes: 1954 to 1965

The first period[11] commenced when scientists confirmed the health risks and injuries from smoking that tobacco's defenders were compelled to deny lest their companies be severely impaired in the marketplace (Hilts 1996, 1–2). Advocates (especially defense lawyers) pursued complementary strategies selected for effectiveness in public relations and litigation. For example, when plaintiffs submitted evidence from recent medical or scientific studies to establish the liability of tobacco companies to individual consumers of their products, the response of tobacco's lawyers was to subordinate manufacturers' image and even their research to the construction of an impregnable defense against lawsuits. In "A Frank Statement to Cigarette Smokers" the industry stated its concern and responsibility for the health of its customers and its dedication to researching scientific and medical uncertainties about the effects of consumption (Kluger 1996, 164). At the same time, however, tobacco's defenders shaped their inside and outside efforts to promulgate the claim that medical and scientific studies were inchoate and that more was unknown about the use of tobacco products than was known.

In table 7, we call this recurring contention the "medical/scientific indeterminacy theme." This theme need not have indicated the tobacco industry's obstinacy or deceit, for in the 1950s medical researchers did not know exactly which compounds in smoke were carcinogenic and to what degrees and under which circumstances. Perhaps more to the point, the public at large had yet to be persuaded that science or medicine had determined that consumption of tobacco was harmful.[12] On the other hand, the claim about the medical/scientific indeterminacy of tobacco's effects was from the beginning an attack on scientific messengers (Hilts 1996, 5) that made little sense outside litigation. Study after study leading to the Surgeon General's report in 1964 reinforced and expanded the original sci-

---

in Kluger's magnum opus (1996). Mather (1998) deftly covers the tactical and strategic implications of the latest wave of litigation. *The Runaway Jury* (Grisham 1996) introduces the trying of tobacco cases in an entertaining but informed manner.

11. Pringle (1998, 5) used the years 1954–73 to mark the first period of tobacco litigation, while Rabin (2001) used 1954–65. We follow Rabin in order to distinguish themes more clearly. The period 1965–83 was a time during which themes characteristic of each of the first two periods were blended. Besides, "[o]f the mere handful of tobacco suits filed in the seventies not one went to verdict" (Zegart 2000, 47).

12. According to Gallup polls, a majority of Americans came to believe that smoking caused lung cancer in or shortly after 1960. Roughly 10–15 percent fewer Americans believed there was an association between smoking and heart disease. See www.gallup.com/poll/topics/tobacco3.asp (last visited February 25, 2002).

ence and anti-tobacco activists' evidence that an industry was poisoning consumers in pursuit of profit—the plaintiffs' major assertion in the "medical/scientific evidence theme" in table 7. Although defenders trumpeted users' rights to choose to use, companies' concern for users' health, and the pleasures and stress-reduction that came from smoking, the first battles of the Tobacco Wars primarily pitted tobacco defenders' theme of medical/scientific indeterminacy against the challengers' theme of medical/scientific evidence, the latter theme passing from "evidence" to "consensus" to "certainty" for many observers.

Expanded Themes: 1983 to 1992

After the Surgeon General reported in January 1964 that consumption of tobacco was related to various diseases, plaintiffs and defendants supplemented their strategic themes. Plaintiffs could now presume that their reliance on the "medical/scientific evidence theme" would be tantamount to the "medical/scientific consensus theme" (see table 7) in many or most disputes, although tobacco's lawyers would continue to argue tactically that the plaintiffs' specific health conditions might be due to other causes. Tobacco plaintiffs updated their tactics: they pooled resources to overcome the burdens of "proving" to the satisfaction of judges and jurors that consuming tobacco caused cancer, and they exploited the intervening shift in technical standards from warranties to products liability torts (Rabin 1993, 118–25). These tactics served the expanded strategic theme that plaintiffs now wielded. Not only could plaintiffs demand compensation based on ever-stronger scientific evidence, but tobacco companies' earlier deceptions and propaganda enabled plaintiffs' attorneys to portray tobacco's defenders as recklessly or deliberately protecting tobacco manufacturers from civil liability for tobacco products. During the first period of tobacco litigation, plaintiffs had asserted that this or that cigarette maker had injured the plaintiff; by the second period, such specific, tactical assertions had become widespread. Litigants now followed a strategy of characterizing tobacco as an unreasonably dangerous product about which consumers had not been adequately warned and tobacco companies had long dissembled. That is, plaintiffs pursued the theme of corporate liability. Tobacco's defenders continued the tactics of attrition crafted during the first campaign—"Scorched Earth, Wall of Flesh" persisted. The industry's vast army of defense attorneys filed myriad motions, appealed adverse procedural or evidentiary rulings, hid evidence behind attorney–client privilege or less exalted means of evading discovery, investigated plaintiffs and their attorneys to learn of vulnerabilities, and otherwise engaged in relentless, remorseless adversarial tactics lest they lose even one case and be beset by far more opponents.

In addition to these battle-tested tactics, industry lawyers pursued two other major strategic themes. They simultaneously argued that no medical experts could say for sure that tobacco caused cancer *and* that everybody knew that use could lead to disease. What tobacco lawyers claimed that scientists could not yet know with certainty the same lawyers maintained that ordinary Americans already knew. This remarkable parlay supplemented their ever-less-persuasive reliance on the "medical/scientific indeterminacy theme" with the potent claim stressing that the deleterious effects of smoking were well known to consumers, who nonetheless elected to use tobacco products and now were suing tobacco producers after years of consumption and enjoyment. This was the "individual responsibility theme," which in legal terms meant that smokers had knowingly assumed the risks of their use and enjoyment of tobacco products (and so is listed in table 7 as the "individual responsibility/assumed risk theme).[13] Outside courts and before a larger jury of popular opinion, spokespeople for tobacco interests argued the less legalistic, more value-based variant on the same compound theme—*freedom of choice.* This seemingly discordant combination of scientific uncertainty, individual responsibility, and assumption of risk severely disadvantaged plaintiffs. Because they had to cite scientific consensus to establish the liability of the defendants, plaintiffs reinforced the defense's claim that everyone knew that tobacco caused diseases, which in turn made them vulnerable to such characterizations as self-victimizing, irresponsible, weak, and fraudulent. If tobacco companies continued to offer a legal product that consumers knew to be bad for them, jurors were unlikely to blame the defendant for the plaintiff's poor choices.[14]

Tobacco lawyers' paradoxical defense worked reasonably well, for by 1995 only one of the more than seven hundred lawsuits filed against tobacco companies had yielded plaintiffs both a winning verdict and an award—*Cipollone v. Liggett Group, Inc.,* which concluded in 1988 (Mather 1998, 904–5). Even that exception proved several rules for the second cam-

13. The Surgeon General's 1964 report publicized health risks so broadly that the "everyone knows" argument became persuasive. Congress provided for warning labels and thereby, according to courts, preempted more stringent state or local efforts.

14. For example, in explaining the unanimous decision denying the wrongful death claim by the widow of a fifty-year-old man (*Horton v. The American Tobacco Co.*), one juror stated, "I think that we probably all felt that [smoking] caused him to be sick, but he was an adult, he knew what he was doing, there was information at that time" (cited in Derthick 2002, 31).

paign of the Tobacco Wars. Rose Cipollone and her survivors were sympathetic plaintiffs hard to portray as chiselers, but the jury awarded no damages on behalf of the late Ms. Cipollone, who was considered by jurors to have chosen to smoke and therefore was held to be personally responsible for the disease that killed her. Individual responsibility, that is, not merely outweighed corporate responsibility but nearly precluded it in the eyes of the *Cipollone* jurors—the preeminent rule in cases before 1993. Jurors did give a verdict and an award to Mr. Cipollone to compensate him for his loss, though. Even this "victory" for plaintiffs, however, reiterated the defense's theme of individual responsibility. Because Mr. Cipollone had not *chosen* to use tobacco but had borne consequences of such use, he was entitled to compensation, the jury said, apparently contrary to a strict reading of law (Rabin 2001, 179). The Cipollones' lawyer, Marc Edell, obtained many more tobacco-industry documents than previous attorneys had been able to wrest from tobacco lawyers, but even establishing what tobacco companies knew about the dangers of smoking and when they knew it could not overcome the "individual responsibility/assumed risk theme" or, outside court, freedom of choice arguments.

Cipollone demonstrated another rule of tobacco litigation before the third period. After the jury had awarded compensation to Mr. Cipollone based on their perception that he had not shirked personal responsibility, the Third Circuit Court of Appeals set the verdict and award aside, and the U.S. Supreme Court sent Marc Edell and the Cipollone survivors back to start the trial anew. Neither Edell's law firm nor the Cipollones had the resources or will to continue the battle,[15] so the more than $50 million that tobacco defendants spent had exhausted the plaintiffs—a dramatic instance of tobacco lawyers' "Wall of Flesh, Scorched Earth" strategy to win through attrition.

The second period of tobacco litigation, therefore, ended with the abandonment of *Cipollone;* the scoreboard read: "Eight hundred and thirteen claims filed against the industry, twenty-three tried in court, two lost, both overturned on appeal. Not a penny paid in damages" (Pringle 1998, 7). Absent a powerful reply to arguments for individual responsibility, assumption of risk, and freedom of choice, plaintiffs appeared unlikely ever to prevail.

---

15. To that point, the litigation had cost Edell's firm more than $3 million; Zegart puts the figure at $7 million (2000, 86). "The *Cipollone* lawsuit involved more than 100 motions, most of which were argued; several key pretrial appeals; a four-month jury trial; two petitions for certiorari to the U.S. Supreme Court, one of which was granted, with argument and then reargument before that Court . . . ." (Mather 1998, 905).

Themes in the Dramatic Third Period: 1993 to the Present

The third period of the Tobacco Wars has been a dramatic, perhaps even revolutionary, reversal of legal fortunes for its disputants in court.[16] These extraordinary changes resulted in large part from the mobilization of vast new resources and new strategic themes by challengers of tobacco products.[17] Private trial lawyers fresh off remunerative assaults on asbestos and attorneys possessed of sufficient resources and expertise to match tobacco's defenders joined one or more frays (Zegart 2000).[18] Attorneys general in nearly all the states—following the lead of Mississippi, Minnesota, and Florida—lent their own credibility, visibility, and resources to such high-profile counsel, enabling plaintiffs to challenge tobacco giants in 1996–97. And some attorneys proved they could compete without huge resources. Most notably, Miami trial lawyer Stanley Rosenblatt tried a class-action suit in 1994 on behalf of sixty thousand flight attendants claiming harms from second-hand smoke, the same year that he filed a class-action lawsuit for all tobacco-related injuries in Florida. Overall, the sheer volume of legal challenges to tobacco manufacturing accelerated rapidly. Between 1993 and June 1998, 807 legal actions were pending against the tobacco industry. These included actions by the states, fifty-five class-action lawsuits, over six hundred individual claims, and various other claims by health care plans, governmental bodies, and Indian tribes (Meier 1998; Mather 1998).[19]

At the same time, a multidimensional shift in tactical advantages enabled plaintiffs to counter defendants' mainstay: individual responsibility and assumption of risk. The argument of corporate liability for compensatory or punitive damages now persuaded some juries, if not citizens outside courtrooms, because evidence gathered for *Cipollone*, well-informed whistleblowers, and even a defecting tobacco CEO made it clear that to-

16. Mather (1998, 898, 899) groups the litigation and trial courts' decisions of this period as having taken place between 1994 and 1998.

17. In addition, plaintiffs reaped the benefits of better organization and increased financing during and after the second period. On the project focusing on tobacco products liability, for example, see Mather 1998, 907. On the pooling of resources for the *Castano* suits, see Zegart 2000, 136–37.

18. Readers familiar with Marc Galanter's classic distinction will recognize immediately that "one-shotter" plaintiffs yielded the field of battle to plaintiffs' attorneys who were "repeat players" (Galanter 1974).

19. These dramatic increases in the numbers of lawsuits against tobacco should not obscure the fact that the industry continued to triumph in most litigation, including various lawsuits by the federal government, foreign nations, insurers, classes, and individuals.

bacco companies had long known that their products caused diseases and addicted users. Tobacco producers' public denials of what even they knew privately, a potent resource in previous litigation campaigns, now supplied challengers with the evidence of corporate indifference, recklessness, or willfulness that punitive damages demanded. Strategies premised on "corporate liability" in the second period expanded during the third period to include "corporate recklessness" and "corporate willfulness." Armed with compelling evidence that tobacco executives and scientists knew that nicotine was an addictive substance and the now unassailable scientific consensus on the health dangers it posed, challengers finally mounted an effective challenge to corporate themes emphasizing freedom of choice and assumption of risk.

Another theme threatened "Big Tobacco"—as the few major tobacco-producing corporations came to be known—with immense punitive damages and intense public condemnation. To the degree that attorneys could amass evidence that nicotine was addictive, they could undermine the "individual responsibility/assumed risk theme" and freedom of choice arguments. Worse, plaintiffs offered arguments and evidence that Big Tobacco's marketing was largely dependent on hooking users at a young age, when they were susceptible to both peer pressure and inadequate foresight, and not yet of the age when Americans usually hold individuals totally responsible for their decisions. Plaintiffs could be portrayed less as weaklings who made personal choices that they now wanted to blame on deep-pocketed defendants and more as naifs who acceded to peer pressure at a vulnerable age only to have much of their freedom of choice negated by addiction. This "addiction/youthful indiscretion theme" (see table 7) was a potent strategy. If anti-tobacco advocates could induce juries and courts to find corporate recklessness or willfulness, defendants once viewed as solid corporate citizens might be re-imagined as corporate culprits who hook children and adolescents on drugs in the interest of financial gain.

In addition to those mutually reinforcing themes backed by voluminous evidence, challengers fashioned two strategic themes to circumvent defenders' use of the theme of individual responsibility and assumption of risk. Anti-tobacco lawyers recruited nonsmoking plaintiffs who could not be argued to have assumed the risks of diseases or to have made irresponsible or unreasonable choices. As was the case (transiently) in *Cipollone,* this "third-parties theme" provided an exception to individual responsibility because those who did not use tobacco had not assumed the risks of choosing tobacco. This was the core of the argument concerning second-hand smoke that caught fire in the early 1990s. Another thematic tactic likewise introduced innocent third parties. State attorneys general sued to-bacco companies seeking compensation for state expenditures to cover the cost of smoking-related diseases. This "public costs theme" presented a body politic that never elected to smoke and therefore had assumed no risks, but that was forced to endure losses from tobacco marketers' know-ing and willful addiction of state citizens. Thus was a negative externality of personal choice (third parties) made into an alleged drag on the public purse (public costs, especially in Medicaid expenditures) and collective welfare. Although tobacco companies could cite economic analyses that showed that smokers as a group saved the states money because smokers died so early (Viscusi 1999), such an argument was more likely to enrage than to assuage jurors and to harm producers if news media made it public.

The outcomes in court or leveraged by litigation were no less unprece-dented than the dramatic developments in mobilized resources and tacti-cal argument. Within a few years, public and private lawyers negotiated on behalf of the states a nearly $250 billion Master Settlement Agree-ment with the tobacco industry, the class-action suit on behalf of all Flor-ida smokers produced a $145 billion punitive damages award *(Engle v. R. J. Reynolds Tobacco Co.)*,[20] and individuals won punitive damages awards from tobacco companies for amounts up to $28 billion (*Betty Bullock v. Philip Morris Incorporated et al.*), among other clear victories for chal-lengers to tobacco products.

20. The road to the Master Settlement Agreement was very complex, but it can be divided into three segments. First was the 1997 settlement worked out as consent decrees among state attorneys general, private tort lawyers, and corporations in the wake of filed claims by four states. This settlement, eventually enlisting most of the states, imposed regulatory con-trols on advertising and obligated industry giants to pay $368.5 billion, but it also insulated them from pending and future lawsuits as well as capped damage awards. However, the deal was rejected by (mostly Democratic) congressional leaders—under pressure from many sides, including ATLA—who were required to enact some of its terms by legislation. This led to a second stage: the far more punitive McCain bill in Congress, which raised industry's cost to $516 billion, eliminated the immunity from future lawsuits, and raised the cap on puni-tive awards along with increased regulatory controls. However, the bill failed in the Senate, as Republicans responded to industry pressure and cited unsupportive (or mixed) opinion polls. The final stage was the Master Settlement Agreement in 1998, which was a moderated version of the original settlement—reducing industry costs to $206 billion over twenty-five years but providing no immunity against private and federal lawsuits and sustaining in-creased regulation plus modest public education measures—negotiated by the attorneys gen-eral and confirmed by forty-six state legislatures and the courts. This "global" settlement was structured like a massive state tax increase on tobacco, in that smokers bore the primary bur-den through higher cigarette costs, industry viability was assured, and the states benefited from revenues that mostly could be used for goals having little to do with the tobacco "prob-lem." Policy experts have hotly debated the implications of the agreement for public health.

Despite tribulations and capitulations, Big Tobacco activated alternative strategies and turned to its allies for support. Tobacco's defenders and trial lawyers' detractors denounced the huge contingency fees that plaintiffs' attorneys might pocket, and raised a number of interesting questions concerning civil justice policy: How much need or should advocates receive to induce trial attorneys to become "private attorneys general" pursuing the interests of states or the public? If attorneys general set up lawsuits and then employed top litigators to push for settlements, how much were the come-lately negotiators due? To whom are such private "enforcers" of the public good accountable? Such theoretically interesting questions, of course, were used to vilify trial lawyers and, by association, those who loosed them on the tobacco industry. Given the millions that tobacco lawyers had reaped in decades of representing tobacco concerns and misrepresenting what Big Tobacco knew, such questions were ironic if not hypocritical. But the impudence of tobacco's advocates was not as available and accessible a story for news media as the newest installments of lawyer bashing, so the "avaricious attorneys theme" often better suited challengers who showed some promise of winning than defenders who had won for almost forty years. Of course, these judgments of news worth were whetted and abetted by years of disparagement of trial lawyers by tort reformers and other detractors.

Attacks on avaricious attorneys for chasing smokers who were not yet in ambulances not only revived long-standing doubts about adversaries and attorneys but also reinforced the chronic efforts to constrict "bottom-up" litigation by portraying consumers' legal efforts as threatening in ways that, for example, suits between or among businesses were not (Abel 1987). If this "avaricious attorneys" counterattack was audacious on multiple levels, it appealed to citizens who believed that civil plaintiffs were chiselers trying to get something for nothing or were indulging in dramaturgical victimization, and it comported with the theme of individual responsibility that had for so long been a mainstay of tobacco's defense. Owing to its appeal to antipathy toward attorneys and its resonance with the social value of individualism, the counterattack on attorneys' fees was well tailored to meet the prerequisites for news coverage and amplification.

The third period of tobacco litigation nonetheless witnessed a dramatic change in the dispute generally, one that went to the detriment of tobacco's defenders inside and outside courtrooms. However advantageous critiques of lawyers' fees might have been before attorney-resenting publics, disparaging those fees was not a useful ploy before judges and jurors. Jurors who chose to punish defendants for spreading disease, dependency, and disinformation appeared little interested in what lawyers were paid to prosecute the cases in court. Judges were likely to know that, however much plaintiffs' attorneys might derive from their crusades, tobacco attorneys have reaped far more for far longer. Thus, complaints about lawyers' windfall gains did not play as well in court as elsewhere.

Why No Tobacco Tort Tales? Too Many Villains, Too Few Heroes

Table 7 and the cases we have briefly surveyed show why observers have described the third tobacco campaign as "dramatic," in both approach and outcome. However, the instrumental strategies and tactics of plaintiffs and defendants alike suggest one reason why fights over tobacco have not, to our knowledge, led to popular stories that lauded plaintiffs, litigation, or the civil system. The outmanned, outgunned, underdog plaintiffs never won until the mid-1990s, so corporations long had established a presumption of relative innocence. Once plaintiffs began to win cases and leverage settlements, developments complicated knowledge and reportage about tobacco disputing. Tobacco merchants were clearly cast as villains, but so were (ostensibly greedy) attorneys for plaintiffs who stood to profit immensely while actual victims were reported to receive little. Moreover, victories provided few clear images of good guys. FDA commissioner David Kessler established himself as a crusader admired by some, but he did not participate in the litigation, his regulatory efforts were actually rebuffed by the Supreme Court, and he was routinely chastised by critics for his moral intransigence (see Derthick 2002). State attorneys generals lent authority to public litigation, but the sheer number of participants and the welter of events confused even diligent observers. Eventual deals struck to settle suits about public costs were so murky and politicized that ordinary folks could not tell whether the deals left tobacco money on the table (a claim that led members of Congress to escalate the Master Settlement of 1997), whether the states were extorting money from corporations, or whether the biggest winners were highfalutin private litigators and wheeler-dealers brought into the disputes at the last moment who reaped awards vastly disproportionate to their contributions or risks.

That both the initial settlement and later Master Settlement were structured to resemble new taxes—securing corporate viability, burdening some but also deterring other (especially young) smokers with higher costs, augmenting state coffers for general spending—was often alleged but seemingly little understood, for better or worse. Indeed, the sheer volume of legal actions flowing forth at one time, the suddenness of the reversals in judgment, and the enormous amounts of money at stake could be cited as evidence confirming the fundamental arbitrariness of the legal system. Given all the mixed messages and finger pointing from all sides, the public had many reasons for bewilderment but few reasons to abandon the commonsense skepticism about litigation cultivated in previous decades.

INSTITUTIONAL COVERAGE OF TOBACCO DISPUTES

Political scientist Lynn Mather collected evidence showing how the developments in tobacco litigation during the mid-1990s rippled through news periodicals to public consciousness. She concluded that the third period of tobacco litigation prompted a dramatic redefinition of the public agenda regarding "the problem of tobacco and the policy alternatives, political mobilization, new legal norms, and new political and legal resources for opponents of tobacco" (1998, 897). Mather used *Reader's Guide to Periodical Literature* to establish that the course of developments of the Tobacco Wars during the mid-1990s were generally reflected in an increased discussion of tobacco litigation in magazines, even if some of those developments proved only transitory. This expansion of the conflict amplified and ramified the novel themes (listed in table 7 as "public costs," "addiction/youthful indiscretion," and "third-parties") designed to overcome defendants' previously successful appeal to individual responsibility and assumption of risk. Moreover, Mather speculated that the initiation of legal action by respected states' attorneys general added legitimacy to challenges once waged only by private tort lawyers. Plaintiffs, Mather maintained, thus began to win the public relations battle in magazines: as anti-tobacco activists used litigation proceedings as new evidence of corporate misconduct, nearly all coverage in the periodical literature of tobacco's image and interest was negative. Mather perceived a shift as well in opinion polls and among jurors against Big Tobacco. Although appeals reversed or reduced every advance by plaintiffs during this third period, she wondered if the new public understanding of the Tobacco wars that had been set in motion and the expanded politicking could be contained by adverse appellate decisions or dissipated by settlements.

If we read Mather's seminal analysis narrowly, it is possible to construct a claim that the latest campaign in tobacco litigation reordered news reporting to raise issues and themes more advantageous to challengers and challenges than to defenders and defenses. We extend this thesis and argue that these recent battles redounded to the benefit not only of Big Tobacco's adversaries but also of those opposing pop tort reform.

We reexamined newspaper reportage during the mid-1990s and after to see if additional evidence supports either the narrow or broad variant of the thesis. Generally, our own findings confirm some of Mather's observation that media representations regarding litigation against tobacco companies had become more positive. However, our larger study of newspaper reportage and public opinion suggests a more complex picture in which traditional news practices and media susceptibility to spin (along with the complexity of events themselves) produced narratives of legal victories that moderated or contradicted the positive shift in the third period of tobacco litigation. We show how instrumental successes during this period both changed and failed to change the penchants of the press.

Did the New York Times *Convey Novel Themes and Shifts in Agenda?*

Before we review data from our sample of five newspapers, we take a quick look at the coverage by what is commonly believed to be *the* newspaper of record in the United States. Between 1985 and 2000, the *New York Times* displayed a shift of themes somewhat consistent with Mather's findings.[21] In figure 8 we array the number of mentions of four themes discussed earlier.[22] Two of those themes dramatically reinforce the thesis about changed coverage. The "individual responsibility theme" appeared regularly and prominently in episodic reports in the *Times* before 1993 but only sporadically thereafter, although that does not signal that individual responsibility, assumption of risk, freedom to use tobacco products, or cognate themes ceased to matter after 1993. As jurors and judges began to validate exceptions to the invocation of individual responsibility, the *New York Times* mentioned public costs prominently after 1993 but not before. This result is hardly surprising given winning themes in the third period of tobacco campaigns. Still, the findings demonstrate that novel strategies did correspond to coverage of themes in mass media. After all, one source of the news is what actually takes place in the world.

Another provenance of the news is news worth. As illustrated by the data in figure 8, the mentions of attorneys' fees (a subset of the derogation of trial lawyers that we dubbed the "avaricious attorneys theme" in table 7) remind us in different ways that newsmakers need not limit their reports to results or strategies in official arenas. Protests about attorneys' fees little advantaged tobacco defendants in court but were repeated in reports in the *New York Times,* almost entirely during the latest phase of the Tobacco Wars. That Big Tobacco's novel attack on challengers would make the

---

21. Jeffrey Dudas coded the *New York Times* and compiled the resulting data.

22. We do not include in figure 8 mentions of shared liability, for which we also coded, because it was so seldomly mentioned. As we remarked earlier, the "medical/scientific indeterminacy theme" had sharply declined as a credible claim by the second and third periods. Although it appeared in the *Times* on occasion, it added more noise than signal to figure 8, and so we deleted it as well. Preliminary screenings of the data did not suggest that either the "third-parties theme" or the "addiction/youthful indiscretion theme" would appear often enough to contribute substantially to analysis, so we did not code for them either.

FIGURE 8 Mentions of key themes by year

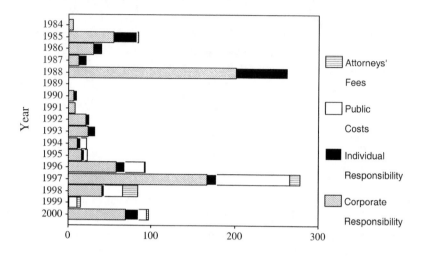

Total Mentions Each Year

Times should not be surprising in light of our discussion in this and earlier chapters. Tobacco's defenders and their sympathizers trumpeted the outlandish fees that some trial attorneys stood to gain. Although the mentioning of attorneys' fees neither undermined the call for corporate responsibility on the one hand nor directly propped up the invocation of individual responsibility on the other, it did spite tobacco's antagonists by attributing the excesses of a few flamboyant, well-heeled, high-priced litigators to advocates afflicting Big Tobacco. Moreover, the theme of attorneys' fees reprised decades of animosity toward lawyers and civil litigants.

The variable prominence of "corporate responsibility" over seventeen years should have been anticipated, for challengers had asserted the liability of tobacco producers for diseases and health care costs since the 1950s. What must be acknowledged in the specific context of tobacco litigation, we believe, is that the *New York Times* had from 1984 through 2000 covered plaintiffs' allegations of corporate liability far more often than any other theme and had in each of those years reported assertions of the responsibility of tobacco manufacturers more often than other themes combined. Institutional and instrumental factors aligned to make tobacco disputes *both* the dramatic, personalized, and discrete but familiar stories that newspapers prefer to convey *and* the ready sources of startling revelations that plaintiffs intended trials to be. The pre-trial discovery of Marc Edell in *Cipollone* and the coordinated efforts of Richard Daynard and the Tobacco

Products Liability Project had exposed what tobacco companies knew and when they came to know it (Kluger 1996, 559–61)—which we take to be an instrumental influence on coverage. The evidence adduced, the testimony heard, and the verdicts rendered in *Cipollone* in 1988 further provided a "news hook"—which we conceive as a mostly institutional influence—that made mentions of corporate responsibility in 1988 even more frequent than mentions during the conflicts that led to the Master Settlement. We find in figure 8, then, an important qualification of the thesis about agenda redefinition: to a greater or lesser extent, in the pages of the *New York Times* plaintiffs had already enjoyed a thematic edge over defendants in period 2.

Did the Five Major Newspapers Convey Novel Themes and Shifts in Agenda?

To get an even richer view of the translation of themes from advocacy to journalism, we assembled data from the five prominent newspapers—*New York Times, Wall Street Journal, Washington Post, Los Angeles Times, and Christian Science Monitor*—in our larger study (see chapter 5). Coders recorded and classified complaints about the civil justice system as a routine part of their scrutiny of *thematic or general* articles (that is, editorials, commentaries, features, and all else except spot coverage of specific cases, which are called *episodic or case-specific* reports in this book) recorded in the sample from 1980 to 1999. Table 8 arrays thirteen complaints about the civil justice system advanced in those thematic articles.[23] The rows of complaints are listed in descending order of frequency of their appearance in the five newspapers during the second period of litigation—from 1980 to 1992[24] (for a slightly different ordering based on frequencies overall, see table 5 in chapter 5). On either side of the listed complaints are three columns of the rounded percentages for each variety of complaint. The left set of columns arrays thematic articles published during 1980–92 and the columns on the right array general articles published during 1993–99. For example, the 265 articles in our thematic sample from 1980 through 1992 contained 481 complaints (see the bottom cell in the leftmost column); 29 percent of these complaints concerned litigation costs. Comparisons between the columns that array all articles in each period (that is, those articles that concerned tobacco plus those articles that did not) suggest some

23. Chapter 5 provides details on how this coding was carried out. Table 8 is based on six fewer articles and seven fewer complaints than table 5 in chapter 5 due to coders' omissions.

24. If the second period commences in 1983, articles prior to 1983 belong to no defined "period."

TABLE 8 Complaints about U.S. legal system in 946 thematic articles, 1980–99

	Period 2: 1980–92				Period 3: 1993–99	
Across all 265 articles prior to 1993	Among 244 articles that *did not* refer to tobacco	Among 21 articles that *did* refer to tobacco	Complaints (cf. table 5 in chapter 5)	Across all 680 articles after 1992	Among 218 articles that *did not* refer to tobacco	Among 462 articles that *did* refer to tobacco
29%	29%	17%	1. Litigation costs	23%	32%	8%
15%	15%	9%	2. Soaring damages	12%	9%	17%
14%	14%	25%	3. Greedy lawyers	25%	17%	37%
12%	12%	0%	4. Too much litigation	9%	11%	6%
6%	7%	0%	5. Defendants ripped off	3%	4%	2%
6%	5%	33%	6. Citizens act like victims	7%	7%	9%
6%	6%	8%	7. Frivolous lawsuits	10%	10%	9%
3%	3%	0%	8. Incompetent/biased jurors	2%	2%	1%
3%	3%	0%	9. Too many lawyers	2%	1%	4%
2%	2%	0%	10. Feckless/biased judges	1%	2%	0%
2%	2%	0%	11. Americans too litigious	3%	3%	3%
1%	1%	17%	12. Greedy litigants	2%	1%	4%
1%	1%	0%	13. Tort taxes irrational	1%	1%	2%
100%	100%	100%		100%	100%	100%
$n = 481$	$n = 469$	$n = 12$	Total complaints	$n = 317$	$n = 481$	$n = 196$

general trends in complaints in each period of litigation. To each period's general trends we may contrast trends specific to articles related to tobacco disputes. This provides a glimpse of how tobacco coverage in the third period diverged from other civil coverage in both the second and third periods. We highlight the most common complaints in table 8 by using boldface type for each row in which the number of complaints exceeded 10 percent of the total number of complaints for either period.

Table 8 reveals a wide array of thematic shifts between the second and third periods,[25] but we call attention to a general trend: *per article, third-period litigation and especially tobacco litigation gave rise to far fewer of the most common complaints about civil justice in America than did second-*

25. We have defined these periods in a manner consistent with descriptions and analyses of tobacco litigation. Pushing out the time spans for each period makes little or no difference in the trends on which we focus in the text. See the Web page associated with this book (www.lawslore.info) for evidence of the robustness of the comparisons and contrasts we make.

period litigation. Among 265 thematic articles between 1980 and 1992 inclusive, we found 481 total complaints; we found 680 thematic articles after 1992 but 513 total complaints. Thematic articles from the second period yielded a mean of 1.82 complaints; thematic articles from the third period yielded a mean of but 0.75 complaints.[26] When articles that concerned tobacco are separated from other period-3 articles, the former average 0.42 complaints per article while the comparable mean for other articles was 1.45 complaints per article. In sum, mean complaints per article dipped from one period to the other in articles not related to tobacco (from an earlier mean of 1.92 complaints per article to 1.45) but complaints per tobacco article were fewer still.

Turning to specific complaints, we see that concerns about the costs and ubiquity of litigation (complaints numbered 1 and 4 in table 8) dipped from 1993 on and dropped far more in articles related to tobacco than in other thematic articles.[27] The modal complaint in period 2—concerns about the costs of litigation—declined by about one-fifth, from 29.2 percent of all articles in the second period to 22.8 percent in the third. However, that general trend resulted from a plummeting of complaints about the costs of tobacco disputes. Thematic articles that did not bring up tobacco disputes complained about litigation costs a bit *more* in the latter era than in the former.[28] Indeed, "Litigation Costs" was, among tobacco-mentioning articles published after 1992, only the *fifth* most common complaint, appearing almost *one-fifth* as often as complaints about avaricious attorneys. Roughly the same percentage of thematic articles that did not involve tobacco mentioned worries about "too much litigation" before and after 1993 (see row 4 of table 8), but the percentage of tobacco-related general articles that raised that complaint was about half as great during 1993–99 (remembering that period-2 tobacco articles numbered but twenty-one). These results conform to Mather's narrow thesis that 1990s

26. Of course, the 513 complaints from the latter period were concentrated within six-and-a-half years while the 481 complaints from the earlier period were spread over twice as many years. However, a glance back at figure 3 in chapter 5 reminds us that most articles during 1980–92 appeared in the latter half of that span.

27. Covariation in at least five sorts of complaints—"Litigation Costs," "Too Much Litigation," "Defendants Ripped Off," and incompetence or bias on the part of jurors or judges—may correspond to the thesis that a revolution in litigation resulted in a revolution in press coverage, at least in these five newspapers of record. We dwell on the two most common complaints because they seem to us the most important politically.

28. The reader might be inclined to point out that the percentage of tobacco-related articles in period 2 that brought up this complaint was far less than other articles in that period. The reader should recall that so few period-2 articles referred to tobacco that 17 percent in table 8 represented *two* thematic articles.

tobacco litigation had relatively or absolutely enhanced the image of tobacco's challengers and to our broader thesis that the third-period litigation
had lessened disapproval of "litigiousness," albeit marginally.

If Table 8 reveals some shifts toward more positive presentations of the
revolutionary litigation, it also indicates contrary trends. While the image
of challengers and especially lawyers who make the cases against Big
Tobacco had improved, complaints about soaring damages and greedy lawyers had swelled as well. The most glaring match between a theme bene-
fiting Big Tobacco and a complaint voiced more often overall and especially often in tobacco-related articles concerned avaricious attorneys, the
third most popular complaint in the second period and the most common
one in the third period.[29] Complaints about "Greedy Lawyers" were nearly
twice as common overall in the latter period and more than twice as common among articles about tobacco as among articles not mentioning tobacco. Among tobacco-related articles after 1992, complaints about avaricious attorneys were the statistical mode by more than twenty percentage
points.[30]

Likewise, complaints about compensatory or punitive awards increased
in tobacco-related articles while declining in other articles (see complaint
2 in table 8: "Soaring Damages"). Although complaints about "Soaring
Damages" were down in articles unrelated to tobacco and way up in articles that mentioned tobacco, the stupendous stakes in tobacco cases
complicate interpretation of that result. Stakes were high before 1993 but
no plaintiffs ultimately collected, and the two transient awards following
positive verdicts did not seize national attention. In contrast, after 1993 the
cases brought by the attorneys general and several private cases involved
vast sums of money. Because awards to challengers in the third period
were breathtaking by any standard, we are disposed to attribute shifts in
that complaint to the "holler of the dollar" rather than to the instrumental
activities of challengers or defenders per se. We take this change to be very
different from complaints about the cupidity of lawyers, which were nec-

29. If this shift in itself suggests that the major post-1990 innovation of tobacco's defenders resonated among journalists, the analyst should keep in mind that distrust and derogation of attorneys predated and guided attacks on avaricious ambulance chasers. In a similar
manner, complaints about frivolous lawsuits (row 7 in table 8) built on tort tales and long-
standing criticisms. Those complaints were slightly less common in tobacco-related articles
than in articles not related to tobacco, but after 1993 complaints about silly suits nearly
doubled by percentage.

30. Far less impressive but consistent with this pattern of drawbacks is the sixth complaint in table 8, "Citizens Act Like Victims." This has been a consistent feature in tobacco litigation over nearly five decades.

essarily more subjective and more directly attributable to a theme of to-bacco's defenders and traditional legal lore.[31]

Moreover, statistical representations almost surely mute the significance of the headlines and rhetoric that infused news in the late 1990s. Our *New York Times* sample turned up numerous referents to lawyers as "pirates," "contestants," and, of course, "ambulance chasers" who regularly engaged in "extortion," "blackmail," and "shakedowns." For example, one article entitled "A Tobacco Case's Legal Buccaneers" (Collins 1995) begins: "Here, in the former playground of pirates (New Orleans), a new alliance of lawyer-buccaneers has banded together in quest of fabulous treasure." Allegations of "greed" and pecuniary motives, not to mention lawyers' disregard for sacred moral values, abound in the article. Other articles trumpet such headlines as "In Tobacco Talks, Lawyers Hold Key," "Record Legal Fees Loom as Major Issue in Tobacco Deal," "House Weighs in on Fees in Lawsuits in Tobacco," "Billion Dollar Legal Fees," and "High-Flying Lawyer Again Inflicts Damage on Tobacco Industry." This telling trend substantially qualifies the generalization that period-3 litigation changed standard coverage of civil litigation to the benefit of those assailing Big Tobacco.

In sum, third-period tobacco disputes may have lessened two of the three most common complaints about litigation—the three sorts of complaints featured in half or more of tobacco-related and tobacco-unrelated articles alike. Such mitigation of civil complaints at the heart of conventional legal lore tends to bolster contentions that news coverage of disputing during the third period favored tobacco plaintiffs relatively. Concerning the "pro-tobacco" theme regarding greedy lawyers, in contrast, the papers offered stark evidence of the effectiveness of defendants and tort reformers in exacerbating long-standing distrust of and animosities toward attorneys. In addition, articles concerning tobacco nearly twice as often referred to soaring damages—the "holler of the dollar" again—as articles that did not mention tobacco.

Thematic Articles Continue to Favor Tort Reform over Its Opponents

Table 9 captures developments yet more ominous for anti-tobacco activists, developments that are contrary to claims that news coverage shifted in favor of plaintiffs in the third period (1993–99). The marked tendency of thematic articles in the five newspapers to marshal arguments or re-

31. Tort reformists have propagated complaints about skyrocketing awards and greedy trial lawyers, but we cannot extricate those influences from the instrumental influences of tobacco's defenders.

TABLE 9 Remarks in 945 thematic articles, 1980–99

	Period 2: 1980–92				Period 3: 1993–99	
Across all 265 articles prior to 1993	Among 244 articles that *did not* refer to tobacco	Among 21 articles that *did* refer to tobacco	Remarks	Across all 680 articles after 1992	Among 218 articles that *did not* refer to tobacco	Among 462 articles that *did* refer to tobacco
41%	43%	15%	Pro-tort reform $n = 1,852$	31%	42%	18%
25%	25%	16%	Anti-tort reform $n = 1,070$	17%	23%	11%
35%	32%	69%	Mixed on tort reform $n = 2,321$	51%	35%	71%
101%* $n = 2,191$	100% $n = 2,013$	100% $n = 178$	All remarks re tort reform $n = 5,243$	99%* $n = 3,052$	100% $n = 1,700$	100% $n = 1,352$

*Total differs from 100% due to rounded entries.

marks that favored tort reform far more frequently than those that opposed tort reform (discussed in chapter 5) was as evident in period 3 as it had been in period 2 (1983–92).[32] Third-period thematic articles that raised tobacco issues included a greater percentage of remarks favoring tort reform than did second-period tobacco articles and a lesser percentage of anti-tort reform remarks than second-period tobacco articles. In each period thematic articles about tobacco were "mixed"—that is, ambivalent or neutral—regarding tort reform in about seven out of ten instances. Whatever the impact of tobacco litigation in the 1990s, tort reform gained ground and its opponents lost ground relative to one another. True, remarks in thematic or general articles appear considerably more balanced overall after 1992, but that new balancing is due to predominance of tobacco-related articles in the latter era, when more than two-thirds of all thematic articles raised tobacco matters (as contrasted with the roughly 8 percent of period-2 articles that concerned tobacco).

32. As we did in table 8, we defined periods 2 and 3 in a manner consistent with descriptions and analyses of tobacco litigation. Shifting the dividing year from 1992 as the end of the second period and 1993 as the beginning of the third would work but marginal differences in table 9 and make no difference in our interpretations. See the Web site associated with this book (www.lawslore.info) for evidence of the robustness of the comparisons and contrasts we make.

Across periods 2 and 3, thematic articles in the five newspapers contained about 1.73 remarks favoring tort reform for every remark opposing it. This ratio of positive to negative remarks regarding tort reform went from 1.66 across all thematic articles during 1980–92 to 1.80 during 1993–99. If we restrict ourselves to articles that did not concern tobacco, the ratio of pro-tort reform to anti-tort reform remarks was 1.70 in the earlier period but 1.88 in the later period, a modest increase. Articles that concerned tobacco manifest a remarkable escalation from a ratio of 0.93 (that is, less than one pro-tort reform remark for every anti-reform remark) to a ratio of 1.61 in period 3. These findings support neither narrow (that is, tobacco-specific) nor broad (that is, across tort disputes) claims about a revolution in coverage during the third period of tobacco litigation.

Why No Tobacco Tort Tales? "Fair and Balanced" Coverage

In general, we have found coverage of tobacco disputes and themes to be more variegated than a focus on innovative tactics by tobacco plaintiffs might lead one to expect. The inventive strategies of challengers yielded some favorable coverage, but that was balanced in print reports by some less favorable coverage. Disputants' strategies and tactics appear to have reshaped coverage in the latest battles, but newspapers' tendencies continued to shape coverage as well. We have presented evidence that instrumental developments were moderated by institutional inclinations of the press. Resulting reportage was more or less fair and more or less balanced relative to mainstream views of the merits, issues, and policies inherent in tobacco disputes,[33] which means that tobacco stories reached readers of the five newspapers (plus those who construct print or broadcast news based on one or more of the five) in forms less amenable to the treatment that creates classic tort tales. If novel litigation strategies seemed to neutralize tort tales, however, they did little to assist the creation of counternarratives—at least that we could find.

Moreover, our findings suggest that coverage that was newly advantageous to opponents of Big Tobacco or tort reform (or both) tended to be offset by aspects of journalism that advantaged Big Tobacco or tort reform

33. For present expository purposes we accept the description of the mainstream on tobacco policy that Kagan and Nelson (2001) have recently offered. Were it not a peripheral issue for our present endeavor, we should point out that Kagan and Nelson so expansively define the mainstream of American opinion that virtually anything short of an all-encompassing victory for either side would count as a middling outcome. We believe that, by any less capacious conception, that mainstream would be far closer to tobacco's bank than to tobacco's adversaries. In that case, media treatment of tobacco fights would be "fair and balanced" according to a quite questionable standard.

(or both). Our survey of themes in the *New York Times* during 1984–2000 disclosed that coverage did convey themes that were newly prominent in the third period, which confirmed at least the narrow version of the hypothesis regarding issue transformation. We found that assertions of public health costs and corporate liability achieved greater prominence while some perspectives that had bolstered tobacco defenders and/or tort reform receded.[34] By contrast, our survey revealed that the *Times* also carried accelerating attacks on avaricious attorneys. Our analysis of complaints from all five newspapers showed some support for the claim that coverage had changed, but at the same time reiterated the prominence of attacks on lawyers for preying on corporate defendants and on plaintiffs for opportunistically playing the victim. Thus, a markedly mixed and matched set of themes and complaints reached readers—hardly the stuff of popular narratives favoring either side. Period-3 tobacco cases also reinforced sentiments in favor of tort reform more than opposition to tort reforms, although many thematic treatments appeared as ambivalent in the latest period as they had in earlier periods. This result undermined the broader implications of moderately changed coverage and suggests limits to the capacity of instrumental developments to alter long-standing institutional viewpoints.

We thus repeat a conclusion similar to that in the previous section of this chapter: disputes and reports of disputes alike have presented neither the heroes nor the underdogs most suitable for popular narratives, nor the unambiguous plot lines that popular narratives commonly reflect. The thematic agenda of news reporting was significantly redefined in this era, but its new terms both favored and slighted tobacco's challengers.

IDEOLOGY, KNOWLEDGE, AND TOBACCO DISPUTES

We have contended thus far that, while foes of tobacco seemed to make huge gains through litigation during the 1990s, the complexity of these legal battles and the standoffs in tactical mobilization of arguments by the key disputants, filtered through standard media practices, produced only modest and scattered public celebrations of the challengers' legal triumphs. Now we turn to the broader cultural and ideological factors that shaped the terms of the public contest itself and its interpretations by various mass audiences. We once more contend that, among the many values at stake, shared commitments to the core principle of individual responsi-

---

34. The fading from news coverage of the theme of individual responsibility, despite the persistent finding that Americans hold users more responsible than producers for the harms of tobacco, reminded us that the themes' or topics' prominence need not imply potency.

bility best explain why no heroic saga of struggles against nicotine have appeared—or, we propose, will appear. We complement attention to this principle with recognition, again, of the widespread ambivalence expressed toward lawyers, which helps to explain why heroes are so hard to come by in tobacco disputing and why the seemingly suitable villains escaped serious scrutiny. Commitments and ambivalences, separately and together, demonstrate a third and reinforcing set of reasons for the absence of popular paeans to third-period tobacco disputes.

Individualism, Victims' Choices, and Users' Responsibilities

It is not clear that one could overestimate the role of individual responsibility themes or freedom of choice arguments in the defense of tobacco's power, privilege, and profits. From the start of disputes over the liabilities of tobacco producers, defenders have asserted the right of users to pursue their pleasures from smoking and the freedom to indulge in what others (and even many users) regard as a health hazard and a vice. Invocations of individual choice existed alongside the "Frank Statement" by the tobacco industry of its responsibilities to consumers of its product, along with the industry's claims that the medical science of tobacco was indeterminate and the facts unclear. As the credibility of tobacco companies' claims to behave responsibly and to be in doubt about the medical dangers of tobacco faded, "freedom of choice" became a dominant theme both in public relations and in litigation (see table 7). Public relations firms that had been engaged by Big Tobacco in the 1950s had not stumbled upon this theme by accident. They and tobacco's advertisers and marketers sought ways to present their product that would resonate with the principle of American individualism, in both rugged and refined versions. The publicists stressed freedom to enjoy life's little pleasures without the fretting of moralists, health zealots, medicos, or other busybodies and pests. Advertising and marketing, of course, conjured images of relatively safe smoking, fantasies in which urban cowboys might ride through Marlboro Country, and allegories in which women had come a long, long way by puffing cigarettes as slim as other cultural artifacts told women they ought to be.

While new findings of medical science and the 1964 Surgeon General's report demonstrated that the pleasures of consuming tobacco were hardly cost-free, tobacco companies found that the principle of individualism, if properly packaged, could accommodate new information about diseases and early death. To the "rugged individualist," tobacco users had decided to take their pleasures as they chose, enjoying them in the short run, even if they should have to pay for those pleasures drastically in the long run. Such users were not entitled to sue over remorse after years of pleasure.

The choice to consume was theirs to make, but users' exercise of such liberty in effect immunized those who marketed addictive, unhealthful nicotine. Filtered through the law, arguments from individualism concluded that plaintiffs had assumed a risk that every reasonable person recognized, despite the industry's denials. To appreciate the potency and even beauty of arguments from individual choice, one must recognize that they held users responsible for their decisions *not despite* but *especially and expressly due to* ample warnings to which reasonable users had access. American individualism, among other corollaries, entailed that free citizens made their choices and chose the consequences. They did not turn liberty into "have it both ways" license by choosing then blaming others for their own choices.

Every account of the Tobacco Wars likewise demonstrates this profound resonance of freedom of choice among jurors, who consistently found for tobacco defendants against plaintiffs repenting of their choices (see Hans 2000). Moreover, this theme persuaded far beyond the courtroom (Derthick 2002; Samuelson 2001, 235–38). In the *New York Times* account of the loss by plaintiff Galbraith in 1985, triumphant spokespersons for R. J. Reynolds were cited repeatedly. "We are gratified that the jury has understood and agree with our position that smoking is a question of individual responsibility and clearly not addictive," claimed one representative. An attorney for the company repeated the point: "I think the verdict(s) . . . demonstrate that the central issue remains the same in these cases: that smoking is an issue of individual responsibility" (December 24, 1985). Five days later, the same attorney was cited in a follow-up article chanting the same mantra: "One is responsible for deciding to smoke or not to smoke. . . . What these cases are about is personal decision-making" (December 29, 1985).

In the 1990s, suits against tobacco companies succeeded by circumventing issues of users' choices. In third-party disputes involving secondhand smoke, plaintiffs alleged that they had been harmed under circumstances that constrained or prevented personal choice or individual sovereignty. In states' cost-recovery suits, attorneys general and their litigators demonstrated nonchoice by means of a fiction that may have been contrary to fact but certainly got around the defense that smokers freely chose to smoke. They noted that states had been left to bear the costs of health care for diseased and dying users who had not "freely consented" to the use of tobacco because of their addiction to it. They were in thrall to nicotine or peer pressure or both, and so could not use good sense in deciding whether to use tobacco.

Even as the focus on responsibility was blurred by other themes in trials and press coverage, there is reason to believe that its status trumped contending norms in American culture. A brief review of public opinion polls demonstrates that tobacco disputes and coverage effectively tapped and solidified long-standing public sentiment.[35] Consider samplings between 1997 and 2001, almost all of the third-period of tobacco litigation. When asked whether tobacco companies or smokers were mostly or entirely to blame for smokers' health problems, respondents blaming smokers mostly or entirely ranged from 55–64 percent of the sample. Between 25 and 30 percent of respondents attributed all or most of the blame on tobacco companies, while 8–14 percent blamed each equally. In two 1998 articles of *The Public Perspective,* Lynda Saad and Everett Carl Ladd respectively confirmed even larger margins of similar differences in public opinion. Ladd noted that "tobacco is, emphatically, not a popular product, and the tobacco companies are indeed unpopular" (1998, 5). However, he cited a 1997 Fox News poll finding that 76 percent of Americans blamed smokers for tobacco-related illnesses, while only 17 percent blamed corporations, when asked to choose. Saad similarly cited a 1998 Time/CNN poll that found a three-to-one public margin supporting the individual right to smoke and a 1998 NBC/WSJ poll finding 72 percent of the public blamed smokers while only 16 percent blamed tobacco companies— figures almost identical to a decade earlier. "Regardless of their personal habits, many Americans seem to be saying that adult smoking is an individual right, choice and responsibility," she concluded (1988, 4). In fact, the percentages of the public opposing a ban on cigarette sales steadily *increased* from 1965 through the late 1990s.

In a similar report drolly entitled "Americans Agree with Philip Morris: Smoking Is Harmful," David W. Moore (1999) reported that 51 percent of those polled supported the Justice Department's suit to recover national health costs from illnesses related to smoking, but 42 percent supported the tobacco companies' contention that the suit should be dismissed. A 1996 Gallup poll found 57 percent of Americans were opposed to any move by the FDA to reclassify tobacco and thus alter the regulations governing its purchase (Saad 1998, 3). Ladd similarly used polling data to demonstrate the leading reasons for public disapproval of the 1998 Senate Tobacco Bill by a 44 percent to 36 percent margin, with 20 percent undecided: (1) opposition to the proposed tax hike; (2) the strong ethos of individual responsibility; and (3) support for freedom of choice (1998, 5–6; see also Derthick 2002, 131–35, 143). If such soundings accurately reflect the views of the citizenry at the height of the anti-tobacco revolution, then

---

35. Unless otherwise indicated, polling results issued from www.gallup.com/poll/topics/tobacco.asp (last visited February 15, 2002). See also the summary in Derthick 2002, 131–35, 143.

the efforts of lawyers and states fell far short of challenging traditional norms invoked in support of Big Tobacco.

Consider as well reactions to a Florida trial in which a jury awarded $145 billion to smokers in July 2000. Of a random national sample, 59 percent disapproved of the Florida verdict while 37 percent approved; 59 percent of respondents blamed smokers more than industry, but only 26 percent blamed industry more than smokers (Newport 2000). Gallup had first asked Americans to assign blame in 1994. The results were 64 percent blaming smokers completely or mostly, 25 percent blaming tobacco manufacturers completely or mostly, and 10 percent blaming producers and smokers equally (Newport 2000). These figures almost exactly matched results from a 1999 poll in which the public placed the blame for shootings more on individuals who misuse guns than on gun manufacturers. If recent litigation has shifted public sympathies against industry and away from holding individuals responsible, we are unable to discern that shift in these data. There is little evidence that the issue agenda among the general public has changed dramatically as a result of dramatic events in the courtroom.

In sum, most Americans seem convinced that tobacco use is a menace, but most also remain convinced that adults should not and need not be prevented from choosing to use. Kagan and Nelson (2001) note that Americans are neither prohibitionists nor libertarians regarding the use of tobacco, and polls reveal a majority perspective that is not so much ambivalent as balanced. A growing majority of Americans have accepted the role of substances in tobacco in the etiology of diseases,[36] but that acceptance only underscores how for most Americans the issue of tobacco use is a matter of rational choices on the parts of individuals. Perhaps four out of five Americans accept the contestable proposition that second-hand smoke is at least somewhat harmful, but no majority of respondents favors banning smoking in hotels, motels, workplaces, or restaurants. Rather, they prefer that public accommodations and workplaces set aside areas for smoking. Clear majorities of respondents report that a person's smoking makes no difference to the respondent's respect for the person and that they sympathize with smokers. Clear majorities of smokers consider themselves addicted and say they would not start smoking if they could choose again, but they also report their belief that they would be able to quit if they so decided.[37]

Thus, even if individual responsibility did not figure as prominently in newspapers during the third period of tobacco litigation as it did earlier

36. Cited in www.gallup.com/poll/topics/tobacco.asp (last visited February 15, 2002).
37. Ibid.

when it was *the* consistently winning theme, variants on that theme continued to bedevil challengers and, as far as we can see, will continue to circumscribe challenges to tobacco manufacturers. Recognition of this deeply rooted value seriously qualifies any claims about drastic changes in coverage of the Tobacco Wars and obstructs triumphal tales about the legal system. If the bulwark of "Fortress Tobacco" (Rabin 2001) seems as impregnable as ever, would-be storytellers have as yet no victory to memorialize. More broadly, the Tobacco Wars can be understood at once to have contested and to have been shaped by the ideological principles at the heart of legal lore in America.

Ambivalence toward Attorneys

If Americans are balanced in their views about tobacco policies and issues, we showed in chapter 4 that they are truly ambivalent about attorneys. As litigation has generally become a more public or at least more publicized means of affecting and effecting policies, litigators increasingly have been held responsible for policies—praised if policy changes are welcomed and damned if changes are unwanted or worse (Friedman 1989, 1598). The emergence of mass, social policy torts has highlighted the extraordinary public power increasingly assumed by private and government attorneys alike (see chapter 4). Traditional ambivalence, if not skepticism, toward litigation generally and toward attorneys specifically, nurtured by politics and the press over recent decades, not surprisingly has been compounded by the high-stakes, high-profile Tobacco Wars. Questions regarding the appropriate motives, roles, influence, and accountability of lawyers have proliferated in the recent era of the Master Settlement and multibillion dollar awards. There are, after all, legitimate reasons to ask whether a handful of private attorneys should reap the huge windfalls of profits ostensibly produced by recent litigation, regardless of arguable social benefits. These questions have been exacerbated by deep divisions among trial lawyers themselves concerning asbestos, tobacco, and related class-action settlements. While these debates turn in part on competing visions of how to achieve fairness, justice, and the public good in legal settlements, they inescapably concern the distribution of huge amounts of money. Amid such high-stakes contests, even plaintiffs' attorneys uninvolved in the third world of litigation may become identified with or tarred by the greedy, self-interested practices attributed to corporate defendants.

As we have already seen, long-standing mass media reliance on dramatic conflict, hollering dollars, and allegations of excessive greed has cultivated this ambivalence about plaintiffs' attorneys generally and, again, particularly in the Tobacco Wars. "The size of the tort lawyers' fees was perhaps the most publicized and controversial feature of the settlement," notes political scientist Martha Derthick (2002, 183). One problem with such media coverage, however, has been its apparent lack of discrimination in identifying large amounts of money with scripted innuendo about greed, or at least irrational fate. Whether or not causes are just or plaintiffs are due recompense, plaintiffs' attorneys have tended to be stereotyped as parasites who prey on plaintiffs and defendants alike (see Rhode 1999).

Several related but different dimensions of media coverage regarding spousal and legal partners Stanley and Susan Rosenblatt, of Miami, Florida, illustrate how media stereotypes of plaintiffs' attorneys work to impress public understanding. The Rosenblatts became anti-tobacco crusaders after they successfully challenged murder charges against a St. Petersburg pathologist in the mercy killing of his wife, who developed terminal lung cancer from smoking. When they subsequently initiated a class-action lawsuit in 1994 against R. J. Reynolds on behalf of sixty thousand flight attendants subjected to second-hand smoke (*Broin v. Philip Morris Co. et al.*), they were regarded by practically everyone as thoroughly mad, in both conventional senses of the word. As Stanley Rosenblatt related to one of us in his modest Miami office,

> Every lawyer that I knew said, "Rosenblatt, you're out of your mind. . . . Stop this Don Quixote stuff." Everyone. Unanimously. . . . I mean, we surely would have been out of our minds to do it for the money. . . . This was the kind of case that you hear horror stories where lawyers go broke. This was absolutely classic. I mean we were in denial. I didn't want to know how much money we owed the bank. We weren't working on other cases; we weren't taking in money; we would just spend it.

Once their trial work generated an unlikely $350 million settlement, however, these principled zealots were widely portrayed in the news as greedy, selfish, and unconcerned about their clients. A CNN report was typical, and was headlined "Flight Attendants Voice Anger over Tobacco Settlement." The story recounted protests by lawyers for class "objectors" who criticized the stupendous attorney award of "$46 million for their legal fees and expenses [while] the settlement included nary a penny for any one of the flight attendants who joined the lawsuit" (see CNN US News, February 6, 1998, www.cnn.com/us/9802/06/flight.attendants.smoke). Tort reformers and tobacco representatives echoing these charges were featured prominently in subsequent coverage.

However, popular reports of fee figures failed to acknowledge the many millions in actual costs incurred by the Rosenblatts at very high risk, or the much smaller actual returns that they enjoyed. These were not lawyers fattened by asbestos or similar litigation but small-time solo attorneys moved by genuinely held, if contestable, ideals. In fact, a U.S. District Judge on appeal affirmed the fees and overall settlement as "fair, reasonable, and adequate and in the best interests of the class." The judge noted that the Rosenblatts took the case "with seemingly insurmountable odds. The likelihood of success was not strong, and if defeated, class counsel would have received no fees and no compensation for approximately $3 million in out-of-pocket costs." Finally, most articles obscured that the lawsuit's novel settlement directed $300 million to research on smoking-related illnesses for public benefit and left open the option for individual lawsuits by members of the class, which the lead attorneys subsequently helped to organize and initiate—all directly authorized by the overwhelming majority of the plaintiffs themselves. Indeed, contrary to the caricature of fringe lawyers trying to grab a piece of the action, tort experts regarded the result as arguably one of the most innovative, client-responsive, and publicly spirited class-action settlements in the tobacco litigation legacy. Trial Lawyers for Public Justice, a public interest watchdog firm that critically polices class actions and social policy torts, named the Rosenblatts "Trial Lawyers of the Year" in 2001, largely for this case.

Nevertheless, news articles following up extensive coverage regarding the objectors' (dubious) challenges prior to the appeal were joined by voices from other critics in and beyond the legal community following the ruling. Such reporting never scrutinized the sources of criticism, nor did it include Rosenblatt's own rejoinders. As he put it to us, "Investment bankers . . . and bond traders, some with no particular brilliance, no particular ability, are making zillions of dollars, and doing little good in the process. . . . And yet the political Right has no trouble focusing resentment on me and my effort to make tobacco companies accountable."

A second and related episode involved the Rosenblatts' even more spectacular trial victory on behalf of nearly seven hundred thousand Florida plaintiffs in *Engle v. R. J. Reynolds Tobacco Co.,* the first private class action tobacco case to be certified in the nation. The decision in the case, which developed over seven years and took two years to try, came in three stages. In July 1999, the jury found that smoking is addictive and causes twenty diseases; each of nine defendant companies was liable for negligence and intentional wrongdoing, thus permitting an entitlement to punitive damages. In April 2000, three class representatives were awarded $12.7 million in compensatory damages for their individual claims. Most stunningly, the jury later that year awarded $145 billion in punitive damages ("a lot of zeroes," commented Judge Kaye), the largest such award in history. Once again, newspapers provided plenty of space for tort reformers, tobacco representatives, and other critics to protest bitterly about the size of the award and likely fees for the attorneys. But another dimension of coverage—rather different and less obvious, but equally problematic—deserves notice. The verdict was followed by a spate of articles that portrayed the Rosenblatts in a manner that was at first glance laudatory but on reflection equivocal. For example, the *New York Times* ran an article on July 15, 2000, titled "High-Flying Lawyer Again Inflicts Damages on Tobacco Industry," focusing on the fortunes in court and in the bank reaped by the unusual mom-and-pop law firm. "Now it's up to Ma and Pa Kettle," a proud Mr. Rosenblatt was quoted. A week later, a second article appeared. Headlined "In the End, Smoke Succumbed to One Man's Fire," its focus was on the male half of the dynamic lawyer duo, and especially on his "righteous anger." Similar articles appeared in local Florida papers like the *Miami Herald* and the *Jacksonville Florida Times-Union*.

The various news reports predictably personalized the lawyers as intriguing Davids who felled a huge Goliath, but each portrayed them in consistently curious ways. On the one hand, the stories recycled Horatio Alger myths: a pair of American immigrants made good; a devoutly religious couple with nine kids triumphed and prospered through intense devotion and hard work. On the other hand, the narratives' focus on the "crazy" gambit of these "lone eagles" against "incredible" and "insurmountable odds" dramatically invoked a favorite metaphor of tort reformers for our allegedly arbitrary legal system—the litigation lottery. Completely overlooking the couple's legal arguments, precedents, evidence, or strategies that convinced the jury during the trial, the stories focused on how this couple by luck or by pluck won big when a wild gamble paid off. They might as well as have won the local Lotto. Such coverage understandably pleased the Rosenblatts. Yet these accounts may have done more to divert than to enhance public understanding about the issues, processes, or power stakes contested in American law. They certainly reinforced tort reform claims about windfall awards to undeserving plaintiffs and plaintiffs' attorneys.

Even more important, news coverage of the initial *Engle* victory, focusing on the wager of a lucky lawyer, provided little preparation for the third chapter of the Rosenblatt saga. In late May 2003, a three-member panel of Florida's Third District Court reversed the trial verdict in *Engle* on half a dozen grounds. The appellate court, among other actions, decertified the class because the effects of corporate deception and medical injuries varied widely and thus should be litigated individually rather than as a common matter of law; ruled that the determination of lump-sum punitive damages was wrongly undertaken prior to, and apart from, a finding of liability for actual harm and determination of compensatory damages for each class member (putting "the cart before the horse"); ruled that the huge jury award violated state law stipulating that punitive damages cannot exceed assets of, and thus "destroy or bankrupt," defendants; ruled that a right to punitive damages was precluded by the Master Settlement Agreement of the states and Florida's separate lawsuit; and lambasted attorney Rosenblatt for "inflammatory," "prejudicial" tactics of using racial analogies and urging the jury "in a subtle way that they should disregard the law" in their search for justice.[38]

It is noteworthy that this momentous reversal received only minimal news coverage. The few major news articles on the subject, moreover, seemed to take delight in reporting the District Court's "withering comments" *(Los Angeles Times)* and "sharply critical" *(New York Times)* rebuke regarding the Rosenblatts' suspect legal tactics, while virtually ignoring the role of the trial judge who supervised the problematic proceedings.[39] We could find no acknowledgment in published articles about how the Rosenblatts were transformed from lottery-winning underdogs to underhanded devils. Our point is not to defend the Rosenblatts but simply to note the swift, simple shift from one familiar stereotype of legal lore to another. Perhaps most important, the fact that the routine legal process completely derailed the alleged "runaway jury" and, in the process, invoked precedents to pronounce that class-action litigation in tobacco disputes was virtually dead barely registered on the media barometer. Alleged litigation lotteries and trial attorneys' avidities proved more newsworthy than consequent legal developments, especially when the latter reestablished the status-quo immunity and dominance of the tobacco industry.

This brings us to our primary point. By focusing on plaintiffs' attorneys, news coverage to a large extent displaces attention from other key issues and actors. The focus on the trial lawyers not only has obscured their high-risk losses of millions of dollars over time, but it has ignored recognition of the defense attorneys who have made millions for saving tobacco companies billions by manipulative tactics, some hardball but others dirty pool. Indeed, entire firms have been nurtured largely on revenues from the defense of tobacco suits, revenues many times greater than those secured by plaintiffs' attorneys in trials (see Kessler 2001, 369). The focus on trial lawyers' gains, whether by greed or good luck, likewise has shifted attention from tobacco companies themselves who produce and market aggressively their harmful products for enormous profits at great costs to the

38. For the record, the Rosenblatts did extract a $700 million settlement from the tobacco companies on a side issue regarding the bond set after the initial trial, which a suspect Florida legislative act attempted to bypass.

39. Rosenblatt was censured for telling the jury truths that few legal scholars would contest and most teach their students. "Let's tell the truth about the law, before we all get teary-eyed about the law," the *New York Times* article repeated from the appellate ruling. "Historically, the law has been used as an instrument of oppression and exploitation" (Meier 2003).

public's health and pocketbook. It also discounts focus on the failures of elected and appointed officials to regulate tobacco and to provide more adequate health benefits to its victims, not to mention their self-interested political maneuverings to take control of windfall returns for purposes unrelated to original goals of the Master Settlement Agreement (Derthick 2002). All in all, by successfully focusing public attention on blaming victims of smoking and their attorneys, tobacco's advocates, mass media, and the ideological principles at the core of inherited legal lore together have greatly impeded substantial redefinition of the public agenda regarding tobacco.

DISPATCHES FROM THE TOBACCO WARS

We have offered three complementary perspectives, each of which significantly qualifies any expectation one might have for a new public agenda concerning tobacco, and together explain why there are few or no tobacco tales that counter the tales of tort reformists. When we reexamined the thematic strategies that challengers and defenders pursued inside and outside courtrooms, we confirmed insights about how litigants had reframed tobacco issues in novel ways in the 1990s. We have argued that plaintiffs' inventive reframing of challenges and defenders' clever responses created a tobacco policy "revolution" far more confusing than reconstructive. When we traced the course of tobacco litigation in the 1990s as reported in five national newspapers, we found that the papers publicized themes from each side. This meant not only that the themes relating to public costs and corporate responsibility were amplified, but that those concerning greedy lawyers and individual responsibility were boosted as well. Further, the papers often treated tobacco issues and cases in a manner similar to their treatments of other tort issues and cases in reports and articles, which meant that some reportage reinforced the pro-plaintiff bent of 1990s cases but that other reportage boomeranged against novel challenges. Challengers may have benefited from the tendency of the press to overreport plaintiffs' legal arguments and victories in case-specific reportage, but defenders benefited from rising dissatisfaction with the civil justice system and increased support for tort reform in thematic articles. Assessing the net gains or losses of that trade-off is a complex matter, although it appears that the benefits to challengers were limited to tobacco cases while the benefits to defenders and tort reformists were broader.

On the largest scale, our data led us to conclude that two powerful frames had survived the latest onslaughts on the part of challengers: the individual responsibility theme and an ambivalence about lawyers that tended to warrant attacks on lawyers' fees, tactics, and clout. Each rests on the manufactured common sense that stigmatized tort litigation during preceding decades, thwarting any progress by challengers to Big Tobacco in mass culture. Even those who have drawn attention to the latest wave of litigation can't help but wonder if it might have crested already; our contribution has been to suggest that, whenever the crest came or will come, it will not sustain plaintiffs in a very long or very high ride.

For at least the three reasons above, we do not expect the "juridico-entertainment complex" to issue many if any powerful narratives celebrating challengers or defenders of tobacco. If we are correct in our analyses and arguments above, any future treatments of high-stakes fights over tobacco are unlikely to improve on Hollywood fare such as *The Insider*.[40] Consequently, the dramatic thunder of tobacco litigation in court during the 1990s is likely to remain but a whisper struggling to be heard amid the familiar chant of American legal lore. More important yet, the Florida District Court's reversal of the enormous *Engle* award comports with other recent decisions in suggesting a new phase has emerged in the Tobacco Wars—a phase in which dramatic legal challenges to Big Tobacco in the courts themselves have been tamed by traditional individualizing logics once again. Class-action claims have been repeatedly rebuffed, while public claims for punitive damage awards have been restricted by federal Supreme Court guidelines generally and by the Master Settlement Agreement specifically in tobacco cases. [41] At the time of this writing, it seems that the narrow individualistic ethic of personal responsibility again governs official legal disputing over deadly carcinogens, while the government consensus to help secure tobacco company profitability in view of

40. Michael Mann's mass-marketed feature film *The Insider* conveyed the courage and principle of whistleblower Dr. Jeffrey Wigand (played by Russell Crowe) and producer Lowell Bergman (Al Pacino), but neither tobacco executives nor lawyers nor news people were portrayed very positively. Trial attorneys Richard Scruggs and Ronald Motley and Mississippi attorney general Michael Moore appeared to be resolute challengers of Big Tobacco, but the first two were first seen in the film flying in a private jet with Mr. Scruggs at the controls—confirming the stereotype of high-flying trial attorneys. Those three lawyers, however, were the most praiseworthy members of the bar according to the film. Almost every other attorney came off as crass, thuggish, or amoral, except for the CBS attorney who informed viewers that the truth of Dr. Wigand's revelations made things far worse legally; she (and the law of tortious interference) seemed surreal. Since tobacco manufacturer Brown and Williamson came across as ominous when not Orwellian, challengers were relatively creditable in the film, but that scarcely made for a counterweight to the accumulated legal lore, trove of tort tales, and assumption of the value of individualism in contemporary American culture.

41. See *Liggett v. Engle* (2003), pp. 10–11, 28. Consult the Web site accompanying this book (www.lawslore.info) for updates of relevant cases.

the large tax benefits and legal payoffs those profits generate has been emphatically reconfirmed. It would be premature to declare that the Tobacco Wars are over, but they may be reduced to no more than sporadic, small-scale guerilla challenges from plaintiffs' lawyers like those that were common prior to the 1990s.

CHAPTER EIGHT

Law through the Looking Glass
of Mass Politics

My general theme isn't society but the discourse of the true and false, by which I mean the correlative formation of domains and objects and of the verifiable, falsifiable discourses that bear on them; and it's not just their formation that interests me, but the effects in the real to which they are linked.

MICHEL FOUCAULT, "QUESTION OF METHOD"

Narrative can contribute to hegemony by functioning as a means of social control instructing about what is expected. . . . Narrative can also contribute to hegemony by colonizing consciousness with well-plotted but implicit accounts of social causality. Finally, . . . to the degree that stories depict understandings about particular persons and events while simultaneously effacing the connections between the particular persons and the social organization of their experience, they hide the grounds of their own plausibility and help reproduce the taken-for-granted hegemony.

PATRICIA EWICK AND SUSAN SILBEY,
"SUBVERSIVE STORIES AND HEGEMONIC TALES"

The American media, the public, and even many judges and lawyers are notably reluctant to consider the validity of "reality frames" other than those that characterize personal injury claimants as selfish and socially destructive. Hostility toward claims for remediation is, if anything, increasing, and asserting a claim is often taken as a negative indicator of the claimant's character and identity. If the prevailing ideology in American social settings continues to reject the very conceptual framework that supports injury victims' claims, then it will be the injurers whose worldviews most profoundly shape the communities in which we live.

DAVID ENGEL, "INJURY AND IDENTITY"

The preceding chapters have evaluated a pervasive form of legal lore contending that proliferating lawsuits, opportunistic plaintiffs, and greedy lawyers have contributed to a growing crisis in the contemporary United

States.[1] We have considered this distinctive legal knowledge from a variety of perspectives.

Our first general concern has been to explore the development and dissemination of familiar narratives bemoaning a lawsuit crisis in the contemporary United States. Throughout our analysis we have contended that the construction of mass legal knowledge is a complex, dynamic, and loosely structured process. We have sought to make sense of this tangled process by identifying and scrutinizing the interplay of its instrumental, institutional, and ideological dimensions, emphasizing in particular the latter two aspects of knowledge production—the proclivities of modern mass media and deeply rooted cultural values—to account for the undeniable lure of this legal lore.

Our second general concern has been to analyze the unique form, content, and character of mass legal knowledge. Realist critics surely are correct that pop tort reformers routinely invoke vivid anecdotes as empirical evidence for suspect claims about the explosion of civil litigation and, especially, frivolous lawsuits. But we contend that the distinctive *normative* appeal to responsible, disciplined, nonlitigious individuals who constitute the imagined "moral community" of America is the most resonant truth in the new common sense preached by reformers and normalized by the media. However insubstantial in empirical foundation, simplistic tort tales and ordinary news coverage together tap deeply held values concerning individualism and suspicion about formal state institutions, reaffirming prevailing understandings about both what is "wrong"—morally, economically, politically, legally—with the contemporary civil law system and what is necessary to right things. Focusing on this normative dimension of narratives, we suggest, renders far more comprehensible the connections between reformers' tilted tales and media news stories as well as the receptivity by news reporters of tort reformers' spin. Moreover, we suggest, a frank accounting of this moralistic appeal further helps to explain why gambits of empirical debunking by realist-minded sociolegal scholars and trial lawyers have posed only modest challenges to the prevailing lore in mass society.

Attention to the subtle manifestations and power of ideology in the complex process of producing knowledge prefigures our final argument. We have provided in preceding chapters a number of observations to suggest the important ways that this mass-produced legal knowledge matters for social, political, and legal practice throughout contemporary Amer-

---

1. We think there is abundant evidence to suggest that this lore about U.S. legal practices thrives throughout much of the world as well, but we have provided just incidental evidence here for such a proposition.

ican culture. Our goal in this final chapter is to address more directly and systematically some of these important implications or effects of the commonsense "truth" about tort law. In doing so, we integrate evidence presented earlier with much additional data, but our primary aim is to outline conceptually useful ways of recognizing and assessing the important ramifications of the prevailing legal knowledge. Just as we have emphasized the particular role of mass media in the production of knowledge, so too do we stress here how media stories of law in particular shape society, politics, and law itself. The diverse types of evidence we marshal are intended primarily to illustrate our interpretive position rather than to prove our points. The discussion thus is more speculative and suggestive than conclusive; it also is, unavoidably, more overtly normative and partisan in its judgments, although our primary aim is analytical. We first briefly address some challenges at stake in such an undertaking before outlining two of the most important ways that prevailing narratives, like the proverbial looking glass, distort—twist, divert, and magnify in fuzzy terms—the politics of law.

HOW DOES LEGAL KNOWLEDGE MATTER?

This study has proposed that narratives about a lawsuit crisis have been used primarily to fortify traditional U.S. cultural norms and social practices against recent advances on the part of those seeking consumer rights and demanding corporate accountability. Hence our insistence on the significant, if little recognized, role of tort reform politics and the alluring legal lore it has mobilized in fomenting the culture wars dividing American society. This in turn highlights the interpretive and empirical challenge at stake for our project: Can we identify reliable evidence that this particular form of mass legal knowledge and its core premises actually have made a notable difference in American political culture?

Perhaps the most conventional resource for answering such a question is public opinion surveys. Indeed, academic literature about tort reform politics frequently cites polling data, most often to show considerable public support for tort reform claims and goals. For example, a much-cited 1986 Roper Center poll conducted for the Insurance Information Institute found that 71 percent of respondents thought plaintiffs' liability lawsuits were justified only half of the time or less; 66 percent agreed that there were too many lawsuits; three of five thought that the litigation rates were rising faster than the nation's population; and 58 percent believed that liability awards and settlements were too high. A follow-up Roper poll for the same institute found almost exactly the same results in 1993. Moreover, a 1985 Roper Center poll found that 5 percent of respondents thought that the civil justice system favored defendants, 48 percent said it favored the injured person, and 31 percent said that it was equally fair to both sides; a whopping 75 percent reported their views that juries tend to rule against big business more than against individuals as defendants in civil cases. Likewise, a 1991 Gallup poll found that consumers believe punitive damages to be usually (32 percent) or sometimes (50 percent) too high. A 1999 poll by Bruskin, Goldring Research found that 44 percent of respondents believed that jury awards "are out of control," while 42 percent find them reasonable.[2]

Polls that we cited in chapter 4 regarding the declining faith in the honesty and ethics of lawyers also are relevant in this regard. And many other polls can be cited from the 1980s and 1990s—such as those we cited in chapter 7 regarding tobacco litigation—that report much the same type of results, thus providing noteworthy evidence regarding belief in legal lore about a lawsuit crisis. As a very sophisticated poll by two political scientists concludes, "the most important conclusion from our work is that the myth of the litigation explosion continues to be widely held and appears to be permanently entrenched" (Meinhold and Neubauer 2001, 112; see also Neubauer and Meinhold 1994).

These data seem to provide powerful support for the thesis that narratives bemoaning a civil lawsuit crisis matter a great deal. We remain wary about exclusive reliance on such findings, however.[3] For one thing, none of the available polls have been repeated over long periods of time so as to provide evidence that public knowledge and judgment have been transformed by the dual influence of increased tort reform advocacy and the media attention paid to it. Moreover, most of these polls were conducted for business groups and tended to ask selective questions that, arguably, shaped the findings. As Diane Colasanto, former president of the American Association for Public Opinion Research, said of one such poll, "You can't measure public opinion research with leading questions like these" (Center for Justice and Democracy 2002). Such polls also notoriously tend to be vague and impressionistic in their queries.

When political scientist Herbert Kritzer (2001) conducted a telephone survey using more specific questions probing citizen knowledge about jury awards, he found the matter to be more complex. Respondents did tend to have an inflated view of jury awards, but the magnitude of the

---

2. These polling results are widely cited in literature on tort reform. All can be found in the RPOLL library on Lexis/Nexis. The most commonly cited report is Mooney 1992.

3. We acknowledge the limits of our own references to polling data in chapter 7, although in most cases the data referred to judgments about specific policies and issues rather than general values.

distortion was far less than standard news reporting might lead us to expect. It is equally important to recognize that, even when questions are well framed by respectable pollsters, they almost always probe discrete responses about litigation in isolation from other values, interests, concerns, and considerations. For example, we noted earlier that consumers express considerable distrust of corporate commitments to protecting consumer safety and are even more distrustful of insurance companies. Indeed, surveys regarding citizen rights to sue negligent corporate producers and health care professionals often show considerable support in various states for the existing civil law system (see Citizens for Corporate Accountability and Individual Rights, memo, April 13, 1999).

In sum, the knowledge tapped by opinion surveys tends to be highly selective, narrow, and decontextualized. The most frequently cited polls on lawsuit abuse provide little insight into how citizens actively think about and make judgments regarding complex practical situations involving multiple types of relevant knowledge and conflicting values, much less whether these modes of judgment have changed over time. By contrast, our social constructionist analysis

> focuses on "common knowledge" as opposed to "public opinion"; what people think and how they think about public issues rather than valence- oriented "opinions" concerning an issue. . . . The use of "knowledge" rather than "opinion" emphasizes the need to organize information into meaningful structures. The phrase "common knowledge" emphasizes that the structuring and framing of information is not unique to each individual but aggregates into the cultural phenomenon of shared perspectives and issue frames. (Neuman, Just, and Crigler 1992, 18)[4]

We especially focus on how such knowledge is manifest in structured practices within particular contexts of institutionalized sociolegal interaction that are likely to matter the most.[5] Specifically, how and how much does mass-produced legal knowledge influence the practical thinking of voters assessing policy issues and political candidates; of elite policymakers confronting legal reform proposals; of jurors or victims in deciding how to assign liability for harms; of attorneys in advising clients handling

---

4. See also Schudson 1995.

5. As Ewick and Silbey (1998) put it, "Consciousness can no longer be understood as something that is individual and merely ideational. It must be constructed as a type of social practice, in the sense that it reflects and forms structure." Hence, they argue, consciousness should be "envisaged as emerging out of, even as it impinges on, social interactions" (225).

disputes and conducting trials; and of institutional managers or consumers engaged in risk assessment and insurance purchases? Can we identify the ways in which the prevailing legal knowledge has and has not been effectively mobilized to provoke particular responses of participants in discrete roles and settings? In the remainder of this chapter we move beyond attention to relatively passive, insular, abstract attitudes about law and focus instead on legal knowledge as it is mobilized in identifiable, consequential social practices by variously situated citizens.

AGENDA SETTING AND MACROPOLITICS

Agenda Setting: Core Insights

Our first general angle of analysis picks up on previous discussions about the macropolitical agenda-setting efforts of the pop tort reform movement and its allies.[6] The essence of *agenda setting* was well enunciated E. E. Schattschneider: "In politics as in everything else, it makes a great difference whose game we play" (1960, 47). In short, the ability to define or control the rules, terms, or perceived options in a contest over policy greatly affects the prospects for winning.

It is worth noting that the dynamic politics of agenda setting can take place in any organizational venue—within specific institutional sites of workplaces and neighborhoods to legislatures and courts, or more broadly throughout society. In contemporary complex societies like the United States, "systemic" or societywide agenda-setting practices tend to focus on the interactions among governmental leaders, nonstate policy advocates, and the mass-media consuming public. One of Schattschneider's (1960) seminal contributions concerned how the scope of a conflict figured into agenda setting-dynamics. In his framework, we noted earlier, powerful groups usually aim to restrict the conflict's scope to a limited number of actors in largely private, insular, and informal processes, while less powerful groups find it in their interest to expand the scope of conflict to include broader audiences and more public, formalized modes of decisionmaking. Subsequent scholarship complicated this picture by demonstrating how expansive public contests accentuated the role of the mass

---

6. Daniels and Martin provided a very useful and compelling analysis of tort reform advocates' strategic efforts from an agenda-setting perspective in their 1995 book. Our discussion here aims to add to that analysis, emphasizing in particular how agendas have actually been shaped and altered interactively through the influence of both tort reformers' strategies and media dissemination of legal lore. However, we offer nothing like a comprehensive theory of agenda setting. For that, see Baumgartner and Jones 1993.

media in communicating competing ideas, understandings, and definitions. As the mass media have facilitated political interaction across greater
expanses of space, so has politics increasingly become a matter of symbolic manipulation of contested constructions that often lack grounding in
the immediate experience of most citizens. In short, the potential for di-
versionary agenda setting, empty "symbolic politics," and empirically ungrounded political lore to dominate the conventional wisdom of public
discourse has become a familiar feature of contemporary public life (see
Edelman 1964, 1988; Bennett 1996). And as this politics of iconic images
and symbolic ideas has developed greater power, so have the most powerful groups—including large business corporations and New Right advocates (Smith 2000)—come to invest heavily in media campaigns aiming to
mold public agendas.

Our analysis throughout this book has offered a host of insights regarding such agenda-setting dynamics in contemporary political contests over
civil law reform and legal knowledge generally. In the next few pages,
we summarize and elaborate on the discursive outcomes that have
emerged from these portrayals of social reality. While legal knowledge has
been contested in each case, we identify how mass-produced knowledge
about the lawsuit crisis has worked to shape significantly the salience and
terms—that is, the mobilized bias—of such public contests over legal policy among elites and before ordinary citizens.

Tort Reform Contests

One primary focus of agenda-setting analysis has concerned the variable
ways that specific policy issues, problems, or responses are constructed by
different parties. Neither problems nor their solutions label themselves,
after all; they must be actively identified, defined, and defended to win
and sustain attention (Gusfield 1981). This type of analysis focuses, in
Deborah Stone's apt words, on how people "fight with ideas," symbols,
metaphors, stories, and evidence to "create different portrayals of the
battle—who is affected, how they are affected, and what is at stake" (1988,
25). The scrutiny in this regard is thus on "strategic representation"—that
is, on narrative constructions motivated by an instrumental purpose or
goal. Stone focuses in particular on one type of agenda-setting practice especially relevant to this study—the contest over what she labels competing "causal stories." "Since our cultural understanding of accidents defines
them as events beyond human control," she contends, "causal politics is
centrally concerned with moving interpretations of situations from the
realm of accidents" to one in which "situations come to be caused by human actions and amenable to human intervention" (1989, 281, 284). In

short, causal stories clash by focusing responsibility on different practices, people, or relations that arguably are harmful and in need of regulatory control or reform. Analysts have further illustrated that problems and solutions are often related in complex, unexpected ways. While different definitions of problems often drive the competition among leaders over alternative policy solutions, the reverse can be true as well. In other words, political actors often "invent" social problems for the purpose of cultivating a perceived need for policy solutions that those actors desire for other (often unarticulated) reasons.

The most direct and obvious way that legal lore production has mattered for this aspect of public agenda setting has concerned contests directly over reform of tort law. Indeed, the tort reform campaign has signaled one of the most well orchestrated "new" efforts of big business and allied think tanks to shape directly public knowledge, discourse, and perceived issue salience. The reformist movement has defined its primary goal as "making the public better aware of the cost and consequences of lawsuit abuse" in order *"to create a climate* for reform of our civil justice system" (emphasis added).[7] We have made it clear earlier in this book (chapter 2), moreover, that the pop tort reform issue has attained significant salience and success in popular campaigns, especially at the state level. Legislation or initiatives mandating various types of tort reform have been passed in more than forty states since the mid-1980s. Federal legislation was repeatedly sponsored between 1988 and 2000; it was one of ten legislative proposals in the GOP's Contract with America in 1994. A comprehensive reform bill was initiated in both houses during 1995 as the Common Sense Legal Reforms Act and was passed by Congress in 1996, although it did not withstand the veto by President Clinton, who nevertheless did sign several more narrowly tailored reform measures. Likewise, to a large degree George W. Bush built his reputation in Texas politics by trumpeting the tort reform theme; both of the major party candidates and their running mates during the 2000 presidential campaign openly supported the cause.

At the time of this writing, new legislative proposals for tort reform and lawsuit control are emerging at both the state and federal level. Piecemeal limitations on the legal liability of airlines, drug makers, teachers, asbestos manufacturers, and makers of anti-terrorism devices were written into law in 2002 to rein in trial lawyers, whom Republican Senate leader Trent Lott labeled a "pack of wolves." A Republican-initiated campaign for far-

7. The first quote is from the Texas Campaign against Lawsuit Abuse (www.tala.com/history.html); the second quote is from a California CALA, cited in Daniels and Martin 2000, 11.

reaching federal medical malpractice reform rose high on the congressional agenda in 2003 (VandeHei 2002).

At every point, we have shown, tort reformers' proposals have been contested. Scholars, advocates for trial lawyers, and policy elites have directly challenged reforms by decrying the simplistic portrayals of anecdotal tort tales as well as the reformers' inflated rhetoric; by marshaling alternative statistical and case study evidence to show the empirical inaccuracy of commonplace claims about a lawsuit crisis; and by exposing the harms imposed and profits gained by unaccountable producers of goods and services. Those opposed to the forces of reform—buoyed by ample financing, lobbying clout, and legal skills of trial lawyers—have succeeded in stopping federal legislation and neutralizing in large part state laws mandating tort reform. However, we also have shown how the best-funded opponents of reform, the trial lawyers, have conducted the bulk of their challenges behind the scenes, mostly conceding the public debate to better-funded supporters of reform. With only a few exceptions, scholarly critics of pop tort reform have remained in the background or been limited to obscure outlets, leaving assorted underfunded consumer groups nearly alone to wage the public battle over ideas. Moreover, we have suggested that opponents of tort reform have waged substantive campaigns that are as inadequate in form and content as they are remote in venue. In instrumental terms, opponents of tort reform have won many policy battles, but the larger cultural war over ideas has been, in Eisenberg and Henderson's words, a "slaughter" (1992, 770; see also Schwartz 1991–92).

Our emphasis on the institutional power of the news media underlines how mass-manufactured legal lore has greatly shaped, even distorted, these struggles over the public agenda on tort reform among the general citizenry. This argument goes beyond recognition of the fact that print news is both the primary *source* of reformers' tort tales and the primary *medium* for disseminating these twice-told tales along with the reformers' policy message. More important, mass-produced news has steadily supplied selective stories about "real" life that provide a narrative foundation and affirmative evidence for the dominant lore. As Gavriel Salomon's research on media and learning confirms, citizens tend to view television news as part of the entertainment media in which it is embedded, while newspaper accounts are thought to be far more serious and reliable, more like textbooks or legal documents that can be accepted as true and objective (Salomon 1979, 1984; see also Neuman, Just, and Crigler 1992). In short, print news more fully naturalizes the selective representations it normalizes. Rapidly increasing instances of front-page news coverage about plaintiffs' winning large monetary awards for vague claims of injury from deep-pocketed defendants thus confirm the tall tales and allegations of reformers that later appear on editorial and opinion pages of the same newspapers. Moreover, as we saw in chapters 6 and 7, such narratives tend to endure; once reporters and editorialists fix on a story frame or opinion, they tend to resist rethinking what they committed themselves to publicly.

We emphasize further the accessibility and adaptability as well as availability of news accounts among the citizenry. As media analysts have led us to expect, stories of civil litigation tend to be simplistic, dramatic, individualized, and decontextualized. Emphasis is routinely directed toward the allegations of disputants and the large monetary awards they seek or win. News accounts stress perfunctory, almost predictable contests of inflated naming, blaming, and claiming, while virtually erasing the complexities of legal evidence, argument, and procedure in the trials that judges and juries witness. The fact that most news stories avoid educating the public about legal principles and processes also renders them more easily understood and enduring. Indeed, such stories contain many of the very framing elements—individualistic focus, the holler of dollars, dramatic conflict, powerlessness at the hands of government—to which citizen consumers of news seem most predisposed and responsive (Neuman, Just, and Crigler 1992; Iyengar 1991).[8] And precisely these elements make news stories resonate with the crude, exaggerated tort tales spun by reformers. If endless repetition of simplistic, selective story lines shapes commonsense knowledge, then routine readers of the news would seem to be extremely well primed for the message of those who criticize our civil law system.

It is worth underlining as well our previous suggestions regarding how the moral appeals of popular narratives have enhanced their status as conventional wisdom. One of the primary arguments advanced by Neuman, Just, and Cigler's compelling book *Common Knowledge* is that mass audiences tend to derive great moral significance from news narratives, while typically overlooking factual details. In their study, the authors found that news media tended to downplay moral themes in the pursuit of balance and objectivity, while the public "relished and drew out the moral dimension in the human impact of issues, and underscored the moral dimension of public policies" (1992, 112). In short, what citizens allow themselves to know is largely shaped by what they have learned to believe. As we have noted, media accounts of civil litigation have varied widely in their degree

---

8. We offer a curious caveat here. Scholars emphasize that readers indulge their preference for and longer remember "human impact" themes of news reporting. Civil litigation coverage often focuses on individual claims and fates in court, but stories tend to be surprisingly impersonal, offering little sympathetic attention to those injured or harmed; injured citizens are treated as adversarial plaintiffs, underscoring the homology to tort tales. See chapter 5.

of explicit moralizing, often but hardly always muting the moralism typical of parallel tort tales. However, even when explicit moral judgments
about individual greed, moral irresponsibility, and arbitrary government
redistribution of wealth have been absent, standard news coverage has invited such inferences. The reason, we noted earlier, is that media coverage
of tort cases tends to efface the human aspects of pain and suffering
among citizens harmed by unsafe products or professional incompetence.
Injured citizens are represented instead primarily as contentious plaintiffs in dramatic legal disputes, contesting similarly depersonalized defendants.[9] Actual experiences of consumer anguish are ignored or eclipsed
by attention to the familiar legal roles of adversaries and the large monetary sums at stake. Moralistic judgments about the relative responsibility,
reasonableness, and character of legal disputants are encouraged by news
practices over assessments that turn on moral sentiments of compassion
and empathy for the "private" injuries of victims. Such framing conventions are hardly likely to inspire faith in the legal process or in legal outcomes favoring plaintiffs.

Two further considerations exacerbate these tendencies of routine news
production. First, as outlined by Ewick and Silbey (1998), citizens understand law through different interpretive "schemas." The two that most uphold popular faith in the prevailing liberal legal order specify particular elements or characteristics of legitimate, properly functioning law. The
"before the law" frame values law above all else for its impartiality and abstract rationality; the "with the law" frame imagines law as a game among
self-interested individuals bound by legitimate rules and norms of responsible action. The relevance for our analysis is that both sets of standards arguably are called into question by serial stories of plaintiffs who
are depicted as winning inexplicably large awards for wild claims lacking
clear, consistent justification. "Litigation lotteries" hardly fit the legitimate,
fair "game" model of law respected by most ordinary citizens, much less
the norm of reasoned impartiality. If Ewick and Silbey are correct, the
rapid increase in news reporting about high stakes civil litigation after the
1980s provided considerable impetus for widespread public concern about

---

9. Routine media stories are very different in this regard from morally complex, ambiguous artistic reflections such as both the book and movie versions of *The Sweet Hereafter*. Indeed, the novelist Russell Banks developed a brilliantly sensitive study of tragic choices in a
small community after a bus accident killing many children that contrasted dramatically
with newspaper coverage of the actual event on which he based his story. For a provocative
account of the movie, see Sarat 2000b. Even the fine, philosophically rich, artistic narratives
paint a negative portrait of the personal injury lawyer and plaintiffs who follow him, however. In fact, to our dismay, students in our university classes often read the movie as essentially another tort tale.

a legal order gone awry. In case the consuming public failed to draw this inference directly from the news, widely circulated tort tales and pervasive commentary from experts, pundits, and editorialists usually have been close at hand to aid the interpretive linkages to skeptical moral themes about individual rapacity and the arbitrary legal sweepstakes. Again, there is much reason to think that the mass-media production of legal knowledge has contributed to systemic agenda setting with respect to the issue of civil litigation.

Second, there is ample evidence from social science to suggest further that the narrowly selective elements structuring news narratives and media commentary have considerable impact on reader perceptions of issues (Bennett 1996; Page 1996). We undertook a modest experiment to probe just how that influence might matter for public representations of civil litigation. On the first day of an introductory undergraduate class in the spring of 2000, we asked 119 college students to read an actual news account of the McDonald's coffee case (see chapter 6). One-half (60) read the short, widely circulated AP "template" article of the case; the other half (59) read Andrea Gerlin's longer, more detailed and complex but little replicated news account—which also omitted crucial evidence from the trial but reported many more facts of the case, the injury, and jury reasoning— in the *Wall Street Journal.* We then asked students to answer a ten-item survey about both this dispute and its implications for civil litigation broadly.[10] The first interesting finding was that over 92 percent of respondents, with little difference between the two groups, reported that they had heard of the case before; the primary sources they listed for previous exposure to the story were television, newspapers, and word of mouth.

The two groups diverged dramatically on most other questions. We first asked a series of questions specifically about the hot coffee case. Readers of the typically succinct AP report consistently were far more negative than readers of the Gerlin account (1) on whether the case should have been heard by courts, by 61 percent to 40 percent; (2) on whether the verdict was unreasonable, by a whopping 65 percent to 18 percent; and (3) on whether the award was unreasonable, by 66 percent to 39 percent. The two groups did not split much on guesses about how much Ms. Liebeck was eventually awarded, but 60 percent overall guessed high, with about one-third guessing more than twice as high as the estimated settlement (see Kritzer 2001). On more general issues, the AP readers agreed that U.S. citizens are too obsessed with their rights by a 43 percent to 30 percent mar-

10. See the Web site accompanying this book (www.lawslore.info) for an accounting of our methodology and statistical results.

gin over the Gerlin readers, with half as many of the former expressing concern that citizens are too indifferent about rights. Finally, both groups expressed great agreement that there was too much litigation in the United States, 72 percent and 68 percent respectively, although the Gerlin readers included many more who disagreed with that position (15 percent to 2 percent for AP readers). These findings are highly suggestive. If we are correct that the reading public is subjected to a steady diet of tort case profiles in the news resembling the AP report, as well as to tort tales and reform rhetoric, earlier reported general poll findings about winners of the agenda-setting contest seem more convincing.[11]

Many other segments of the nation's population share perceptions of a litigation crisis and other beliefs common among our undergraduates. Ethnographic studies of small communities (Greenhouse, Yngvesson, and Engel 1994), in-depth interviews with citizens in urban areas who have suffered discrimination (Bumiller 1988; Nielson 2004), and surveys of legal actors in many contexts verify findings of opinion polls that ordinary legal knowledge is amply suffused with lore that confirms the tort reform agenda. It is difficult to know for sure how much of the responsibility for these predispositions belongs to media reporting, but there can be little doubt that the media have skewed the public agenda in ways that invest tort reform with considerable salience as a policy issue and privileges its supporters in contests over the merits.

Evidence for the power of legal lore in shaping the *public agenda among elites* is equally suggestive. We offer several examples. It is relevant to remember that, by 1994, the momentum of the national tort reform movement was flagging. A decade of failure to pass major national legislation in Congress had sapped energies and nurtured frustration, while widespread state reforms were being undone by legal appeals to state constitutional courts. The hopes of supporters rose when forty-four senators from across the political spectrum sponsored the Products Liability Fairness Act in 1994, although they knew from previous experience that a bitter battle would follow. In late July, moderate Republican John C. Danforth stood to make a passionate case to his colleagues about why a lawsuit reform bill must be passed. Danforth—an ordained Episcopal priest, a lawyer, a former attorney general from Missouri, and a pillar of moral authority—narrated a story lifted from a newspaper account as the centerpiece of his argument about how our products liability system that had spun out of control:

---

11. We did code responses for variations in race and gender of respondents. The former produced too small of a number to consider, while the latter produced no noteworthy differences.

There was a famous case a few years ago of a 70-year-old man who lost the eyesight in his left eye. Now, the loss of eyesight in one eye is not a minor matter. But what is the just result of a 70-year-old man losing eyesight in one eye? What is the reasonable compensation that such an individual should receive? Should it be in the thousands of dollars? In the tens of thousands of dollars? The hundreds of thousands of dollars? Should it be in the millions of dollars? This person filed a lawsuit, a products liability case, against Upjohn Co., and his recovery was $127 million.[12]

This anecdote, of course, had all the elements of a classic tort tale. While the facts listed about *Proctor v. Davis* were literally accurate, the senator's homily explicitly impugned the reasonableness of the plaintiff's claim and focused nearly all the attention on the enormous, seemingly arbitrary monetary award. Many critical facts aired at the trial, but typically left unreported in the news, went unmentioned in Danforth's account, such as the fact that nearly all of the initial $127 million award was in punitive damages against Upjohn for well-documented "outrageous conduct" in unscrupulously marketing the unsafe steroid Depo-Medrol; the $3 million in compensatory damages was not merely for "loss of sight in one eye," but for the pain, disability, and emotional suffering caused by three unsuccessful surgeries and eventual removal of the entire eye; the punitive damages were reduced by the trial judge to $35 million, later by an appellate court to $6 million, and probably by even more in an eventual settlement under pressure of continuous appeals by the profitable corporation.

This was just one of many beguiling stories excerpted from the news and recycled by reform advocates to elevate the lawsuit crisis on the congressional agenda and prefigure its eventual outcome. Anecdotes about legal liability costs for girl scout cookies, pajama manufacturers, high school sports programs, and milkshake vendors far outweighed references to systematic studies in the congressional record (see our Web site accompanying this book—www.lawslore.info). The most important of these stories, of course, was the McDonald's coffee case, which reached court just weeks after Danforth's sermon and flooded the newspapers for months prior to congressional hearings the next spring. No other news story could have provided a more powerful boost to the cause. "Everybody in America is fed up with being sued by everybody for everything. I just have to refer to the case of the lady that sued and won for having been scalded by a cup of cof-

---

12. We uncovered Danforth's address in our study of congressional floor debates. Most of our account regarding omitted facts and issues surrounding this case were taken later from Bogus (2001, 6–17).

fee she bought in McDonald's 5 minutes earlier," proclaimed Representative Kasich as Republicans geared up to take action to limit frivolous lawsuits in 1994 (140 Cong. Rec. H9766, September 27, 1994).

An electronic subject search of the congressional debates in 1995 confirmed that the McDonald's coffee case dominated political discourse. Between February 1 and May 9, we found eighty-four references to "McDonald's coffee" and seventeen to "Stella Liebeck," the plaintiff; these allusions were most numerous between March 31 and May 9, when floor debates on proposed tort reform bills commenced. Most references to the case were negative, simplistic, and factoid-ridden. For example, Representative Michael Oxley, chairman of the House Energy and Commerce Committee, discussed the "frivolous lawsuit" problem just a few days later in a public statement: "Whenever the public reads about a woman who spills coffee in her lap and gets $3 million, most people say this doesn't make a whole lot of sense" (quoted in Ruiz 1995). The remark by Representative Porter J. Goss is typical of the commentary during the hearings: "I would guess that most Americans probably agree that the $3 million judgment recently awarded to a woman who spilled hot coffee in her lap was unreasonable. While the plaintiff in that case, and likely her lawyer too, now may rest comfortably on that judgment, the rest of America can expect to pay more for lukewarm coffee in the future" (141 Cong. Rec. H2661, March 6, 1995).

Opponents of the bill like Ralph Nader and Senator Ernest Hollings protested, of course, often laboring to explain the facts of the case to the legislators as the realist script prescribed. But their protests reiterated how the selectively reported news story of an atypical lawsuit redefined the agenda of the U.S. Congress, forced opponents to maneuver on hostile discursive terrain, and required only token amplification by business-supported lobbyists. Tort reform again became a salient issue, and the debate was dramatically stacked in favor of reformers by a new epitome of a long-developing conventional wisdom (see Gordon 1995). Based on debates grounded overwhelmingly in anecdotal common sense and polls showing constituent support, national tort reform legislation passed both houses of Congress for the first time.

Evidence also suggests that belief in the conventional wisdom among elites has proved difficult to dislodge and disrupt. Consider political scientist Donald Songer's study of how legislators, attorneys, and medical doctors responded to rigorous social scientific evidence demonstrating that there was no explosion of lawsuits and large awards in South Carolina during the 1980s. Songer (1988) conducted a survey, followed by selective interviews, of 408 such elites during 1986–87. He found that all three groups, and doctors by a huge margin, greatly overestimated the rise in litigation levels, sizes of awards, percentages of cases that went to jury trial, and the percentage of those latter cases won by plaintiffs. A second survey was taken the following year after a summary of empirical findings showing that actual tort practice did not fit critics' allegations was widely reported in major newspapers. His hope was "that the publication of the jury verdict study would produce a significant increase in the accuracy of the perceptions of all three types of elites." However, "the survey data did not fulfill this hope." Elite accuracy about actual litigation patterns did not change, and in fact actually *worsened* in some regards, after exposure to the social scientific data. One plausible explanation was that the academic study—"a collection of charts, graphs, and statistical data"—required detailed, intensive study that elites had no time, patience, or capacity to undertake (600). As our earlier discussion would have predicted, an "avalanche of information" thus had little impact on the elites' moralistic, anecdotally grounded, commonsense understandings. "The perceptions of most legislators were consistent with the claims of those who bewailed the existence of a crisis produced by skyrocketing jury awards and an explosion of litigation," despite clear evidence to the contrary (602). Tort reform eventually failed in the South Carolina legislature that year only because a few policymakers at the last minute deferred to a handful of trusted judiciary subcommittee experts who had actually read and understood the studies.

There thus is much reason to think that the tort reform debate over competing causal stories has been significantly shaped by the conventional wisdom routinely confirmed by mass-produced "real" news and fictional entertainment. The agenda-setting dynamics surrounding the tort reform issue thus well confirm the prediction of policy scholar Deborah Stone:

> Assertions of a causal theory [13] are more likely to be successful—that is, become the dominant belief and guiding assumption for policy makers—if the proponents have visibility, access to media, and prominent positions; if the theory accords with widespread and deeply held cultural values; if it somehow captures or responds to a "national mood"; and if its implicit prescription entails no radical redistribution of power or wealth. (1989, 294)

Our primary contribution to this astute assessment is recognition that the "national mood" itself is hardly authentic or natural, but is itself a product

---

13. Stone uses the term "causal story" far more often in her work, which better comports with our usage.

of ubiquitous processes by which mass media manufacture knowledge.[14] And through this process the familiar narratives *about* law have increasingly become translated through reform measures *into* official law itself.

Agenda Diversion and Displacement

A second, more general dynamic identified by agenda-setting analysts concerns the process by which some *specific issues, problems, or solutions come to dominate the agenda to the exclusion of other issues.* As Frank Baumgartner and Bryan Jones (1993) have contended, humans possess limited capacities for attention. Because the cognitive "space" for policy consideration is limited, therefore, issues that command attention end up marginalizing or diverting attention that might be directed to other potentially salient public issues. Political actors recognize this matter of "issue salience" and typically spend as much time attempting to draw attention away from their opponents' agenda and to their own preferred issues as they do in responding to the problems and solutions that opponents outline. Hence the struggle over defining which issues do and do not command attention in a policy sphere is every bit as pressing as the struggle to define how those salient issues are understood and addressed most effectively.[15] Such contests over policy attention can be important, for policy reforms, processes, and institutional mechanisms created to address high-profile issues often remain in place long after the original issues themselves decline in salience, giving way to yet new agendas.[16]

Our social constructionist analysis has identified a variety of important issues and understandings that contorted legal narratives have tended to diminish or even displace. The very fact that a lawsuit "crisis" has been declared by public elites and widely reported as such in the news should be

14. We think that Murray Edelman (1988) gets it right: "News . . . is not so much a description of events as a catalyst of political support and opposition in the light of the spectator's sensitivities, areas of ignorance and ideological stance. . . . By definition a spectacle highlights the obtrusive current news that captures its audience and seems to have a self evident meaning. The meaning and the development itself are typically expressions and vivid reinforcements of the dominant ideology that justifies extant inequalities. They divert attention from historical knowledge, social and economic analysis and unequal benefits and sufferings that might raise questions about the dominant ideology" (93–94, 125).

15. This is what Schattschneider (1960) referred to as the "mobilization of bias . . . in favor of the exploitation of certain types of conflict and the suppression of others. . . . Some issues are organized into politics while some are organized out" (71). See also Bachrach and Baratz 1970; Gaventa 1980.

16. Baumgartner and Jones (1993) define a model of "punctuated equilibrium" to make sense of this process. One need not accept the model per se to understand the dynamics that they explain.

enough to alert the critical observer on this score. As Murray Edelman (1988) argued, a media-defined "appearance of a crisis is a political act, not a recognition of a fact or of a rare situation" (31). Invocations of crisis aim to command immediate and total attention, to divert interest from other competing issues, and to reinforce deference to traditional political arrangements and norms. In short, proclaiming the existence of a crisis is itself a gambit to refocus the public agenda. We identify at least three general ways in which the lawsuit crisis rhetoric, advocated by tort reform elites and supported by mass-produced news, has narrowed the discursive terrain of politics in contemporary America.

The first and most obvious way in which that rhetoric has redefined the terms of issue selection and salience is by *diverting attention away from injurious corporate behavior and toward the alleged irresponsibility of individual lawyers and plaintiffs*. It is worth recalling in this regard that the business-sponsored tort reform movement developed in the late 1970s precisely to halt and, if possible, to reverse the momentum of liberal "public interest" reforms aiming to increase "access to justice" and to challenge the often reckless, unaccountable pursuit of profit by corporations at the expense of public health (McCann 1986). This counterreformist political agenda advanced a "different kind of class politics" that focuses on demonizing cultural elites, especially trial lawyers, who were not on the approved list of corporate chiefs, oil barons, heirs to large fortunes, successful entrepreneurs, or conservative religious leaders (Dionne 2003). The new legal lore has at once facilitated and symbolized that systemic shift of agendas in the culture wars. Indeed, we have shown that increased attention to the greed of lawyers and plaintiffs, to the recklessness of individual consumers, and to the fecklessness of jurors has routinely displaced public attention to the harms caused by corporate greed or indifference. We have illustrated, for example, how media coverage of both the McDonald's coffee case and decades of tobacco litigation focused attention on themes of individual plaintiff irresponsibility. The result in each case was to insulate corporations from responsibility for their negligent and sometimes callous, even rapacious, production of harmful products, blaming instead the victims for both their careless use of products and subsequent wanton litigiousness. By presenting injured consumers as adversarial plaintiffs, news coverage and tort tales reverse the logic of victimization determined in many trials by juries and judges.

This diversion has been nowhere more evident than in the series of so-called insurance crises that have been blamed on soaring legal liability costs over the last thirty years. Concerns over rising costs of liability insurance allegedly necessitated by exploding litigation and skyrocketing jury awards, we saw earlier, was one of the most powerful catalysts to the success of state tort reform efforts. A Reagan era Justice Department report in 1986, which prompted extensive media coverage, stated the position concisely: "The increase in the number of tort lawsuits and the level of awarded damages (or settlements) in and of itself has an obvious inflating effect on insurance premiums" (quoted in Hayden 1991, 100; see also Van Fossen 2002). Many studies, however, including one by the National Association of Attorneys General, have demonstrated that the fluctuating fates of the insurance industry are tied primarily to the ups and downs of (mostly bond) investment markets. The common pattern is for insurance corporations to engage in competitive price cutting during boom times so as to maximize the dollars they have to invest. When the economy falters and investment markets decline, insurance companies are hurt by both declining investment returns and by the low premiums that they collect. The common response is to increase premiums to offset losses and restore profit margins.

To divert attention from their erratic practices in changing market conditions, insurance companies have found it convenient to externalize blame on familiar culprits stigmatized by legal lore—greedy lawyers, devious plaintiffs, and duped jurors. This has been effective, despite the empirical evidence showing that claims that have been paid for medical malpractice per doctor have tracked medical inflation closely; paid claims were slightly above inflation from 1975 to 1985 and fairly flat since. In short, jury verdicts have had only modest impact on the system's overall cost since 1975 (Oster and Zimmerman 2002; Hunter and Doroshow 2002). Even some of those who represent the interests of big business have openly acknowledged the accuracy of these findings and the need for more regulation of the insurance sector.[17] "I don't like to hear insurance-company executives say it's the tort [injury law] system—it's self-inflicted," says Donald J. Zuk, chief executive of a leading malpractice insurer in California (quoted in Oster and Zimmerman 2002, 8). Nevertheless, well-funded public campaigns disseminating legal lore along with intensive lobbying efforts have continued to focus public media attention on the alleged lawsuit crisis (Hayden 1991).

The material impact of tort reform has similarly born out the assessments of other experts. A study by J. Robert Hunter (1999), former Texas Insurance Commissioner and Federal Insurance Administrator under Presidents Ford and Carter, found that tort reform produced only a fraction of the promised savings in insurance premiums for Texas consumers and

17. See *Forbes* 1986; *Economist* 1986. More recently, see Oster 2002, A1: "The higher premiums . . . are the legacy of a decade of imprudence among insurers—a period that combined a relentless price war with aggressive risk-taking." See generally Hayden 1991; Baker 2003.

businesses alike. These modest savings were no greater than, and in some cases were less than, savings in those states that passed no tort reform. And the reasons for these savings were largely demographic changes and an increase in safe products and safe product use. At the same time, profits of insurance companies in Texas rose dramatically, by an uncontested figure of $3 billion. However, evidence of this sort that defied the conventional wisdom about the liability crisis failed to make it into national news coverage, as far as we could find, even though tort reform was one of the major policy achievements touted by then Governor George Bush when running for presidential office. In short, spotlighting the lawsuit crisis primarily served once again to displace attention from corporate investment practices and other schemes to maximize profits.

This same pattern repeated itself even more dramatically following the stock market decline in the first few years of the twenty-first century. In many states throughout the nation, insurance premiums rose rapidly for consumers, businesses, and especially for doctors. As an Oregon newspaper analyzed the problem in the summer of 2002, "insurance companies and doctors blame one factor above all else: limitless jury awards in liability cases." If a difference exists in later news reporting, it is that there has been more explicit attention to contrary evidence showing declines in legal claims against doctors and to the market sources of insurance industry vicissitudes (see Rojas-Burke 2002). But the latter complexities are hardly the primary message of such coverage, which remains hostage to the widely publicized common sense of prominent elites like U.S. Health and Human Services Secretary Tommy Thompson. "There is a problem for America's doctors—and a danger to all Americans," he wrote in a report released to the media on July 24, 2002. "Americans are paying the price of excessive lawsuits through higher health insurance premiums, difficulty in getting a doctor when they need one, higher taxes and missed opportunities to improve patient safety. We must put an end to the malpractice litigation lottery that favors a handful of powerful personal injury lawyers . . . ."[18] Such is the logic supporting federal malpractice reform submitted to Congress (specifically HR 4600) at the time of this writing. President Bush has repeated this logic—that "what we want is quality health care, not rich trial lawyers"—repeatedly (Dionne 2003).[19] Senator Edward Kennedy's lengthy retort that "[t]his amendment has nothing to do with . . .

18. Available at www.hhs.gov.news/press/2002pres/20020724a.html.

19. President Bush elaborated on July 24, 2002: "The cause of the medical liability crisis is a badly broken system of litigation that serves the interest of specialized trial lawyers, not patients" (quoted in Thomas 2003, B10).

the insurance premiums of doctors [and] everything to do with the profits of the insurance industry" not surprisingly received almost no media attention.[20]

This is not to say that news media glorify corporations as entirely responsible and virtuous. After all, the clear majority of news accounts about tort litigation does report that corporate producers and professionals have been found legally liable for harms to consumers. But the framing of most news coverage has focused on legal disputes and large monetary awards, reducing the spotlight on corporations, their motives, and their practices as well as on the plights of injured citizens. Occasionally, a book such as Jonathan Harr's *A Civil Action* or a movie like *Erin Brockovich* does give greater attention to corporate wrongdoing and its victims. But even such populist dramas rarely treat lawyers as noble or the legal system as a bastion of rational justice. It also is true that news coverage amplified the triumph of the public health costs frame in tobacco cases for a few years, but we demonstrated in chapter 7 how that story line was quickly neutralized by refocused attention on greedy lawyers, arbitrary awards, and exploited plaintiffs.[21] Even more telling is the relative absence of newspaper articles documenting the fact that the most dramatic litigation explosion during the last few decades was initiated by corporations suing each other and government, not by consumers (Cheit 1991). News conventions are remarkably consistent over time, and for the most part they have generated legal narratives supporting the prevailing lore in which corporate greed, recklessness, litigiousness, and unaccountability play little role.[22]

In equally important if more subtle ways, prevailing currents of legal knowledge *have encouraged particular ideological framings of events while deterring or displacing other equally plausible interpretive frames from contesting parties.* As we have argued throughout this book, the prevailing legal lore has reinforced American tendencies to evaluate social problems largely in terms of individual responsibility and moral character. The result is not only that the presumed legal wisdom about hyperlexis has reinforced reformers' assaults on consumers and lawyers, but also that it has

---

20. Available at www.senate.gov/~kennedy/statements/02/07/2002730306.html.

21. It is worth recalling that the parties most responsible for diverting settlement money from plaintiffs to self-serving, dubious purposes were politicians. This too received very little attention.

22. It may seem that the corporate scandals set off by Enron in the early years of the twenty-first century belie this claim, but media attention to the "crisis" burned out quickly, surely more rapidly than did the tort litigation "crisis," which has been less dramatically but more steadily in public attention. In any case, the point is not that corporate greed is never a media issue, but it has been insulated by attention directed to the lawsuit crisis narrative.

reduced the scope of debate over legal justice itself to one that is almost exclusively about apportioning liability to discrete parties.[23] After all, we have seen that liberal critics of tort reform have been as quick to blame corporate motives, character, and choices as reformers have been to blame lawyers and plaintiffs. The result is a familiar "blame game" in which each side stakes its hopes on stigmatizing the other, pinning a tale of responsibility on an allegedly contemptible ass. The motivation in each case is not only to extract payment for incurred harms, but also to punish wrongdoing. Such a punitive logic is justified primarily by goals of deterrence, yet the motive of retribution against a mistrusted "other" is often evident. Again, this betrays a narrowly individualistic and moralistic logic of social ordering and risk management that is all too familiar in U.S. culture (Rose 1999). We saw this at work in the tobacco cases, where greedy corporations, rapacious lawyers, and dying victims all fight in righteous tones over who is most to blame. Even opponents on the liberal Left, like activist Ralph Nader and leading social scientists, repeatedly have been lured into an instrumentalist blame game that impedes attention to more complex dimensions of the issues at hand.

The news media, of course, have contributed mightily to these tendencies. The stock plot of articles focusing on legal disputants in and after formal adversarial trial proceedings reinforces the individualizing framework. It is amplified further in the tendentious moralizing we see in spot news as well as in editorials and thematic articles. For example, while recent news coverage has included more attention to the institutional, market-based sources of the so-called insurance crisis, such points are routinely framed in a "fair and balanced" format that highlights contesting political perspectives over individual legal claims. "Doctors say" this, "lawyers say" that, "insurance companies claim" yet something else (see Rojas-Burke 2002). In this way, news ethics of objective reporting justify routine "rituals" of predictable, safe adversarialism among familiar viewpoints that exclude genuinely divergent perspectives and thwart complex understandings (Bennett 1996, 149–53).

This format was well illustrated by an *ABC Nightline* special in the summer of 2002 about the health insurance crisis, provocatively entitled "A Dying Practice: What Happens When Doctors Go Out of Business?" Chris Bury, the host, began with a series of allegations from doctors about the reasons for high insurance costs. After the doctors had spoken for themselves, Bury continued: "The fair solution, of course, is a matter of perspec-

23. One could argue that media coverage just reinforces settled tort law doctrine in this regard. However, much law permits identification of injuries, wrongs, and problems that require action even in the absence of a clear perpetrator.

tive. So is the question of who's at fault. Like the president, the insurance companies blame outrageous jury verdicts and greedy trial lawyers; the lawyers in turn point to bumbling doctors and incompetent insurance companies." Reporter Deborah Amos then chimed in: "The blame game is fierce. Doctors blame lawyers, lawyers blame doctors, and yet others say it's insurance companies that are to blame for this health care crisis." The rest of the show reveled in the combat, tossing allegations of fault like fresh meat to hungry lions but posing or provoking no alternatives to a contest of adversaries in a "reasoned debate."

So what is excluded by this individualistic, fault-fixated agenda?[24] For one thing, the focus on individualizing blame obscures the complex context of interdependent institutional power at stake in most products liability and medical malpractice cases. Simply put, routinely treating individual plaintiffs and corporate defendants as co-equal disputants in a moral battle distorts the gross power asymmetries among adversaries. It discounts the enormous instrumental resources of money, expertise, counsel, and advertising available to corporations, not to mention the structural leverage that follows their control over the supply of jobs, tax revenues, and products and services essential to social welfare in our economic system. The resource imbalance in tobacco litigation has been only the most dramatic example. An outside counsel described the defense team in these words:

> They had the most powerful law firms in the country representing them, good law firms, outstanding lawyers. In our case, thirty law firms, 600 lawyers, being paid every day at $500 an hour. . . . They said in court under oath that they spent over $100 million just producing the privileged documents in our case. RJR said it spent over $95 million producing its document index. Who did that money go to? In defending their right—and they have a right to have that type of defense. . . . But how are you going to take them on? Who is going to take them on? (Ciresi 1999, 2827, 2837)

Our point is that such factors of radically unequal wealth and disproportionate power for the few are notably absent from most news coverage,

---

24. Our point here is not that the question of relative responsibility should be abandoned in political discourse and policy. Rather, it is that a narrowly individualistic logic of responsibility too often trumps and displaces more complex, nuanced understandings of social relations. Alternative conceptions might reconstruct the ethos of responsibility to recognize social interdependence as well as identify different understandings or standards outside the responsibility logic itself. Subsequent pages develop this point.

thus burying the question of whether "individual moral character" is really the most or only important issue at stake in legal disputes.

At the same time, news coverage almost entirely overlooks the limits on the practical options available to injured citizens. It obscures the fact that most lawsuits for products liability, medical malpractice, and workplace injuries represent a last (not a first) resort for many citizens lacking sufficient personal resources to purchase adequate private insurance, absorb damages, cover health costs from injuries, survive unemployment, and the like. Indeed, the primary examples of plaintiffs in this book—retirees like Stella Liebeck whose low-wage job provided scant savings, a meager retirement fund, and inadequate health care coverage; widows and widowers of smokers or workers subjected to asbestos; women victimized by unsafe, unethically marketed contraceptives, high absorbency tampons linked to toxic shock syndrome, and products like silicone breast implants promising to enhance esteem or appeal;[25] low-income citizens who cannot buy high-priced products, live in environmentally unsafe areas, and labor in unsafe workplaces—are hardly atypical of those who turn to legal action for lack of alternatives in addressing injuries, diseases, and disabilities. It is worth noting in this regard that the impersonal, abstract stereotype of the "litigious plaintiff" masks the racial, gendered, and class features of those claimants, claims, and contexts that it commonly targets. Likewise, the stigma of excessive litigation indirectly undermines legal mobilization strategies by broader rights-based movements—for environmental justice, affirmative action, disability accommodations, abortion, environmental protection, and health insurance, among others—lacking clout in other political arenas. The fact that newspaper coverage, like tort reform rhetoric, often conflates these different areas of law only broadens the likely stigmatizing impact (see chapter 5).[26] In sum, conceptions of justice that focus on relations of power and powerlessness, on inequalities inherent in our society, are systematically erased by blame-game narratives highlighting decontextualized contests over relative individual responsibility and moral character (see Ewick and Silbey 1995, 217–19). To quote Edelman (1988) again, news "spectacles" highlight

---

25. As Lucinda Finley (1997) summarized, "Reproductive or sexual harm caused by drugs and medical devices has a highly disproportionate impact on women, because far more drugs and devices have been devised to control women's fertility or bodily functions associated with sex and childbearing than have been devised for men" (855). See also Bender 1990.

26. That generalized, impersonal attacks on litigiousness and "rights talk" obscure the specific types of claimants and claims under assault is evident in quasi-intellectual works such as Mary Ann Glendon's *Rights Talk* (1991) and Charles Sykes's *A Nation of Victims* (1992).

the obtrusive current news that captures its audience and seems to have a self evident meaning. The meaning and the development itself are typically expressions and vivid reinforcements of the dominant ideology that justifies extant inequalities. They divert attention from historical knowledge, social and economic analysis and unequal benefits and sufferings that might raise questions about prevailing ideology. (125)

It follows, finally, that the prevailing forms of media-supported knowledge about hyperlexis *deflect attention from issues of collective responsibility and the failures of "democratic" government institutions to address adequately the issues of risk and harm in contemporary life.* Indeed, by focusing attention on an alleged excess of individual litigation and appeals to courts, legal lore has worked to divert potential criticism from the inaction by alternative governmental units and processes that might more effectively address the basic welfare of citizens. In particular, focus on the putative lawsuit crisis has worked to draw attention away from the lack of legislative policy mandates securing adequate health care coverage, coordinated medical drug development and production, family leave, unemployment benefits, and related social services or benefits—the types of goods for which many of the most controversial tort suits are often directed—for all citizens across the nation. In the same way, the critique of skyrocketing punitive damages focuses attention on a still relatively rare and exotic legal mechanism, in turn diverting discussion about the need for bolstering our more conventional, legislatively authorized bureaucratic structures of social and economic regulation.

Advocates for more expansive health care, social welfare, and regulatory policy do persist and receive press coverage, of course. But they must increasingly fight tort reform advocates for attention, either by ceding the tort reform issue altogether or becoming routinely sidetracked into debating the merits of the agenda defined by reform advocates. We saw earlier that trial lawyers, for example, have invested in battling tort reform but generally have withheld active political endorsement of increased social insurance, health coverage, and regulation policies, which are not really "their issues."[27] Conversely, many of the social scientists and policy ac-

---

27. Some attorneys responded to questions about state regulation in words like these: "I'm not the guy who should be the spokesman for the 'gee, we trial lawyers are doing a great job—', I'm not the guy for that. Because I have a lot of misgivings, but I think the fundamental answer to that question is that regulators have not been doing a great job. And many times they've become a captive of the industry they're supposed to regulate. And then you've got that revolving door thing that when the regulators retire, they quit, or a new administration

tivists whose empirical scholarship has challenged legal lore have in the process muted their long-standing advocacy of more expansive social justice policies. In short, the new common sense about law ironically has forced progressives into a defense of the civil legal system that they identified as inaccessible in process and inadequate in its substantive guarantees just a generation ago (see McCann 1986). Yet other traditional liberal Democrats like George McGovern and "New Democrats" like Al Gore and Joseph Lieberman have embraced tort reform in ways that dilute or displace previous public commitments to expanding rights-based, social welfare and corporate regulatory policies nearly altogether.

Politicians, policymakers, and pundits who advocate tort reform—mostly but not all identifying with the Republican Party—in turn have explicitly exploited fears of the alleged lawsuit crisis to divert a slew of specific social policy initiatives in the last two decades. For example, while the Clinton administration was pressing its ambitious plan to overhaul and expand national health care starting in 1993, conservatives responded with their Contract with America program that prominently featured tort reform. Not only did the Common Sense Products Liability Act and related bills compete early on with health care on the agenda, but the fears of a lawsuit epidemic it posed, amplified by the McDonald's coffee case, became a primary ground for challenging the administration's proposal. A host of business interests and mostly Republican opponents immediately accosted the rights-based logic of the plan. Even though the Clinton plan gave in quickly by including explicit caps on medical malpractice damage awards, opponents used the fear of increased litigation to undermine and divert focus from the plan's substantive goals. "The bill will toss a T-bone steak to the plaintiff's bar, and a sop to doctors, while snatching the plate away from potentially millions of workers who will see their health coverage dropped or scaled back as employers seek to avoid exposure for decisions over which they have no control," wrote House Majority Leader Dick Armey in a much cited position paper.[28]

Other initiatives to legislate a "patient's bill of rights" have been repeatedly neutralized by the specter of feeding the lawsuit frenzy. In fact,

---

comes in they oftentimes go to work as consultants or whatever for the very industry. No, ideally that would be the way to go—government regulation, but by virtue of the fact—the trial lawyers, in my judgment, fill a very important gap in that respect."

28. Army 1997, 3. Along with many other lawsuit-related salvos, the Armey memo quotes Duke law professor Clark Havighurst as declaring, "I know of no other piece of health-care legislation that would be . . . as beneficial to plaintiffs' lawyers as this bill would be" (3). Not surprisingly, the House leader's GOP alternative included a more market-based approach that privileges "reforming medical malpractice to bring down wasteful 'defensive medicine' costs" as one of its three primary goals (4).

George W. Bush used this tactic successfully to halt, then delay, and then dilute such legislation while governor in Texas (Ivins and Dubose 2000), and then repeated the strategy at the national level as president. As indicated above, halfway through President Bush's term the entire national debate about health care insurance had become inseparable from the task of reducing tort liability litigation of health providers, while limiting products liability litigation and awards has become a cornerstone of economic health and security discourse (Dionne 2003).[29] "[T]he problem of those unnecessary costs don't start in the waiting room or the operating room. They're in the courtroom," proclaimed Bush in a high-profile, if typically twisted, speech justifying federal medical malpractice reform on January 16, 2003. "We're a litigious society; everybody's suing, it seems like. There are too many lawsuits in America, and there are too many lawsuits filed against doctors and hospitals without merit" [sic] (Bush 2003; Lindlaw 2003). Proposals for public investment in more expansive social welfare and regulatory policies repeatedly have been diverted and displaced, when not deterred, by the bogeymen of excessive litigation.

The news media have routinely participated in and reinforced these gambits of agenda displacement. As we noted earlier, during late 1994, in the midst of a protracted debate about national health care, the mass media immediately and uniformly constructed the McDonald's coffee case according to the conventional plot line of tort tales. Hence our query in chapter 6: Why was this not a story about inadequate health care and retirement benefits for the aged, about the absence of family leave policy that would have paid Stella Liebeck's daughter while she tended to her mother, or about more vigilant regulation of product safety? We also noted that the dominant story line in tobacco litigation coverage has been the stress on individual responsibility, interrupted only briefly by the dramatic innovation of the state attorneys' general public health cost logic. Why has media coverage not treated tobacco litigation—and that concerning asbestos, for that matter—as an opportunity to ask questions about the institutional failures of Congress to regulate effectively or ban lethal products rather than leaving claims of the injured to fester in the courts for

---

29. President Bush's 2002 budget proposal speech requested that Congress pass "civil justice reform to help restore America's economy." The president included the lawsuit issue in his routine discourse on the economy, as in an Alabama speech in early 2002, when he promised to promote jobs, but "not jobs for trial lawyers. . . . You ought to have your day in court, no question about it. But we've got to make sure that these junk and frivolous lawsuits stop running up the cost of doing business and make it harder for people to employ people here in America." Available at www.whitehouse.gov/news/releases/2002/07/20020715.html. A Council of Economic Advisors report, relying heavily on ATRA and other sources, supported this position. See www.whitehouse.gov/cea/tortliabilitysystem_apr02.html.

decades? Indeed, why are lawyers and plaintiffs routinely treated with
mistrust for exposing and addressing undeniable health dangers clearly
known but ignored by government officials? That these questions are
so seldom asked—whether by social welfare liberals, trial lawyers, left-
leaning policy advocates, communitarians, or news reporters—confirms
the power of the reigning common sense about hyperlexis and the complex forces that have produced it.

A quite different but equally revealing example is illustrated in political scientist Anne Bloom's study of transnational litigation by harmed foreign workers against U.S. multinational corporations (2003, chap. 5). *Alfaro v. Dow Chemical* concerned a personal injury lawsuit brought on
behalf of several dozen Costa Rican farm laborers who had been rendered
sterile by exposure to a pesticide used on a plantation owned by a U.S.
company. The Texas Supreme Court ruling affirmed the right of foreign
workers to sue their employers in Texas courts. Shortly after the ruling, the
Texas legislature began to consider legislation to overturn the court's decision. After a struggle, the corporate interests promoting reversal eventually reached a compromise with the lawyers for the workers and legislation
to overturn *Alfaro* was passed in 1993. Media coverage was extensive but,
despite the central substantive issue of worker health, focused on the business concern that Texas was becoming the "courthouse of the world." Of
the more than fifty local articles, only one in eight quoted a worker plaintiff, his attorney, or a workers' rights advocate. Most commentators instead
proclaimed the key issue was not the specific actors involved in this case
but trial lawyers and their clients more generally. A typical example appeared in an article entitled "Milking the Cash Cow." The author began
with the usual argument that the *Alfaro* ruling amounted to the Texas
Supreme Court's inviting "the world to Texas—for the purpose of suing
someone." Article after article about *Alfaro* conveyed similar arguments
redefining the workers' case through the lens of tort reform. Ultimately,
this construction was so powerful that many news articles about *Alfaro* began to include coverage of related tort reform issues, such as caps on punitive damage awards. A 1993 article in the *Dallas Morning News*, for example, combined coverage of the legislation to overturn *Alfaro* with a story on
other legislation that would ban some product liability lawsuits in Texas
and greatly restrict others. The headline for this article was "Business Interests Expect Victory on Tort Reform Bills" (Camp 1993). In sum, the
press almost completely subordinated the workers' rights issues of physical injury and environmental harm to business' anxieties about the lawsuit
crisis.

Such complicity has not been complete. One counterexample concerned a rider inserted by Republicans into the 484-page Homeland Secu-

rity bill in late fall 2002 that blocked efforts by thousands of parents to sue pharmaceutical manufacturers of children's-vacccine additives, including especially the mercury-containing preservative thimerosal, which have been alleged to cause autism.[30] The sponsors' justification for the provision was that such lawsuits, which could rival asbestos claims in scope, might undermine corporate capacity to produce vaccines necessary in the aftermath of possible biotechnical terrorist attacks. But critics—who prominently included Congressman Dan Burton—decried the covert policy as nothing but a corporate protection scheme that lets manufacturers off "scot-free," limits compensation for victims, removes deterrents for use of unsafe additives, provides no incentives to develop alternative additives, and does nothing to rationalize production of vaccines that the nation needs now or later. An unusual article in *Newsday* cited Lawrence Gostin of the Center for Law and the Public's Health: "If the sole concern was the national interest, there would have been a full and open debate about the best way to ensure that national vaccines are produced" (Frank 2002, 4). This was a noteworthy case in which the specter of a lawsuit crisis did not entirely distract coverage from voices urging affirmative national policies to deal with medical risks. In early 2003, the measure insulating vaccine manufacturers from lawsuits was repealed (Reuters 2003).

Summary Judgment about the Reform Agenda

The multiple implications of the tort reformers' commonsense distortions can now be fully appreciated. Repeated admonitions about the threats of excessive litigation have supported institutional reforms—elevating evidentiary standards for demonstrating liability, placing caps on compensatory and punitive damages, lowering incentives and raising risks for attorneys—that reduce the access to potential legal remedies for injured citizens that have been created by liberal rights-based programs over the last fifty years. At the same time, invocations of lawsuit frenzy have neutralized calls for new, more expansive social welfare and regulatory programs that might address harms incurred by consumers and workers. Finally, both of these previous dynamics have worked to advance the fundamental ideological appeals advocating increasing individual responsibility for internalizing risk of injury and harm. Instead of collectively organized compensation and regulatory schemes, neoliberals have joined

---

30. The alleged causal linkages to autism are a subject of conflicting scientific studies, and parents could file claims with a federal compensation fund that pays medical costs and up to $250,000 for pain and suffering. For a review of the science and related legal actions, see www.thimerosal-info.com/articles-news.html.

neoconservatives in endorsing increased reliance on personal insurance, greater self-discipline to minimize exposure to risks, voluntary local collaboration to increase security, and growing obligations to assume the costs of accident and misfortune beyond control.

Of course, the alleged lawsuit crisis has represented just one narrative among many discourses supporting the contemporary corporate order. We should be careful not to exaggerate its influence in the grander scheme of things. However, we also have stressed how the individualistic ethos of "social control as self control" has been at the core of a larger conservative campaign to roll back the moderately collectivist "social rights" agenda advocated by liberals during the half century following the New Deal—an agenda that is barely audible in U.S. discourse (Rose 1999; Baker and Simon 2002). Indeed, the ethos of personal responsibility underlying tort reform and the new legal lore has been greatly amplified by linking them to other major policy agendas assailing affirmative action, welfare benefits, liberal criminal justice policies, progressive tax policy, health and safety regulation, environmental regulation, and public health insurance—all part of the raging culture wars. This ethos is not so much opposed to citizens' laying claim to their rights, as has sometimes been argued, as a campaign to shift prevailing discourses away from universalistic "social rights" and toward rights that are contingent on and promote personal displays of proper moral discipline and resource capacity (Handler 2004).[31] Again, the abstract assault on frivolous litigation and irresponsible litigants has obscured the targeting of specific rights-based policies, groups, and power relations. Effectively revitalizing long-standing American ideals of self-governed, autonomous individuals and anti-paternalistic suspicion of state-sponsored redistributive efforts, the lawsuit crisis narrative effectively diverts attention from its own anti-egalitarian implications, its punitive conceptions of justice, its romance with selves rigidly ordered by uniform internalized constraints, and its sweeping politicization of judicial institutions in the name of restoring legal impartiality and integrity.

Our critical standpoint has not turned on a wholesale defense of the existing tort system. Indeed, we have been frank in recognizing that the existing civil law regime is inadequate in many ways and that litigation is often not the best process by which to fashion social policy. Nor have we

---

31. Rosanvallon (2000) concisely explains the larger logic of neoliberal retrenchment: "With the knowledge of the predisposition for certain diseases or with certain behaviors (e.g. smoking), the risks of ill health are no longer common; rather, they are individualized and, thus, commonly applied insurance becomes *'redistribution.'* Similarly knowledge now reveals the varied and individual nature and causes of social exclusion. Thus the veil of ignorance (underlying old collectivism) is torn. . . . On all sides, 'irresponsible' society is denounced, and individuals are called upon to take responsibility for themselves" (4, 23).

rejected the principle of individual responsibility in general, which surely is a valuable if limited moral and legal norm for modern society. Our point instead has been that the prevailing commonsense lore about the lawsuit crisis has impeded sophisticated discourse about the complexities of tort law practice, about the most important recent developments in those practices, about alternative modes of productive legal reform, and about a wide array of socially responsible, just, and effective policy options for dealing with risks of harm experienced by citizens. Agenda-setting analysis alerts us to the ways in which media-supported common sense has been mobilized effectively to privilege and protect the position of powerful corporate interests over others, to divert debates into a narrow range of largely misleading or trivial concerns, and hence to deter or displace alternative visions of egalitarian social justice and collective responsibility that would enrich serious democratic deliberation. The problem is not just that moralism per se impedes rationality, as realists imply; the problem is the particular inegalitarian moral vision that legal lore insinuates into our polity's conventional wisdom.

This reductionist effect of the prevailing legal lore is important, for scholars have long demonstrated that the penchant for rights-based litigation must be understood in relationship to the larger institutional and cultural features of U.S. politics. As historical institutionalist scholars have contended, the limited social welfare state and heavy reliance on individual litigation for risk management in the United States are interrelated attributes of a polity characterized by fragmented state structure, winner-take-all elections, and voluntaristic social values. Legislators in such contexts are often unable to legislate due to partisan stalemate and the power of money, as illustrated by both asbestos and tobacco settlements (see Derthick 2002). These factors account, at least in part, for the uniquely limited substantive content of uniform social insurance entitlements and regulatory policy in the United States. When Congress does manage to legislate, moreover, it typically passes vaguely worded "symbolic" laws that mollify diverse constituents but defer or delegate substantial policy construction and implementation authority to the courts (Burke 2002; Graber 1993; Lovell 2003). By focusing attention on allegedly litigious Americans, therefore, the lawsuit crisis narrative exploited by tort reformers diverts attention from the chronic tendency of U.S. political institutions to leave so much for the judiciary to do in formulating and administering social policy.

It is noteworthy that policy advocates on the Left have supported this logic since the New Deal as much as conservative, pro-business elites did prior to the New Deal (McCann 1986). The irony of this legacy is that the very same politicians who most loudly decry excessive litigation today also routinely delegate or defer the most important issues of policy development and administration to individual litigation in the courts. In any case, serious discussion about reducing our nation's dependence on litigation for social policy development and individual remedies thus would probably require deliberation about broad, perhaps radical reforms of our larger political system (Burke 2002; Kagan 2001). Once again, however, neither the anecdote-based debate over tort reform nor the individualized, decontextualized media coverage of civil litigation has had much to say about such complex institutional dynamics in U.S. politics. The prevailing legal lore has only added yet another brick to the formidable wall that impedes advances toward a more informed democratic discourse within and about law.

EVERYDAY LEGAL PRACTICE IN MASS CULTURE

The new common sense about excessive litigation arguably has become an equally imminent force *within* the daily lives of many, perhaps even most, U.S. citizens, including those who view mass politics as a distant, impersonal, even abstract domain of engagement. We cite below a sample of the evidence verifying that legal lore has substantially permeated legal knowledge and practice in many institutional sites of micropolitics throughout the nation. These data show that many Americans routinely exhibit in their ordinary conduct the new commonsense skepticism about lawyers, litigation, and citizens' rights, embodying the conventional wisdom in their roles as legal subjects. The "litigious plaintiff" and "greedy lawyer" have effectively expanded the catalog of stigmatized "Others"—welfare queens, minority street criminals, welfare poor, deadbeat dads, amoral liberals, slackers of all kinds—deserving harsh judgment, demanding disavowal, and demarcating the codes of appropriate action by good citizens. As such, the *juridical* force of official tort reform in legal rules is paralleled by the related *disciplinary* force of ordinary legal knowledge that compels individual self-regulation and legal restraint (Foucault 1979).

This should hardly be surprising. From the start, tort reformers focused their energies on shaping the broader cultural milieu of tort law practice—asking, for example, what is perceived as an injury; whether and whom to blame for an injury; what to do about it; and even how to respond to what others (especially plaintiffs and lawyers) do with regard to naming and blaming—as much as on reforming official legal rules and policies (Daniels and Martin 2000, 2). Specifically, we suggest, manifestations of the social logic encouraging voluntary risk reduction, private insurance, and especially reluctance to assert legal rights claims for redress of harms is quite palpable within many domains of ordinary legal activity. Our brief, partial review of the copious scholarly literature on these matters suggests that what is alleged to be the new common sense about civil litigation has had considerable impact and is, again, truly reconstituting law itself in American society.

Legal Consciousness in Action

We begin with what we know about ordinary Americans who serve as *jurors*. Abundant scholarly studies since the late 1970s have confirmed that juries have generally been less pro-plaintiff, more pro-defendant, and overall more thoughtful and reasonable than pop tort reformers have alleged. That said, studies have also increasingly shown clear evidence that the reigning common sense about the lawsuit crisis has seized the imagination of jurors. Consider a 1991 study by Greene, Goodman, and Loftus of jurors' attitudes about civil litigation and damage awards. From a survey of 213 experienced or potential jurors in Seattle, they found that 91 percent agreed there are too many lawsuits, 78 percent blamed lawyers as a leading reason for lawsuits, and 62 percent thought that jury awards were too high. When asked about the source of their understandings, most interviewees cited the mass media, with more mentioning newspapers (58 percent) than television (44 percent). Most subjects realized that the media exaggerate the number of high jury awards and emphasize sensational cases, but this recognition did not seem to dilute the impact of such coverage on the respondents' general perceptions.

Hans and Lofquist (1992) reported similar findings. Interviewing 269 jurors in thirty-six trial court cases, the scholars found that jurors were "generally favorable toward business, skeptical more about the profit motives of individual plaintiffs than of business defendants, and committed to holding down awards." Moreover, interviewees expressed strongly negative views about the frequency and integrity of civil lawsuits. A stunning 83 percent of polled jurors think there are "far too many frivolous lawsuits," and 81 percent agreed with the statement that "People are quick to sue, rather than trying to solve disputes in some other way" (93). Hans and Lofquist also found clear evidence that the saturation of mass media and politics with messages about the lawsuit crisis "captured the public's (and jurors') attention because it resonated strongly with preexisting standards of responsibility" (109). A highly respected book by Professor Hans (2000) subsequently reinforced this analysis in much greater detail.

Many regional studies have provided further evidence of similar trends and juror tendencies. For example, studies in Texas by Jury Verdict Research found that median jury awards dropped 59 percent, mostly in soft-tissue injury awards, in the years after 1991. The primary reason was not tort reform policies, most interviewees claimed, but the "climate" caused by adverse publicity and media messages. As one Dallas plaintiffs' attorney, Frank L. Bransom, summarized, "I know the process of selecting juries is more difficult not only because of the law changes, but because of the adverse publicity that the tort reformers have spent millions on. They have spent literally tens of millions lobbying to the people who sit on juries" (quoted in Ward 1997, 1). An earlier article in *Texas Lawyer* cited much the same observation from other personal injury attorneys about the huge "pendulum swing" among jurors. "It's a big change. In the late 1970s, you didn't get those kinds of responses. . . . There's an attitude almost of disdain toward people who have the temerity to go to court and seek compensation for injuries," observed one attorney (quoted in Calve 1996, 17). The primary reason for this change, the article's author concluded (at 15), was "summed up in two words: hot coffee," referring again to the case of *Liebeck v. McDonald's* (see chapter 6). Stephen Daniels and Joanne Martin compiled additional systematic evidence for these shifts in understanding in Texas. In their poll of Texas attorneys, 84 percent reported that juries were less likely to find for a plaintiff than five years previously, 71 percent assessed that juries were less likely to award economic damages, and 89 percent said that juries were less likely to award non-economic damages (2000, 28). They elsewhere excerpt interviews with Texas trial lawyers at length, such as the following:

> What I see as the most severe impact (of tort reform) is right over there, when I go to pick a jury. And juries have gotten mean, real mean. They've been convinced that everything in their lives, from heart attacks to hemorrhoids, is because of a system that is out of control. And when you have a tort reform advocate on the jury panel and you're asking questions, all you have to do is listen to the phraseology. It's all the same: too many frivolous lawsuits, outrageous jury awards, greedy trial lawyers. The guy is repeating the mantra. (Daniels, Van Hoy, and Martin 1999, 10)

Most of the empirical studies of jury practice noted above conclude that the single biggest indicator of jury decisions is what jurors understand and believe about the alleged lawsuit crisis. "Those who are most concerned about a lawsuit crisis tend to favor lower awards," notes Valerie Hans (2000, 195; see also Diamond, Saks, and Landsman 1998). Most such studies examine that issue of causality only indirectly, it is true. One early study by Elizabeth Loftus, though, provides direct experimental evidence that even minimal exposure to insurance company ads about the lawsuit crisis in magazines can dramatically lower the amount that a juror is willing to recognize as fair damages (1979). None of this, of course, suggests that jurors mindlessly act in a way that is predetermined by tort reform propaganda and media stories. Quite the opposite. The primary conclusion offered in these studies about the rationality of jurors is that, despite increasing predispositions of hostility to plaintiffs and big awards, jurors often decide for victims and even occasionally award large damages when presented evidence at trial—exactly what we witnessed in the McDonald's coffee case and several tobacco cases.

We also can cite at least some minimal evidence about changes in the perspectives and practices of *lawyers*. All of the plaintiffs' attorneys whom we talked to registered this point. Reed Morgan, the attorney for Stella Liebeck in her suit against McDonald's, was the most dramatically affected—because of the publicity surrounding the case, he suffered personally, professionally, and financially. But many other attorneys also registered unmistakable dismay about how tort reform and, especially, the broader public assault on tort litigation had negatively affected their practices. Besides increasingly skeptical juries predisposed against plaintiffs and inclined to lower damages awards, the assault on junk science in courts ironically has required plaintiffs to produce more and better paid experts, which further escalates costs (Risinger 2000). The result is a significant increase in the risks of mounting a lawsuit but a decline in the likely returns for lawyers. This dynamic discourages legal representation especially for plaintiffs who are highly needy but not the most severely injured. In short, small cases get priced out of the market as the awards in a few exceptional cases grow ever larger. As one Michigan attorney put it to a *New York Times* reporter, "I've had plenty of defective products, clearly defective, where I won't talk to the people because their injuries aren't severe enough. . . . If they're not quadriplegic, or paraplegic or losing some part of their body, there's no way I'm going to take their case." Another attorney added, "I can't take cases on any more unless I am absolutely positive that I have one worth at least $2,000,000. . . . I can no longer afford to spend $300,000 trying a case that is only worth $500,000, and that's ridiculous" (Winter 2001).

The articles from *Texas Lawyer* cited earlier support these findings of the effects of tort reform on personal injury lawyers. In one of them, a defense attorney noted the swing of the pendulum against plaintiffs and commented, "I think it's sad. . . . I see hard times for the plaintiffs' firms. They are dramatically hurt" (quoted in Calve 1996, 15). This article also reiterated something we repeatedly heard in our own interviews: for years after 1995, attorneys had to build into every trial an effort to neutralize the dominant image in jurors' minds regarding defective products lawsuits—namely, the $2.9 million award for spilled coffee. "It comes up all the time. . . . The McDonald's case has entered into American folklore. It has become the poster child for tort reform," summarizes James Burgund, a jury consultant with Jury Selection Sciences in Dallas (quoted in Greenlee 1997, 703). In fact, during the later 1990s ATLA sponsored seminars for lawyers on how to overcome jury bias that specifically addressed the notorious *Liebeck* case that would not die in mass-mediated culture.

The findings in these articles were reinforced and expanded in the late 1990s by the analytical studies of Daniels and Martin (2000). In a survey of Texas plaintiffs' lawyers, they found that 91 percent believed tort reform campaigns had a negative (25.9 percent) or strongly negative (65 percent) effect on their practices. The biggest impacts were clearly on the "bread and butter" personal injury practices of lawyers at the lower end of the income scale. These lawyers overwhelmingly reported increasingly negative jury responses to their cases; 73.5 percent in the survey said that average value of their contingency fees declined over the previous five years, with only 15.6 percent reporting a rise. The result is that many lawyers have changed their practices, either by abandoning, reducing, or becoming far more selective in their involvement with personal injury claims. Again, this impact on attorneys matters greatly in that it reduces the availability of legal advocates for citizens with the lowest incomes as well as the least health care and social insurance.

We have less evidence about changing inclinations of *judges,* but the data that exist suggest parallel trends. In this regard it is worth recalling that federal appellate judges, led by Supreme Court chief justice Warren Burger, were among the earliest leaders in assailing trends in litigiousness and calling for reform, not least to reduce their workload. The classic study by Theodore Eisenberg and James Henderson (1992, 794) concluded, moreover, that a "widespread, independent shift in judicial attitudes continues to be the likely major source of decline" in tort plaintiffs' rates of success. The reasons, they argued, were the political campaigns of tort reformers directed at legal authorities as well as increasingly conservative judicial appointments. But the fact that such trends have been, as they put it, "truly national" rather than regional or jurisdictional (774) also underlines to us the likely broader influence of mass media. Studies of select state and national appeals judges have confirmed a clear anti-plaintiff bias in appellate cases. At the national level, scholars Kevin Clermont and Theodore Eisenberg (2000) found a 31 percent reversal rate for defendants, and only 13 percent reversal rate for plaintiffs, largely based on "misperceptions" of appellate judges about the trial process (see also Bloom 2001, chap. 6).

It stands to reason, furthermore, that the biggest impacts are felt not by lawyers but by *accident victims* who are left to fend for themselves. "You can't get beyond a jury that says, 'Well, why weren't you watching where you were going?' " a lawyer in Texas confirmed (quoted in Calve 1996, 20).

Evidence regarding filings of cases, escalating the sense of grievance into a formal claim, again is sparse. The diagnosis of Eisenberg and Henderson (1992) of the "quiet revolution" in products liability was that cases "began to plummet" and success rates continued to fall (from 56 percent to 39 percent in published opinions) during the decade after 1979 (see also Mooney 1992). This declining rate accelerated in the late 1990s. The number of products liability cases filed in federal court dropped by more than half during 1997–2000—from 32,856 to 14,428—in the last four years of the 1990s, while the size of median and highest awards jumped (Winter 2001). Studies in select regions of Texas show that state filings decreased in number after 1990, as did the size of awards (Daniels and Martin 2000).

These trends surely reflect the increasing selectivity of attorneys in taking cases as much as inclinations of the aggrieved, but the stakes in most cases are greater for the latter than the former. At the same time, high-profile coverage of some tort lawsuits actually has *encouraged* opportunistic legal action on the part of some citizens, such as those with injuries from hot liquids. The fact that some cases generate copycat legal action may ironically produce the opposite effect of that intended by tort reformers. Our interviews echoed those of other scholars in repeatedly producing accounts from attorneys regarding the inflated damages that some injured consumers expect to reap from litigation, largely as a result of the highly publicized exceptional cases. In short, it is quite possible that legal lore about skyrocketing damage awards actually has encouraged more frivolous lawsuits while discouraging ordinary citizens with the most reasonable and just reasons for action from claiming their legal rights!

We also expect that distorted lore about the litigation explosion might affect *managers of private business and public organizations* in important ways. As Edelman, Abraham, and Erlanger (1992) have demonstrated, narratives about organizational risk disseminated through both targeted professional communications and mass media can significantly influence the choices of managers about measures to reduce liability. In this regard, the study by Bailis and MacCoun (1996) regarding skewed coverage of tort litigation in business-oriented magazines becomes an important complement to our own findings reported in previous pages. That tort tales and selective news coverage are even more common in the business press underscores findings of opinion polls and surveys that professional elites—doctors, business owners, corporate executives—are most convinced of the reality of the lawsuit crisis (Songer 1988).

The interrelationships suggested here have been most fully and convincingly explored through the recent systematic empirical studies of political scientist Charles Epp (2001). He examined the practices of administrative policy elites throughout the nation, particularly the adoption by

police departments, parks and recreation departments, and human resources departments of policies regarding, respectively, the excessive use
of force, playground safety, and sexual harassment. Epp found that "senior
city administrators, in particular, appear to believe that city governments
face heavy threats from litigation . . . and they also appear to believe that,
in response, cities have instituted a range of substantive changes in their
administrative structures, policies and procedures." Epp's extensive survey
of managers showed that increased adoption of intrusive, often costly administrative policies to reduce risk correlated significantly with several
factors, including most prominently the existence of local support networks which pressed liability issues and the diffusion of professional
knowledge highlighting liability concerns. By contrast, action to reduce
risk showed no meaningful relationship to variations in official law. In
short, the politics of constructed expectations seemed to be the primary
determinant of policy choices.

These findings also have several ironic implications. On the one hand,
the managerial behavior associated with inflated perceptions of risk advance the goals of neoliberal policy—anticipatory reduction in risk-related
behavior, aversion to formal adversarial relations, and willingness to pay
more for liability insurance. On the other hand, such constructed perceptions may, ironically, extend the regulatory impact of tort law and legal
proceedings (Epp 2002). By increasing perceptions of risk, ubiquitous narratives about a lawsuit crisis actually may augment the power of civil litigation in ways that that reformers bemoan but defenders of our civil law
system find gratifying.

Finally, increased perceptions of liability and its related costs ostensibly imposed by civil litigation have been closely linked to other changing
patterns of practice among lawyers, big business, government, and insurers. Perhaps the most palpable of these implications has been the *alternative dispute resolution movement* (ADR) in the United States over the last
two decades. Emanating from both within and beyond the legal profession, this movement began from the commonsense contention that Americans had become obsessed with litigation and "adversarial legalism" (see
Adler 1995; Harrington 1985). Many scholars have suggested, quite rightly
we think, that this movement was a direct reaction to the rights-based liberal activism challenging traditional hierarchies in the 1960s. As anthro-
pologist Laura Nader (1995) has contended, "The concerns were not with
justice, but with harmonious relations, with community. . . . The concern
with harmony was accompanied by the silencing of disputes . . . and
achieved by the movement against the contentious, the movement to control the disenfranchised" (448). Its impulses, in her terms, derived from es-

tablished elites and aimed for therapeutic pacification at the cost of denied access to justice (see also Nader 2002). As such, ADR and tort reform again reflect well-funded, interconnected movements embracing an individualistic disciplinary message aiming to alter the terms of collective power in modern society.

Narratives of Avoidance and the Moral Community

The core questions that led to our writing this book were raised in part by a provocative study of legal practice in three American towns by Carol Greenhouse, Barbara Yngvesson, and David Engel (1994). Critical reflections on their individual case studies led the authors to identify a common ethos, what they label "narratives of law avoidance," at work in local practices involving personal injuries. In their words:

> A pervasive form of nonlitigiousness was apparent in many of these narratives, contrary to popular perception that American society had become completely enamored of litigation. Although law and order were highly valued . . . so was the ethic of rejecting law and embracing forms of social order based on self-discipline and tradition rather than law enforcement. (118–19)

These narratives were routinely voiced and enacted by ordinary citizens, but the authors contend that they were especially endorsed, even enforced, by official local legal actors such as lawyers, court clerks, judges, jurors, insurance representatives, and the like. Although widely shared among differently situated citizens, moreover, these stories were grounded in a myth of communal harmony that masked unequal power and injustice. The narratives were, the authors concluded, a means by which "some attempted to create or impose order within the community, to define or deflect change, and to articulate a philosophy of individualism and equality that could also be reconciled with their tenacious defense of the status quo" (119). In particular, legal disputes became opportunities for invocation of these narratives to distinguish between appropriate and inappropriate legal action, between responsible and irresponsible persons, between disciplined insiders and reckless outsiders. Such narratives are inherently fluid, flexible, and indeterminate in meaning, but they nevertheless primarily work to insulate traditional power hierarchies and norms from challenge.

Our findings significantly expand these authors' account regarding the power of such narratives. The trio of anthropologists interpreted these powerful myths as largely the product of responses by small-town elites to the forces of suburbanization—to the "alien invasion" of large corporate institutions, more diverse working-class populations, and mass commercial culture. Such changes were viewed by denizens as bringing some benefits, but they also posed threats to deeply rooted romantic images of a harmonious past and traditional group solidarities. Our study of legal lore, by contrast, has identified these same narratives of avoidance *within* the very corporate-controlled, commercially driven processes of mass-produced knowledge. This suggests that myths of legal harmony do not just thrive among citizens hoping to insulate their local communities from mass culture; these myths are embedded in the discursive logics—at once available, accessible, adaptable, and actionable[32]—that inform and shape mass commercial culture itself. Disciplining legal Myths R Us, it seems. No doubt Greenhouse, Yngvesson, and Engel are correct that such understandings are reinforced through the practices of local elites and ordinary citizens within what Foucault calls the "capillary" sites of social power. However, recognition of the broader sources of legal knowledge production in mass media significantly augments our understanding about the ubiquity and power of these ideologically coded narratives in our legal culture.

It has become commonplace to think of "individual responsibility" as a hegemonic ideology in the United States that generally supports but, because indeterminate, also provides resources for contesting dominant relations.[33] At this point in our study, a case can be made that contemporary commonsense narratives about the lawsuit crisis drawing selectively on that ideology qualify for hegemonic status as well (see Hayden 1991). Legal lore contributes to hegemony to the extent that it sustains a pervasive taken-for-granted, commonsense knowledge on which the prevailing order rests. This conventional wisdom naturalizes and reinforces the status-quo order by narrowing the range of citizens' expectations and filling their imaginations with selective accounts of social causality; it ensures that what we know and what we are encouraged to believe about law are closely intertwined. The common sense about law does not preclude or determine contests over legal meaning, but it works to deter some conflicts while channeling others into safe, manageable trajectories and venues. In particular, legal lore, like many expressions of liberal ideology, defines both

---

32. We refer readers back to chapters 2–4.

33. Many of the references cited throughout this book provide evidence for this claim about the implications of prevailing individualistic norms in the United States. We explicitly choose to align our analysis with that of law and society scholars such as Scheingold 1991; Sarat 2001; Merry 1990; and Greenhouse, Yngvesson, and Engel 1994.

causes and evidence of failure in individualistic terms that efface attention to larger patterns of harm, systematic analysis of power relations that structure interaction, and collective responses to shared loss, gain, and aspiration.

The new legal lore advances, furthermore, a contradictory image of law that shields its mythical character from challenge (see Ewick and Silbey 1998). In retrospect, it relates a story of law's corruption, a tale that identifies greedy lawyers and irresponsible plaintiffs with the "litigation lottery" that the lore says the distorted system of civil law has become. Prospectively, it posits a redemptive ideal of law linked to a mythic past of communal harmony among morally restrained individuals, but also imminent among those virtuous citizens exploited by the irresponsible and rapacious. As in the small towns studied by Greenhouse, Yngvesson, and Engel, these categories serve as ambiguous, mutable, even arbitrary signifiers of moral assessment rather than as clearly defined standards for judging behavior. At least in elite venues and news accounts, mega-corporations thus become victims at the hands of aged widows; smokers are blamed for the deceitfully poisoned products that kill them; lawyers who expose health dangers are vilified while congressional leaders reap tax windfalls for avoiding responsibility; and jurors who overcome their internalized suspicion of rights claimants upon hearing case facts are dismissed as naïve, soft-headed dupes. This is not just hegemony at work, but a hegemonic order in which it is the "injurers whose worldviews most profoundly shape the communities in which we live" (Engel 2001).

At the same time, we again caution against both exaggerating the scope and relative salience of this common wisdom in contemporary U.S. culture and overdetermining the meanings that derive from familiar narratives. Hegemonic narratives are not unequivocal or undifferentiated in meaning; hegemony is always variable, incomplete, contested, dynamic, unstable (McCann 1994; Ewick and Silbey 1998). Legal lore surely resonates with differing degrees of intensity and shades of meaning depending on the context in which it is related. We doubt neither the capacity of variously situated citizens to evade, subvert, or challenge the prevailing logic nor the ironic implications of mass legal knowledge that may be unwelcome to its proponents. It is worth noting that even we applaud some likely implications of the conventional legal wisdom. To the extent that the new common sense amplifies judicial regulatory power in deterring dangerous products and professional practices, we relish the inherent irony. To the extent, moreover, that legal lore discourages simplistic faith in law as inherently just, dependence on legal elites and the state as empowering, and complacency about unfair legal outcomes, we find some undeniable merit. But to the extent that legal lore also suppresses a more sophisticated politics of rights (Scheingold 1974), a politics of aspiration that demands social justice from and through law while remaining appropriately skeptical about the constraints of legal elites, institutions, and language, we fear a profound loss in the potential for advancing justice and democracy in our society.

References

ABC John Stossel Special. 1995. "The Blame Game: Are We a Country of Victims?" Broadcast August 17, 1995.
———. 1996. "The Trouble with Lawyers." Broadcast August 17, 1997.
ABC Nightline. 2002. "A Dying Practice: What Happens When Doctors Go Out of Business?" Broadcast July 25, 1996.
Abel, Richard L. 1981. "A Critique of American Tort Law." *British Journal of Law and Society* 8:199–231.
———. 1987. "The Real Tort Crisis—Too Few Claims." *Ohio State Law Journal* 48:443–67.
———. 1989. *American Lawyers.* New York: Oxford University Press.
———. 2001. "Torts." Chap. 20 in *The Politics of Law: A Progressive Critique,* ed. David Kairys, 445–70. 3d ed. New York: Basic Books.
Accord Publishing. 2001. *Legal Lunacies 2002 Calendar.*
Adler, Peter S. 1995. "The Future of Alternative Dispute Resolution: Reflections on ADR as a Social Movement." In *The Possibility of Popular Justice,* ed. Sally Engle Merry and Neal Milner, 67–88. Ann Arbor: University of Michigan Press.
Aetna Life and Casualty. 1978. "Too Bad Judges Can't Read This to a Jury." Advertisement.
AIR (Americans for Insurance Reform). 2002. "Stable Losses, Unstable Rates." October 10. Available at www.insurance-reform.org.
Andresky, Jill, Mary Kuntz, and Barbara Kallen. 1985. "A World without Insurance?" *Forbes,* July 15, pp. 40–42.
"Are Lawyers Running America?" 1995. Broadcast on PBS *Think Tank,* November 17.
Arizona Republic. 1994. "McDonald's Coffee: Sending the Wrong Message." August 22, p. B4.
Armey, Dick. 1997. "Health Care Quality: Bureaucracy or Consumer Choice? Available at www.freedom.house.gov/library/healthcare/healthcare.asp (last visited October 30, 2002).
Asimow, Michael. 1996. "When Lawyers Were Heroes." *University of San Francisco Law Review* 30:1131.
———. 2000a. "Bad Lawyers in the Movies." *Nova Law Review* 24 (winter): 533–84.
———. 2000b. "Divorce in the Movies: From the Hays Code to Kramer vs. Kramer." *Legal Studies Forum* 24:221–67.
Associated Press. 1994. "Woman Burned by Hot McDonald's Coffee Gets $ 2.9 Million." AM Cycle. Located via "Academic Universe."
ATRA (American Tort Reform Association). 1999a. Press release.

———. 1999b. American Tort Reform Association Web Page www.atra.org:80/atra/ATH .HTM#Pickled (visited July 15, 1999).

Auerbach, Jerold S. 1976. *Unequal Justice: Lawyers and Social Change in Modern America.* New York: Oxford University Press.

Bachrach, Peter, and Morton S. Baratz. 1970. *Power and Poverty: Theory and Practice.* New York: Oxford University Press.

Bagdikian, Ben H. 1992. *The Media Monopoly.* 4th ed. Boston: Beacon Press.

Bailis, Daniel S., and Robert J. MacCoun. 1996. "Estimating Liability Risks with the Media as Your Guide: A Content Analysis of Media Coverage of Tort Litigation." *Law and Human Behavior* 20:419–29.

Baker, Tom. 2003. "Insuring Liability Risks." Unpublished paper, University of Connecticut.

Baker, Tom, and Jonathan Simon, eds. 2002. *Embracing Risk: The Changing Culture of Insurance and Responsibility.* Chicago: University of Chicago Press.

BarCharts. 2000. "Quick Study: Torts." Boca Raton, Fla.: BarCharts, Inc.

Barry, Dave. 1995. "A Great Year for Victims." *Dallas Morning News,* January 1, p. 2f.

Baumgartner, Frank R., and Bryan D. Jones. 1993. *Agendas and Instability in American Politics.* Chicago: University of Chicago Press.

Baumgartner, M. P. 1984. "Social Control in Suburbia." In *Toward a General Theory of Social Control,* vol. 2, ed. Donald Black. New York: Academic Press.

Beckett, Katherine. 1997. *Making Crime Pay: Law and Order in Contemporary American Politics.* New York: Oxford University Press.

Bell, Peter A., and Jeffery O'Connell. 1997. *Accidental Justice: The Dilemmas of Tort Law.* New Haven: Yale University Press.

Bellah, Robert Neely, Richard Madsen, William M. Sullivan, Ann Swidler, and Steven M. Tipton. 1985. *Habits of the Heart: Individualism and Commitment in American Life.* Berkeley: University of California Press.

Bender, Leslie. 1990. "Feminist (Re)torts: Thoughts on the Liability Crisis, Mass Torts, Power, and Responsibilities." *Duke Law Journal* 1990:848–63.

Bennett , W. Lance. 1996. *News: The Politics of Illusion.* 3d ed. White Plains, N.Y.: Longman.

———. 2001. *News: The Politics of Illusion.* 4th ed. White Plains, N.Y.: Longman.

Berendt, John. 1993. "The Lawsuit." *Esquire,* May, pp. 37–38.

Bergman, Paul, and Michael Asimow. 1996. *Reel Justice: The Courtroom Goes to the Movies.* Kansas City: Andrews and McMeel.

Bird, Donald Allport. 1976. "A Theory for Folklore in Mass Media: Traditional Patterns in the Mass Media." *Southern Folklore Quarterly* 40:285–305.

Birnbaum, Jess. 1991. "Crybabies: Eternal Victims." *Time,* August 12, p. 17.

Black, Amy E., and Stanley Rothman. 1998. "Shall We Kill All the Lawyers First? Insider and Outsider Views of the Legal Profession." *Harvard Journal of Law and Public Policy* 21 (summer): 835.

Black's Law Dictionary. 1968. 4th ed. St. Paul: West Publishing Group.

Bloom, Anne. 2001. "Taking on Goliath: Why Personal Injury Litigation May Represent the Future of Transnational Cause Lawyering." In *Cause Lawyering and the State in the Global Era,* ed. Austin Sarat and Stuart Scheingold, 96–116. Oxford: Oxford University Press.

———. 2003. Taking on Goliath: Can U.S. Courts Give Workers a Transnational Voice? Ph.D. diss., University of Washington.

Bogus, Carl T. 2001. *Why Lawsuits Are Good for America: Disciplined Democracy, Big Business, and the Common Law.* New York: New York University Press.

Boon, Andrew. 2001. "Cause Lawyers in a Cold Climate: The Impact of Globalization on the

United Kingdom." In *Cause Lawyering and the State in the Global Era,* ed. Austin Sarat and Stuart Scheingold, 143–85. Oxford: Oxford University Press.

Boot, Max. 1998. *Out of Order: Arrogance, Corruption, and Incompetence on the Bench.* New York: Basic Books.

Bourdieu, Pierre. 1977. *Outline of a Theory of Practice.* Translated by Richard Nice. New York: Cambridge University Press.

Brakel, Samuel Jan. 1996. "Using What We Know about Our Civil Litigation System: A Critique of 'Base-Rate' Analysis and Other Apologist Diversions." *Georgia Law Review* 31:77–200.

———. 2000. "'Besting' Tort Reform in Illinois (and Other Misnomers): A Reform Supporter's Lament." *Capital University Law Review* 28:823–35.

Brennan, Troyen A., Lucian L. Leape, Nan M. Laird, Liesi Herbert, A. Russell Localio, Ann G. Lawthers, Joseph P. Newhouse, Paul C. Weiler, and Howard H. Hiatt. 1991. "Incidence of Adverse Events and Negligence in Hospitalized Patients: Results of the Harvard Medical Practice Study." *New England Journal of Medicine* 324 (6): 370–76.

Brill, Steven. 1996. "Address to Texas Law Review Association on March 29, 1996." *Texas Lawyer,* April 15, p. 18.

Brill, Steven, and James Lyons. 1986. "The Not-So-Simple Crisis." *American Lawyer,* May, pp. 1, 12–17.

Broder, Ivy E. 1986. "Characteristics of Million Dollar Awards: Jury Verdicts and Final Disbursements." *Justice System Journal* 11:349–59.

Brunvand, Jan Harold. 1968. *The Study of American Folklore.* New York: Norton.

———. 1999. *Too Good to Be True: The Colossal Book of Urban Legends.* New York: Norton.

———. 2001. *Encyclopedia of Urban Legends.* New York: Norton.

Bryant, Arthur H. 1999. "Chrysler Air-Bag Verdict as Victory for Consumers." *USA Today,* March 18, p. 14A.

Bumiller, Kristin. 1988. *The Civil Rights Society: The Social Construction of Victims.* Baltimore: Johns Hopkins University Press.

Burke, Thomas F. 2002. *Lawyers, Lawsuits, and Legal Rights: The Battle over Litigation in American Society.* Berkeley: University of California Press.

Burns, Thomas. 1969. "Folklore in the Mass Media: Television." *Folklore Forum* 2 (4): 90–116.

Bush, George W. 2003. "President Calls for Medical Liability Reform: Remarks by the President on Medical Liability Reform, University of Scranton." January 16. Available at www.whitehouse.gov/news/releases/2003/01/20030116–1.html.

Calve, Joseph. 1996. "Poured Out." *Texas Lawyer,* December 16, pp. 1, 15–20.

Camp, Charles B. 1993. "Business Interests Expect Victory on Tort Reform Bills; Consumer Groups Say Proposals Protect Firms' Misdeeds." *Dallas Morning News,* February 20, p. 1A.

Campbell, Bruce, and Talarico, Susette M. 1983. "Access to Legal Services: Examining Common Assumptions." *Judicature* 66:313–18.

Caplow, Stacy. 1999. "Still in the Dark: Disappointing Images of Women Lawyers in the Movies." *Women's Rights Law Reporter* 20 (spring/summer): 55–71.

Carlson, Darren K. 2001. "Half of Americans Say Second-Hand Smoke Is 'Very Harmful.'" Gallup News Service, July 25. Available at www.gallup.com/poll/releases/pr010725c.asp (last visited February 15, 2002).

Carroll, Robert Todd. 2000. "The Skeptic's Dictionary: Electromagnetic Fields (EMFs)," available at http://skepdic.com (visited October 20, 2003.

Casper, Jonathan D. 1993. "Restructuring the Traditional Civil Jury: The Effects of Changes in Composition and Procedures." In *Verdict: Assessing the Civil Justice System*, ed. Robert F. Litan, 414–59. Washington, D.C.: Brookings.

Center for Justice and Democracy. 2002. "Mythbuster: Biased 'Tort Reform' Polls and Surveys: What They Really Show." New York.

Chaptman, Dennis, and Richard P. Jones. 1999. "Tobacco Accord Worth $2,583 Hourly to Firms." *Miwaukee Journal Sentinel,* July 12, online.

Charen, Mona. 1996. "What Has Happened to Thinking of Others?" *St. Louis Post-Dispatch,* July 26, p. 7B.

Chase, Anthony. 1986a. "Lawyers and Popular Culture: A Review of Mass Media Portrayals of American Attorneys." *American Bar Foundation Research Journal* 281–300.

———. 1986b. "Toward a Legal Theory of Popular Culture." *Wisconsin Law Review* 1986: 527–69.

———. 1999. "Civil Action Cinema." *Law Review of Michigan State University–Detroit College of Law* 1999 (winter): 945–57.

Cheit, Ross E. 1991. "Corporate Ambulance Chasers: The Charmed Life of Business Litigation." In *Studies in Law, Politics, and Society,* vol. 11, ed. Austin Sarat and Susan S. Silbey, 119–40. Greenwick, Conn.: JAI Press.

Chesebro, Kenneth J. 1993. "Galileo's Retort: Peter Huber's Junk Scholarship." *American University Law Review* 42:1637–1726.

Chibnall, Steve. 1977. *Law-and-Order News: An Analysis of Crime Reporting in the British Press.* London: Tavistock.

Chicago Sun-Times. 1994. "Hot Coffee." December 2, p. 56.

Chicago Tribune. 1993. "Striking a Blow at 'Junk Science.'" Editorial. July 12, p. 12.

Chin, Audrey, and Mark A. Peterson. 1985. *Deep Pockets, Empty Pockets: Who Wins in Cook County Jury Trials?* Santa Monica: RAND Institute for Civil Justice.

Ciresi, Michael. 1999. "Panel Discussion: The Tobacco Litigation and Attorneys' Fees." *Fordham Law Review* 67:2827–57.

Cincinnati Enquirer. 1994. "Spilled Coffee: The Rest of the Story about McDonald's $3 Million Claim." September 6, p. A6.

Civil Justice Association of California. 1999. "Research: 1998 Campaign Contributions by California Trial Lawyers." Available at www.actr.com/research.index.hmtl.

Clermont, Kevin M., and Theodore Eisenberg. 1992. "Trial by Jury or Judge: Transcending Empiricism." *Cornell Law Review* 77 (July): 1124–77.

———. 2000. "Anti-Plaintiff Bias in the Federal Appellate Courts." *Judicature* 84:128–34.

Coffee, John C. 1995. "Class Wars: The Dilemma of the Mass Tort Class Action." *Columbia Law Review* 95:1343–1465.

Cohen, Neal M. 1991. "Busting Liability Reform Dike." *Journal of Communications,* September 30, p. 12a.

Cohen, Stanley. 1987. *Folk Devils and Moral Panics: The Creation of the Mods and Rockers.* Oxford: Basil Blackwell.

Collins, Glenn. 1995. "A Tobacco Case's Legal Buccaneers." *New York Times,* March 6, p. D1.

Congressional Record. 1994. September 27, 140, H9766m.

———. 1995a. March 6, 141, H2661.

———. 1995b. May 2, 141, S5956.

Conley, John M., and William M. O'Barr. 1990. *Rules versus Responsibility: The Ethnography of Legal Discourse.* Chicago: University of Chicago Press.

Cook, Timothy. 1998. *Governing with the News: The News Media as a Political Institution.* Chicago: University of Chicago Press.

Cooper, Mark. 1995. "The Verdict Is In: Jury Awards Unchanged over 30 Years." *Citizen Action,* April.

Cox, Gail Diane. 1992. "Tort Tales Lash Back." *National Law Journal,* August 3, pp. 1, 36.

Cramton, Roger C. 1996. "What Do Lawyer Jokes Tell Us about Lawyers and Lawyering?" *Cornell Law Review* 23 (1): 3–9.

Cross, Frank B. 1998. "Lawyers, the Economy, and Society." *American Business Law Journal* 35 (summer): 477–513.

Curran, Barbara A. 1977. *The Legal Needs of the Public: The Final Report of a National Survey.* Chicago: American Bar Foundation.

Daniels, Mitchell. 1986. "The Young Must Lead in Repair and Reform." *National Law Journal,* August 18, p. S13.

Daniels, Stephen. 1989. "The Question of Civil Jury Competence and the Politics of Civil Justice Reform." *Law and Contemporary Problems* 52:269–310.

———. 1990. "Tracing the Shadows of the Law: Jury Verdicts in Medical Malpractice Cases." *Justice System Journal* 14 (1): 4–30.

———. 1999. "'It's Darwinism—Survival of the Fittest': How Markets and Reputations Shape the Ways in Which Lawyers Obtain Clients." *Law and Policy* 21 (4) 377–99.

Daniels, Stephen, and Joanne Martin. 1995. *Civil Juries and the Politics of Reform.* Evanston: Northwestern University Press.

———. 2000. "'The Impact That It Has Had Is Between People's Ears': Tort Reform, Mass Culture, and Plaintiffs' Lawyers." Unpublished paper, American Bar Foundation.

———. 2002. "It Was the Best of Times, It Was the Worst of Times: The Precarious Nature of Plaintiffs' Practice in Texas." *Texas Law Review* 80 (7): 1781–1828.

Daniels, Stephen, Jerry Van Hoy, and Joanne Martin. 1999. "Clouds and Silver Linings: The Response of Plaintiffs' Lawyers to Tort Reform." Paper delivered at the annual meeting of the Law and Society Association, in Chicago.

Danzon, Patricia A. 1985. *Medical Malpractice: Theory, Evidence, and Public Policy.* Cambridge, Mass.: Harvard University Press.

Darnton, Robert. 1975. "Writing News and Telling Stories." *Daedalus* 104:175–94.

Dateline NBC. 1999. Broadcast November 12.

Davis, Richard. 1994. *Decisions and Images: The Supreme Court and the Press.* Englewood Cliffs, N.J.: Prentice-Hall.

Deal, Carl, and Joanne Doroshow. 2002. *The CALA Files: The Secret Campaign by Big Tobacco and Other Major Industries To Take Away Your Rights.* New York: Center for Democracy and Justice.

De Frances, Carol J., and Marika F. X. Litras. 1999. *Civil Justice Survey of State Courts, 1996: Civil Jury Cases and Verdict in Large Counties, 1996.* Washington, D.C.: Bureau of Justice Statistics Bulletin NCJ 173426 (September).

De Frances, Carol J., Steven K. Smith, Patrick A. Langan, Brian J. Ostrom, David B. Rottman, and John A. Goerdt. 1995. *Civil Justice Survey of State Courts, 1992: Civil Jury Cases and Verdicts in Large Counties.* Washington, D.C.: Bureau of Justice Statistics Bulletin NCJ 154346 (July).

Denvir, John, ed. 1996. *Legal Reelism: Movies as Legal Texts.* Urbana-Champagne: University of Illinois Press.

Derthick, Martha A. 2002. *Up in Smoke: From Legislation to Litigation in Tobacco Politics.* Washington, D.C.: C Q Press.

Dezalay, Yves, and Bryant Garth. 1997. "Law, Lawyers and Social Capital: Rule of Law vs. Relational Capitalism." *Social and Legal Studies* 6 (1) 109–41.

Diamond, Shari, Michael Saks, and Stephan Landsman. 1998. "Juror Judgments about Liability and Damages: Sources of Variability and Ways to Increase Consistency." *DePaul Law Review* 48 : 301–25.

DiGirolama, Michele. 1986a. "Judge Throws Out $986,000 Jury Award to 'Psychic.'" UPI, August 9.

———. (1986b) "Psychic Gets $1 Million in Damages." UPI, March 29.

Dillard, Kirk W. 1996. "Illinois' Landmark Tort Reform: The Sponsor's Policy Explanation." *Loyola University of Chicago Law Review* 27 (summer): 805–17.

Dionne, E. J. 2003. "Stimulating Class Warfare." *Seattle Times,* January 8, p. B6.

Dirck, Joe. 1993. "Let's-Sue Syndrome: It Wasn't My Fault." *Cleveland Plain Dealer,* May 2, p. 11H.

Discovery Inquiry. 1996. November: 5 (5): 11.

Donzelot, Jacques. 1977. *The Policing of Families,* trans. Robert Hurley. Baltimore: Johns Hopkins University Press.

Douglas, Mary. 1992. *Risk and Blame: Essays in Cultural Theory.* London: Routledge.

Douglas, Mary, and Aaron Wildavksy. 1982. *Risk and Culture: An Essay on the Selection of Technical and Environmental Dangers.* Berkeley: University of California Press.

Dowie, Mark. 2002. "A Teflon Correspondent." *Nation,* January 7/14, pp. 36–39.

Downie Jr., Leonard, and Robert G. Kaiser. 2002. *The News about the News: American Journalism in Peril.* New York: Knopf.

Drechsel, Robert E. 1983. *Newsmaking in the Trial Courts: Newspaper Reporters and Sources in Courts of Original Jurisdiction.* New York: Longman.

Dundes, Alan. 1990. *Essays in Folklore Theory and Method.* Madras: Cre-A.

Dunworth, Terence. 1988. *Product Liability and the Business Sector: Litigation Trends in Federal Courts.* Santa Monica: Rand Institute for Civil Justice.

Eckstein, Paul F. 1994. "Can Products Liability Cases be Secret?" *Litigation* 20 (3): 23–24.

Economist. 1986. "The Guilty Parties in the Great Liability Insurance Crisis." March 22, p. 23.

———. 1987. "A Survey of Insurance." June 6.

Edelman, Lauren B., Steven E. Abraham, and Howard S. Erlanger. 1992. "Professional Construction of of the Legal Environment: The Inflated Threat of Wrongful Discharge Doctrine." *Law and Society Review* 26 : 47–83.

Edelman, Murray. 1964. *The Symbolic Uses of Politics.* Urbana: University of Illinois Press.

———. 1988. *Constructing the Political Spectacle.* Chicago: University of Chicago Press.

Eisenberg, Theodore, and James A. Henderson. 1992. "Inside the Quiet Revolution in Products Liability." *UCLA Law Review* 39 : 731–810.

Eisenberg, Theodore, John A. Goerdt, Brian J. Ostrom, and David B. Rottman. 1995. "Litigation Outcomes in State and Federal Court: A Statistical Portrait." Paper presented at the annual meeting of the Law and Society Association, Toronto.

Eisenberg, Theodore, John Goerdt, Brian Ostrom, David Rottman, and Martin T. Wells. 1997. "The Predictability of Punitive Damages." *Journal of Legal Studies* 26 (2) 623–61.

Engel, David. 1984. "The Oven Bird's Song: Insiders, Outsiders and Personal Injuries in an American Community." *Law and Society Review* 18 : 551–82.

———. 2001. "Injury and Identity: The Damaged Self in Three Cultures." In *Between Law and Culture: Relocating Legal Studies,* ed. David Theo Goldberg, Michael Musheno, and Lisa C. Bower, 3–21. Minneapolis: University of Minnesota Press.

Entman, Robert M. 1989. *Democracy without Citizens: Media and the Decay of American Politics.* New York: Oxford University Press.

———. 1993. "Framing: Toward Clarification of a Fractured Paradigm." *Journal of Communication* 43 : 51–58.

Epp, Charles R. 2001. "The Fear of Being Sued: Variations in Perceptions of Legal Threat among Managers in the United States." Paper presented at the annual meeting of the Law and Society Association, in Budapest.

———. 2002. "Legal Liability as a Form of Regulation: A Comparison of Police, Playgrounds, and Personnel." Paper presented at the annual meeting of the American Political Science Association, in Boston.

Epstein, Edward Jay. 1973. *News from Nowhere: Television and the News*. New York: Vintage.

Ericson, Richard V., Patricia M. Baranek, and Janet B. L. Chan. 1991. *Representing Order: Crime, Law, and Justice in the News Media*. Buckingham, UK: Open University Press.

Erwin, Diana Griego. 1994. "Big Bucks for Dumb Luck? Coffee Is Hot and Life Is Full of Risks—Deal With It." *San Diego Union-Tribune*, August 25, p. B11.

Esler, Gavin. 1996–97. "Hey, Buddy, I'm the Victim Here!" *New Statesman*, December 20–January 3, pp. 98–100.

Esquire. 1995. "Dubious Achievement Awards of 1994." 123 (1): 35.

Evans, Rowland, and Robert Novak. 1994. "America's Most Powerful Lobby." *Reader's Digest* April: 131–35.

Ewick, Patricia, and Susan S. Silbey. 1995. "Subversive Stories and Hegemonic Tales: Toward a Sociology of Narrative." *Law and Society Review* 29 : 197–226.

———. 1998. *The Common Place of Law: Stories from Everyday Life*. Chicago: University of Chicago Press.

Felstiner, William L. F., Richard L. Abel, and Austin Sarat. 1980–81. "The Emergence and Transformation of Disputes: Naming, Blaming, and Claiming." *Law and Society Review* 15 : 631–55.

Fine, Gary Alan. 1992. *Manufacturing Tales: Sex and Money in Contemporary Legends*. Knoxville: University of Tennessee Press.

Finley, Lucinda. 1997. "Female Trouble: The Implications of Tort Reform for Women." *Tennessee Law Review* 64 : 847–880.

Fishman, Mark. 1980. *Manufacturing the News*. Austin: University of Texas Press.

Forbes. 1986. "The Tort Reform Quagmire." August 11, pp. 76–79.

Foucault, Michel. 1979. *Discipline and Punish: The Birth of the Prison,* trans. Alan Sheridan. New York: Vintage Books.

———. 1980. *Power/Knowledge: Selected Interviews and Other Writings, 1972–1977*. New York: Pantheon Books.

———. 1991. "Questions of Method." In *The Foucault Effect,* ed. Gordon Burchell, Colin Gordon, and Peter Miller, 73–86. Chicago: University of Chicago Press.

Frank, Thomas. 2002. "Bill Rules Out Lawsuits against Vaccine Maker: Protection for Drug Tied to Autism." *Newsday* article reported in *Seattle Times,* October 25, p. A4.

Frankel, Alison, and John E. Morris. 2000. "Traitor to His Class: Watch Out World." *American Lawyer* (January): 1–9.

Freedman, Michael. 2002. "The Tort Mess: It's Even Worse Than You Think." *Forbes* 169 (11): 90–96.

Freedman, Monroe. 1975. *Lawyers' Ethics in an Adversary System*. Indianapolis: Bobbs-Merrill.

Friedman, Lawrence. 1989. "Law, Lawyers, and Popular Culture." *Yale Law Journal* 98 : 1579–1606.

Fritschler, A. Lee, and James M. Hoefler. 1996. *Smoking and Politics*. 5th ed. Englewood Cliffs, N.J.: Prentice-Hall.

Galanter, Marc. 1974. "Why the 'Haves' Come Out Ahead: Speculations on the Limits of Legal Change." *Law and Society Review* 9 (8): 95–160.

———. 1983. "Reading the Landscape of Disputes: What We Know and Don't Know (and

Think We Know) about Our Allegedly Contentious and Litigious Society." *UCLA Law Review* 31:4–71.

———. 1992. "Pick a Number, Any Number." *American Lawyer,* April, p. 82.

———. 1993a. "News from Nowhere: The Debased Debate on Civil Justice." *Denver University Law Review* 71:77–113.

———. 1993b. "The Regulatory Function of the Civil Jury." In *Verdict: Assessing the Civil Justice System,* ed. Robert F. Litan, 61–102. Washington, D.C.: Brookings.

———. 1993c. "The Tort Panic and After: A Commentary." *Justice System Journal* 16 (2): 1–5.

———. 1994. "Predators and Parasites: Lawyer-Bashing and Civil Justice." *Georgia Law Review* 28:633–81.

———. 1996a. "The Day after the Litigation Explosion." *Maryland Law Review* 46:3–39.

———. 1996b. "Real World Torts: An Antidote to Anecdote." *Maryland Law Review* 55:1093–1160.

———. 1998a. "The Faces of Mistrust: The Image of Lawyers in Public Opinion, Jokes, and Political Discourse." *University of Cincinnati Law Review* 66:805–45.

———. 1998b. "An Oil Strike in Hell: Contemporary Legends about the Civil Justice System." *Arizona Law Review* 40:717–52.

———. 2002. "The Turn against Law: The Recoil against Expanding Accountability." Paper presented at the annual meeting of the Law and Society Association, in Vancouver.

Galanter, Marc, and Mia Cahill. 1994. "Most Cases Settle: Judicial Promotion and Regulation of Settlements." *Stanford Law Review* 46:1339–391.

Galanter, Marc, Bryant Garth, Deborah Hensler, and Frances Kahn Zemans. 1994. "How to Improve Civil Justice Policy: Systematic Collection of Data on the Civil Justice System Is Needed for Reasoned and Effective Policy Making." *Judicature* 77 (4): 185.

Gamson, William. 1989. "News as Framing." *American Behavioral Scientist* (November/December): 157–61.

———. 1992. *Talking Politics.* New York: Cambridge University Press.

Gamson, William, and Andre Modigliani.1989. "Media Discourse and Public Opinion on Nuclear Power: A Constructionist Approach." *American Journal of Sociology* (July): 1–37.

GAO (General Accounting Office). 1989. *Product Liability: Verdicts and Case Resolution in Five States.* Pub. No. GAO/HRD-89-99.

Garber, Steven, and Anthony G. Bower. 1999. "Newspaper Coverage of Automotive Product Liability Verdicts." *Law and Society Review* 33:93–122.

Garry, Patrick M. 1997. *A Nation of Adversaries: How the Litigation Explosion Is Reshaping America.* Boulder: Perseus Publishing.

Gaventa, John. 1980. *Power and Powerlessness: Quiescence and Rebellion in an Appalachian Valley.* Urbana: University of Illinois Press.

Gentile, Gary. 2002. "Former Smoker Wins $28 Billion." Associated Press, October 4. Available at www.story.news.yahoo.com/news?

Gerlin, Andrea. 1994. "A Matter of Degree: How a Jury Decided That a Coffee Spill Is Worth $2.9 Million." *Wall Street Journal,* September 1, p. A1.

Geyelin, Milo. 1992. "Tort Bar's Scourge: Star of Legal Reform Kindles Controversy but Collects Critics." *Wall Street Journal,* October 16, p. A1.

Gibeat, John. 1998. "Secret Justice." *ABA Law Journal* (April): 52.

Gifis, Stephen H. 1975. *Law Dictionary.* Woodbury, N.Y.: Barron's Educational Series.

———. 1998. *Dictionary of Legal Terms: A Simplified Guide to the Language of Law.* 3d ed. Woodbury, N.Y.: Barron's Educational Series.

Gilens, Martin. 1999. *Why Americans Hate Welfare: Race, Media, and the Politics of Antipoverty Policy.* Chicago: University of Chicago Press.

Glaberson, William. 1999. "State Laws Limiting Injury Suits Are Falling Like Dominoes." *New York Times,* July 16, sec. 1, p. 1.

Glaberson, William B., and Christopher Farrell. 1986. "The Explosion in Liability Lawsuits Is Nothing but a Myth." *Business Week,* April 21, p. 24.

Glendon, Mary Ann. 1991. *Rights Talk: The Impoverishment of Political Discourse.* New York: Free Press.

————. 1996. *A Nation under Lawyers: How the Crisis in the Legal Profession Is Transforming American Society.* Cambridge: Harvard University Press.

Goldfarb, Lewis H. 1999. "Air Bags: Why Let Facts Get in the Way?" *Wall Street Journal,* March 26, p. A23.

Goodbye Lover. 1999. Directed by Roland Joffé. Written by Ron Peer, Joel Cohen, and Alex Sokolow. Produced by Arnon Milchan, Gotham Entertainment Group, Lightmotive, and Regency Vision. Distributed by Warner Brothers.

Gordon, Marcy. 1995. "Injury Victims Lobby against GOP Damages Bill; Supporters Run Ads." Associated Press, March 2, PM cycle.

Graber, Mark A. (1993) "The Nonmajoritarian Difficulty: Legislative Deference to the Judiciary." *Studies in American Political Development* 7 : 35–73.

Greene, Edith, Jane Goodman, and Elizabeth F. Loftus. 1991. "Jurors' Attitudes about Civil Litigation and the Size of Damage Awards." *American University Law Review* 40 : 805–20.

Greenhouse, Carol. 1982. "Nature Is to Culture as Praying Is to Suing: Legal Pluralism in an American Suburb." *Journal of Legal Pluralism* 20 : 17–37.

Greenhouse, Carol, Barbara Yngvesson, and David M. Engel. 1994. *Law and Community in Three American Towns.* Ithaca: Cornell University Press.

Greenlee, Mark B. 1997. "Kramer v. Java World: Images, Issues, and Idols in the Debate over Tort Reform." *Capital University Law Review* 26 : 701–38.

Gregory, Leland H. 1998. *Presumed Ignorant! An Uncensored Guide to Disorder in the Courts—So Funny It Oughta Be Illegal.* New York: Dell.

Griffin, C. W. 1996. "Warning: Scientific Evidence Can Be Soporific." *Washington Post,* December 11, p. A25.

Grisham, John. 1996. *The Runaway Jury.* New York: Doubleday.

Guay, Paul, and Stephen Mazur. 1997. *Liar, Liar.* Directed by Tom Shayac. Produced by James D. Brubaker, Michael Bostick, and Brian Glazer. Distributed by Universal Pictures.

Gusfield, Joseph. 1981. *The Culture of Public Problems: Drinking, Driving, and the Symbolic Order.* Chicago: University of Chicago Press.

Haimes, Allen Nelsen. 1990. *Judith: The Story of Judith Richardson Haimes.* Seminole, Fla.: Pentacle Publications.

Haltom, William. 1998. *Reporting on the Courts: How Mass Media Cover Judicial Actions.* Chicago: Nelson-Hall.

Haltom, William, and Michael McCann. 1998. "Law and Lore: Media, Common Knowledge, and the Politics of Civil Justice." Paper presented at the annual meeting of the American Political Science Association, Boston.

————. 2000. "Hegemonic Tales and Subversive Statistics: A Twenty Year Study of News Reporting about Civil Litigation." Paper presented at the annual meeting of the Law and Society Association, in Miami.

————. 2001. "Hegemonic Tales and Everyday News: How Newspapers Cover Civil Litigation." Paper presented at the annual meeeting of the American Political Science Association, San Francisco.

Hamilton, V. Lee, and Joseph Sanders. 1996. "Corporate Crime through Citizens' Eyes: Stratification and Responsibility in the United States, Russia, and Japan." *Law and Society Review* 30:513–47.

Handler, Joel F. 2004. *Social Citizenship and Workfare in the United States and Western Europe: The Paradox of Inclusion.* Cambridge, UK: Cambridge University Press.

Hans, Valerie P. 1993. "Attitudes toward the Civil Jury." In *Verdict: Assessing the Civil Jury System,* ed. Robert F. Litan, 248–81. Washington, D.C.: Brookings.

———. 2000. *Business on Trial: The Civil Jury and Corporate Responsibility.* New Haven: Yale University Press.

Hans, Valerie P., and William S. Lofquist. 1992. "Juror's Judgments of Business Liability in Tort Cases: Implications for the Litigation Explosion Debate." *Law and Society Review* 26 (1): 85–115.

Harrington, Christine. 1985. *Shadow Justice: The Ideology and Institutionalization of Alternatives to Court.* Westport, Conn.: Greenwood Press.

Hayden, Robert M. 1991. "The Cultural Logic of a Political Crisis: Common Sense, Hegemony, and the Great American Liability Insurance Famine of 1986." In *Studies in Law, Politics, and Society,* ed. Austin Sarat and Susan S. Silbey, 95–117. Greenwich, Conn.: JAI Press.

Heinz, John P., Edward O. Laumann, Robert L. Nelson, and Paul S. Schnorr. 1977. "The Constituencies of Elite Urban Lawyers." *Law and Society Review* 31:441–72.

Heinz, John P., and Edward O. Laumann. 1982. *Chicago Lawyers: The Social Structure of the Bar.* New York: Russell Sage.

Heinz, John P., Robert L. Nelson, Edward O. Laumann, and Ethan Michelson. 1998. "The Changing Character of Lawyers' Work: Chicago in 1975 and 1995." *Law and Society Review* 32:751–75.

Henderson, James A., and Theodore Eisenberg. 1990. "The Quiet Revolution in Products Liability: An Empirical Study of Legal Change." *UCLA Law Review* 37:479–553.

Hengstler, Gary A. 1986. "Psychic's Case to Be Retried." *American Bar Association Journal* 72:23.

———. 1993. "Vox Populi: The Public Perceptions of Lawyers: ABA Poll." *American Bar Association Journal* 79:60–65.

Hensler, Deborah, James S. Kakalik, and Mark A. Peterson, 1987. *Trends in Tort Litigation: The Story Behind the Statistics.* Santa Monica: RAND Institute for Civil Justice.

Hensler, Deborah, et al. 1991. *Compensation for Accidental Injuries in the United States.* Santa Monica: RAND Institute for Civil Justice.

Hensler, Deborah, with Bonnie Dumberg-Moore, Beth Giddens, Jennifer Gross, Erik K. Moller, and Nicholas M. Pace. 2000. *Class Action Dilemmas: Pursuing Public Goals for Private Gain.* Santa Monica: RAND Institute for Civil Justice.

Hertsgaard, Mark. 1988. *On Bended Knee: The Press and the Reagan Presidency.* New York: Schocken Books.

Hilts, Philip J. 1996. *Smoke Screen: The Truth behind the Tobacco Industry Cover-up.* Reading, Mass., Addison-Wesley.

Houck, Oliver A. "With Charity for All." *Yale Law Journal* 93 (July): 1415–1562.

Hobbie, K. R. 1992. *World's Wackiest Lawsuits.* New York: Sterling.

Horwitz, Morton. 1979. *Transformation of American Law, 1780–1860.* Cambridge: Harvard University Press.

Howard, Philip K. 1994. *The Death of Common Sense: How Law Is Suffocating America.* New York: Random House.

———. 2001. *The Lost Art of Drawing the Line: How Fairness Went Too Far.* New York: Random House.

Huber, Peter. 1988. *Liability: The Legal Revolution and Its Consequences.* New York: Basic Books.

———. 1990. "Cockroaches in Court." *Forbes,* October 1, p. 248.

———. 1991a. *Galileo's Revenge: Junk Science in the Courtroom.* New York: Basic Books.

———. 1991b. "Junk Science in the Courtroom." *Forbes,* July 8, p. 68.

Hunter, James Davison. 1991. *Culture Wars: The Struggle to Define America.* New York: Basic Books.

Hunter, J. Robert. 1999. "Texas Tort Reform's Incredible Shrinking 'Savings.'" Available at www.consumerfed.org/txtort.pdf.

Hunter, J. Robert, and Joanne Doroshow. 2002. "Premium Deceit—The Failure of 'Tort Reform' to Cut Insurance Prices. Executive Summary." Available at www.centerjd.org/press/release/990713,html.

Ivins, Molly, and Lou Dubose. 2000. *Shrub: The Short but Happy Political Life of George W. Bush.* New York: Vintage.

Iyengar, Shanto. 1991. *Is Anyone Responsible? How Television Frames Political Issues.* Chicago: University of Chicago Press.

———. 1992. "The Accessibility Bias in Politics: Television News and Public Opinion." In *The Mass Media in Liberal Democratic Societies,* ed. Stanley Rothman. New York: Random House.

Jacobson, Peter D., Jeffrey Wasserman, and Kristiana Raube. 1992. *The Political Evolution of Anti-Smoking Legislation.* Santa Monica: RAND.

Jarvis, Robert M., and Paul R. Joseph, eds. 1998. *Prime Time Law: Fictional Television as Legal Narrative.* Durham: Carolina Academic Press.

Joseph, Paul. 2000. "Law and Popular Culture." *Nova Law Review* 24:527–69.

Jost, Kenneth. 1992. "Tampering with Evidence: The Liability and Competitiveness Myth." *American Bar Association Journal* 78:44–50.

KABC. 1994a. 4 P.M. news on August 18. Located via "Academic Universe."

———. 1994b. 11 P.M. news on August 18. Located via "Academic Universe."

Kagan, Robert A. 2001. *Adversarial Legalism: The American Way of Law.* Cambridge, Mass.: Harvard University Press.

Kagan, Robert A., and William P. Nelson. 2001. "The Politics of Tobacco Regulation in the United States." In *Regulating Tobacco,* ed. Robert L. Rabin and Stephen D. Sugarman, 11–38. New York: Oxford University Press.

Kagan, Robert A., and David Vogel. 1993. "The Politics of Smoking Regulation: Canada, France, the United States." In *Smoking Policy: Law, Politics, and Culture,* ed. Robert L. Rabin and Stephen D. Sugarman, 22–48 (New York: Oxford University Press).

Kalven, Harry. 1964. "The Dignity of the Civil Jury." *Virginia Law Review* 50 (October): 1055–75.

Kammen, Michael. 1999. *American Culture, American Tastes: Social Change and the 20th Century.* New York: Knopf.

Kaplan, David. 1986. "What America Really Thinks about Lawyers." *National Law Journal,* August 18, pp. S1–19.

Katz, Roberta. 1996. "Is It Time to Reform the Adversarial Civil Justice System?" *Discovery Inquiry* 6 (5): 11.

Kennedy, John H. 1992. "Secrecy Orders Put New Burdens on Legal System," *Boston Globe,* February 5, p. 53.

Kessler, David. 2001. *A Question of Intent: A Great American Battle with a Deadly Industry.* New York: Public Affairs.

Kingdon, John. 1995. *Agendas, Alternatives and Public Policies.* 2d ed. New York: Harper Collins.

Kluger, Richard. 1996. *Ashes to Ashes: America's Hundred-Year Cigarette War, the Public Health, and the Unabashed Triumph of Philip Morris.* New York: Knopf.

Koenig, Thomas. 1998. "The Shadow Effect of Punitive Damages on Settlements." *Wisconsin Law Review* 1998 (1): 169–209.

Koenig, Thomas, and Michael Rustad. 1995. "His and Her Tort Reform: Gender Injustice in Disguise." *Washington Law Review* 70 : 1–88.

Kolata, Gina. 1992. "Secrecy Orders in Lawsuits Prompt States' Efforts to Restrict Their Use." *New York Times,* February 18, p. D10.

Koniak, Susan F. 1995. "Feasting While the Widow Weeps: *Georgine v. Amchem Products, Inc.*" *Cornell Law Review* 60 : 1045–1168.

Kristol, Irving. 1995. " 'The Culture Wars in Perspective': Walter B. Wriston Lecture at the Manhattan Institute." November 16. Available at www://manhattan-institute.org/html/w11995.htm (last visited October 17, 2003).

Kritzer, Herbert M. 1986. "Adjudication to Settlement: Shading in the Gray." *Judicature* 70 : 161–65.

———. 1997. "Contingency Fee Lawyers as Gatekeepers in the Civil Justice System." *Judicature* 81 : 22–29.

———. 1999. "The Professions Are Dead, Long Live the Professions: Legal Practice in a Post-Professional World." *Law and Society Review* 33 : 713–59.

———. 2001. "Public Perceptions of Civil Jury Verdicts." *Judicature* 85 (2): 79–82.

KTTV. 1994. 10 P.M. news on August 18. Located via "Academic Universe."

Kurtz, Howard. 1998. "The Democrat Who Switched and Fought: Former Gore Confidant Formulated Industry's Effective Ad Blitz." *Washington Post,* June 19, p. A1.

———. 2003. "A Little Snag in Those Frivolous Suits; U.S. News's Examples Were 'Myths.' " *Washington Post,* June 23, p. C01.

Ladd, Everett Carl. 1998. "The Tobacco Bill and American Public Opinion." *Public Perspective* (August/September): 5–19.

Lakoff, George. 2002. *Moral Politics: How Liberals and Conservatives Think.* Chicago: University of Chicago Press.

Landers, Ann. "McLawsuit Plaintiffs Should Wake Up and Smell the Coffee." *Fresno Bee,* October 6, p. F2.

Landes, William, and Richard Posner. 1986. "New Light on Punitive Damages." *Regulation* 10 : 33–36, 54.

Lawrence, Regina. G. 2000. *The Politics of Force: Media and the Construction of Police Brutality.* Berkeley: University of California Press.

Lawyers 2002 Calendar—Jokes, Quotes, and Anecdotes. 2001. Kansas City: Andrews McMeel Publishing.

Lears, T. J. Jackson. 1985. "The Concept of Cultural Hegemony: Problems and Possibilities." *American Historical Review* 90 (26): 567–93.

Lebedoff, David. 1997. *Cleaning Up: The Exxon Valdez Case, the Story behind the Biggest Legal Bonanza of Our Time.* New York: Free Press.

Lempert, Richard. 1993. "Civil Juries and Complex Cases: Taking Stock after Twelve Years." In *Verdict: Assessing the Civil Justice System,* ed. Robert F. Litan, 181–247. Washington, D.C.: Brookings.

———. 2001. "Activist Scholarship." *Law and Society Review* 35 (1): 29–31.

Leo, John. 1995. "The World's Most Litigious Nation." *U.S. News and World Report,* May 22, p. 24.

Lichter, S. Robert, Linda S. Lichter, and Stanley Rothman. 1991. *Watching America: What Television Tells Us about Our Lives.* New York: Prentice-Hall.

Lieberman, Jethro. 1983. *The Litigious Society.* New York: Basic Books.

Lieberman, Trudy. 2000. *Slanting the Story: The Forces that Shape the News.* New York: New Press.

Lindsey, Robert. 1985. "Businesses Change Ways in Fear of Lawsuits." Special to *New York Times,* November 18, p. A1.

Lindlaw, Scott. 2003. "Bush Pushes for Medical-Malpractice Caps." Associated Press, January 17.

Lipschutz, Ronnie D. 1998. "From 'Culture Wars' to Shooting Wars: Cultural Conflict in the United States." In *The Myth of "Ethnic Conflict": Politics, Economics, and "Cultural" Violence,* ed. Beverly Crawford and Ronnie D. Lipschutz, 394–433. Berkeley: Research Series, International and Area Studies, University of California Press.

Litras, Marika F. X., and Carol J. DeFrances. 1999. *Federal Justice Statistics Program: Federal Tort Trials and Verdicts, 1996–97.* Bureau of Justice Statistics Bulletin NCJ 172855 (February; revised May 3, 1999).

Litras, Marika F. X., Sidra Lea Gifford, Carol J. DeFrances, David B. Rottman, Neil LaFountain, and Brian J. Ostrom. 2000. *Civil Justice Survey of State Courts, 1996: Tort Trials and Verdicts in Large Counties, 1996.* Bureau of Justice Statistics Bulletin NCJ 179769 (August).

Lofquist, William S. 2002. "Closing the Courthouse Door: Constructing Undeservingness in the Tort and Habeas Corpus Reform Movements." *Sociological Spectrum* 2: 191–233.

Loftus, Elizabeth. 1979. "Insurance Advertising and Jury Awards." *American Bar Association Journal* 65 (January): 68–70.

London Times. 1994. "Café au Loi." August 20, n.p.

Los Angeles Times. 1986a. "Says Her Powers Vanished, 'Psychic' Awarded $988,000 in Hospital CAT-Scan Lawsuit." March 30, p. 20.

———. 1986b. "Psychic's $988,000 Award Voided." August 9, p. 20.

Lovell, George. 2003. *Legislative Deferrals: Statutory Ambiguity, Judicial Power, and American Democracy.* New York: Cambridge University Press.

Luban, David. 1988. *Lawyers and Justice: An Ethical Perspective.* Princeton: Princeton University Press.

Lukes, Steven. 1974. *Power: A Radical View.* London: Macmillan.

Macauley, Stewart. 1989. "Popular Legal Culture: An Introduction." *Yale Law Journal* 98: 1545–1558.

MacCoun, Robert. 1993. "Inside the Black Box: What Empirical Research Tells Us about Decisionmaking by Civil Juries." In *Verdict: Assessing the Civil Justice System,* ed. Robert E. Litan, 137–80. Washington, D.C.: Brookings.

Magee, Stephen P., William A. Brock, and Leslie Young. 1989. *Black Hole Tariffs and Endogenous Policy Theory: Political Economy in General Equilibrium.* Cambridge: Cambridge University Press.

Mailer, Norman. 1975. *Marilyn: A Biography.* New York: Warner Paperback Library.

Malott, Robert. 1986. "America's Liability Explosion: Can We Afford the Cost?" *Vital Speeches of the Day* 52: 190.

Manning, Bayless. 1977. "Hyperlexis: Our National Disease." *Northwestern University Law Review* 71 (6): 762–82.

Martin, John. 1994. "ABC Takes Aim at the 'Blame Game.'" *Providence Journal-Bulletin,* October 26, p. 5E.

Martin, Steve. 2000. "The Third Millennium: So Far, So Good." *New York Times,* January 1, sec. 2, pp. 1–8.

Mather, Lynn. 1998. "Theorizing about Trial Courts: Lawyers, Policymaking, and Tobacco Litigation." *Law and Social Inquiry* 23 (fall): 897–937.

Mather, Lynn, and Barbara Yngvesson. 1980–81. "Language, Audience, and the Transformation of Disputes." *Law and Society Review* 15 (3–4): 775–821.

Matthews, Jay. 1995. "Torts and a Tug on the Heartstrings: In the Battle over Liability Law, Ad Puts Emotion on the Front Line." *Washington Post,* May 10, p. F1.

May, Marilyn, and David Stengel. 1990. "Who Sues Their Doctors? How Patients Handle Medical Grievances." *Law and Society Review* 24 : 105–20.

McCann, Michael W. 1986. *Taking Reform Seriously: Perspectives on Public Interest Liberalism.* Ithaca: Cornell University Press.

———. 1994. *Rights at Work: Pay Equity Reform and the Politics of Legal Mobilization.* Chicago: University of Chicago Press.

McCann, Michael W., William Haltom, and Anne Bloom. 2001. "Java Jive: Genealogy of a Juridical Icon." *University of Miami Law Review* 56 (1) 113–78.

McCann, Michael W., and Tracey March. 1995. "Law and Everyday Forms of Resistance: A Socio-Political Assessment." In *Studies in Law, Politics, and Society,* ed. Austin Sarat and Susan S. Silbey, vol. 15, pp. 207–36. Greenwich, Conn.: JAI Press.

McGirr, Lisa. 2002. *Suburban Warriors: The Origins of the American New Right.* Princeton: Princeton University Press.

McLuhan, Marshall. 1951. *The Mechanical Bride: Folklore of Industrial Man.* New York: Vanguard.

Medved, Michael. 1993. *Hollywood vs. America.* New York: Random House.

Meier, Barry. 1998. "Tobacco Bill's Death Is Likely to Prompt Litigation Landslide." *New York Times,* June 19, p. A24.

———. 2003. "Huge Award for Smokers Is Voided by Appeals Court." *New York Times,* May 22, p. A20.

Meinhold, Stephen S., and David W. Neubauer. 2001. "Exploring Attitudes about the Litigation Explosion." *Justice System Journal* 22 (2): 105–15.

Menkel-Meadow, Carrie. 1998. "The Causes of Cause Lawyering: Toward an Understanding of the Motivation and Commitment of Social Justice Lawyers." In *Cause Lawyering: Political Commitments and Professional Responsibilities,* ed. Austin Sarat and Stuart Scheingold, 3–30. New York: Oxford University Press.

Merry, Sally Engle. 1979. "Going to Court: Strategies of Dispute Management in an American Urban Neighborhood." *Law and Society Review* 13 : 891–925.

———. 1990. *Getting Justice and Getting Even: Legal Consciousness among Working Class Americans.* Chicago: University of Chicago Press.

Mezey, Naomi. 2001. "Out of the Ordinary: Law, Power, Culture, and the Commonplace." *Law and Social Inquiry* 26 (1): 145–67.

Mill, Don Harper. 1978. "Medical Insurance Feasibility Study—A Technical Summary." *Western Journal of Medicine* 128 : 360.

Miller, Richard E., and Austin Sarat. 1980–81. "Grievances, Claims, and Disputes: Assessing the Adversary Culture." *Law and Society Review* 15 (3–4): 525–65.

Mindes, Marvin, and Alan Acock. 1982. "Trickster, Hero, Helper: A Report on the Lawyer Image." *American Bar Foundation Research Journal* 6 : 177–233.

Mollenkamp, Carrick, Adam Levy, Joseph Menn, and Jeffrey Rothfeder. 1998. *The People vs. Big Tobacco.* Princeton: Bloomberg Press.

Moller, Erik. 1996. *Trends in Jury Verdicts since 1985.* Santa Monica: RAND Institute for Civil Justice.

Montgomery, Scott. 1994. "Lay Blame: It Is the Name of the Game." *South Bend Tribune,* December 18, p. F1.

Mooney, Sean F. 1992. *Crisis and Recovery: A Review of Business Liability Insurance in the 1980s.* New York: Insurance Information Institute.

Moore, David W. 1999. "Americans Agree with Philip Morris: Smoking Is Harmful." Gallup News Service, October 14. Available at www.gallup.com/poll/releases/pr991014.asp (last visited February 15, 2002).

———. 2002. "Nine of Ten Americans View Smoking as Harmful." Gallup News Service, February 5. Available at www.gallup.com/poll/releases/pr991007.asp (last visited February 16, 2002).

Morgan, S. Reed. 1994. "Verdict against McDonald's Is Fully Justified." Letter. *National Law Journal,* October 24, p. A20.

Morone, James A. 2003. *Hellfire Nation: The Politics of Sin in American History.* New Haven: Yale University Press.

Munger, Frank. 1993. "Sociology of Law for a Post-Liberal Society." *Loyola of Los Angeles Law Journal* 27:89–125.

Nader, Laura. 1995. "When Is Popular Justice Popular?" In *The Possibility of Popular Justice,* ed. Sally Engle Merry and Neal Milner, 435–52. Ann Arbor: University of Michigan Press.

———. 2002. *The Life of the Law: Anthropological Projects.* Berkeley: University of California Press.

Nader, Ralph, and Wesley J. Smith. 1996. *No Contest: Corporate Lawyers and the Perversion of Justice in America.* New York: Random House.

NBC Nightly News. 2003. "Debate over Whether Juries Award Excessive Amounts in Punitive Damages." January 3.

Neubauer, David W., and Stephen S. Meinhold. 1994. "Too Quick to Sue? Public Perceptions of the Litigation Explosion." *Justice System Journal* 16 (3): 1.

Neuman, W. Russell, Marion R. Just, and Ann N. Crigler. 1992. *Common Knowledge: News and the Construction of Political Meaning.* Chicago: University of Chicago Press.

New York Times. 1986. "Around the Nation; Woman Wins $1 Million in Psychic Power Suit." March 29, sec. 1, p. 6.

———. 1995. "OUTLOOK 1995: THE ECONOMY—Highlights—A Simple Pleasure, Made Complicated." January 3, p. C3.

Newport, Frank. 2000. "Americans Disapprove of Florida Jury's Dramatic $145 Billion Verdict against Tobacco Industry." Gallup News Service, July 18. Available at www.gallup.com/poll/releases/ pr000718.asp (last visited February 15, 2002).

Newsweek. 2002. "For the Common Good." Web Exclusive: May 1.

Nielson, Laura Beth. 2004. *License to Harass: Law, Hierarchy, and Offensive Public Speech.* Princeton: Princeton University Press.

Norton, Anne. 1993. *Republic of Signs: Liberal Theory and American Popular Culture.* Chicago: University of Chicago Press.

Nye, Peter. 1992. "The Great Debate." *Public Citizen* (November/December).

O'Hanlon, Ann. 1995. "Woman Scarred by Stomping of Songbirds Is Awarded $135,000." *Washington Post,* December 1, p. B1.

Oakland Tribune. 1995. "A Nation of Lawyers." May 5, p. A14.

Olson, Theodore B. 1995. "Was Justice Served?" *Wall Street Journal,* October 4, p. A16.

Olson, Walter K. 1991. *The Litigation Explosion: What Happened When America Unleashed the Lawsuit.* New York: Truman Talley Books.

———. 2002. *The Rule of Lawyers: How the New Litigation Elite Threatens America's Rule of Law.* New York: Truman Talley Books.

Omaha World Herald. 1996. "Another Outrageous Jury Award." June 5, p. 18.

Onishi, Norimitsu. 1996. "The Courts, and Not Grades, May Decide a High School's Valedictorian." *New York Times,* June 12, p. A5.

Oster, Christopher. 2002. "Business' Insurance Costs Surge, but They Shouldn't Blame September 11th." *Wall Street Journal,* April 11, p. A1.

Oster, Christopher, and Rachel Zimmerman. 2002. "Insurers' Missteps Helped Provoke Malpractice 'Crisis.'" *Wall Street Journal,* June 24, p. 8.

Ostrom, Brian J., David B. Rottman, and John A. Goerdt. 1996. "A Step Above Anecdote: A Profile of the Civil Jury in the 1990s." *Judicature* 79 (March–April): 233–37.

Page, Benjamin I. 1996. *Who Deliberates? Mass Media in Modern Democracy.* Chicago: University of Chicago Press.

Paletz, David L. 1999. *The Media in American Politics: Contents and Consequences.* New York: Longman.

Paletz, David L., and Robert M. Entman. 1981. *Media Power Politics.* New York: Free Press.

Parikh, Sara. 2001. "Professionalism and Its Discontents: A Study of Social Networks in the Plaintiff's Personal Injury Bar." Ph.D. diss., University of Illinois at Chicago.

Patterson, Thomas. 1993. *Out of Order.* New York: Knopf.

Pelline, Jeff. 1994. "Excuses, Excuses—Sun Gets in the Eyes of Corporate America." *San Francisco Chronicle,* December 29, p. D1.

Percelay, James. 2000. *Whiplash! America's Most Frivolous Lawsuits.* Kansas City: Andrews McMeel Publishing.

Perkins, Joseph. 1992. "A Pestilence of Lawsuits: Tort Reform Is Needed to Stop 'Wheel of Fortune.'" *San Diego Union-Tribune,* September 18, p. B7.

———. 1997. "Time to Toast the Winners of Stella Awards." *San Diego Union-Tribune,* December 19, p. B9.

Peterson, Mark. 1987. *Civil Juries in the 1980s: Trends in Jury Trials and Verdicts in California and Cook County, Illinois.* Santa Monica: RAND Institute for Civil Justice.

Peterson, Mark, Syam Sarma, and Michael Shanley. 1987. *Punitive Damages: Empirical Findings.* Santa Monica: RAND Institute for Civil Justice.

Picturing Justice, The Online Journal of Law and Popular Culture. Available at www.usfca.edu/pj/index.html.

Post, Robert C. 1987. "On the Popular Image of the Lawyer: Reflections in a Dark Glass." *California Law Review* 75 : 379.

President's Council on Competitiveness. 1991. *A Report: Agenda for Civil Justice Reform in America.* Washington, D.C.: Government Printing Office.

Press, Aric, with Ginny Carroll and Steven Waldman. 1995. "Are Lawyers Burning America?" *Newsweek,* March 20, pp. 32–35.

Pressley, Leigh. 1994. "Great Gobblers: 1994 Turkeys of the Year." *Greensboro News and Record,* November 24, p. D1.

Priest, George, and Benjamin Klein. 1984. "The Selection of Disputes for Litigation." *Journal of Legal Studies* 13 : 1–55.

Pringle, Peter. 1998. *Cornered: Big Tobacco at the Bar of Justice.* New York: Henry Holt.

Quayle, Dan. 1994. "Address to the Annual Meeting of the American Bar Association." In Dan Quayle, *Standing Firm: A Vice-Presidential Memoir,* 375–80. New York: HarperCollins.

Queenan, Joe. 1992. "Birth of a Notion: How the Think Tank Industry Came Up with an Issue That Dan Quayle Could Call His Own." *Washington Post,* September 20, p. C1.

Rabin, Robert. 1988. "Some Reflections on the Process of Tort Reform." *San Diego Law Review* 25 : 13–42.

———. 1993. "Institutional and Historical Perspectives in Tobacco Tort Liability." In *Smoking Policy: Law, Politics, and Culture,* ed. Robert L. Rabin and Stephen D. Sugarman, 110–30. New York: Oxford University Press.

———. 2001. "The Third Wave of Tobacco Litigation." In *Regulating Tobacco,* ed. Robert L. Rabin and Stephen D. Sugarman, 176–206. New York: Oxford University Press.

Rabin, Robert L., and Stephen D. Sugarman, eds. 2001. *Regulating Tobacco.* New York: Oxford University Press.

———. 1993. *Smoking Policy: Law, Politics, and Culture.* New York: Oxford University Press.

Radin, Max. 1946. "The Ancient Grudge: A Study in the Public Relations of the Legal Profession." *Virginia Law Review* 32 : 734.

Ramsey, Maja, Justine Durrell, and Timothy W. Ahearn. 1998. "Keeping Secrets with Confidentiality Agreements." *Trial* (August): 38, 40.

Random House. 1999. *Random House Webster's Unabridged Dictionary.* CD-ROM Version 3.0.

Reagan, Ronald. 1987. *Public Papers of the Presidents* (April 1).

Reed, Douglas S. 1999. "A New Constitutional Regime: The Juridico-Entertainment Complex." Paper presented at the annual meeting of the Law and Society Association, in Chicago.

Reuters. 2003. "U.S. Congress Votes to Repeal Vaccine Provision." February 14. Accessed at www.safeminds.org/recent/reutersrepeal/reutersrepeal.html.

Rheingold, Paul D. 2000 "Analysis and Perspective: Who Are the Real Plaintiffs' Lawyers?" *Bureau of National Affairs* 1 (6): 216–18.

Rhode, Deborah L. 1999. "A Bad Press on Bad Lawyers: The Media Sees Research, Research Sees the Media." In *Social Science, Social Policy, and the Law,* ed. Patricia Ewick, Robert A. Kagan, and Austin Sarat, 139–69. New York: Russell Sage.

Risinger, D. Michael. 2000. "Defining the 'Task at Hand': Non-Science Forensic Science after *Kumbo Tire Co. v. Carmichael.*" *Washington and Lee Law Review* 57 (3): 767–800.

Rojas-Burke, Joe. 2002. "Doctors Take Big Cuts as Insurance Costs Rise." *Oregonian,* June 26, pp. A1, 8.

Rooney, Andy. 2002. "I'm Going To Sue." Broadcast on *CBS 60 Minutes,* October 27. Available at http://www.cbsnews.com/stories/2002/10/25/60minutes/rooney/main527005 .html.

Rosanvallon, Pierre. 2000. *The New Social Question: Rethinking the Welfare State.* Princeton: Princeton University Press.

Rose, Nikolas. 1999. *The Powers of Freedom: Reframing Political Thought.* Cambridge: Cambridge University Press.

Rosen, Mike. 1994. "Coffee and $ 2.9 Million to Go." *Denver Post,* August 26, p. B11.

Rossie, Dave. 1994. "How About a Hot Cup of Coffee?" *Denver Post,* August 28, p. G5.

Roth, Jonathan, and Andrew Roth. 1988. *Poetic Justice: The Funniest, Meanest Things Ever Said about Lawyers.* Berkeley: Nolo Press.

Rottman, David. 1990. "Tort Litigation in the State Courts: Evidence from the Trial Court Information Network." *State Court Journal* 14 (4): 4–18.

Ruiz, Paul. 1995. "Crying over Spilled Coffee: Media Deform the Legal Reform Debate." *Extra! (Journal of Fairness and Accuracy in Reporting),* May/June, www.fair.org.extra/ 9505/legislation.

Rustad, Michael. 1992. "In Defense of Punitive Damages in Products Liability: Testing Tort Anecdotes with Empirical Data." *Iowa Law Review* 78 : 1–88.

———. 1996. "Nationalizing Tort Law: The Republican Attack on Women, Blue Collar Workers, and Consumers." *Rutgers Law Review* 48 : 673–81.

Rustad, Michael, and Thomas Koenig. 1993. "The Historical Continuity of Punitive Damages Awards: Reforming the Tort Reformers." *American University Law Review* 42 : 1269–1333.

———. 1995. "Reconceptualizing Punitive Damages in Medical Malpractice: Targeting Amoral Corporations, Not Moral Monsters." *Rutgers Law Review* 47 : 975–1083.

———. 2002. "Taming the Tort Monster: Ideology and Utopia in the American Civil Justice System." *Brooklyn Law Review* 68 (1): 1–122.

Saad, Lydia. 1998. "A Half-Century of Polling on Tobacco: Most Don't Like Smoking but Tolerate It." *Public Perspective* (August/September): 1–4.

Said, Edward. 2001. "The Public Role of Writers and Intellectuals." *Nation,* September 17. Available at www.thenation.com/doc.mhtml?i=20010917&s=essay.

Saks, Michael J. 1992. "Do We Really Know Anything about the Behavior of the Tort Litigation System—And Why Not?" *University of Pennsylvania Law Review* 140:1147–1292.

———. 1993. "Malpractice Misconceptions and Other Lessons about the Litigation System." *Justice System Journal* 16 (2): 7–19.

———. 1994. "Book Review: Medical Malpractice: Facing Real Problems and Finding Real Solutions." *William and Mary Law Review* 35 (winter): 693–726.

———. 1998. "Public Opinion about the Civil Jury: Can Reality Be Found in the Illusions?" *DePaul Law Review* 48:221–45.

Salant, Jonathan D. 2003. "Votes in Congress Mostly Follow the Money." *Seattle Times,* July 10, p. A.4.

Salomon, Gavriel. 1979. *Interaction of Media Cognition and Learning.* San Francisco: Jossey Bass.

———. 1984. "Television Is 'Easy' and Print Is 'Tough': The Differential Investment of Mental Effort in Learning as a Function of Perceptions and Attributions." *Journal of Educational Psychology* 76 (4): 647–58.

Samborn, Randall. 1993. "Tracking Trends: Anti-Lawyer Attitude Up," *National Journal,* August 9, 1, 20–23.

Samuelson, Robert J. 2001. *Untruth: Why the Conventional Wisdom Is (Almost Always) Wrong.* New York: Random House.

San Diego Union-Tribune. 1994. "Java Hijack." Editorial. August 20, p. B6. Located via "Academic Universe."

———. 2001. "Court Secrecy Threatens Public Safety." June 6, p. B9.

Sarat, Austin. 2000a. "Exploring the Hidden Domains of Civil Justice: 'Naming, Blaming, and Claiming' in Popular Culture." *DePaul Law Review* 50:425–52.

Sarat, Austin. 2000b. "Imagining the Law of the Father: Loss, Dread, and Mourning in *The Sweet Hereafter.*" *Law and Society Review* 34 (1): 3–46.

———. 2001. *When the State Kills: Capital Punishment and the American Condition.* Princeton: Princeton University Press.

Sarat, Austin, and William L. F. Felstiner. 1995. *Divorce Lawyers and Their Clients: Power and Meaning in the Legal Process.* New York: Oxford University Press.

Sarat, Austin, and Stuart Scheingold. 1998. "Cause Lawyering and the Reproduction of Professional Authority." In *Cause Lawyering: Political Commitments and Professional Responsibilities,* ed. Austin Sarat and Stuart Scheingold, 3–30. New York: Oxford University Press.

Sarat, Austin, and Jonathan Simon. 2001. "Beyond Legal Realism: Cultural Analysis, Cultural Studies, and the Situation of Legal Scholarship." *Yale Journal of Law and the Humanities* 13:3–32.

Schattschneider, E. E. 1960. *The Semisovereign People: A Realist's View of Democracy in America.* New York: Holt, Rinehart and Winston.

Scheingold, Stuart A. 1974. *The Politics of Rights: Lawyers, Public Policy, and Political Change.* New Haven: Yale University Press.

———. 1984. *The Politics of Law and Order.* New York: Longman.

———. 1991. *The Politics of Street Crime: Criminal Process and Cultural Obsession.* Philadelphia: Temple University Press.

Schuck, Peter H. 1991. "Introduction: The Context of the Controversy." In *Tort Law and the Public Interest: Competition, Innovation, and Consumer Welfare,* ed. Peter H. Schuck, 17–43. New York: Norton.

Schudson, Michael. 1995. *The Power of News.* Cambridge: Harvard University Press.

Schwartz, Theresa M. 1991–92. "Product Liability Reform by the Judiciary." *Gonzaga Law Review* 27:303.

Schwartz, Victor, Mark A. Behrens, and Mark D. Taylor. 1997. "Who Should Make America's Tort Law: Courts or Legislatures?" Washington Legal Foundation monograph.

Schwartz, Victor, Kathryn Kelly, and David F. Partlett. 2001. *Torts: Cases and Materials,* 10th ed. New York: Foundation Press.

Seattle Times. 2000. "Lesson from Woman's Lawsuit—Next Time, Hold the Pickles." October 8, p. 12.

Seinfeld. 1995. Episode 112 "The Postponement" (Kramer's coffee spill in the theater) aired September 28, 1995; Episode 113 "The Maestro" (Kramer's settled suit) aired October 5, 1995.

Serrin, William. 2000. *The Business of Journalism: 10 Leading Reporters and Editors on the Perils and Pitfalls of the Press.* New York: New Press.

Shamir, Ronen. 1995. *Managing Legal Uncertainty: Elite Lawyers in the New Deal.* Durham: Duke University Press.

Shanley, Michael G., and Mark A. Peterson. 1987. *Posttrial Adjustments to Jury Awards.* Santa Monica: RAND Institute for Civil Justice.

Sherwin, Richard K. 2000. *When Law Goes Pop: The Vanishing Line between Law and Popular Culture.* Chicago: University of Chicago Press.

Sigal, Leon. 1973. *Reporters and Officials: The Organization and Politics of Newsmaking.* Lexington, Mass.: D. C. Heath.

Silbey, Susan, and Austin Sarat. 1987. "Critical Traditions in Law and Society Research." *Law and Society Review* 21:167–74.

Silverstein, Ken. 1996. "APCO: Astroturf Makers." *Multinational Monitor* 17 (3). Accessed at www.multinationalmonitor.org/hyper/mm0396.09.html.

Sloan, Frank, Penny Githens, Ellen Clayton, Gerald Hickson, Douglas Gentile, and David Partlett. 1993. *Suing for Medical Malpractice.* Chicago: University of Chicago Press.

Sloan, Frank, and Chen Ruey Hsieh. 1990. "Variability in Medical Malpractice Payments: Is the Compensation System Fair?" *Law and Society Review* 24:997–1039.

Slotnick, Elliot E., and Jennifer A. Segal. 1998. *Television News and the Supreme Court: All the News That's Fit to Air?* Cambridge, U.K.: Cambridge University Press.

Smith, Mark A. 2000. *American Business and Political Power: Public Opinion, Elections, and Democracy.* Chicago: University of Chicago Press.

Smith, Willam C. 1999. "Prying Off Tort Reform Caps." *America Bar Association Journal* (October): 29–30.

Snow, David A., and Robert D. Benford. 1997. "Master Frames and Cycles of Protest." In *Social Movements: Perspectives and Issues,* ed. Steven M. Buechler and F. Kurt Cylke Jr., 456–72. Mountain View, Calif.: Mayfield Publishing.

Songer, Donald R. 1988. "Tort Reform in South Carolina: The Effect of Empirical Research on Elite Perceptions concerning Jury Verdicts." *South Carolina Law Review* 39:585.

Speiser, Stuart M. 1993. *Lawyers and the American Dream.* New York: M. Evans.

Squires, James D. 1994. *Read All about It! The Corporate Takeover of America's Newspapers.* New York: Times Books.

St. John, Bill, and Marty Meitus. 1994. "Despite Lawsuit Brew-haha, Hot Coffee No Burning Issue." *Denver Rocky Mountain News,* August 21, p. 28A.

Stark, Steven D. 1987. "Perry Mason Meets Sonny Crockett: The History of Lawyers and the Police as Television Heroes." *University of Miami Law Review* 42:229.

Stavropoulos, William S. 1998. "Tort Reform." *Executive Speeches* (October/November): 27–31.

Stefancic, Jean, and Richard Delgado. 1996. *No Mercy : How Conservative Think Tanks and Foundations Changed America's Social Agenda.* Philadelphia: Temple University Press.

Steiner, Benjamin D., William J. Bowers, and Austin Sarat. 1999. "Folk Knowledge as Legal Action: Death Penalty Judgments and the Tenet of Early Release in a Culture of Mistrust and Punitiveness." *Law and Society Review* 33:461–506.

Stone, Deborah A. 1988. *Policy Paradox and Political Reason.* Glenview, Ill.: Scott, Foresman.

———. 1989. "Causal Stories and the Formation of Policy Agendas." *Political Science Quarterly* 104 (2): 281–300.

Strasser, Fred. 1987. "Tort Tales: Old Stories Never Die." *National Law Journal,* February 16, p. 39.

Studdert, David M., and Troyen A. Brennan. 2000. "Beyond Dead Reckoning: Measures of Medical Injury Burden, Malpractice Litigation, and Alternative Compensation Models from Utah and Colorado." *Indiana Law Review* 33:1643–86.

Sykes, Charles J. 1992. *A Nation of Victims: The Decay of the American Character.* New York: St. Martin's Press.

Taragin, Mark, Laura Willett, Adam Wilzek, Richard Trout, and Jeffrey Carson. 1992. "The Influence of Standard Care and Severity of Injury on the Resolution of Medical Malpractice Claims." *Annals of Internal Medicine* 117:780–84.

Tejada, Carlos. 1999. "Incensed by Soot: Decorative Candles Ignite a Crusade." *Wall Street Journal,* March 31, p. A1.

Thomas, Helen. 2003. "Curtailing Consumer Protection." *Seattle Times,* January 12, 2003, p. B10.

Time. 1986. "Sorry, Your Policy Is Cancelled." March 24, pp. 16–26.

Torry, Saundra. 1995. "Tort and Retort: The Battle over Reform Heats Up." *Washington Post,* March 6, p. F7.

Tuchman, Gaye. 1978. *Making News: A Study in the Construction of Reality.* New York: Free Press.

Tulsky, Frederic N. 1986. "Did Jury's Award Consider Psychic's Loss of 'Powers'?" *National Law Journal,* April 14, p. 9.

Tversky, Amos, and Daniel Kahneman. 1973. "Availability: A Heuristic for Judging Frequency and Probability." *Cognitive Psychology* 5:207–32.

Twiggs, Howard. 1997. "How Civil Justice Saved Me from Getting Burned." *Trial* (June): 9.

U.S. Department of Justice. 1986. *Report on the Causes, Extent, and Policy Implications of the Current Crisis in Insurance Liability.* Washington, D.C.: Government Printing Office.

Underwood, Doug. 1993. *When MBAs Rule the Newsroom : How the Marketers and Managers Are Reshaping Today's Media.* New York: Columbia University Press.

USA Today. 1986. "Hold Down Awards to Ease the Crisis." June 6, p. 12A.

———. 1999. "$58 Million Award for Minor Injury Invites Many Deaths." March 8, p. 12A.

Vakil, Mili. 1994. "Merchant Shouldn't Take Heat for Dumb Act." *Cleveland Plain Dealer,* October 10, p. 2E.

Van Fossen, Anthony B. 2002. "Risk Havens: Offshore Financial Centres, Insurance Cycles, the 'Litigation Explosion,' and a Social Democratic Alternative." *Social and Legal Studies* 11 (4): 503–21.

Van Natta Jr., Don, and Richard Oppel Jr. 2000. "The 2000 Campaign: The Contributions; Memo Linking Political Donation and Veto Spurs Federal Inquiry." *New York Times,* September 14, p. A1.

VandeHei, Jim. 2002. "GOP Plans New Caps on Court Awards; Piecemeal, Republicans Have Limited Lawsuits against Some Businesses." *Washington Post,* December 29, p. A5.

Vetter, Craig. 1986. "Psychic Whiplash." *Playboy* (August): 33.

Vidmar, Neil. 1995. *Medical Malpractice and the American Jury.* Ann Arbor: University of Michigan Press.

———. 1999. "Maps, Gaps, Sociolegal Scholarship, and the Tort Reform Debate." In *Social Science, Social Policy, and the Law,* ed. Patricia Ewick, Robert Kagan, and Austin Sarat, 170–209. New York: Russell Sage.

Vidmar, Neil, Felicia Gross, and Mary Rose. 1998. "Jury Awards for Medical Malpractice and Post-Verdict Adjustments of Those Awards." *DePaul Law Review* 48:265–99.

Viscusi, W. Kip. 1989. "Toward a Diminished Role for Tort Liability: Social Insurance, Government Regulation and Contemporary Risks to Health and Safety." *Yale Journal on Regulation* 6:65–97.

———.1991. *Reforming Products Liability.* Cambridge: Harvard University Press.

———. 1999. "A Post-Mortem on the Cigarette Settlement." *Cumberland Law Review* 29:523–54.

Wall Street Journal. 1994. "McDonald's Settles Lawsuit over Burn from Coffee." December 2, p. B6.

———. 1997. "Louisiana Jackpot." September 18, p. A14.

Walmac, Amanda. 1996. "The Best Way to Protect Yourself and Your Assets against a Lawsuit." *Money* (August): 29.

Walsh, Elsa, and Benjamin Weiser. 1988. "Court Secrecy Masks Safety Issues." *Washington Post,* October 23, p. A1.

Ward, Angela. 1997. "Surveys Show Jury Awards Declining in Injury Cases." *Texas Lawyer,* September 22, p. 1.

Washington Post. 1986. "Liability Reform Is Coming." April 1, p. A18.

———. 2000. "Chicken McNoggin, Hold the Fries." December 1, p. C01.

Webb, Cindy. 1995. "Boiling Mad: Food Chains Are Awash with Suits over Hot-Drink Burns." *Business Week,* August 21, p. 32.

Werth, Barry. 1998. *Damages: One Family's Legal Struggles in the World of Medicine.* New York: Simon and Schuster.

Will, George F. 1994. "Elevating Newt, Depreciating Chesty, and Other Wonders of 1994." *Newsweek,* December 26, p. 134.

Winter, Greg. 2001. "Jury Awards Soar as Lawsuits Decline on Defective Goods." *New York Times,* January 30, p. A1.

Yin, Robert K. 1994. *Case Study Research: Design and Methods.* 2d ed. Thousand Oaks: Sage Publications.

Zegart, Dan. 2000. *Civil Warriors: The Legal Siege on the Tobacco Industry.* New York: Bantam/Delta.

Zemans, Frances Kahn. 1983. "Legal Mobilization: The Neglected Role of the Law in the Political System." *American Political Science Review* 77:690–703.

Zitrin, Richard A. 1999. "The Case against Secret Settlements (or, What You Don't Know Can Hurt You)." *Journal of the Institute for Legal Ethics* 2:115.

Zitrin, Richard A., and Carol M. Langford. 1999. "Don't Settle for Secrets." *Legal Times,* April 12, p. 22.

Index